Incredible Phenomena

Incredible Phenomena

Edited by Peter Brookesmith

GUILD PUBLISHING
LONDON

Acknowledgements

Pictures were supplied by: Klaus Aarsleff, Aberdeen Journals, Aldus Archives, Heather Angel, K.M. Andrew, Archives of the University of Pennsylvania, Associated Press, Australian Information Services, Herbert Ballard, Clive Barda, Chris Barker/RAF Museum Hendon, BBC Hulton Picture Library, John Beckett/A. Hart-Davis, Bildarchiv Preussichar Kulturbesitz, Birmingham Public Library, Bodleian Library, Janet and Colin Bord, Borough of Brighton, Bridgeman Art Library, Bristol Evening Post, British Library, British Museum, Brooke Bond Oxo, Bruce Coleman, Richard Burgess, Canada Press, Jean-Loup Charmet, Colorific!, Private Collection/Joe Cooper, Culver Pictures, Dawson and Mason, Richard Deacon, Department of the Environment, Paul Devereux, Hylton Edgar, Robert Estall, Mary Evans Picture Library, Mary Evans Picture Library/Harry Price Library, George Ewart Evans, Fate Magazine, George Feifer, Fiji Visitor's Bureau, Joel Finler, Maria L. Finton, Werner Forman Archive, Fortean Picture Library, Leif Geiges, Giraudon, Glaister and Rentoul, Gregorian University of Rome, Henry Gris, Elmer Gruber, Sonia Halliday, Robert Harding, Norma Harvey, Hebridean Press Agency, Nancy Heinl, Sunday Herald, Hertford Museum, John Hillelson/Sygma, Hans Hinz, F. Hodgson/Ann Ross, Toby Hogarth, Michael Holford, Robert Hunt Library, Hutchinson Publishing Group, Alan Hutchison, Illinois State Historical Library, Japanese National Tourist Office, Stephen Kerry, Keystone, Kobal Collection, Brian Larkman, Cyrus Lee, London Features International, Susan Lund, William MacQuitty, Dr. J.A. Macrae, City of Manchester Art Galleries, Mander and Mitcheson, Mansell Collection, Marshall Cavendish Picture Library, Miller Services, Frederick Muller Publishers, NASA, National Film Archive, National Museum of Scotland, Natural Science Photos, Newcastle Chronicle and Journal, Peter Newark's Western Americana, Nostell Priory Wakefield, Public Archives of Nova Scotia, Novosti, S. Ostrander, Photo Associates, Photri, Picturepoint, Popperfoto, Press Association, Dr. H. Puthoff/Stanford Research Institute, Raymonds of Derby, W.C. Reeves, Rex Features, Edward Rice, John Richell, David Robson, Ann Ronan Picture Library, Routledge and Kegan Paul, Royal Academy of Arts, The Royal Collection, Royal Commission on Ancient Monuments of Scotland, Robert Runge, Scala, Science Photo Library, Paul Screeton, Ronald Sheridan Picture Library, Paul Sieveking, Tom Smith/Fortrose Town Council, Sovfoto, Space Frontiers, Spectrum Colour Library, State Library of Victoria Australia, Homer Sykes, Syndication International, Tampa Times, Tao Ch'i Chuan Kung Fu, John Topham Picture Library, D. Towersey, Transworld Feature Syndicate, University of Chicago Library, University of Leeds, UPI, Roger Viollet, Charles Walker, Graham Whitlock, White House Historical Association, Harold T. Wilkins, David Williamson, Willis Wood, Xinhua News Agency, Yorkshire Evening Press, Yorkshire Post, ZEFA.

Consultants	**Deputy Editor**	**Picture Researchers**	**Designer**
Professor A.J. Ellison	Lynn Picknett	Anne Horton	Richard Burgess
Dr J. Allen Hynek	**Executive Editor**	Paul Snelgrove	**Art Buyer**
Brian Inglis	Lesley Riley	Frances Vargo	Jean Morley
Colin Wilson	**Sub Editors**	**Editorial Manager**	**Production Co-ordinator**
Editorial Director	Mitzi Bales	Clare Byatt	Nicky Bowden
Brian Innes	Chris Cooper	**Art Editor**	**Volume Editor**
Editor	Jenny Dawson	Stephen Westcott	Lorrie Mack
Peter Brookesmith	Hildi Hawkins		

The publishers would like to thank the following authors for contributing to this book:
Paul Begg 96–99, 114–117; David Christie-Murray 172–174; Joe Cooper 124–134; Richard Deacon 163–166; Beale McIver 194–195; Graham Fuller and Ian Knight 118–122, 200–202, 204–207, 249–253; Fred Gettings 135–140; Frederick Goodman 208–213; Michael Goss 46–49; Elmer Gruber 184–187; Melvin Harris 110–113, 167–170; Douglas Hill 160–162; Edward Horton 234–245; Francis King 67–78; Perrott Phillips 150–159; Bob Rickard 9–30, 54–57, 100–103, 142–149, 175–183; Ian Ridpath 214–220; Paul Screeton 92–95; Paul Sieveking 50–53, 79–87, 221–233; Frank Smyth 31–45, 59–66, 89–91, 105–109, 188–193, 196–199.

Contents

Introduction

The classification of what is, and what is not, worthy of investigation as a genuinely paranormal phenomenon is not yet fully established. Of the many mysteries that confront us in the world, not all are paranormal; sceptics – a dwindling minority, but still common in the academic world – tend simply to deny the existence of the paranormal, and to dismiss its study, parapsychology, as 'pseudoscience'. Even psychical researchers are often guilty of a subtler, but more invidious rejection of many unexplained phenomena as fit subjects of investigation; as the young discipline of parapsychology struggles to establish itself, its researchers, anxious to acquire respectability in the eyes of academic colleagues, often set unnecessarily narrow limits to what should be examined.

The problem is not a new one. The founder members of the Society for Psychical Research (SPR) for example, believed in telepathy, but were inclined to dismiss clairvoyance as unimportant, and to turn their backs on physical mediumship as somehow embarrassing. Today, some of the SPR's members feel the same way about UFOs, and these members would not cross the road to examine a fall of fish after a storm – not, that is, in their capacity as psychical researchers. Such phenomena, they believe, are not in their brief for investigation, and they are inclined to explain them away as a meteorological freak. This they may well be – but at present this is no more than a hypothesis, which can be established only by full investigation.

In this collection, my own interest is most attracted by the 'Human Enigma' section. If I were asked to name the area of research that, given unlimited time and funds, I should most like to see explored, it would be the mystery of human combustibility and incombustibility. Why, and how, do people suddenly burn to death with no apparent cause? What, in other words, is the explanation of spontaneous combustion?

There is no better description of the phenomenon than Dickens' in *Bleak House*. Guppy and Weevle go down to Krook's room, where they find, 'a smouldering suffocating vapour' and the walls coated with grease, but no sign of a fire except a small burnt patch of floor and some white ash. Suddenly it dawns on them that

> *O Horror, he is here! And this from which we run*
> *away, striking out the light and overturning one*
> *another into the street, is all that represents him.*

Dickens' description of what remains after spontaneous combustion has been repeatedly reinforced, not least by Prof. David Gee of Leeds University Department of Forensic Medicine, who has done considerable work in this field. Well-attested, too, is the fact that the course taken by such combustion is not like that taken by any 'natural' fire. A human body cannot burn in a room without destroying everything inflammable in its vicinity – the temperature required is far too high. And yet, again and again, reports of human combustibility describe the surroundings as untouched by fire and undamaged by smoke.

At the same time, some people seem to have acquired immunity to fire, and this is just as baffling. It is always tempting to dismiss the Old Testament miracles as myths, but the story of Shadrach, Mesach and Abednego contains some interesting side-lights. The assembled company observed that not merely did the three men survive unscathed, but their clothes did not burn either. This was also a feature of the occasions in the 1860s when the medium Daniel Dunglas Home was able literally to play with fire, plunging his hands into live coals and bathing his face in them. When he handed them to witnesses, they did not suffer burns either, nor did their clothes. Home could put a live coal on a handkerchief, and it would not even be singed.

Heat is a form of energy, as are light and electricity, both of which can play equally odd tricks. The French astronomer Camille Flammarion made a special study of the ways in which lightning strikes, and found that it can behave not just unpredictably, but almost maliciously, burning off the clothes of some victims, while leaving them uninjured; burning others, but leaving their clothes undamaged.

These phenomena appear to have struck at random, to have had nothing whatsoever to do with the personal qualities of their victims. But there are also so-called 'electric people', people who are constantly surrounded by glow of what appears to be electric light, or who can influence the performance of electrical equipment in spectacular ways. One of these was the 19th-century French teenager Angelique Cottin, whose 'electricity' (as contemporary investigations took it to be) was examined by some of the leading scientists of the day, and accepted as genuine.

Angelique was lucky. Her gifts had some trying consequences for her personal life – furniture moved away from her when she went towards it to sit down – but she did not do anything dangerous that might have landed her in jail. Two centuries earlier, such dangerous phenomena would have sent her to the stake to be burned as a witch. This last observation deserves consideration: one practical reason for seeking to establish the reality of spontaneous combustion, and of other similar phenomena ('invulnerability', the resistance of certain individuals in certain states to blows that ordinarily would kill them, surely belongs in the same category) is to give some protection to those unlucky people who are unwittingly responsible for psychic phenomena, unrecognised as such, that cause alarm and may be attributed to mental disorder. In the case of spontaneous combustion, victims may unjustly be accused, because the circumstantial evidence points to them as guilty of arson.

The existence of such 'freak' abilities and phenomena offers a challenge to orthodox science. When a coelocanth was discovered in the sea off Madagascar in 1938, the initial reaction of the 'experts' was that a mistake must have been made, as the species had been extinct for millions of years; and the discoverer would have been derided as a dupe or a knave had he not been able to produce the specimen. But when it *was* produced, the specimen did not demand any drastic change in the structure of conventional biology; simply the switch of one species from the 'extinct' list in text-books to the 'extant'.

Acceptance of the existence of either spontaneous combustion or incombustibility, on the other hand, would give bio-chemists, physiologists and the rest a fearful headache. It is possible to show that a human subject who can be put under hypnosis will not merely feel no pain when a match is held under his finger, but will not suffer from after effects such as blistering either. This has been grudgingly accepted as evidence of the power of the mind in a condition of suggestibility, to enforce its will upon the flesh. But that this power should extend to enabling people literally to bathe in fire seems as inconceivable, under present dogmas, as does the notion that a body can mysteriously consume itself by heat.

I am continually asked, when such issues come up in conversation, whether I believe in spontaneous combustion, or witchcraft, or toads emerging from ancient rocks. 'Believe' strikes me as the wrong word, since it carries the implication of faith, dividing people into believers and sceptics, and blocking objective investigation.

The classic example of the way in which belief and scepticism can delay the acceptance of phenomena relates to meteorites. For millennia, it was assumed by the believers that such 'thunderbolts' were an instrument of divine vengeance to smite down sinners. As a result, when astronomy began to emerge as a science in the 17th century, its practitioners assumed that their existence was a superstition. Later, scientists went further, and argued that the existence of any kind of thunderbolt was impossible, because it was contrary to the laws of nature.

Members of the French Academy of the Sciences, for example – the great chemist Lavoisier was one of them – issued a memorandum in 1772 that concluded 'the falling of stones from the sky is physically impossible'. A few years later, when a meteorite was actually seen to fall by many people in a French town, the eminent scientist Claude Berthollet commented how sad it was that an entire municipality should have put folk tales into an official record. The Swiss astronomer Jean Deluc (1727–1817), the first man to have the idea of measuring the height of mountains by utilising barometric pressure, said bluntly, 'if I saw a meteorite fall, I would not believe my own eyes'. Even when meteorites which had been reported were actually found, the scientists who examined them would report that they must be stones dug up by some practical joker.

There have been countless examples since of the way in which ingrained scepticism can warp judgment, and sometimes promote actual dishonesty. In the late 1960s the University of Colorado was offered funds by the United States Air Force to investigate UFOs. The man who was to be put in charge of the investigation made clear in a memorandum that it would be conducted as if it were genuinely impartial, but he would ensure that its real purpose would be simply to accumulate material to provide 'an impressive body of evidence that there is no reality to the observations', which was in fact what the study (called the Condon report) claimed. It might still be taken seriously, had not somebody 'leaked' the memo to the press.

To proclaim belief in many of the phenomena in this collection strikes me as unwise – but less unwise than to deny their existence on the ground that they are impossible. Most of them constitute, at the very least, a legitimate field for exploration.

Take the case of the 'Cottingley Fairies'. *The Unexplained* was first to publish the admission by the two girls – now old ladies – who took the remarkable fairy photographs that the whole affair was largely a hoax. If past experience is any guide, the tendency will now be to put the case into the file labelled 'explained', and to assume that it was all a childish prank. But even leaving aside the issue of whether the recollections of the two old ladies, nearly 60 years after the events they describe, are to be trusted (particularly as they are not in harmony) the problem remains that as children they believed they saw, and communicated with, fairies – as many respectable men and women have also believed. Unquestionably people have believed that they have seen, and heard, and actually felt, fairies. Are they real – in the sense of having an existence, perhaps on a slightly different plane from the human race, but capable of moving in and out of the reach of our senses in much the same way as an amphibian moves between land and water? Or are they hallucinations?

It would be unfortunate, too, if the hoax element in the Cottingley case were allowed to cast doubt on the existence of a genuine psychic component in some photographs. Here, the evidence collected by American psychologist Professor Jule Eisenbud and others during their investigations of the thought photographs of Ted Serios has sufficed to silence even that arch debunker of paranormal science, the stage magician James – 'The Amazing' – Randi, who had eventually to back down when he claimed that he could fake similar pictures in test conditions.

What is surely obvious is that a great many phenomena exist for which conventional science has been unable to provide any plausible explanations and that it is consequently disposed to dismiss as invention, or to ignore. Charles Fort performed a public service by simply chronicling their existence – a tradition still maintained by *Fortean Times*.

Inevitably, some of the phenomena investigated will be found to be hoaxes, or the delusions of the mentally unbalanced; and in other cases we may find that our limitation is the compass of human intelligence. But others, surely, will in time be given room in the house of science, just as meteorites have been.

There is always the need to beware of glib purveyors of the kind of explanation provided in, say, *Chariots of the Gods* by Erich von Däniken, or Charles Berlitz's *The Bermuda triangle*. Such works play into the hands of detractors of investigation of the paranormal by giving them the excuse, when they show up the flaws in the presentation of the case, to imply that the phenomena are as bogus as are the theories about them.

Again, it is one thing to accept evidence for phenomena because of the quantity and quality of the reports relating to them; quite another blindly to believe in some hypothesis assembled to account for them. The evidence needs to be scrutinised dispassionately, if we are not to fall victims to the same vice (though for the opposite reason) as Deluc, and as the man who rigged the Colorado 'investigation' of UFOs.

Brian Inglis

The human enigma

We tend to perceive the limitations and characteristics of the human mind and body as known and immutable, but there are many well-recorded cases where the rules we accept so unquestioningly do not seem to apply. Occurrences such as spontaneous human combustion and the survival of live burial suggest that our knowledge of ourselves is still in its infancy.

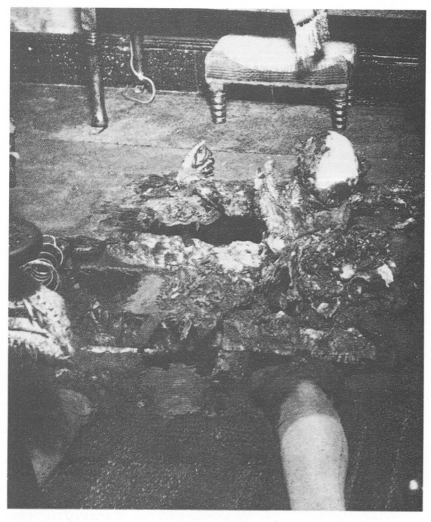

The aftermath of spontaneous human combustion. The fire has reduced most of the body to ashes, leaving only parts of the lower legs, the left hand and portions of the skull, and was intense enough to burn a hole in the floor. Enormously high temperatures must have been involved, yet for some mysterious reason the fire has been contained, causing little further damage to the surroundings

Ashes to ashes

Of all the strange and inexplicable fates that may befall a person, perhaps the most bizarre is to burst into flames without warning and without apparent cause. These cases, although rare, continue to defy science

PEOPLE HAVE LONG BELIEVED that in certain circumstances the human body can burst into flames of its own accord. Flames, furthermore, of such ferocity that within minutes the victim is reduced to a heap of carbonised ashes. This idea – some call it a superstition – has been around for centuries, smouldering in the belief in divine retribution. 'By the blast of God they perish,' says the author of *Job*, 'and by the breath of his nostrils are they consumed.'

This Gothic horror was hugely popular in the 18th and 19th centuries, and its literary use is still extensively discussed in the pages of *The Dickensian*, stimulated by Charles Dickens' own fascination with the subject. Dickens had examined the case for spontaneous human combustion (SHC) 'as a Judge might have done', and knew most of the early authorities and collections of cases. He probably based his description of Krook's death in *Bleak House* (1852–3), upon the cases of Countess Bandi and Grace Pett.

The death of the 62-year-old Countess Cornelia Bandi, near Verona, is perhaps one of the first of the more reliable reports of SHC. According to a statement by Bianchini, a prebendary of Verona, dated 4 April 1731, the Countess had been put to bed after supper, and fell asleep after several hours' conversation with her maid. In the morning the maid returned to wake her and found a grisly scene. As the *Gentlemen's Magazine* reported: 'The floor of the chamber was thick-smear'd with a gluish moisture, not easily got off . . . and from the lower part of the window trickl'd down a greasy, loathsome, yellowish liquor with an unusual stink.'

Specks of soot hung in the air and covered all the surfaces in the room, and the smell had penetrated adjoining rooms. The bed was undamaged, the sheets turned back, indicating the Countess had got out of bed.

Four feet [1.3 metres] from the bed was a heap of ashes, two legs untouch'd, stockings on, between which lay the head, the brains, half of the back-part of the skull and the whole chin burn'd to ashes, among which were found three fingers blacken'd. All the rest was ashes which had this quality, that they left in the hand a greasy and stinking moisture.

A hole burnt in the floor

Bianchini could have been describing some of our modern cases. The diligent researches of Larry E. Arnold unearthed the fate of Dr J. Irving Bentley, a 93-year-old retired physician of Coudersport, Pennsylvania. Gas company worker Don Gosnell discovered the remains after smelling a 'light-blue smoke of unusual odor'. The fire had been so intense that it almost totally consumed the old man. John Dec the deputy coroner said: 'All I found was a knee joint atop a post in the basement, the lower leg from the knee down, and the now-scattered ashes 6 feet [2 metres] below.' And yet the fire had, mysteriously, been contained; firemen testified to the existence of a few embers around the hole, and a slight scorching on the bathtub about a foot (30 centimetres) away was the only other sign of this fiercely fatal fire. The burns on the bath were still visible when Arnold investigated nine years later.

It was suggested that Bentley was a careless smoker – small burns riddled his everyday clothes and the bedroom floor – and that he had wakened to find himself on fire, struggled to the bathroom in search of water, and there collapsed and died. Arnold, in his report on the case in the journal *Pursuit*, 1976, points out that there are several inconsistencies in this account, though it was accepted by the local newspaper and the coroner.

Bentley's pipe had been 'carefully placed' on its stand by his chair; not the action of a man on fire. A broken hip six years before had left him with no feeling in his left leg, and he walked with difficulty – his 'walker' can be seen fallen across the hole. He was enough of a doctor to realise that his only chance of survival, had his clothes been on fire, would be to take them off there and then, rather than risk the precarious trip to the bathroom.

It is more likely that whatever happened to Bentley occurred when he visited the bathroom for some other reason, and that he was beginning to burn before he took off his robe, setting fire to it in the process – it was found smouldering in the bathtub. The autopsy was a mere formality, yet despite having so little to go on – just half a leg; the ashes

A villain meets his end

In chapter 32 of *Bleak House*, Charles Dickens' characters, William Guppy and Tony Weevle, discover that the evil Krook has been mysteriously burned to a few charred lumps and ashes, filling the room with 'hateful soot' and objects coated with an offensive 'thick yellow liquor'. 'Call the death by any name . . . attribute it to whom you will, or say it might have been prevented how you will, it is the same death eternally – inborn, inbred, engendered in the corrupt humours of the vicious body itself, and that only – Spontaneous Combustion, and none other of all the deaths that can be died.'

were never analysed – the coroner decided that Dr Bentley had died of *asphyxiation*, probably because that is the usual cause of death during fires.

Primarily due to the efforts of Charles Fort, the pioneer collector of accounts of strange phenomena, and the small number of people and journals who continue his work, we have accumulated a respectable number of records, from newspapers and medical journals, of SHC right up to the present. Very few of the accounts mention SHC, because officially there is no such phenomenon, and coroners and their advisers have the unenviable task of dealing with evidence that seems to contradict accepted physical laws and medical opinion. Inevitably, suppositions are made about knocked over heaters, flying sparks, careless smoking, and in the case of child victims, playing with matches. Faced with the alternative – a nightmare out of the Dark Ages – it is not surprising that they are accepted.

There are occasional exceptions, which are far more useful to those who truly wish to solve the enigma, like the report in *Lloyds Weekly News* of 5 February 1905. A woman asleep by a fireplace woke to find herself in flames and later died. The honest coroner said he could not understand: the woman had gone to sleep facing the fire, so any cinder that shot out from the grate would ignite the front of her clothes. Yet it was her back that bore the severe burns.

Fear of the truth

At worst, a story may be rejected out of fear or disbelief, as in the case of the elderly spinster, Wilhelmina Dewar, who combusted near midnight on 22 March 1908, in the Northumberland town of Whitley Bay. Wilhelmina was found by her sister Margaret who, in a shocked state, managed to summon her neighbours. In the house they found the severely charred body of Wilhelmina in an upstairs bed. The bedclothes were unscorched and there was no sign of fire anywhere else in the house.

When Margaret told this story at the inquest, the coroner thought it preposterous and asked her to think again. Repeatedly she said she was telling the truth and could not change her story – even after a policeman testified that Margaret was so drunk she couldn't have known what she was saying. As Fort points out, the policeman 'was not called upon to state how he distinguished between signs of excitement and terror, and intoxication.' The coroner adjourned the inquest to give her more time to think. When it was reconvened a few days later it was obvious that a great deal of pressure had been placed upon poor Margaret.

Both sisters were retired school teachers and, up until then, lived respectably. Now the coroner was calling her a liar, the papers called her a drunk, and friends and neighbours turned away, leaving her to face a hostile court. Not surprisingly, she said she had been inaccurate. This time she told a story of finding her sister burned, but alive, in a lower part of the house. Then she helped her upstairs to bed, where she died.

This sounded superficially more plausible, was accepted, and the proceedings promptly closed. The court was not interested in how Wilhelmina was transformed from someone who could be helped upstairs into the cindered corpse with charred abdomen and legs; or how, if she continued to smoulder after being helped into bed, there was no mark of fire in the house. 'But the coroner was satisfied,' wrote Fort sarcastically. 'The proper testimony had been recorded.'

Yet it was medico-legal interest that kept alive the notion of SHC, with pathologists endorsing the phenomenon, then rejecting it in favour of 'preternatural combustibility'. In addition, there was the perennial possibility that a murderer may simulate SHC to hide his crime. One of the earliest test cases occurred in Rheims in 1725 when an innkeeper, Jean Millet, was accused of having an affair with a pretty servant girl and killing his wife. The wife, who was often drunk, was found one morning about a foot (30 centimetres) away from the hearth.

'A part of the head only, with a portion of the lower extremities, and a few of the vertebrae, had escaped combustion. A foot and a half (45 centimetres) of the flooring under the body had been consumed, but a kneading-trough and a powdering tub very near the body sustained no injury.' A young assistant doctor, named Le Cat, was staying at the inn and managed to convince the court that this was no ordinary fire death but a 'visitation of God' upon the drunken woman, and an obvious result of soaking one's innards with spirits. Millet was vindicated, and Le Cat went on to qualify with distinction, and publish a memoir on SHC.

Spontaneous human combustion received its severest criticism from the great pioneer chemist, Baron Justus von Liebig, who wrote a spirited refutation of both spontaneous and preternatural combustion, on the grounds that no one had seen it happen. As a scientist he saw the historical evidence as an unsupported record of the *belief* in SHC, rather than actual proof of spontaneous burning deaths. Further, he lamented the lack of expert witnesses, and dismissed the accounts generally because they 'proceed from ignorant persons, unpractised in observation, and bear in themselves the stamp of untrustworthiness.'

Despite Liebig's assertion, however, there is plenty of evidence from both medical and police sources. Many of these bear witness to the ferocity of the phenomenon, as in the case investigated by Merille, a surgeon in Caen, recorded in Trotter's *Essay on drunkenness* (1804). On 3 June 1782, Merille was asked by 'the king's officers' in the city to report on the death of Mademoiselle Thaurs, a lady of over 60 who had been observed, that day, to have drunk three bottles of wine and one of brandy. Merille wrote:

The body lay with the crown of the head resting against one of the hand-irons . . . 18 inches [45 centimetres] from the fire, the remainder of the body was placed obliquely before the chimney, the whole being nothing but a mass of ashes. Even the most solid bones had lost their form and consistence. The right foot was found entire and scorched at its upper junction; the left was more burnt. The day was cold but there was nothing in the grate except two or three bits of wood about an inch in diameter, burnt in the middle.

Dr Wilton Krogman, who investigated a famous case of SHC, and experimented with

Left: the great chemist Baron Justus von Liebig. He rejected tales of spontaneous human combustion because of the lack of expert witnesses – and because his attempts to make flesh burn with the same intensity as SHC were, without exception, a dismal failure

Below: an anonymous victim of SHC lies with its apparently unburnt head resting in a grate. An electric fire is also visible – but how did the body burn so thoroughly without setting fire to the rest of the room?

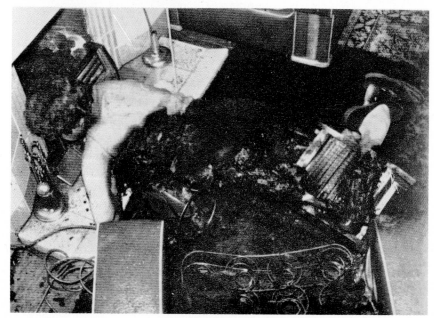

The burning of Dr Bentley

Dr J. Irving Bentley, a retired physician, lived on the ground floor of an apartment building in Coudersport, northern Pennsylvania. On the cold morning of 5 December 1966, Don Gosnell entered the building's basement to read the meter for the North Pen Gas Company. In the basement a 'light-blue smoke of unusual odor' hung in the air. Scattering an unfamiliar heap in the corner with his boot, Gosnell found it was ashes. There had been no answer to his greeting on the way in, so he decided to look in on the old man. There was more strange smoke in the bedroom but no sign of Bentley. Gosnell peered into the bathroom and was confronted with a sight he will never forget. A large hole had burned through the floor to the basement, exposing the joists and pipework below. On the edge of the hole he saw '. . . a brown leg from the knee down, like that of a mannequin. I didn't look further!' Gosnell fled from the building.

sophisticated crematorium equipment, said: 'Only at 3000°F (1650°C) plus have I seen bone fuse or melt so that it ran and became volatile.' Such a heat would certainly char everything within a considerable radius and set the house ablaze, yet the meticulous Merille writes:

> None of the furniture in the apartment was damaged. The chair on which she was sitting was found at the distance of a foot from her, and absolutely untouched . . . the consumption of the body had taken place in less than 7 hours, though according to appearance, nothing around the body was burnt but the clothes.

Reluctant admissions

Modern researchers into SHC readily quash the idea that the phenomenon is as rare as some commentators suggest. Similarly, there is a growing number of cases testified to by doctors and pathologists, and this number would probably increase if the fear of ridicule could be completely removed. A Dr B. H. Hartwell reported to the Massachusetts Medico-Legal Society an unusual case of SHC that he witnessed while driving through Ayer, Massachusetts, on 12 May 1890.

He was stopped and called into a wood where he saw a horrible sight. In a clearing a woman was crouching 'in flames at the shoulders, both sides of the abdomen, and both legs.' Neither he nor the other witnesses could find an obvious cause for the fire.

This doctor's experience was not unique. Support for the suspicion that many a doctor would be able to tell of an encounter with mysterious and fatal fires comes in a coincidental and roundabout way. Maxwell Cade and Delphine Davis, authors of the imaginative study of ball lightning *Taming of the thunderbolts* (1969), confessed they themselves would not have put much faith in the above story, or in the existence of SHC, 'if a doctor friend had not told us of a lecture which he attended at the Massachusetts Medico-Legal Society, where several such cases were discussed. When we expressed cautious doubts, the doctor assured us that he had been called to a similar case himself as recently as the autumn of 1959.'

When Dr D. J. Gee of the University of Leeds delivered his well-known paper on 'A case of spontaneous combustion' he was surprised by the candid discussion that followed. He is quoted as saying:

> Dr George Manning described his experience of several similar cases, and indicated that the phenomenon was certainly not as rare as might be supposed from the literature. This view was supported by Dr David Price, who said that he met with this phenomenon approximately once in every four years.

A strange unnatural fire

The idea that human beings can burst into flames of their own accord is odd enough. But, in fact, everything about spontaneous human combustion is bizzare

Spontaneous human combustion strikes with astonishing speed, yet the heat generated is sufficient to char even the bones of the victim. In contrast, a body can take hours to burn away in the sustained fire of a crematorium – and even then only the flesh is thoroughly destroyed

PERHAPS THE MOST common characteristic of SHC is the sheer speed with which it strikes. Many victims were seen alive only a few moments before the fire struck from nowhere. An Italian surgeon called Battaglio reported the death of a priest, named Bertholi, in the town of Filetto, in 1789. Lodging with his brother-in-law, he had been left alone in his room reading a prayerbook. A few minutes later he screamed. People came running to find him on the floor surrounded by a pale flame, which receded as they approached.

Bertholi wore a sackcloth under his clothes, next to his skin, and it was immediately apparent that the outer clothes had burned away leaving the sackcloth intact. Under the sackcloth the skin on the man's trunk was not burned, but detached from the flesh and hung in shreds.

Some writers deduce that the fire develops with particular rapidity, from the fact that the victims are often discovered still sitting calmly, as though nothing had happened.

A dramatic example is given in Ron Willis's article on SHC in *INFO Journal* 8 (1972). In 1960, five charred bodies were found in a burned-out car near Pikeville, Kentucky. The coroner commented: 'They were sitting there as though they'd just gotten into the car. With all that heat it seems there'd be some sort of struggle to escape. But there hadn't been.'

Another almost universal characteristic of SHC is the extreme intensity of heat that is involved. Under normal circumstances the human body is very hard to set alight, especially if still alive, and people who die in fires usually sustain only partial or superficial damage to the body. Reduction to a pile of calcined ashes, experts all agree, demands a fierce heat which needs to be externally fuelled and maintained for hours, and even so crematoria still have to grind up the bones that remain afterward.

The death of Mrs Reeser (see box) was investigated by Dr Wilton M. Krogman, a renowned forensic anthropologist from the University of Pennsylvania School of Medicine, who has researched and experimented the causes and effects of deaths by and during fires. He said he has watched bodies in a crematorium burn for over 8 hours at 2000°F (1110°C) without any sign of the bones becoming ashes or powder; and that it takes a heat of about 3000°F (1650°C) to make bone melt and become volatile. Willis mentions the case of Leon Eveille, aged 40, found burnt to a crisp in his locked car at Arcis-sur-Aube, France, on 17 June 1971. The heat had melted the windows. It was estimated that a burning car normally reaches about 1300°F (700°C), but to melt glass the temperature must have been over 1800°F (1000°C).

Time and again in cases of SHC, we encounter a further strange effect: the confinement of the heat. Charred bodies are found lying in unscorched beds, sitting on slightly singed chairs, or with their clothing intact.

In 1905 the *British Medical Journal* reported the death of 'an elderly woman of intemperate habits'. Authorities broke into a house from which smoke was issuing to find

a small pyramidal heap of broken calcinated human bones, on the top of

Dr Wilton Krogman, an expert on the effects of fire on the human body. He was astonished by the state of Mrs Reeser's corpse, and constructed an elaborate theory to account for it

which was a skull, on the floor in front of a chair. All the bones were completely bleached and brittle; every particle of soft tissue had been consumed, and yet a tablecloth within three feet of the remains was not even scorched. . . . Curiously, the ceiling was scorched, as if the woman had become a pillar of fire.

Fort, in his *Complete books* (1941) gives two startling cases. The first, from the *Daily News* of 17 December 1904, describes how Mrs Thomas Cochrane, of Falkirk, was found in a bedroom burned to death 'beyond recognition'. There had been no outcry, and little else burned, with no fire in the grate. Her charred corpse was found 'sitting in a chair, surrounded by pillows and cushions'. The second is from the *Madras Mail* of 13 May 1907 concerning a woman in the village of Manner, near Dinapore. Flames had consumed her body, but not her clothes. Two constables had found the corpse in a room in which nothing else showed signs of fire, and had carried the smouldering body to the District Magistrate.

In 1841 the *British Medical Journal* reported an address by Dr F. S. Reynolds to the Manchester Pathological Society on the subject of SHC. Although rejecting the idea of 'spontaneous' combustion, he admitted there were baffling cases, and gave an instance from his experience of a woman of 40 who fell near a hearth. She was found next morning still burning. What astonished him was the damage to the legs: inside unharmed stockings her femora was carbonised and knee-joints opened.

Some chroniclers of SHC have drawn attention to the lack of outcry and struggle by victims. 'In their grim submission,' Fort wrote, 'it is almost as if they had been lulled by the wings of a vampire.' There is more to it than being overcome by drink and fumes – some psychic or psychological component of the phenomenon prefaces or accompanies the burning, and this may explain the lack of escape, and the inability of surviving victims to tell what happened to them.

For example, the *Hull Daily Mail* of 6 January 1905 describes how an elderly

The destruction of Mary Reeser

Workmen are seen here clearing away the remains of the chair in which Mrs Mary Reeser, a widow of 67, of St Petersburg, Florida, departed this life on a pillar of fire, during the night of 1 July 1951. Damage to the surroundings was minimal. The overstuffed chair was burned down to its springs, there was a patch of soot on the ceiling above and a small circle of carpet was charred around the chair, but a pile of papers nearby was unscorched. Dr Wilton Krogman, a forensic scientist who specialised in fire deaths, was visiting in the area and joined the investigation. He said:

I cannot conceive of such complete cremation without more burning of the apartment itself. In fact the apartment and everything in it should have been consumed. Never have I seen a human skull shrunk by intense heat. The opposite has always been true; the skulls have been either abnormally swollen or have virtually exploded into hundreds of pieces . . . I regard it as the most amazing thing I have ever seen. As I review it, the short hairs on my neck bristle with vague fear. Were I living in the Middle Ages, I'd mutter something about black magic.

Police considered every likely theory, and a few unasked-for ideas from cranky members of the public: suicide by petrol, ignition of methane gas in her body, murder by flame-thrower, 'atomic pill' (whatever that meant), magnesium, phosphorus and napalm substances . . . and even a 'ball of fire' which one anonymous letter-writer claimed to see. In the end the coroner accepted the FBI theory, that she had fallen asleep while smoking and set her clothes alight.

Dr Krogman himself proffered the idea that Mrs Reeser had been burned elsewhere by someone with access to crematorium-type equipment or materials, then was carried back to the apartment, where the mystery assailant had added the finishing touches, like heat-buckled plastic objects, and a door-knob that was still hot in the morning. A year later, the police confessed the case was still open.

woman, Elizabeth Clark, was found in the morning with fatal burns, while her bed, in the Trinity Almshouse, Hull, was unmarked by fire. There had been no outcry or sounds of struggle through the thin partitions. She was 'unable to give an articulate account' of her accident, and later died. Of course that could mean that the authorities – not for the first time – simply didn't believe her account.

In *Lo!* (1930), Fort describes the complex fires that plagued Binbrook Farm, near Grimsby, in the winter of 1904–5. One incident involved a young servant girl who was burning without her knowledge, and might have been another SHC statistic had not her employer roused her from her daydreaming (or trance). According to a local newspaper, the farmer said:

> Our servant girl, whom we had taken from the workhouse . . . was sweeping the kitchen. There was a very small fire in the grate; there was a guard there so that no one can come within 2 feet [0.6 metres] or more of the fire, and she was at the other end of the room, and had not been near. I suddenly came into the kitchen and there she was, sweeping away while the back of her dress was on fire. She looked around as I shouted, and seeing the flames, rushed through the door. She tripped and I smothered the fire out with wet sacks.

The girl had obviously been on fire for some time and was 'terribly burned'.

As we have seen in the Pikeville car case, several people have combusted together, but such cases are extremely rare. Baron Liebig thought that the occurrence of multiple SHC cases disproved the 'disease' theory (see box), since in his experience a disease has never run the same course in two or more people, detail for detail, culminating in their simultaneous death. Certainly none of the 'diseases' that are suggested by the theory's apologists has done so.

Willis describes the case of the Rooneys who lived in a farmhouse near Seneca, Illinois:

> On Christmas Eve 1885, Patrick Rooney and his wife and their hired man, John Larson, were drinking whiskey in the kitchen. Larson went to bed and woke up Christmas morning feeling sick. Downstairs in the kitchen he found everything covered with an oily film, and on the floor, Patrick Rooney dead. Larson rode to get help from Rooney's son John, who lived nearby. Back at the farm the two men noticed that there was a charred hole next to the kitchen table. Looking into the hole they found, on the earth under the kitchen floor, a calcined skull, a few charred bones and a pile of ashes. Mrs Rooney had been obliterated by a fantastically hot fire that had not spread beyond her immediate area.

The coroner soon found that Patrick had been suffocated by the smoke of the burning body of his wife.

Charles Fort, who spent a lifetime collecting reports of SHC and other inexplicable occurrences. Fort wondered if SHC might be connected with demonology: 'I think our data relate not to "spontaneous combustion of human bodies" but to things or beings, that with a flaming process consume men and women, but like werewolves or alleged werewolves, mostly pick women.'

Fuelling the human fireball

Among the early pathologists the theory arose that in certain circumstances the body may produce gases that combust on exposure to quantities of oxygen. The distinguished scientist Baron Karl von Reichenbach wrote of the 'miasma of putrefaction' of human bodies, for instance. But Liebig could find no evidence of such a gas, 'in health, in disease, nay not even in the putrefaction of dead bodies.'

Dixon Mann and W.A. Brend, in their *Forensic medicine and toxicology* (1914) give the case of a fat man who died two hours after admission to Guy's Hospital, London, in 1885. The following day his corpse was found bloated, the skin distended all over and filled with gas, although there was no sign of decomposition. 'When punctures were made in the skin, the gas escaped and burnt with a flame like that of carburetted hydrogen; as many as a dozen flames were burning at the same time.' Had the man died at home near a fire, another case of 'spontaneous combustion' would have been reported to confuse researchers further.

However, gases within the body tissues of the sort suggested would be fatally toxic, and the victim would have been gravely ill or dead. And generally there are no such symptoms: victims have often been seen alive shortly before their flaming. Nor does this theory account for the observed fact of clothes that are left unburnt on a charred corpse.

As an alternative to the disease theory, we might consider organic or mechanical malfunctions of normal processes within the body. Ivan Sanderson and, before him, Vincent Gaddis, speculated about the build-up of phosphagens in muscle tissue, particularly the vitamin B10, vital to normal energy supplies. A technical paper in *Applied Trophology* (December 1957) included this relevant paragraph:

> Phosphagen is a compound like nitro-glycerine, of endothermic formation. It is no doubt so highly developed in certain sedentary persons as to make their bodies actually combustible, subject to ignition, burning like wet gunpowder under some circumstances.

This may explain the readiness of some bodies to blaze, but we still have to identify the source of ignition.

An unmistakable case of simultaneous SHC is summarised by Fort, of an elderly couple named Kiley, who lived near Southampton. On the morning of 26 February 1905, neighbours heard a curious 'scratching' and went next door to investigate. They entered the house and found it in flames inside. Kiley was found burned to death on the floor. Mrs Kiley, burned to death, was sitting in a chair in the same room, 'badly charred but recognisable'. Both bodies were fully dressed,

judging by the fragments of clothes, indicating they had been burned before their time for going to bed . . . the mystery was that two persons, neither of whom had cried for help, presumably not asleep in any ordinary sense, should have been burned to death in a fire that did not manifest as a general fire until hours later.

There are on record two cases of SHC which coincided with suicide attempts, the implication of which is obscure unless one presupposes some form of the 'psychic suicide' theory in which victims combust because they have given up on life.

On 13 December 1959, 27-year-old Billy Peterson, of Pontiac, Michigan, said goodbye to his mother and drove to his garage where he hooked a pipe from the car's exhaust into the car itself. Only 40 minutes after Billy had left his mother, a passing motorist saw the smoke and investigated. Inside the car Billy was dead from carbon monoxide poisoning, but it was the condition of his body that puzzled pathologists. His back, arms and legs were covered in third-degree burns, and some parts of him were charred to a crisp. Despite all this, his clothes and underclothes were quite unharmed.

On 18 September 1952, Glen Denney, 46, a foundry worker in Louisiana, cut the arteries in his left arm and both wrists and ankles, but he had died from inhaling smoke. When found, he was a 'mass of flames' with nothing else in the room ablaze. The coroner guessed that he had poured kerosene over himself and lit a match, though no container was found, and just how he could hold, let alone light, a match with arterial blood pumping over his hands at about 4 per cent of body volume per second was not explained. The investigator, Otto Burma, wrote: 'There is no doubt in my mind that Denney did in fact attempt suicide. But while in the process of carrying out this act his body caught fire due to some unknown cause.'

Many other aspects of SHC would reward investigation. There are, for instance, demonstrable connections with poltergeist phenomena, which frequently involve mysterious spontaneous fires. Then there are people who are fire-prone, in whose presence fires repeatedly break out. Examining these and other facts that surround SHC may lead us nearer to understanding the phenomenon – and perhaps to identifying its causes.

The end of an old soldier

On 19 February 1888, Dr J. Mackenzie Booth, a lecturer at Aberdeen University, was called to the loft of a stable in Constitution Street, where he found the charred corpse of a 65-year-old pensioner. There was considerable damage to the body: most of the fleshy parts had burned away exposing the calcined ends of bones. The floor around the man had burnt through so that the corpse rested on a charred beam. The heat had also burned the roofing slats above him, causing some slates to fall onto his chest and damage his brittle form further. He was last seen going into the loft with a bottle and lamp the previous evening.

It was thought that he had knocked the lamp over and then been overcome by drink and smoke. (Booth's report describes the 'old soldier' as being 'of inebriate habits'.) But the lamp had been seen to go out shortly after he went into the loft, and no fire was seen during the night. Furthermore, it is clear from this engraving (from the *British Medical Journal* of 21 April 1888, and based directly on a photograph of the scene) that the bales of hay surrounding the man did not catch fire. The carbonised face retained recognisable features, from which, and from 'the comfortably recumbent attitude of the body' Booth noted that 'it was evident that there had been no death struggle.'

Mysteries of the human bonfire

Medical men and scientists have long doubted that spontaneous human combustion actually occurs. But the facts stubbornly refuse to fit their conventional explanations. This chapter suggests that behind the mysterious burning lies a rare and complex series of events

DEATHS THAT APPEAR to have been caused by spontaneous human combustion (SHC) have always been an embarrassment to the medical profession. The refusal to believe in SHC is not the result of a deliberate conspiracy to suppress the evidence, however. Rather there has been a turning away, a wish not to think about such an outrage of accepted medical and scientific knowledge.

If SHC is mentioned at all, it is only to be dismissed as a belief mistakenly held by the uninformed, or as a superstition lingering from less enlightened times. J. L. Casper, for example, in his *Handbook of the practice of forensic medicine*, complained: 'It is sad to think that in an earnest scientific work, in this year of grace 161, we must still treat of the fable of "spontaneous combustion".' And opinion today is hardly less compromising. Dr Gavin Thurston, the coroner for Inner West London, has said that 'no such phenomenon as spontaneous combustion exists, or has ever occurred'.

At the same time, those scientists and doctors who have examined the effects closely, acknowledge that there have been cases of death by burning that are genuinely inexplicable. But since SHC officially does not exist, some other reason has had to be found for the same effects. And so the notion of

'preternatural combustibility' was born.

The next step was to identify the causes of such a combustibility – and, in any given case, to discover its source of ignition. So, in the middle of the 19th century, a typical SHC victim was thought to be almost certainly a drinker and a smoker; most likely an elderly, solitary, corpulent woman of sedentary habits. Alcohol was both the physical and the moral cause of conflagration. Horrific tales circulated about divine punishment for inebriation, in which the lambent and inextinguishable flames were but a foretaste of the everlasting hellfire to come. Boineau, a French priest, reported the 1749 case of an 80-year-old woman reduced to a carbonised skeleton as she sat sipping brandy. As Baron Justus von Liebig noted sarcastically, 'The chair, which of course had not sinned, did not burn.'

Liebig, in fact, sceptical of SHC though he was, utterly discredited the notion that there was any connection between the phenomenon and drinking. Liebig showed conclusively that alcohol-saturated flesh will burn only until the alcohol is used up; and fatty tissue behaves in the same way – when it can be set alight.

In his 1965 article in *Medicine, science and the law*, Dr D. J. Gee, a lecturer in forensic

Top: Only the legs remain of Mrs E.M., a widow who died on 29 January 1958. Was she burnt by the fire in the grate, or did she combust of her own accord?

Above: Dr Gavin Thurston, who has firmly stated that SHC has never taken place

medicine at Leeds University, described his own experiments following his examination of a charred corpse in 1963. Dr Gee successfully set light to small quantities of fat, but the burning could be sustained only by placing the sample in a strong draught. Even this resulted in no more than a slow smouldering, not the spectacular blaze typical of SHC. However, this has only made it necessary for investigators of what would otherwise be admitted as cases of SHC to look for the 'explanatory' sustaining draught, and prompted some writers to highlight victims who were found in or near a fireplace, where there would be such an updraught.

The readiness with which coroners have adopted these suggestions seems to indicate a strong desire to terminate the proceedings as quickly, conveniently and 'reasonably' as possible, rather than admit a bizarre and frightening mystery. Some verdicts are far from satisfactory. Consider the case of Grace Pett, a fishwife of Ipswich, who was found on the morning of 10 April 1744, lying on the floor near the grate, and burning 'like a block of wood . . . with a glowing fire without flame'. After the fire was put out, Grace was seen to be 'like a heap of charcoal covered with white ashes'. That Grace was a regular smoker, and had the previous evening 'drunk plentifully of gin' in welcoming a daughter

home from Gibraltar, were sufficient for the advocates of temperance and preternatural combustibility.

There are several details in this case, however, that afford these apologists no comfort. According to the account in Sir David Brewster's *Natural magic* (1842) there had been no fire at all in the grate, and a candle, in use that fateful evening, had burnt down safely overnight in its candlestick. And worse: 'The clothes of a child on one side of her, and a paper screen on the other were untouched', and the wooden floor beneath her burning body 'was neither singed nor discoloured'.

Can we, in the 20th century, offer an alternative explanation for SHC besides 'preternatural combustibility'? The savants of the 19th century can be forgiven for thinking only in terms of conventional fire. But since the admirable Liebig's day the physical and medical sciences have made enormous progress. Today we know of many forms of death that can penetrate a man's body silently and invisibly. Military research into 'radiation weapons' has supplemented nuclear radiation with beamed ultrasound, x-ray lasers, microwave projectors and other horrors, all of which can cook a man inside his clothes. But the spirit of Liebig exhorts us to be rigorous: even if we credit the idea of an

Sir David Brewster, whose account of one fire death bears all the marks of a case of SHC. The coroner, however, thought otherwise

A burning rage

Reviewing the cases of SHC in his book *Mysterious fires and lights* (1967), veteran Fortean Vincent Gaddis noted that a high proportion of victims had apparently given up on life. 'Some were alcoholics, and alcoholism is a form of escape from reality . . . Most were elderly with lowered resistance and perhaps tired of life. Many were invalids or poverty-stricken, dying in rest homes or almshouses. Many led idle, sedentary lives.' Charles Fort and his successors have also observed a significant number of 'no-hopers' among SHC victims. In *Fire from heaven* Michael Harrison suggests that

there are several kinds of SHC, one of which is self-induced by people who are depressed, lonely, deprived, frightened and perhaps resentful. Harrison wonders if normally controlled reserves of physical and psychical energy are not suddenly released in a fatal conflagration, as a kind of 'psychic suicide'.

Suicide by fire has always had symbolic overtones, and has been used to make a political gesture. That a massive build-up of rage or despair may result in a spontaneous blaze is appealing, but it is highly conjectural. Besides, it would account for only some cases.

ubiquitous madman recently on the loose with a death ray, we still have to account for the instances from the past.

There are in fact a number of theories that might account for SHC, though not all are equally attractive. Among the least likely are the 'psychic suicide' theory (see box), and the proposition that people whose clothes are set alight catch fire themselves.

This was the suggestion in the case of Phyllis Newcombe. At midnight on 27 August 1938 she and her fiancé were leaving the dance floor of a Chelmsford ballroom, when she suddenly screamed. Her crinoline dress had become a mass of flames. It was put out with some difficulty – and too late, for Phyllis died in hospital a few hours later. At the inquest it was suggested that a discarded cigarette had set the dress alight. The material flamed when a lighter was put to it, but failed to catch fire when lit cigarettes were thrown at it. The coroner expressed his puzzlement and gave a verdict of accidental death. Puzzled he might have been, since in any case external fires cannot produce burns as extensive as those in SHC cases unless large quantities of fuel and oxygen are supplied over a considerable period of time. Even when these conditions are met, the body is burnt from the outside *in*. But there are many cases of SHC in which the burning takes place *within* the flesh, and the clothes or surroundings remain unharmed.

Another somewhat unsatisfactory thesis is the 'corrosive liquid' theory, and it likewise attempts to explain *away* certain cases of death by fire. Nevertheless this was the reason suggested for the death of Madge Knight. At about 3.30 a.m. on 19 November

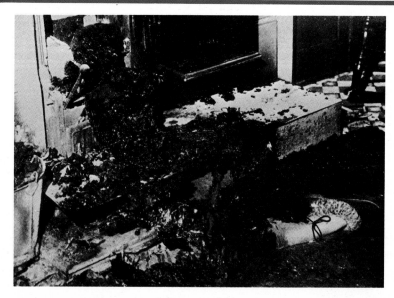

The scorching of a slim lady

Photographic evidence of bizarre burning deaths is very rare and not readily accessible even to the dedicated and bona fide researcher. The charred remains shown here are of 'a slim lady, 85 years old, who was in good health' when she was consumed by flames in November 1963. The case was investigated by Dr D. J. Gee. Because of extensive damage to the body (but to little else) it was assumed that the victim had been in a state of unusual combustibility, and was set alight by an ember or a spark – a theory that would accord with the results of Dr Gee's experiments and the theory of preternatural combustibility.

Conflagration of a clergyman

While away from his parish in Stockcross, Newbury, England, the Reverend Mr Adams burned to death in a hotel room in New York, in 1876, apparently as a result of spontaneous combustion. In *Fire from heaven*, Michael Harrison remarks that 'ecclesiastics, as a class' seem strangely vulnerable to SHC and other paranormal heat phenomena.

1943 she was asleep alone in the spare room of her house in Aldingbourne, Sussex. She awoke feeling as if she were on fire. Her screams brought her husband and others who were sharing the house.

Madge was naked under the bedclothes, but she was in agony because extensive burning had removed most of the skin from her back. A doctor administered morphine, and, bemused, called in a Harley Street specialist. The specialist later told the coroner that he thought the burns must have been caused by a corrosive liquid because there was no sign of fire on the sheets or anywhere else in the room, and no smell of burning. Madge was repeatedly questioned but could not, or would not, say what had happened before she died in hospital in Chichester, on 6 December.

The lack of any sign of fire in many cases has led some researchers to theorise about substances that can burn without flame. In Madge Knight's case, no trace of any corrosive chemical could be found, nor any possible container for it. The notion that Madge hid the evidence before crawling into bed is too absurd to contemplate.

Perhaps the most fruitful clue to the

nature of the phenomenon came in 1975, with Livingston Gearhart's article in the Fortean journal *Pursuit*. He had discovered that a significant number of SHC cases took place on or near a peak in the geomagnetic flux. The strength of the Earth's magnetic field rises and falls quite dramatically in relation to solar activity. Global averages of the daily figures are gathered for astronomers and geophysicists, and these show a distinct correlation between the incidence of SHC and high geomagnetic readings. This seems to indicate that SHC may be the result of a very complex chain of events, in which there is an interaction between certain astronomical conditions and the state of an individual's body. These in turn form the preconditions for the 'ball lightning' theory.

Ball lightning has been offered as one possible culprit for Mrs Reeser's demise. And hers is not the only case. According to an article in *Fate* (April 1961) by the Reverend Winogene Savage, a friend's brother awoke one morning to his wife's screams. Rushing to their living room he found her on the floor, ablaze, with a strange fireball hovering over her blackened form. With the help of neighbours and several buckets of water the flames were put out; but the lady later died, and her husband suffered burns from his ministrations. Witnesses noted that although the wife's clothes had been burnt off, there was no scorching on the rug where she had collapsed, and no other sign of fire damage in the room.

Death from natural causes

Maxwell Cade and Delphine Davis include this account in their 1969 study of ball lightning, *Taming of the thunderbolts*, and note its similarity to the records of spontaneous human combustion. They review the theories of several physicists who suggest that the huge energies of ball lightning could, in certain circumstances, manifest short radio waves of the kind used in microwave ovens. And they speculate:

> If this theory is correct . . . it is possible for victims to be burned to death, not merely within their clothes, but even within their skin, either by the proximity of a lightning ball or by having a ball form within their body, or just by the action of the intense radio-frequency field which, in the absence of their body, would have formed a lightning ball at that place.

As it is a natural phenomenon, and because ball lightning is notoriously capricious, it is the best candidate so far for the cause of SHC cases, whether ancient or modern. It would also account for the victims being fried from the inside out. Microwave diathermy can heat different materials at different rates, and this may explain the curious phenomenon of selective burning that is associated with SHC.

Not one of these theories can account by

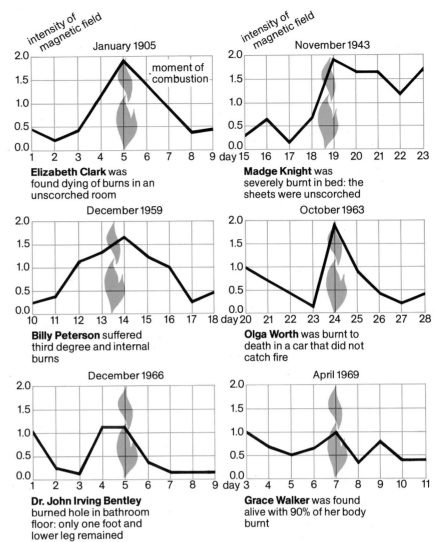

January 1905
moment of combustion
Elizabeth Clark was found dying of burns in an unscorched room

November 1943
Madge Knight was severely burnt in bed: the sheets were unscorched

December 1959
Billy Peterson suffered third degree and internal burns

October 1963
Olga Worth was burnt to death in a car that did not catch fire

December 1966
Dr. John Irving Bentley burned hole in bathroom floor: only one foot and lower leg remained

April 1969
Grace Walker was found alive with 90% of her body burnt

itself for the bizarre varieties of burning that have been authoritatively recorded. The fact that SHC occurs infrequently (if not so rarely as some writers claim) also suggests that it requires special circumstances to come about, and depends on the correct conjunction of many necessary factors. Some we can guess at; others remain unknown. But we can at least offer the following synthesis.

Age and sex seem less important than the victim's psychic and physiological state. We may imagine a lonely, sedentary person, incapacitated by illness or injury, or psychically by despair, fear, depression and perhaps resentment. This incapacity may psychosomatically affect the body and its metabolism, causing an imbalance of phosphagens and erratic behaviour in the body's heat-regulating mechanisms. Normally, this state would pass unnoticed. But imagine that it should happen a few days after intense sunspot activity, with a magnetic storm pushing up the value of the geomagnetic field to abnormal heights for the victim's locality. Now all that is needed is a trigger: a cosmic ray, a natural burst of low-frequency energy, or a lightning ball. And then we have a human bonfire.

The force of the Earth's magnetism is surprisingly uneven. It is unequally distributed around the globe, and fluctuates in intensity (measured in gausses). These six charts show the curious relationship between a high reading on the geomagnetic scale and the incidence of SHC

Resting in peace

To most people the idea of being buried alive is pure nightmare. But some have perfected the art of staying buried alive for long periods – for fame and fortune, or even to gain enlightenment. This chapter looks at a curious way of passing the time

SOMETIME IN THE mid 17th century an astonishing incident occurred in the outskirts of Amritsar, in north-west India. Workmen, digging a ditch in a layer of brittle shale, found they had accidentally broken into an unsuspected tomb. Inside they found the dust-covered – and apparently mummified – body of a young yogi, sitting cross-legged in faded orange robes. They decided to bring the body to the surface and, so the story goes, when the Sun's rays first touched the body's dry skin, it began to change. The yogi gradually stirred and within a short time was talking to the workmen, seemingly not much affected by the ordeal of being buried alive. But he had an even greater shock to impart to his saviours. His name was Ramaswami, he said, and he had descended voluntarily into his tomb about 100 years previously.

Within a month news of the yogi's resurrection had spread far and wide in the subcontinent, and was taken by many Indians to be confirmation, if such were needed, of the reality of yogic powers. No one challenged Ramaswami, so universal was the belief in this feat. On the contrary, one famous historian, Arjun Singh, even journeyed to Amritsar to learn more of life in the previous century from one of its alleged

former denizens. If Ramaswami was a charlatan, he was no ordinary one, because the historian came away impressed.

However, the story of Ramaswami, while providing the prototype for the phenomenon of living burials, is quite unsatisfactory as evidence. Further details are locked away in obscure publications in the Indian languages and are generally inaccessible to the Western researcher; and should one discover a reference it will almost certainly lack the kind of corrobative details that a Westerner would find convincing, partly because these have always seemed incidental to the Indian mind, preoccupied as it has been with philosophical or spiritual truths. Far more satisfactory are the records of a fakir called Haridas, who appeared in the Jammu region of India's north-west frontier in the late 1820s.

Haridas first came to prominence when Raja Dhyan Singh, a government minister, published a description of a four-month

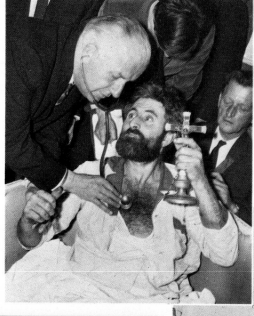

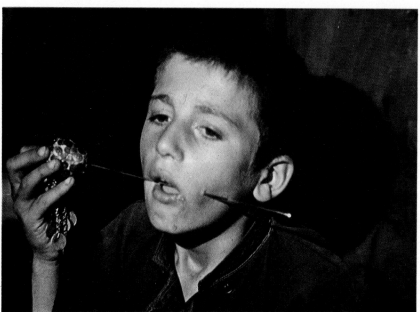

burial endured by Haridas that he himself had witnessed. This was independently confirmed by at least one European doctor. When news of further triumphs in Jasrota and Amritsar reached the ears of the Maharaja of Lahore, an educated sceptic, he invited Haridas to his palace for a carefully controlled experiment. Several English doctors, and French and English military personnel were also invited, the latter being asked to scrutinise the proceedings.

According to a lengthy account in the *Calcutta Medical Times* in 1835, the doctors had immediately discovered that Haridas had cut away the muscles under his tongue so that it could be doubled back to seal off the nasal passages at the back of the throat. For some days before his immurement Haridas consumed only milk and yoghurt and bathed in hot water. Finally he fasted completely, and before all the witnesses performed several extreme yogic ablutions to clean out his

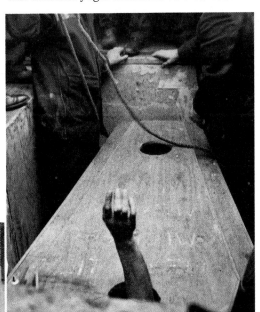

The capacity of Indian yogis – or holy men – to endure even the most hideous self-inflicted pain without flinching (bottom, far left), and to alter their metabolism at will, has long been the stuff of travellers' tales. But the mystic East does not have the monopoly of mind over body. In 1968 Mike Meaney, an Irish barman from Kilburn, London, was buried in a wooden coffin for a record-breaking 61 days. As the coffin was lowered he was in exuberant spirits (left); when he was exhumed, in front of an enormous crowd (below left), he was pronounced by a doctor to be 'in excellent condition' (far left). Others aim to get above ground as fast as possible – in 1955 escapologist Derek Devero freed himself from his manacles and a mailbag underground in Pollokshields, Glasgow, in just five minutes (above)

alimentary canal, including, we are told, swallowing a 30-yard (27-metre) strip of linen and regurgitating it. He closed his nose and ears with wax – a defensive measure against insects – settled into a cross-legged position and rolled his tongue back. The physicians found that within seconds his pulse was undetectable. 'He was physically dead,' declared one.

As the barley sprouts above

Haridas was wrapped in linen and placed in a large, padlocked chest, which was then sealed with the Maharaja's personal seal. The chest was buried and barley sown in the soil above it. Then a wall was built around the site and guards were posted around the clock. Forty days later the guests gathered again, this time to witness the fakir's unearthing. In the meantime, the barley had sprouted undisturbed, and the seal and locks had remained intact. Inside his shroud Haridas was found in the same pose.

According to one of the witnesses, Sir Charles Wade, the fakir had all the appearance of a dead man – his legs and arms had shrunk and were rigid, his head lolled on one shoulder, and there was no detectable pulse in arm or temple. Haridas was massaged all over for minutes before signs of life returned. Doctors pulled back his tongue, unbunged his nose and ears and inflated his lungs with bellows. He was back to normal within the hour. The Maharaja gave him a handful of diamonds; after that he was lionised and showered with gifts wherever he went – for a while. For despite performing several more times – without ever being proved a fraud – he was ignominiously drummed out of Indian high society for deflowering several of his female followers. He was never heard of again.

About a year after Haridas's successful performance at Lahore, there was a report in the *Indian Journal of Medical and Physical*

The human enigma

In the 1930s the United States and Europe were treated to repeated demonstrations of live burials by three Egyptians, Tara Bey, Rahman Bey and Hamid Bey. While in England Rahman Bey effected various 'mysterious' feats under the auspices of psychical researcher Harry Price, including a live burial at Carshalton, Surrey, in July 1938 (right). Although he emerged in good condition some time later (below right) his 'miraculous' abilities were later shown to be only average tricks by Harry Houdini, who outdid every trick the Beys performed

Below: the appropriately named Lucky, a tomcat, was found in a sealed drain in Bristol in June 1982. Workmen had blocked the drain five weeks before – with Lucky in it. His only injury was a stiff neck. After a hearty meal he was able to pose with kennelmaid Joyce Alsworth for the press

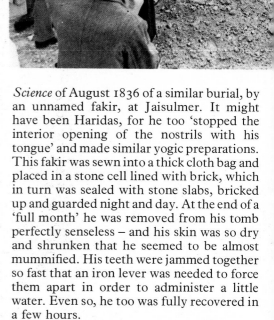

Science of August 1836 of a similar burial, by an unnamed fakir, at Jaisulmer. It might have been Haridas, for he too 'stopped the interior opening of the nostrils with his tongue' and made similar yogic preparations. This fakir was sewn into a thick cloth bag and placed in a stone cell lined with brick, which in turn was sealed with stone slabs, bricked up and guarded night and day. At the end of a 'full month' he was removed from his tomb perfectly senseless – and his skin was so dry and shrunken that he seemed to be almost mummified. His teeth were jammed together so fast that an iron lever was needed to force them apart in order to administer a little water. Even so, he too was fully recovered in a few hours.

In the 1920s three self-styled Egyptians – Tara Bey, Rahman Bey and Hamid Bey – aroused considerable interest in their tour of Europe and the USA. They performed live burials attended by newsmen and physicians, and in the ground of the witnesses' choosing. In what might be called the classic manner, they stopped their ears and noses with cotton, and consciously diminished their breathing and pulse rate. Tara Bey claimed this was achieved by willpower, together with pressure on 'certain' nerve centres in the head and neck and retraction of the tongue to the back of the throat. Recovery was aided either by the attentions of his assistants or through something akin to post-hypnotic suggestion. Despite achieving apparently genuine burials for short periods – for obviously they were not in the same league as Haridas – they were accused at every turn of trickery.

Houdini triumphs again

Their tour ended in a double disgrace. To scotch the rumours of fraud Rahman Bey agreed to lie in a coffin in the Hudson River, but for some reason came up after only 19 minutes, just a few minutes longer than the world record for breath holding. Harry Houdini saw his chance to expose the fakir as a fraud: using his own not inconsiderable powers of breath control, he spent one and a half hours in a steel coffin at the bottom of a swimming pool at the Hotel Shelton, New York. Tara Bey, too, was trounced, but by a Frenchman called Heuzé who was buried in an ordinary coffin for an hour. There was no need for mystical trances, he said, because by keeping absolutely still and breathing slowly there had been enough air.

It is easy enough to explain the burial feat by presupposing trickery, as openly advocated by the psychologist D. H. Rawcliffe in *Illustrated magic* (1931) – or as implied in Ottaker Fischer's speculation in the same work that fakirs must have dug concealed tunnels leading to hollow trees, or used coffins with false bottoms or sliding panels.

The fact that most of the mendicant jugglers and magicians calling themselves fakirs have been revealed to be cunning tricksters has not helped matters either. In 1955 the pioneering ufologist John Keel, then aged about 25, was a syndicated journalist drifting about India seeking out *jadoo wallahs* – performers of black magic and miracles. In his search for genuine mysteries, which was recorded in his first book *Jadoo* (1957), he saw very few and gradually became more cynical about the alleged accomplishments and motives of the self-styled 'living gods' and their ilk:

> Even though India is filled with tales about men who presumably equalled Haridas' performances, there is no solid record of them. Fakirs who tried the stunt afterwards were just imitators and they devised all kinds of tricks to do it. . . . More sincere holy men attempted the feat without trickery, and when they were dug up they were really dead.

These fatalities were so frequent that in 1955, while Keel was looking for someone to perform the feat for him, the Indian government was obliged to outlaw the practice.

But even the cynical John Keel found enough evidence to suggest that there were genuine fakirs with authentic powers – but they were solitary, secretive men who could not be found unless they wished it. This view had been confirmed by Louis Jacolliot, former Chief Justice in the then French Indies, who spent some time wandering through India in search of true fakirs. As Jacolliot explains in his *Occult science in India* (1884), he met several who, naked and without trickery or any kind of apparatus, demonstrated a variety of paranormal phenomena on demand.

If yoga is the means to the goal of *samadhi*, a superconscious state of union with the totality of existence, then the Islamic fakir and his counterpart, the Hindu *sadhu*, differ from more philosophical or spiritual yogis by

Right: an Indian fakir reclines on a bed of sharp nails, his emaciated body showing signs of previous self-torture. It seems that anything, from sticking knives in oneself to firewalking, is possible while entranced. The vital bodily functions can also be slowed until barely perceptible. It is under such conditions that yogis can remain underground for a considerable time

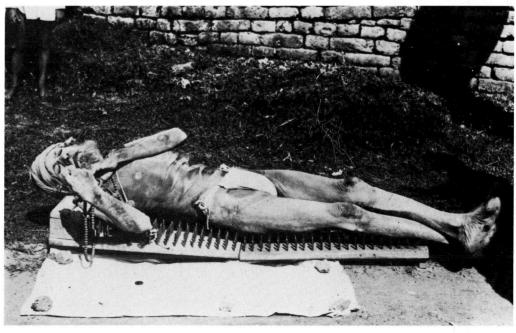

hibernating animal and can similarly be buried alive for days'. The comparison between the fakir's self-induced cataleptic state and animal hibernation was first proposed by James Braid, the physician who coined the term 'hypnosis', and the connection is clearly implied in the title of his *Observations on trance, of human hibernation* (1850), in which he discusses live burials. He concluded that yogis had perfected their control through the use of self-hypnosis, which released extraordinary subconscious powers.

This association with animal hibernation is an enduring and obvious one, and has engendered a splendid piece of American folklore, referred to by Ivan Sanderson in *Things* (1967), that from colonial times pioneer folk in the hard mountain winters would systematically chill their old folk in freezing draughts, then pack them in snow until the spring thaw. However, laboratory studies cited by Andrija Puharich in *Physiological psychology* (1950) show that although the yogi does indeed reduce his oxygen consumption and heartbeat, 'the two states are quite unlike.' For example, Puharich claims that in hibernation the basal metabolic rate is low and in yogic trance it is high; in hibernation blood sugar supply is much reduced whereas in yogic trances it remains more or less the same or can even rise. He concludes: 'Therefore, although trance and hibernation may appear to an outsider to be very much the same condition, they are, physiologically speaking, directly opposite conditions.'

Yet the fact remains that 'impossible' feats of suspended animation have been witnessed by many people of integrity over the centuries, in Africa as well as India.

concentrating on the means and not the goal. Their aim is nothing less than mastery of their immediate existence by absolute control of their bodies, minds and psychic forces. This, they claim, can be accomplished only by years of gruelling discipline bordering on self-torture. This single-minded persistence pays off with conscious control of the body's autonomic nervous system, which governs our involuntary functions, and through which the adept can demonstrably control his pulse rate, breathing, sexual function, metabolism, kidney activity, body temperature and so on. This fine control would extend to involuntary muscle functions; another form of the yogic ablutions used by Haridas to cleanse his alimentary tract is the reversal of normal peristaltic motion so that water may be drawn up through the bowel and bladder.

In *The living brain* (1953) the neurologist Dr W. Grey Walter agreed that conscious control of autonomic processes would enable an adept to reduce his body 'to the state of an

The buried fakir's self-induced cataleptic state seems to bear a resemblance to that of hibernating animals, such as the dormouse (above), or to the instinctive behaviour of some creatures, such as the Australian frog *Lymnodynastes ornatus* (right), that hide in the ground. Yet according to Andrija Puharich, the yogi's state is quite unlike that of a hibernating animal; for example, in hibernation the basal metabolic rate is dramatically lowered – but in trance it rises. Puharich summed up: 'they are, physiologically speaking, directly opposite conditions'

A grave condition

In Dahomey, West Africa, certain tribesmen are drugged, wound in a sheet (left) and buried for long periods. During this time they are supposed to be in touch with magical or archetypal forces that will benefit the whole tribe. Some Indian yogis, who go through similar ordeals, have been tested by Western scientists, such as Dr Elmer Green of the Menninger Foundation (below), and discovered to be 'elsewhere' mentally, and possibly aware of events outside time and space. The Russian mentalist Wolf Messing (bottom) apparently gained his bizarre gifts only after a prolonged, 'psychic' sleep, or trance

How can a man – even a trained adept, such as an Indian yogi – suspend his bodily functions in such a way that he is, in effect, simulating death? This curious phenomenon of prolonged suspended animation is still practised in some places today

IT SEEMS IMPOSSIBLE to Westerners that men can deliberately put themselves in a state of suspended animation – by controlling their autonomic bodily functions, in a way not understood – and remain buried underground for hours, days, or – so it is rumoured – even years and emerge alive. Yet for centuries reliable witnesses have reported many such 'impossible' feats performed by Indian fakirs or yogis – but why do they choose such an extreme form of self-mortification?

The yogi has developed these disciplines to minimise inner and outer distractions (the latter by controlling his sensory channels) in his quest for the attainment of higher consciousness. But it appears that the Indian fakir uses them simply to control his body rather than to reach some nebulous *samadhi*, or ecstasy. To him the live burial becomes the supreme demonstration of his power over his body and mind. According to Andrija Puharich, the fakir is not unconscious in the ordinary sense, since one of his aims is to maintain full control of the four states –

waking, sleeping, dreaming and the biological shutdown of the 'false death' of catalepsy, which in the fakir's case is often self-induced. During the period of burial he does not lose consciousness but enters a deep state of meditation.

Just how and why the practice first originated is lost in the mists of time. The physician James Braid, at least, was sure of its antiquity. In his *Observations of trance, of human hibernation* (1850), he cites a passage from the *Dabistan*, a Persian classic on Indian religion: 'It is an established custom amongst the yogis that, when malady overtakes them, they bury themselves.' This implies that self-inhumation may have its

The human enigma

Augustine, for example, writing in the 6th century, described the ability of a priest named Rutilut, who could deliberately stop his pulse and respiration and who was insensitive to pain during his self-induced trances.

Whatever the origins of live burial, instances similar to those of India do occur in other countries where they are part of the physical phenomena of ritualised trance – as described in M. Eliade's *Shamanism* (1972). In *More things* (1969) Ivan Sanderson tells of a burial of an unnamed fakir for 24 hours under two truckloads of gooey earth on the main plaza of Belize, British Honduras, supervised by five doctors, including a British Senior Medical Officer.

And in Japan there existed a strange cult of self-mummification, described in Carmen Blacker's *The Catalpa bow* (1975). These Buddhists would vow to complete fasts lasting up to 4000 days, beginning with a severely restricted diet and gradually diminishing to a total fast with the goal of dying on the last day of the fast. At least two members of this 'interesting and now extinct' group are recorded as entering their tombs alive. Provided only with a breathing tube, they too

origin in attitudes towards death and illness, the technique being learned from the survivors who undoubtedly reported that the extreme form of isolation hastened their cure or enhanced their ecstasies. Comparisons might be drawn here with the therapeutic sleep of patients at the temple-hospitals dedicated to the god Asclepius in 5th-century Greece – such as the one that flourished at Epidaurus, Peloponnese – and the practice, common in oriental mystery cults, of keeping an initiate in darkness or underground for a period of instruction, or in a trance-like sleep, induced by drugs or exhaustion, in order to obtain visions.

A different origin might have been the imitation of spontaneous instances of suspended animation – indeed the medical historians G. Gould and W. Pyle, in their *Anomalies and curiosities of medicine* (1896), compare the fakir's feat to cases of recovery from hanging or drowning involving either long periods of unconsciousness or the pathological form of catalepsy that has frequently led to the horrors of premature burial. This latter form, also called narcolepsy, contributed to the growth of the evil and grisly vampire legend. To this we might add the hysterical catalepsy that preceded the arrival of paranormal abilities in a significant number of cases, such as the Russian telepathist Wolf Messing who was unconscious for three days.

Gould and Pyle discuss other cases in the literature of abnormal psychology from the 19th century either in connection with diseases or as 'spontaneous mesmeric sleep'.

The ability to simulate death is rare – though not unknown – in the West. St

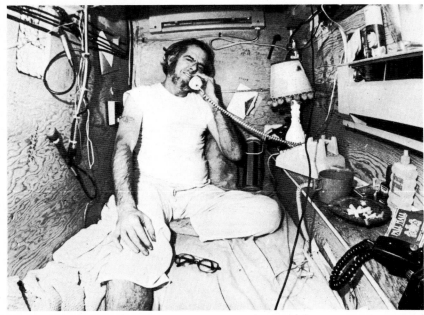

Top: in 1974 an Indian yogi buried his head in earth for many long minutes, with a pulse rate of just two beats per minute – but he survived. And a US stuntman, Bill White (above), attracted attention by staying underground for 134 days, two hours and five minutes in 1978, passing the time by telephoning the press – including the public relations officer of *The Guinness book of records* (in which he found a place)

eventually joined the ranks of mummified abbots in the temples on Mount Yudono.

According to the South African *Pretoria News* in late 1974, a Togolese jujuman, named Togbui Siza Aziza, was buried for three hours in Accra in an ordinary coffin. Stone slabs covered the box, then a layer of mortar topped with more slabs. After two hours the crowd began to panic and pleaded with Aziza, whose muffled voice could still be faintly heard. Finally, the ground shook and Aziza burst through the mortar, easily shoving the slabs aside. But the coffin was found nailed shut. Interestingly, Aziza, who tours with a group promoting African mysticism, Afrika Azzeu, says that he gains his magical

The legendary feats of Indian holy men include being buried with arms protruding from the ground (left), and keeping one's arms above one's head for 30 years (below). It seems likely that many such tales are mere rumour, but some of them may well be based on fact

powers, which include the ability to heal the sick, understand animals and be impervious to pain, by meditating underground.

Among other accounts of suspended animation from Africa, mention must be made of the 'walkers for water', who were first drawn to the attention of Ivan Sanderson in 1932 by the British Resident Mr N. H. Cleverley in Calabar, British Cameroons. The Resident had dispatched a senior official and a sergeant of the Native Bush Police to investigate the refusal of several villages in the Ibibio tribal territory to pay their taxes. The villagers were nowhere to be found on their large swamp-surrounded islands, until the native sergeant doffed his uniform and went 'under cover'. Then he made a startling discovery.

Peering over a 6-foot (1.6-metre) cliff the sergeant saw 'the entire community (over a hundred souls, men, women and children, *and* their pets, which were confined in open-work baskets and appeared to be asleep) sitting motionless at the bottom of the water with their backs to the bank.' The sight of his sergeant shaking with fear – and failing to 'wake up' the villagers, in 8 feet (2.4 metres)

Stephen Pile's bestselling *Book of heroic failures* (1979) includes 'The most unsuccessful lying in state' and 'The funeral that disturbed the corpse'. The first concerns the 'late' Bishop of Lesbos who, in 1896, after two days lying in state, suddenly sat up and demanded to know what the mourners were staring at. In the second story a missionary called Schwartz who 'died' in New Delhi in the 1890s joined in the hymn singing from his coffin during his funeral.

In the context of Pile's book both are hilarious stories, yet premature burial was – and still is – a grim business. In the days when doctors merely felt the pulse

Death when is thy sting?

or held a mirror to catch the mist of breath, cataleptic patients had a horrifyingly high chance of being certified dead and duly buried – alive. In primitive areas knocking sounds emitting from freshly dug graves might be taken as ghostly manifestations and therefore ignored.

But, despite today's medical sophistication, the actual moment of death is the subject of hot debate; are we 'dead' if our hearts stop beating or only when our brains cease to register electrical activity? And is the heart that is transplanted an organ that is torn from the living or from the dead?

of water, was too much for the European, who fled back to Calabar. His report was not dismissed by his superiors, who were 'old Coasters' and well acquainted with the bizarre practices of the region. A second, more experienced team was dispatched, but by the time they arrived village life was back to normal and the sergeant had collected the taxes. This was not 'a yarn', Cleverley assured Sanderson; the incident had been soberly recorded at the Resident's court in Calabar.

This story is not unrelated to the live burial of fakirs. Either the African villagers could suspend their vital functions spontaneously, or they prevailed upon some shaman skilled in techniques akin to hypnotism. But there is a record of at least one yogi who performed a very similar phenomenon by an act of his own will in Bombay, on 15 February 1950, according to a report in the

Above: December 1953, and yogi Count Ostoja induces a trance in order to endure being buried alive; he duly survived. Even stranger desires caused a now extinct cult of Japanese Buddhists to fast unto death – but release came only when they took up a position in what was to be their tomb (left). Some even timed this feat so exactly as to die the same day they entered the tomb

Lancet for that year signed by a Dr R. J. Vakil. Before a huge crowd, and under Dr Vakil's supervision, 'an emaciated middle-aged sadhu called Shri Ramdasji' was sealed into a small underground cubicle for 56 hours. The chamber measured 5 by 8 feet (1.5 by 2.4 metres) and was made of concrete studded with large nails, and plugged with more concrete. At the end of the 56 hours a hole was bored in the lid and 1400 gallons (6400 litres) of water poured in through a firehose, and the hole re-sealed. The watery tomb was broken open nearly seven hours later and the sadhu discovered completely submerged. He had survived.

For 15 years after hearing the story of the Ibibio villagers from Cleverley, Sanderson tried to find out more about their astonishing feat, but in vain. 'Trouble is,' he wrote, 'I can't find anybody in our world who will even discuss the matter sensibly and from a scientific point of view. One would have thought that this would be a golden opportunity for liars and other storytellers. Perhaps it is too big a lie; perhaps they just don't have the imagination. Perhaps, however, it is the truth. . . .'

The human salamander

Fear of fire is deeply rooted in the human psyche – but some rare people are totally immune to both heat and flames. This chapter begins an examination of the history of human incombustibility

THE BELIEF that the blacksmith is 'Master of Fire' is common in both ancient cultures and modern primitive societies, and at various times has been current in central Europe, Asia, Africa and North and South America; a fact which lends extra interest to an extraordinary story published in the *New York Herald* of 7 September 1871.

Nathan Coker was blacksmith in Easton, Maryland, and had long held the reputation of being immune to heat. A committee of local citizens and members of the press asked if they might put him to the test, and he agreed. First, a shovel was heated in his forge until it became white-hot and incandescent. Coker 'pulled off his boots and placed the hot shovel on the soles of his feet, and kept it there until the shovel became black.'

Next, lead shot was heated until molten. Coker swilled it around his teeth and tongue

like a mouthwash, until it solidified. Then Coker plunged his hands into the blazing forge and calmly picked out glowing coals, which he showed to the onlookers on the palms of his hands. As a finale, he casually handled a piece of red-hot iron.

'It don't burn,' he told the reporter nonchalantly. 'Since I was a little boy, I've never been afraid to handle fire.'

Coker was neither a showman nor a religious fanatic. To him, the startling phenomenon was simply a fact of life.

A blacksmith was involved in a similar report made by a New York physician, Dr K. R. Wissen, in 1927. While on a hunting trip in the Tennessee mountains, the doctor met a shy backwoods boy who could hold burning firebrands without feeling pain or suffering physical injury. The boy told Wissen that he had discovered his mysterious ability as a child, when he had picked up a red-hot horseshoe from a forge. Like Coker, he took his gift entirely for granted.

The immunity of certain people to extreme heat – whether cultivated, as in the

The human enigma

Previous page, left: a modern Balinese trance dancer seems to be in imminent danger of incinerating himself over a fierce fire – but escapes totally unscathed

Previous page, right: the Old Testament tells how King Nebuchadnezzar threw Shadrach, Mesach and Abednego into the fiery furnace – and they emerged unhurt

Right: an early 19th-century engraving showing a traditional Thai firewalker treading a pit of super-heated stones. Only 'special' people, those few who are born incombustible, or others who undergo secret magical rites – perhaps involving auto-hypnosis – can expose their flesh to intense heat without feeling, or showing, any ill effects

case of shamanist societies, for instance, or apparently fortuitous, as in the case of such individuals as Nathan Coker – has been a source of wonder and bafflement to observers of the phenomenon for centuries. The very ubiquity, across ages and continents, of these 'human salamanders' adds to the mystery. The Biblical story of Nebuchadnezzar's burning fiery furnace and its three intended victims Shadrach, Mesach and Abednego, for example, strikes a familiar chord when compared with modern fire-walking in Trinidad or Polynesia. The fire was so hot that it killed the men who put Shadrach and company into it, yet

> 'the princes, governors and captains, and the king's counsellors, being gathered together, saw these men, upon whose bodies the fire had no power, nor was an hair of their head singed, neither were their coats changed, nor the smell of fire had passed on to them.'

Classical writers such as Plato and Virgil recorded instances of people walking unscathed on hot coals, while in the third

century AD the Neoplatonist Porphyry and his pupil Iamblichus investigated the phenomenon as part of a thorough and objective survey of divination, spirit raising, and trance states. Certain 'possessed' mediums, they noted, felt no pain and suffered no injury when 'thrown into fire, or passed through fire'.

The annals of the early and medieval Church are littered with accounts of such saintly activities as levitation, miracle healing and teleportation as well as immunity to fire. And though the majority of them are based on hearsay evidence, a handful stand up to scrutiny. Among these are accounts of 'ordeal by fire', a favourite way of settling ecclesiastical differences. In 1062 the Bishop

of Florence was accused by the saintly Peter Aldobrandini of having bribed his way into office. A long, narrow corridor was paved with red hot coals, with a bonfire at each end. Peter walked through one bonfire, along the coals, and out through the further flames, his flesh and clothing remaining unburned. The Bishop declined to follow him, and resigned instead. Later, in the mid 13th century, another monk with a reputation for holiness, Giovanni Buono, made a habit of demonstrating his faith by shuffling his feet in burning coals 'as if washing them in a brook, for as long as it took to say half a *miserere*'.

In 1637 the French Jesuit, Father Paul Lejeune, was very impressed – although at the same time considerably annoyed – by what he saw among the Huron Indians near Quebec. Lejeune was heading a mission to the Indians, but the tribal medicine men were in no mood to be converted and put on what appeared to be a special show for him: a sort of healing by fire ceremony. He wrote:

> You may believe me, since I speak of a thing that I saw with my own eyes – they [the medicine men] separated the brands, drew the stones from the midst of the fire, and holding their hands behind their back took them between their teeth, carried them to the patients, and remained some time without loosening their hold . . . not only these persons but even the sick were not burned. They let their bodies be rubbed with glowing cinders without their skin appearing in the least affected.

Even Lejeune's phlegmatic Jesuitry could not compete and he retired from the scene temporarily defeated.

In 1731 the lay authorities and the Catholic Church joined forces to examine an outbreak of hysterical possession that had

Above: firewalking as a modern tourist attraction: holidaymakers eagerly photograph local volunteers stepping out casually over white-hot stones outside the Korolevu Beach Hotel in Fiji

Right: Saints Alexander and Eventius are joined by Theodulus to celebrate their triumph over the flames into which they were thrown by Aurelius, persecutor of Christians

Below: an Indian fakir exhibits his technique of mind-over-matter by hanging upside down over a fire

followed the death of the Jansenist heretic François de Paris four years previously. De Paris's followers, congregating around his grave at St Medard, were reported to have gone into convulsions, during which they spun like tops, twisted their limbs into impossible positions, and levitated. Louis xv ordered the cemetery closed, and appointed a magistrate, Carré de Montgeron (an agnostic), to head the examining board.

One meticulously detailed report compiled by Montgeron, two priests and eight court officials told of the incombustible Marie Souet. Naked, apart from a linen sheet, Marie had gone into a trance that rendered her body rigid. In this condition she had been suspended over a blazing fire for 35 minutes, and although the flames actually lapped around her, neither she nor the sheet was damaged. The free-thinking Montgeron was so astounded by what he saw that he began a sympathetic examination of spiritism, annoying the authorities and landing himself in the Bastille for his pains.

The famous English diarist John Evelyn wrote of seeing 'Richardson the fire-eater' perform after dinner at Lady Sunderland's house in London on 8 October 1672. His account is all the more convincing for the slight note of scepticism at the end:

He devoured brimstone on glowing coals before us, chewing and swallowing them; he melted a beer glass and ate it quite up; then taking a live coal on his tongue he put on it a raw oyster, the coal was blown on with bellows till it flamed and sparkled in his mouth, and so remained until the oyster gaped and was quite boiled; then he melted pitch and wax with sulphur, which he drank down as it flamed; I saw it flaming in his mouth a good while. He also took up a thick piece of iron, such as laundresses use to put in their smoothing bokes, when it was fiery hot, held it between his teeth, then in his hand and threw it about like a stone, but this I observed he cared not to hold very long.

Another celebrated 'after-dinner' performer whose feats attracted considerable attention in Victorian society was the medium Daniel Dunglas Home. Lord Adare, an army officer and war correspondent, and H. D. Jencken, a barrister, told how, at a seance in 1868, Home stirred up a glowing fire in the grate and 'placed his face right among the burning coals, moving it about as though bathing it in water'. It seems that Home could confer his immunity to onlookers too; after making passes over their hands he would hand them burning embers without them suffering injury. More startlingly, at a seance at the home of Mr and Mrs S. C. Hall, a couple who combined prominence in the art world with membership of the Society for Psychical Research, Home took 'a huge lump of live burning coal, so large that he held it in both hands', and placed it on top of Mr Hall's

head. Mr Hall said that the coal felt 'warm but not hot'.

According to Mrs Hall, Home 'then proceeded to draw up Mr Hall's white hair over the red coal; Mr Home drew the hair into a sort of pyramid, the coal, still red, showing beneath the hair'.

Even while Home was startling such establishment figures as Adare and Sir William Crookes, tales of firewalking and firehandling feats from far-flung corners of the Empire were becoming commonplace. Basil Thompson, for instance, in his *South Sea yarns*, related how he watched a group of Fijiian islanders walking over a long pit of super-heated stones. Thompson touched a pocket handkerchief to one of the nearer stones and it immediately scorched, and yet not only did the near-naked Fijiians walk over the pit with impunity, but 'their ankle fillets of dry fern remained untouched.'

In 1904, members of Sir Francis Younghusband's expedition to Tibet told of Buddhist monks who could not only stand motionless and unharmed in the midst of blazing

fires but sit for hours, clad only in a thin saffron robe, in sub-zero temperatures. Over and over again such stories were told, often by intelligent and unbiased witnesses, only, more often than not, to have them dismissed by the scientific establishment.

Professor E. R. Dodds, in his *Supernormal phenomena in classical antiquity*, outlines the difficulty of collating ancient accounts of paranormal happenings. A useful purpose, he suggests, may be served by examining surviving evidence to see whether the phenomena described are consistent with those from other periods of history; if they are strikingly different, it could be argued that each age is the victim of its own superstitions.

In the case of the 'human salamanders', the many similarities between accounts from all ages and countries must mean that the student of the paranormal has at least a sound basis from which to work.

The mastery of fire

People who are proof against fire can be found all over the world – on every continent and in every kind of society. But where did the tradition of 'fire mastery' have its roots? And what does it mean to those who practise its unlikely rituals?

GEORGE SANDWITH was fascinated, like many a Westerner before him, by the fire-walking ceremonies he saw while working as a British government surveyor on the island of Suva in the Fijiian group. Local adherents of one of the many Hindu sects made a practice of walking over red-hot embers, laid down in special trenches 30 to 40 feet (9 to 12 metres) long, to celebrate the feasts of Hindu deities.

After his retirement in the 1950s, Sandwith wrote a book, *The miracle hunters*, in which he gave details of what he had witnessed. He also recorded the reaction of a fellow European, a banker, who was watching the phenomenon for the first time:

> Very grudgingly he admitted the fire-walking was genuine, for he had thrown something on the pit and it caught fire at once, but he was strongly of the opinion that the Government ought to stop it! When asked why he became very annoyed replying that it does not conform with modern scientific discoveries. When I suggested that something of value might be learned from the firewalkers, he was so furious that he turned on his heel and left me.

While the banker's 'rationalist' attitude may be understandable it is one that has been adopted by scientists in the face of 'fire phenomena' for well over a century. More interestingly, it is paralleled by the attitudes of the leaders of those religions – Hinduism, Buddhism and Shintoism, for instance – whose followers practise 'firehandling'. To them, such activities occupy a peripheral place, at best, in relation to orthodox religion

Above: Jatoo Bhai, a 'fakir' from Calcutta, dances in the midst of a blazing fire – and will emerge unscathed

Below: during the ritual of preparation for the firewalk, Jatoo Bhai goes into an attitude of prayer

and are not encouraged. They do not fit in with established thought.

Occasionally an example of 'fire power' turns up in a primitive society that has no tradition of such esoteric skills, and here again the practitioner is often viewed with disapproval. The late Frank Clements, a journalist and rancher from what was then Southern Rhodesia, and who served as Mayor of Salisbury during the 1950s, gave an account of one such isolated instance that he encountered among the Shona tribe. He and a veterinary surgeon had been inoculating Shona cattle and were invited for a meal. Afterwards, squatting by the fire, Clements lit a cigarette with a Zippo lighter. As he recalled afterwards:

> It was an old one and was slightly over-fuelled, and the resulting flame was, I

suppose, rather spectacular to those of the tribe who were not familiar with cigarette lighters – mostly the younger children. But there was a tribal elder present who had taken rather a dislike to my companion and me. As if showing what *he* could do, he plucked a burning brand from the fire and, holding it up to his grey-bearded face, licked the flame slowly, letting it flicker around his cheeks and nostrils. Then he quenched the flame quite deliberately between his palms, gave a snort of contempt in our direction, and tossed the stick away. He seemed to suffer no injury and his beard was not even singed.

Interestingly, the Shona are an agricultural people whose traditions lack any element of fire mastery – unlike, for instance, the Katanga, the BaYeke, the Mosengere and other tribes of the Congo area who are metalworking people and practise complex fire rituals and initiation rites. The Shona 'fire-eater' appears to have been unique among his people: an individual who either had learned his skill from a wandering expert or was one of those born with the gift.

Anthropologically, it is possible to trace

Below: Jatoo Bhai works himself into a state of religious ecstasy as part of the 'fireproofing' process

Bottom: handling fire, before the dance in the flames

the activities of most fire ritual societies back to a probable central source – the Iron Age shamanists of central Asia. These, Tartars, Mongols and Yakuts, thought of fire as one of the greatest of nature's mysteries, to be feared and revered. 'The first smith, the first shaman, and the first potter were blood brothers,' says an ancient Yakut proverb, referring to their importance in the community; but beyond doubt the smith was held in the highest esteem. He was 'master of fire' and he proved it by swallowing burning coals, walking on hot embers, and holding red-hot iron in his hands: significantly, the greatest Tartar hero of all, Ghengis Khan, was said to have begun life as a blacksmith, and to have flown his leather apron as a battle pennant at the peak of his lance when riding

to war. As a corollary to fire mastery, the smith could also endure intense cold by cultivating 'inner heat' or 'spiritual heat', so that by overcoming both extremes of temperature he was, in the eyes of his community, super-human and on the level of a spirit or demi-god.

Over the course of centuries the knowledge and practice of firehandling filtered out from Asia during prehistoric migrations. By about 500 BC, it had spread to China and Japan, Tibet and the Indian sub-continent. While in Bulgaria and Greece the ancient Cabiri peoples were being described as 'masters of the furnace' and 'mighty in fire'. Their secret knowledge eventually found its way all around the eastern Mediterranean and down into Africa.

Fire mastery was easily absorbed into the practices of Hinduism on the Indian sub-continent. The word 'Hindu' is simply the Persian for 'Indian'; to the Indians themselves their religion was 'Sanatana', roughly translating as 'eternal and ageless'. The aim of devout Hindus is to achieve the 'Brahman', or essential self, and they attempt this by following one or more of the 10 or so 'yoga' paths of self discovery. Hatha yoga, perhaps the most familiar form to Westerners, is the way to both physical control and mastery of the occult. The initiate works his way through seven stages of hatha yoga until he reaches the eighth stage, *samadhi*, which cannot be taught but is recognised by the practitioner achieving it. *Samadhi* brings with it preternatural abilities, or *siddhis*, and the men who achieve these are known as *sadhus* – erroneously known to Europeans as *fakirs*, a word that properly denotes an Islamic holy man.

The majority of *sadhus* seem content to remain in one place and quietly meditate. It is the more eccentric 'fakir' types who capture the popular imagination. Some of these are genuinely sincere, setting themselves dramatic but apparently pointless tasks in their search for holiness; they may set out to bathe in as many sacred rivers and waterholes as possible, or sit motionless in a thorn

fakir will arrive at a village and order the trench to be prepared and filled with hot stones. He then leads the 'faithful' across. There are many accounts of Europeans having joined in the walks, and remarkably few instances of serious injury. 'The idea is,' explained one commentator, 'that the *sadhu* takes on all the pain to himself and then negates it by willpower. The stones are genuinely hot, the bodies of the walkers untreated by any artificial preparation. There seems to be no rational explanation. . . .'

Significantly, it is among the Hindu sects that the firewalkers of Polynesia, Malaya and Tahiti flourish. But the Buddhists of China, Tibet and Japan go in for almost exactly similar practices, while in Hong Kong firewalking feats are an out-and-out tourist attraction. Shintoism, the ancient nature and ancestor worship of the Japanese, also has its firewalking devotees.

E. G. Stephenson. a professor of English literature, attended a Shinto ceremony in Tokyo during which a 90-foot (27-metre) blazing trench was prepared. Professor Stephenson bravely asked if he might try. The officiating priest took him to a temple nearby and sprinkled salt over his head, after which the professor 'strolled over the trench in quite a leisurely way', feeling only a 'faint tingling' in the soles of his feet.

There is a strong element of showmanship about many of the voodoo rituals of the West Indies, in which fire mastery in various forms plays an important part. In Trinidad, fire-eaters and firewalkers abound, but it is in Haiti, where voodoo still forms the basis of

bush for years until the spiky growth completely enfolds them, or permanently clench their fists so that their finger nails grow into the palms of their hands. Some, on the other hand, set out on what amounts to a deliberate circus career, and it is from among these that most of the fire masters of India are drawn. To devout and sophisticated Hindus these 'showmen' are anathema, and yet the genuineness of their powers is never doubted: a contradiction that has caused a good deal of Western scepticism. It is almost as if a medieval saint were to have levitated, exhibited stigmata, and performed miracles of healing in the market place for cash.

Fire-trench walking seems to be among the most popular of the fakirs' feats. On the feast day of a local Hindu deity – there are dozens of Hindu sects and numerous gods – a

Above: Jatoo Bhai dances in the flames at the climax of his ritual

Right: after the dance, the fakir displays his unburnt feet – and, equally remarkable, his unscorched clothing

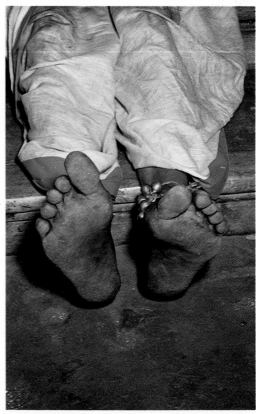

most political, social and religious activity, that fire masters are most spectacular.

Dr William Sargant, author and psychiatrist, made Haitian voodoo the subject of close study for several years. Briefly, he came to the conclusion that most of the phenomena took place after the participants had worked themselves into a state of deep trance. Interestingly, Haitian voodoo practices can be traced back by way of the African Congo, Arab traders, Asia Minor and Persia to the Mongol and Tartar shamans.

Many West Indian slaves were exported from the Congo, among them great numbers of Yoruba. The principal god of the Yoruba tribe was Ogun, a celestial smith who taught his people to handle fire and work with metal. The Yoruba secret society Ogboni still has Ogun as its patron, and practises firehandling and eating. In Haiti, Ogun has become Ogun Badagris, the 'bloody warrior' who demands that his followers cultivate immunity to both 'inner' and 'outer' fire.

They fulfil these requirements quite literally, first by dancing on live coals, and second by drinking prodigious quantities of fiery white rum into which ground cayenne pepper has been liberally poured. At one all-woman ceremony, Dr Sargant saw the participants not only consume this apparently lethal mixture without collapsing, but rub it into their open eyes without damaging their sight in any way. Haitian voodoo is a complex admixture of African and European influences, and Dr Sargant was interested to note that some of the women dancers wore modern welders' and metal-workers' goggles, which they removed only to anoint their eyes with the rum and pepper.

The North American Indians are a Mongol race in origin; their prehistoric ancestors were nursed in the same Asiatic cradle as the Tartars, and carried shamanism and its accompanying fire mastery with them from Siberia to Alaska and from there down

Above: the Buddhist fire-walking festival *hi watari*, which is held every year at the foot of Mt Takao in Japan. The ceremony is dedicated to prayers for peace – and to the health of the onlookers, who rub their ailing parts with wooden boards before throwing them on to the fire

Below: the Navajo fire dance, as depicted by the painter William Leigh

the American continent. Literally every Indian tribe has at least the remnants of fire worship as part of its culture. Father Lejeune's Canadian Hurons have retained the old skills more or less intact, as have the Apaches of the South West and several of the Plains Indians such as the Sioux and Cheyenne. Some tribes, the Blackfoot and Pueblo for instance, less dramatically smear themselves with ashes, which they regard as the 'seeds of fire', in purification rituals.

Perhaps the most intriguing fire purification ceremony among North American Indians is that practised by the Navajo, which combines elements of shamanism with those of the Finnish sauna. The village people prepare themselves for purification by building a roaring fire in the *hogan* or ritual hut. The tribe strip naked and, led by the shaman, enter and circle the fire while the shaman makes offerings of incense to the four quarters. A ritual dance follows, during which the women shuffle around the edge of the fire, while the men leap over and run through it. When this is over, the men and women segregate themselves, and the shaman heats long stakes of wood until they are charred and glowing; these he applies first to his own legs and then to the legs of his patients. Anyone suffering burns is considered to be in need of extra prayers. Each person then drinks a bowl of salt water, and vomits into a bowl of sand; again, anyone who does not vomit is considered to be impure and undergoes the ritual again. Finally the doorway of the *hogan* is sealed, and shaman and followers sit around the fire until the flames die down and the ashes cool.

The ashes are later mixed with the vomit, taken outside and left to dry and be blown away on the wind. The purification is over for another year.

Trial by fire

Incombustibility was, until recently, thought of as being essentially an Eastern 'trick' – but, with application, Europeans can also learn the ancient art of making themselves immune to fire

SOME FIREWALKERS ARE born with the gift, some attain the gift, and some have the gift – literally – thrust upon them. But exactly how men avoid being seriously burned while walking across banked stones heated to up to 800°F (430°C), modern science has yet to explain.

Is fakery involved? In the 1890s, a New Zealand magistrate named Colonel Gudgeon, his friend Dr T. N. Hocken, and two other Europeans were determined to find out once and for all. While they were watching (rather sceptically) a demonstration of fire-walking by a shaman in Raratoa, Polynesia, the shaman challenged them to accept the protection of his *mana* – or power – and try the walk themselves. Colonel Gudgeon and friends accepted the challenge, removed

Above: a spectacular exhibition of firewalking put on by 40 fanatical Brahmins in 1912 for the entertainment of their European audience. They carry sacred objects to reinforce their mood of heightened religious ecstasy, which seems to make them impervious to the incandescent pit

their shoes and socks, and made the perilous journey. According to Gudgeon's report later, one of the party, 'who, like Lot's wife, looked behind him, a thing against all the rules', was badly burned. Gudgeon himself had his doubts as he approached the pit and felt the waves of heat. 'My impression', he said, 'was that the skin would all peel off my feet'. Nevertheless all he felt when he got to the other side was 'a tingling sensation not unlike electric shock'.

When his own personal sally was successfully over, Dr Hocken began making tests. He had brought along a thermometer capable of readings up to 400°F (205°C), which he suspended six feet (two metres) above the trench. The mercury rapidly climbed the glass and would have burst, according to the doctor, if the solder had not melted first. Afterwards, he made a thorough examination of the native walkers' feet, finding them soft and pliable and in no way unduly leathery. He took scrapings for 'foreign protective substances', which proved negative, and finally licked the soles of the feet with his tongue. They were, he announced, completely free of any chemical protection, and he was of the opinion that trickery could not account for what he had seen.

Despite Dr Hocken's carefully scientific approach, his conclusions were unacceptable in some quarters. For instance, Edward Clodd, the president of the Folklore Society, poured scorn on firewalking reports in his presidential address for 1895.

'The whole thing is a trick', he declared. 'I don't pretend to know how it is done. But it is well known that the soles of people who go barefoot acquire a callosity which enables them to endure what we could hardly tolerate

in our boots.' He went on to suggest that the feet might be 'rendered insensible' by treating them with diluted sulphuric acid or alum. 'And it is well known', he repeated, 'that a man may hold his hand in a stream of molten iron so long as the hand is kept moist. The intense heat causes the moisture to retain its spherical form, so that there is a sort of film between the hand and the metal, rendering the heat perfectly bearable.'

Clodd's outburst brought forth a lengthy and brilliant rebuke from Andrew Lang, one of the most prominent of late-Victorian historians and anthropologists. Mentioning reports of similar phenomena in Virgil, in books of travel, saintly legends, trials by ordeal, and so on, Lang pointed out that anthropology had 'treasured' such accounts:

Why she should stand aloof from analogous descriptions by . . . living witnesses, the present writer is unable to

An experiment at Carlshalton, England, in April 1937, proved that, even under strictly observed conditions, both Indians and Europeans could walk the fiery pit – and emerge unscathed. First over the embers was Ahmed Hussein (top) and next came Reginald Adcock (above). Both had their feet examined before and after the walk to check for any artificial protection or – afterwards – any burn-marks. Neither were found to exist. This experiment followed that of September, 1935 (also at Carlshalton) when a Moslem, Kuda Bux, was carefully watched by scientists and psychical researchers as he walked over fiery embers

imagine. The better, the more closely contemporary the evidence, the more a witness of the abnormal is ready to submit to cross examination, the more his testimony is apt to be neglected by Folklorists.

Of course, he went on, he was not maintaining that there was anything 'psychical' in firewalking or firehandling, and as far as anyone knew it might well be a trick. But:

As a trick it is so old, so world-wide, that we should ascertain the *modus* of it. Mr Clodd . . . suggests the use of diluted sulphuric acid, or of alum. But I am not aware that he has tried the experiment on his own person, nor has he produced an example in which it was successfully tried. Science demands actual experiment.

In fact, experiment continued into the next few decades. Doctors like T. N. Hocken carefully noted the effects without having an inkling as to the cause. Dr John G. Hill of

Tahiti, for instance, had examined a white man who had walked the fiery local pit. His face had peeled in the heat, but his boots, socks and feet were unmarked. Dr. B. Glanvill Corney, chief medical officer of the Fijiian Islands, gave the results of an extensive survey he had made in a paper published in February 1914. He had watched five mass walks over genuinely super-heated stones, and had examined the feet of every individual taking part before and after the walk, without finding trace of trickery – or burning.

Although not conducted under rigid scientific rules, the firewalk which took place in 1921 at Madras must surely have been among the most spectacular ever recorded. The Roman Catholic Bishop of Mysore had asked his friend, the sophisticated local Maharaja, to organise a firewalk demonstration. According to the writer Oliver Leroy, the Maharaja hired a Moslem 'fakir' to cast a sort of mystical blanket of protection over those entering the fire. To the strains of the Maharaja's military brass band – all of whom were Christians – the first voluntary walkers crossed the flames. The Moslem 'fakir' physically threw a number of unwilling participants onto the burning embers, whose looks of horror changed to astonished smiles. Finally the entire brass band were induced to make the trip and walked through, twice.

Firewalking in England

The only damper cast on the proceedings came when the Maharaja finally called a halt; the Moslem organiser screamed in agony and threw himself writhing upon the ground. It was explained to the Bishop that all potential pain had been visited upon the fakir himself.

Fourteen years later, in September 1935, an attempt was made to organise a truly scientific experiment with firewalking under the aegis of the University of London. A 24-foot (7-metre) fiery trench was prepared at Carlshalton, Surrey – its average temperature being 800°F (430°C). A young Indian Moslem named Kuda Bux strode across the length of the trench four times, and again was found to be free of any artificial protection. Despite the stringent tests made to guard against trickery, the onlookers included several diehard sceptics. Harry Price, the famous ghost hunter, rationalised that Kuda Bux was able to do the impossible because he made but brief contact with the burning wood, which anyway had low thermal conductivity. An unnamed doctor sneered to observer Harold S. W. Chibbett that 'anyone could do it'. Invited to try, he replied that he was not suitably dressed.

In the face of the cumulative evidence, such jibes and ill-informed 'rationalisations' are meaningless: certain people, individually and in groups, do have a mysterious ability to walk on hot coals and handle burning embers without mechanical trickery being involved. But does the secret lie in a 'trickery' of the

When Professor Stephenson undertook his 30-yard (27-metre) walk along a burning trench in Tokyo, he was prepared by a Shinto priest who took him to a temple and sprinkled salt on his head. As he walked across he felt a mild tingling in his feet – and, at one point, a sudden brief stab of pain. Later he found a slight cut on his foot, as if made by a sharp stone, which seems to indicate that the salt sprinkling ceremony protected him only from the heat, and not from *all* pain. Dr Harry B. Wright reported a similar observation after watching a firewalk at Viti Levu in Fiji. Though the walkers appeared to be in a state of ecstasy during the walk itself, they reacted sharply – and normally – when he jabbed their feet at random with a pin and a lighted cigarette before and after the ceremony. Similarly St Polycarp of Smyrna – who was martyred in about AD 155 – was sentenced to the stake, but the flames had no effect on him; finally a soldier stabbed him with a spear – and killed him.

There are several recorded instances of the officiating priest or shaman taking on the pain of the walkers himself – as in the cases of Colonel Gudgeon and the Maharaja of Mysore mentioned earlier.

In such circumstances it would appear that the officiant is able to hypnotise – or literally entrance – his followers: if the spell wears off or faith wavers, the fire resumes its power to burn.

Many of the North American Indian rituals involve preparations of dancing, chanting and either feasting or abstinence. Hindus, Buddhists and followers of Shinto call upon their gods, saints, and ancestors. Every year on the feast days of St Constantine and St Helena, Greek villagers of Langadas perform a firewalk over hot coals while holding icons of the two saints aloft, thus ensuring themselves protection. In these cases a form of self-hypnosis seems to

Above: though a stage act, the fire immunity is real

Opponents – Edward Clodd, (above) thought firewalking an easy trick; Andrew Lang (below) wanted Clodd to prove his theory personally but Clodd refused to try

play a major role. Certainly the accounts of D. D. Home making 'passes' with his hands before handing onlookers red-hot coals to hold smacks of the 'hypnotic passes' of stage mesmerists.

But the boots burned off . . .

That there could be substance in the 'natural ability' explanation of fire immunity is borne out by John Evelyn's description of Richardson, the fire-eater, who made no claim to magical or spiritual powers – but could quite simply eat fire. Into this category comes the account, by Max Freedom Long, of a fairground fire-eater who impressed him in the 1940s. The writer fixed up a private performance to which he invited a dentist. The fire-eater played 'the hottest flame of a welding torch over the inside of his mouth, keeping his jaws wide open to allow close inspection'. He also heated a rod of metal until it was flexible and bent it between his teeth. Both Long and the dentist believed that the phenomenon was authentic.

But the sceptic's biggest stumbling block is not the immunity of the fire handler himself, but that of his clothes. A state of trance hypnosis may well protect a person's skin, but how does one hypnotise a pair of socks and shoes? The fully clad brass band of the Maharaja of Mysore walked through their flames and came out as smartly uniformed as when they went in; the saffron robes of Buddhist fire dancers in Hong Kong remain cool, dry and totally uncharred. And long before that, St Catherine of Sienna regularly went into ecstatic trances and lay for hours across the kitchen fire. The wonder was not so much that she remained unincinerated but that her clothes did. Even odder was the selectivity of the fire towards the Jansenist hysteric Marie Souet: while lying over a blazing hearth, she and the sheet which wrapped her went unburned though her stockings and shoes burned quite normally.

Dr W. T. Brigham of the British Museum consented to go on a firewalk on the volcanic island of Kona in the South Seas. It was a walk with a difference, for the volcano had just erupted, and his protectors, three Kahunas or local magicians, proposed that he should stroll with them across the glowing, molten lava. First, they suggested, he should take off his boots, as they would not be covered by the magical protection. The professor hesitated, and finally the magicians pulled him onto the lava with them. He was forced to walk across 50 yards (46 metres), while the three magicians laughed heartily at the glowing scraps left behind as his boots and socks burned off. His feet – and the rest of his clothes – were completely unharmed.

After his Fiji experiments, Dr Glanvill Corney reported that neither psychical nor psychological theories alone can account for what happens in the case of fire immunity, and that some physical phenomenon takes place which is yet to be explained.

Their master's voice

A maddened horse suddenly quiet and tame . . . a tired old nag turned into a prancing thoroughbred . . . a horse obedient to commands that are not even uttered . . . what is the secret of such amazing control? This chapter reveals the old art of the Horse Whisperers

IN 1873 A DILETTANTE historian named William Smith visited Lee Gap horse fair near Dewsbury, Yorkshire, and came away convinced that he had seen a magician in action. He wrote in his diary:

> A gypsyman there had what was described as the 'horse-sense': this being the ability to control horses from a distance without any word of command, but with a slight gesture of the hand seeming to bid them now come, now stay, now run, canter or gallop as he wished. His companions averred that this gift was not common to all gypsies, and that horsemen without gypsy blood also have it, but that it is rare.

Smith noted that the 'gypsyman' seemed able to influence not just his own animals but those of casual visitors to the fair, including carriage horses. 'I was told,' he concluded,

Above: William Smith, an amateur historian, diarist and antiquarian of the late Victorian period. He left an account of the seemingly magical control over horses demonstrated by a 'Horse Whisperer' at a fair in 1873

Below: the horse fair at Skirling in Scotland, painted by James Howe in the 19th century. Such events were natural gathering places of the Horse Whisperers

'that the art lies in a charm or amulet which possesses some preternatural efficacy over the beasts; and . . . I could not doubt it.'

The twin fairs of Lee Gap and Latter Lee, chartered by Henry II in the 12th century, are still held every August and are among the few centres of Romany horse trading left in the north of England. But, sad to say, nothing as spectacular as that witnessed by Smith has been reported in recent years. What Smith saw was a 'Horse Whisperer' about his mysterious business, and today the 'preternatural' art is all but dead, and may even be totally extinct. Yet the Horse Whisperers were once widespread in England and Scotland.

For about 1000 years before the Norman Conquest, the only horses indigenous to the British Isles were the shaggy ponies such as the Shetland, Connemara, and New Forest breeds that still thrive today. The Romans imported cavalry mounts, probably of Arab and Persian stock, but the main draught animals of the Anglo-Saxons were oxen, and remained so in most parts of the country until the early 17th century. For many hundreds of years, therefore, a man would have to be either a military farrier or in the service of a nobleman to gain skill at horse handling.

A hundred years after the Conquest, plate armour began to supplement the light chain mail and leather of the Norman cavalryman, and 'heavy' horses were imported from France to carry the knights in their new and bulky gear. Gradually such horses as the Percheron were crossed with others to produce native breeds: the Suffolk Punch, Cleveland Bay, Shire, and Clydesdale – shaggy-footed giants ideal for working in harness. Compared with the oxen of earlier years, they were highly intelligent animals, readily responsive to training. It was with them, perhaps during the 16th century, that the Horse Whisperers perfected their skills.

The date of the appearance of the Horse Whisperers has to be speculative, for little was written about them before the 18th century. By then they had become a 'free-masonry' in their own right, with passwords, salutes, and possibly secret handshakes. Almost certainly they were the lineal descendants of the privileged military horse-handlers of medieval times.

The reason for their self-imposed secrecy, to begin with at least, was two-fold: first, to guard their skills from outsiders, and second, to avoid charges of witchcraft. It seems likely that the Whisperers came into the 'cunning man' category of primitive magic workers, most of whom seem to have escaped the rigorous persecutions of the 17th century. The Essex born 'Cunning Murrell' was much sought after by farmers for his healing powers and control over various animals, including the horse.

Dan Wickett, who died in his native Polperro, Cornwall, in the mid 1960s and was famous as a wart healer, worked as a ploughboy in his youth and was said to have had 'The Word', another term for the Horse Whisperer's skill. Another contemporary possessor of The Word was the unfortunate Charles Walton who worked as a ploughman in Warwickshire in the early part of the present century. His power over animals

Above: the Lee Gap horse fair in Yorkshire, where Smith was so impressed with one 'gypsyman's' special skills in horse handling

Below: 'Cunning Murrell' (right) at an Essex forge, producing magical bottles to counteract diabolical influences. He was also known for his healing powers and control over horses

extended to cattle, toads and birds, and it was apparently fear of these occult skills that caused an unknown assailant to drive a pitchfork through his throat at Lower Quinton in 1945. This gives him the dubious distinction of being the last 'witch' to be 'executed' in England.

The last English stronghold of the Whisperers was East Anglia, where, even after the introduction of the petrol-driven tractor, the monotonously flat lands made ploughing with a horse team both relatively easy and economical. Here, in the dying years of the craft, folklorists such as George Ewart Evans were able to record the tradition through stories from the older generation.

'Thus I command'

The East Anglian Whisperers certainly shared many of the attributes of the 'cunning men'. Their secret phrase of power was said to be *sic iubeo* – 'thus I command' – but whether this was simply a password among themselves, or was supposed to have a direct effect on their horses, is not clear. Their main power lay in talismans, one for attracting or 'drawing' the horses, and the other for repelling or 'jading' them. The drawing charm was the milt – called the pad in Scotland – a spongy wedge of tissue found in a foal's mouth just after birth. The Whisperer removed the milt, which called for dexterity because the foal usually swallows it immediately, then dried it and impregnated it with aromatic oils.

The jading amulet was rather more mysterious. According to tradition a frog, or sometimes a natterjack toad, was killed and impaled on a whitethorn to dry out, then buried for a month till the flesh rotted away. The bones were then carefully collected and thrown onto the surface of a running stream.

An early 20th-century photograph of a member of the Scottish 'Brotherhood of the Horseman's Word' – or Horse Whisperers – taken in West Lothian. The pose of the horses indicates the high degree of control the horseman has over them

The one bone that floated and drifted against the current was kept for the talisman.

According to Evans in his book *The pattern under the plough* (1966), this bone was the ilium or main bone in the frog's pelvic girdle, which looks rather like a chicken wishbone. More importantly, it closely resembles the 'frog' or v-shaped band of horn on the underside of a horse's hoof. Being both a visual and a verbal pun, it is a powerful piece of imitative magic. Explaining the amulets further, Evans wrote in the limited circulation magazine *Pentagram* in 1968:

There were, I learned, two classes of herbs and substances used by certain horsemen. The first class strongly attracted a horse by their pleasant odour

Above: George Ewart Evans, the folklorist who has recorded the tradition of East Anglian Horse Whisperers

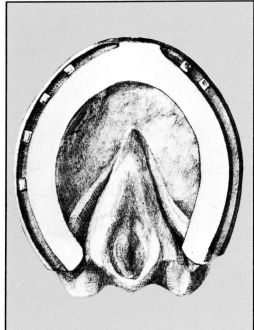

Left: the underside of a horse's hoof showing the 'frog', which is a v-shaped band of horn. The v-shaped pelvic bone of a frog is used by the Horse Whisperers in a charm to repel, or 'jade', a horse. Being both a visual and a verbal pun, the frog bone becomes a powerful piece of imitative magic

or taste . . . the milt came under the class of 'drawing substance' though only among the horsemen of the inner ring [the Whisperers]. The horsemen who had the 'word' or 'know' as it was called in Suffolk, first steeped the milt in one of the sweet-smelling substances so that it was used as a 'drawing' charm. . . .

The plants used to impregnate the milt included sorrel, bryony, cinnamon, rosemary and tansy. The frog bone, on the other hand, was carried in a leather pouch or linen wrapping along with either a piece of raw flesh or a gobbet of animal grease – substances that offended the horse's sensitive sense of smell so much that it would not go near the horseman with the amulet.

As well as these rudimentary drawing and jading devices, the Whisperers used their shrewd understanding of horse psychology and physiology to achieve startling effects – and some of their tricks were simple to the point of crudity. For instance, even a tired old nag could be made to arch its neck and prance like a thoroughbred by slipping a piece of raw ginger under its tail – an old horseman's wile that eventually found its way into everyday language in the phrase 'to ginger things up'. And in order to operate on the horse's hindquarters or legs, the Whisperer would nip its upper lip tightly with a piece of wire known as a 'twitch'. Curiously, the horse tends to concentrate on the head pain, largely ignoring what is happening to its quarters.

George Rowe, a former farrier from Dartford in Kent, explained:

If a fire breaks out in a cowshed you open the doors and the cows simply file out. If a fire breaks out in a stable the horses go berserk, thrashing around in

Bryony is one of the sweet-smelling herbs used by the Horse Whisperers in an amulet to 'draw', or attract, horses. It is made into an aromatic oil and poured onto the milt, a spongy tissue in the mouth of a new-born foal

their stalls, kicking out at anything that moves, even break their legs – anything but walk out in an orderly manner. The thing to do when they are in that sort of mood is frighten them in a different way; it's a difficult thing to explain but the fears tend to counteract each other and the horse stands petrified with fright. One can then handle the animal with relative ease.

There are many stories of farmers who were foolish enough to dismiss a Whisperer, or otherwise annoy him, only to find that their horses could not be moved from the stable. In these cases, Evans thinks that the Whisperer would have smeared a jading substance over the threshold, making the horse frightened to cross it.

Interwoven with their plain 'horse sense' was a mystique that the Whisperers cultivated, perhaps deliberately, in order to make their talents seem special. There are numerous stories of horsemen binding wounds with cheese rind, strips of mouldering harness leather or spiders' webs to cure inflammation and protect against infection – and it was not until the discovery of penicillin in mould cultures that the principle behind such medication became apparent. The Whisperer was often called upon to doctor humans, his reputation probably helped by folk memories of the magical powers of the blacksmith and, in Celtic mythology, of the horse itself. He would weave necklets of horsehair to cure goitre, or powder the hair on mouldy bread to make a potion to banish worms.

But the enduring mystery of the Horse Whisperers lies in the apparent sophistication of their brotherhood. Though few

clues remain as to the East Anglian society, Evans does speak of the 'inner ring', a term having a definite masonic sound to it. And the Latin tag *sic iubeo* is surely not a term that an 18th-century agricultural worker would ordinarily use. If the Whisperers did have their roots in a medieval craft guild, however, such a phrase might just have endured through the years.

The Scottish 'Brotherhood, or Society, of the Horseman's Word' survived into the late 19th century, and possibly on into the 20th, for much the same reasons as its East Anglian counterpart: horse power was economically feasible in Aberdeenshire, Morayshire and parts of the Lowlands for much later than elsewhere. The sophistication – and masonic influence – of the north-eastern horsemen is immediately apparent in their 'Oath', which dates from at least 1780. In it, the novice horseman declares:

I of my own free will and accord solemnly vow and swear before God and all these witnesses that I will heal, conceal, and never reveal any part of the true horsemanship which I am about to receive at this time. Furthermore I solemnly vow and swear that I will neither write it nor indite, cut it nor carve it on wood or stone, nor yet on anything movable or immovable under the canopy of heaven, nor yet so much as wave a finger in the air to none but a horseman.

The initiate goes on to 'vow and swear' that he will neither 'give it nor see it given' to a 'tradesman of any kind save to a blacksmith or a horse-soldier'. The oath goes on to keep the secret from 'a farmer or a farmer's son unless he be working his own or his father's

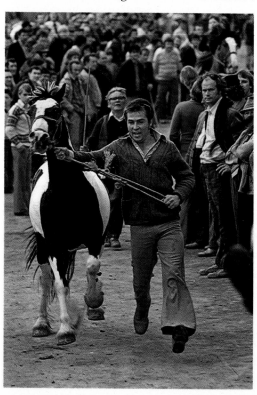

A horseman (right) taking his horse through its paces at Appleby horse fair (far right) in Cumbria. Who knows whether among the throng there is one who still uses the special, secret skills of the Horse Whisperers?

horses, a fool or a madman, my father, mother, sister, brother or any womankind,' the last including 'my wife, daughter nor yet the very dearest ever lay by my side'.

The 'true horsemanship' is not to be revealed to anyone 'after sunset Saturday night nor before sunrise Monday morning'. Furthermore, the novice swears:

> . . . neither to abuse nor bad use any man's horses with it and if I see a brother do so I will tell him of his fault. Furthermore I will never give it . . . to any under the age of 16 years nor above that of 45 years . . . unless there be three or more lawful sworn brethren present after finding them to be so by trying and examining them.

The final vow

Nor, he promises with an Aberdonian touch, will he give it 'for less than the sum of £1 sterling or value thereof'. He swears never to refuse to attend a meeting if notified within three days except in 'case of riding fire or going for the doctor'. The final vow is:

> If I fail to keep these promises may my flesh be torn to pieces with a wild horse, and my heart cut out with a horseman's knife, and my bones buried on the sands of the seashore where the tide ebbs and flows every 24 hours, so that there be no remembrance of me amongst lawful brethren. . . .

According to a 19th-century account of such a 'swearing in' ceremony, the final chilling oath was followed by the investiture of the blindfolded novice with the 'regal crown, the royal robe, and the sacred sword belt of the Brotherhood'. When his blindfold was removed he discovered that these were an old

Charles Walton, said to possess 'The Word' giving power over horses, could also control other animals. He was murdered in 1945 – probably by someone who feared his occult powers

hat bedecked with imitation horse's ears, a horse blanket, and a girth-strap. He then ate bread and salt, and 'the evening degenerated into drunkenness and true horseplay.'

There is a sinister footnote to the history of the Scottish brotherhood, which is unlikely to be coincidence. The horsemen often referred to their meetings as 'kuklos' from the Greek meaning 'circle'. On Christmas Eve in 1865, six young Confederate cavalry officers, all of Scottish descent, met together in Pulaski, Tennessee, to form a 'drinking' brotherhood. Casting around for a name, they came up with 'kuklos' and added the word 'clan' spelled with a κ for alliterative effect. Today, the initiation rites of the Ku Klux Klan include the robing of a new member with the 'sacred crown, robe and sword belt' – which are in fact an old hat, blanket, and leather strap.

Many secret societies sprang up in Britain during the 18th century, each with its regalia, its oath, and its password, and it is at least possible that the Horse Whisperers, whether English or Scottish, inspired one or two of them. In Scotland itself the skilled horse-handler has for centuries been regarded with a certain awe. The Aberdeenshire dialect phrase for him is 'orra loon' – meaning 'odd or misplaced lad'.

And the 'Horseman's Toast' used as a skipping rhyme among schoolchildren in the Grampian district still lends the 'orra loon' and his art an air of biblical unease:

> Here's tae the horse wi' the four white feet,
> The chestnut tail and mane,
> A star on his face and a blaze on his breast
> And his master's name was Cain.

The gentle art of murder

Some masters of the martial arts are said to possess the ability to commit the perfect murder, using a forbidden technique that is known only to a handful of initiates, and many mysterious claims have accumulated around the delayed death touch

George Dillman, an American karate teacher, smashes three ice blocks, each weighing 300 pounds (136 kilograms), with a single blow of his elbow. We are familiar with such well-publicised feats by masters of oriental martial arts – but is there also a secret art in which a covert 'blow', almost unnoticed by the victim and by third parties alike, can kill the victim after a long delay?

ANYONE WHO HAS SEEN A KARATE expert demolish piles of bricks, boards, tiles or concrete slabs with a single blow will testify to the lethal potential of a human body when it has undergone the right kind of training and conditioning. When a man such as George Dillman, an American master of karate, shatters simultaneously 10 ice blocks, each weighing 100 pounds (45 kilograms), stacked on top of each other, he leaves no doubt as to the reality of the feat: the splintered rubble that is left behind is proof enough.

But it is another matter to believe that some martial arts experts can cause internal injuries, unconsciousness and death by the briefest of pressures on certain apparently non-critical points of a victim's body – and that these effects can be deferred until hours, days or even months have passed. Yet this is exactly what has been alleged of the almost

legendary art of *dim mak*, the 'delayed death touch'.

It was in search of the truth behind stories of dim mak and other fabled unarmed combat systems that a Western martial arts expert, John F. Gilbey, roamed from continent to continent. He finally encountered the delayed death touch technique in Taiwan in 1957. There, with all the reluctance that is natural when closely guarded and dangerous knowledge is imparted to an outsider, a boxing master named Oh Hsin-yang gave him a demonstration. The human guinea-pig used in the experiment was his son, Ah Lin.

The blow was a light, seemingly harmless touch delivered just below the victim's navel. For the three days following, Gilbey was able to keep Ah Lin under the closest surveillance. His health was seemingly unimpaired; his spirits were lively. The master did not come near his son until noon on the third day. He appeared just in time to revive him with herbal medicine and massage – for, as

Mourners crowd around the coffin at a Hong Kong funeral (below). Their grief is for the superstar Bruce Lee (bottom), the hero of numerous kung fu films. He probably died from a freak reaction to a tranquilliser – but many fans believed their hero had been killed by a delayed death touch from some unknown rival

Bottom right: Dr John 'Biff' Painter allegedly showing the reality of *ch'i* force: he 'applies it to the auric field' of his blindfolded colleague – and the man sways back, even though no physical contact has been made

Oh Hsin-yang had anticipated, his son had suddenly and unaccountably collapsed into unconsciousness.

When Ah Lin had recovered (though he faced three months' convalescence to get over his experience completely) Gilbey left Taiwan convinced that he was one of the very few Westerners who had been privileged to witness the delayed death touch in operation.

Despite Gilbey's own expert status, this evidence remains anecdotal, as do most accounts of dim mak. Until 1980 no work even remotely approaching Western laboratory standards was available and the only masters said to possess the skill refused to demonstrate it, even under the most informal conditions.

Instrument of perfect murders

In consequence the delayed death touch remains the focus of wild fantasies: it is the supposed instrument of 'perfect murders', in which the victim dies of causes unknown, with symptoms suggesting severe, incomprehensible yet natural illness. In the East any unexpected death of a notable person can provoke rumours of a dim mak assassination. The untimely death of the martial arts superstar Bruce Lee in July 1973 had precisely this effect.

Stories of the delayed death touch occur all over south-eastern Asia, but particularly in China, where the skill reputedly reached a zenith during the T'ang Dynasty (AD

618–906). Although the term is applied somewhat loosely to a number of techniques, purists are careful to distinguish it from *tieh chang*, the iron palm (involving toughening of the hands), and from *tu wu shou*, the poison hand (involving the anointing of the hand with harmful substances). The true delayed death touch is not a ferocious movement like a karate 'chop', or one of the whiplash punches found in many styles of kung fu: it is more like a short-distance prod with, apparently, not enough force behind it to leave so much as a bruise.

Students of the 'forbidden art' must remember that a victim's vulnerability fluctuates according to the temperature and hour of the day. This is consistent with an Eastern tradition that the circulation of the blood through the body varies hourly. A Western karate master, Alan Lee, states that the circulation passes via 36 major, 72 minor and 108 subsidiary 'blood gates', and that the expert, knowing both their location and the times when the flow of blood through each is at its maximum, can use light pressure on a strategic point to cause a fatal disruption of the flow – by, for example, a blood clot. Such knowledge took years to acquire; once they were in possession of it, masters could reduce their own susceptibility to attack by regulating the pulse at crucial times.

According to Dr John 'Biff' Painter, an American master, the Chinese martial art technique of *duann mie*, a blow directed

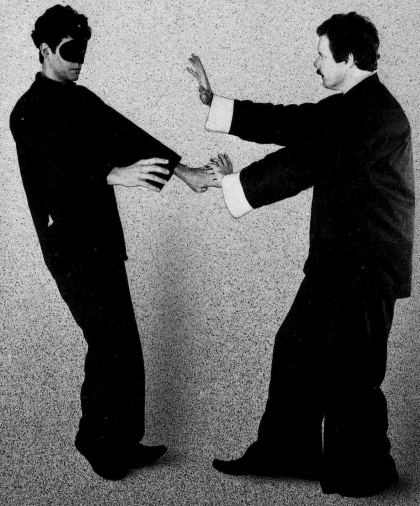

against veins or muscles, can cause the wasting and death of important organs by an interruption of the blood supply to them. At first the victim suffers only minor discomfort, but later succumbs as the affected organ is starved of its blood supply.

But some writers attribute the efficacy of the true death touch to its interference with the mysterious 'intrinsic' or 'internal' energy of the human body, *ch'i*. This energy – *ch'i* in Chinese, *ki* in Japanese – is fundamental to a number of oriental disciplines of healing and of combat that Western researchers have viewed with increasing interest since about 1960. The technique of acupuncture is a notable example. The energy is thought to pervade the human body, circulating in a 24-hour cycle along channels called meridians and feeding the organs. Although it is never entirely absent from each channel, it is subject to a kind of tidal effect, approaching and receding from them according to the hour of the day. Oriental therapists regard illness as imbalance or blockage of *ch'i* and seek by use of needles or by manipulations to restore the overall harmony.

The ability to control *ch'i* and to generate extra surges of it is alleged to enable martial artists to perform feats well beyond their normal ability, and many styles of fighting feature, during their more advanced stages, exercises designed to stimulate the flow of *ch'i*.

The martial arts student may also be taught the 708 points on the meridians to which pressure can be applied to enhance or retard *ch'i*, allegedly preventing it from feeding the vital organs. The result of such an attack would again be a kind of starvation – but of energy rather than blood. Unconsciousness and eventually death would ensue, without any physical clue to connect the antagonist with the damage.

Disrupting the energy flow

John Painter puts the odds against an untrained attacker successfully making a lethal dim mak strike by pure chance at 10,000 to one. It is not enough merely to know the right points to strike, to gauge the right moment from knowledge of the timetable governing the *ch'i* circulation and to hit the target with unerring accuracy – taking into account such factors as the body temperature and muscular build of the victim. The attacker must then, according to the theory, be able to generate the requisite amount of internal energy. He must disrupt the victim's *ch'i* flow by transferring a certain 'voltage' of his own *ch'i* through his fingers at the moment of the strike.

Painter estimates that if the discharge of *ch'i* is 'light', the victim's end may be deferred by up to two weeks. A heavy blow might kill him in as little as 12 to 24 hours. Light-to-moderate attacks create a partial blockage of the meridians, augmented each time the *ch'i* reaches the affected point on its diurnal

circulation, until the meridian comes to resemble a choked water pipe. The process can be reversed only by the ministrations of someone with a superior knowledge of Chinese medicine, such as a skilled acupuncturist. However, Dr Painter regards some dim mak strikes as incurable: the victim 'should begin his funeral preparations', he grimly advises.

Many people in the East have a deeply rooted belief in the existence of the death touch. Could such a person be killed by the mere suggestion that the touch he had just received would be fatal?

The victim's belief in the efficacy of dim mak certainly figured strongly in a strange story carried in English newspapers on 17 February 1976. During a brawl aboard the Royal Fleet Auxiliary *Empire Gull*, anchored at Marchwood, Hampshire, a Chinese cook, aged 48, stabbed to death an elderly compatriot who had hit him. His statement to the police suggested that he believed the blow had been imbued with more than physical force – that it was a delayed death touch. He remarked: 'He died first and I will die later.' And indeed he was suffering from a mysterious, undiagnosable illness that is said to have baffled three doctors. Was the illness due to his own evident conviction that the blow was to prove lethal?

But there are several reliable modern accounts of martial arts experts selectively breaking one brick or tile in a stack of several, leaving those above and below unharmed. Such feats make it more credible that a blow could be delivered to a human body and cause internal injury without leaving any external marks – but there can be no question of bricks and tiles being influenced by suggestion.

But just what evidence is there that the delayed death touch is more than a comic book fantasy?

John Painter gave a demonstration during a lecture on acupressure in November 1980 that goes some way towards conforming with scientific requirements. The experiment was

Above: the delayed death touch in action? Dr Painter is shown administering a mild blow, too gentle to be painful, to a volunteer. The symptoms that followed included rising temperature, fluctuating pulse rate, profuse sweating and trembling. Dr Painter claims that 'severe damage' would have occurred had he not taken remedial action

Left: the Chinese 'body clock': in each organ the *ch'i* flow is strongest at particular times. (The 'triple warmer' supposedly controls the harmony of the system)

Body clock diagram:
- 1–3a.m. liver
- 3–5a.m. lung
- 5–7a.m. large intestine
- 7–9a.m. stomach
- 9–11a.m. spleen
- 11a.m.–1p.m. heart
- 1–3p.m. small intestine
- 3–5p.m. bladder
- 5–7p.m. kidney
- 7–9p.m. pericardium
- 9–11p.m. triple warmer
- 11p.m.–1a.m. gall bladder

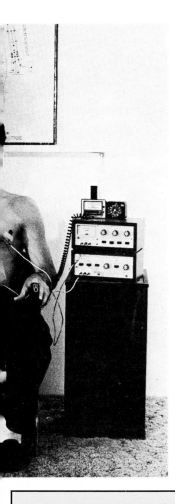

electronically monitored and carried out before an audience that included medically qualified witnesses. The event was striking – in more ways than one.

A healthy volunteer was connected to equipment monitoring his pulse rate, temperature, blood pressure and other physiological factors. He was not informed the exact nature of the experiment, only that it was intended to display a 'special type of acupressure'. After the initial readings had been taken Painter applied a moderate strike to a point called *hui kui hsueh* in the chest. The subject reported no pain but said that his body felt numb and his right arm heavy.

During the next half hour he experienced a variety of unusual symptoms as, according to Dr Painter's thesis, the *ch'i* flow began to pass through the site of the strike. Within 10 minutes he was suffering abdominal discomfort; within another five minutes his body temperature had climbed from 98.6°F (37°C) to 100°F (37.8°C). After 20 minutes the pulse rate – which had been 62 beats per minute at the start of the test – was fluctuating wildly from less than 50 to more than 160. The subject suffered constriction of the chest muscles, profuse perspiration and trembling of the limbs. His blood pressure soared. When Dr Painter judged that it was approaching a dangerous level he ended the experiment by massaging the site of blockage and administering a herbal medicine. One

hour later the subject was back to normal. The onlookers accepted that, left unchecked, the dim mak process would have resulted in severe damage to the human guinea-pig; Dr Painter himself believed the man would have died within two days.

Sceptics might object that the trial did not wholly exclude the possibility of the subject's expectations or the experimenter's suggestions playing a part. But the symptoms recorded seem too extreme to be accounted for solely in those terms. That a person's pulse should race because of suggestion or excitement is highly probable; that it should vary between 50 and 160 from those causes alone is less probable. Still, one isolated experiment will not satisfy Westerners that the delayed death touch truly exists; it would be preferable to study a number of dim mak masters demonstrating their skills in a laboratory. But such persons are rarely encountered and when they are identified they habitually refuse to impart their learning to others. Painter concludes:

> Such power in the hands of the unenlightened is like a chimpanzee with a bazooka. Such power corrupts and distorts reality. It is for this reason that those who possess the full power in such arts refuse to speak of it, and why many of the wise ones regret acquisition of such knowledge and have carried their arts . . . to their graves.

The karate expert C. W. Nicol wrote an account of his martial arts training in Japan in which he relates an almost incredible incident bearing on the delayed death touch. His master was a sixth-dan black belt, Hirokazu Kanazawa (right). One day, when with a few students, he placed three bricks on the floor and broke them with a single blow. But that, he said, was nothing. He put down another pile of three bricks. He determined to put his *ki* (the Japanese term for *ch'i*) into the middle brick. With a shout he brought his fist down on the pile – and only the middle brick cracked. This was in accord with the belief of

Feeling the full force

many martial artists that 'mind-force could project itself further and deeper than the actual physical presence of the fist, and could of itself alone alter the state of matter.'

This is certainly the belief of Dr John Painter, who runs a martial arts institute in Arlington, Texas, USA. He believes that every human being possesses an aura consisting of *ch'i*, and that through certain forms of mental control, such as meditation, it is possible to increase the 'vibratory rate' of the aura. The 'vibrations' can be increased to a point where they are disruptive of any other living matter that comes within a certain radius of influence – up to 12 feet (3.6 metres). The power of this control of *ch'i* can also be demonstrated on a candle flame (far left). Dr Painter explains that it took 10 minutes to extinguish this flame. He believes that beyond the delayed death touch, *dim mak*, there exists a higher art – that of killing from a distance, without the need even to touch the victim. However, there is no need to fear this skill: a condition of acquiring it is to 'clear the mind of all sensual and egotistical desires . . . like a beautiful flower, it must be nurtured and cultivated. . . .' So this fearful power is possessed only by those who are beyond all desire to do harm.

Humans that have a visible glow excite wonderment and interest – and their strange luminescence cannot be explained. This eerie phenomenon seems to be exclusive to the holy and the sick

American psychical researcher, tells of a child whose body, after death from acute indigestion, was surrounded by a blue glow.

The only case of a glowing human who was otherwise healthy comes from a letter to the *English Mechanic* of 24 September 1869:

> An American lady, on going to bed, found that a light was issuing from the upper side of the fourth toe on her right foot. Rubbing increased the phosphorescent glow and it spread up her foot. Fumes were also given off, making the room disagreeable; and both light and fumes continued when the foot was held in a basin of water. Even washing with soap could not dim the toe. It lasted for three quarters of an hour before fading away, and was witnessed by her husband.

When it comes to luminescent animals, such as the glow worm and firefly, the scientific explanation is that they light up as the result of chemical reactions within the body involving oxygen, luciferase, luciferin and adenosine triphosphate (ATP). But this kind of chemical reaction has not been offered as the reason that humans glow.

The human glow worms

A BLUE GLOW EMANATED from the ill woman's breasts as she lay asleep. It happened regularly for several weeks, and each time the luminescence lasted for several seconds. No one could explain it.

The woman was Anna Monaro, an asthma sufferer who lived in Italy. When she started to glow during an attack in 1934, she became a news sensation for a time as the 'luminous woman of Pirano'. The blue light was recorded on film and was also witnessed by many doctors. One psychiatrist said that it was caused by 'electrical and magnetic organisms in the woman's body developed in eminent degree', which did little to clarify the matter. Another doctor speculated that she had an abnormally high level of sulphides in her blood because of her weak condition and also her fasting, inspired by religious zeal. These sulphides, he said, were stimulated into luminescence by a natural process of ultraviolet radiation. Even if this were true, it did not explain why the glow came only from the breasts and only while the woman slept.

Data on glowing humans is found in medical literature, religious writings and folklore. Many toxicology textbooks discuss 'luminous wounds', and in their encyclopedic collection of *Anomalies and curiosities of medicine* (1897), Dr George Gould and Dr Walter Pyle described a case of breast cancer that produced a light from the sore strong enough to illuminate the hands of a watch several feet away. Hereward Carrington, an

Above: a celestial light in the form of a cross and stars were seen to glow around the corpse of Jane Pallister, who died in 1833. Her son and other witnesses attributed this wonder to her virtue and worthiness

Above right: luminescence of the body was involved in Christ's transfiguration and St Paul's conversion (inset)

Right: the common European glow worm has a relatively bright light in its tail. Scientists know *how* the glow worm lights up – it is as a result of a chemical reaction – but they do not know *why* some glow worms light up at all

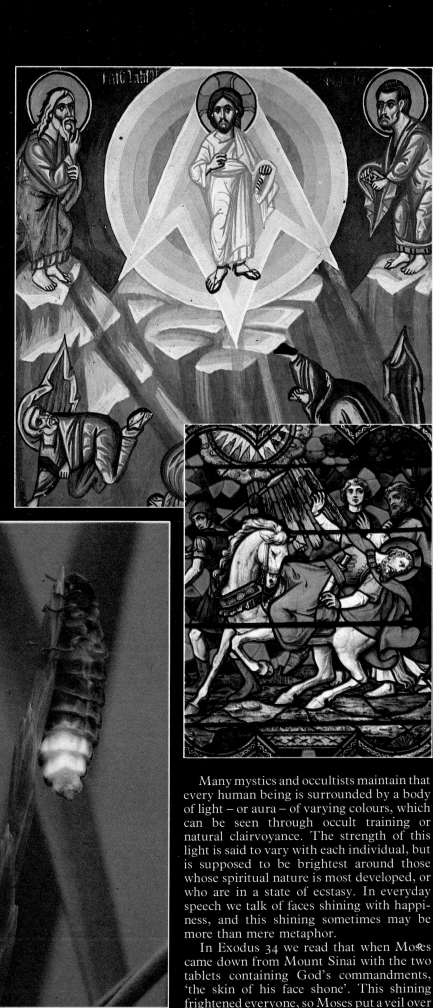

Many mystics and occultists maintain that every human being is surrounded by a body of light – or aura – of varying colours, which can be seen through occult training or natural clairvoyance. The strength of this light is said to vary with each individual, but is supposed to be brightest around those whose spiritual nature is most developed, or who are in a state of ecstasy. In everyday speech we talk of faces shining with happiness, and this shining sometimes may be more than mere metaphor.

In Exodus 34 we read that when Moses came down from Mount Sinai with the two tablets containing God's commandments, 'the skin of his face shone'. This shining frightened everyone, so Moses put a veil over

his face till he had finished speaking with his people. Similar glowings are described in the Bible with regard to St Paul's vision at the time of his conversion, and in the transfiguration of Christ, when his raiment shone so brightly no fuller on earth could whiten it.

Nandor Fodor, the writer on parapsychology, tells us that medieval saints and mystics distinguished four different types of aura: the nimbus, the halo, the aureola and the glory. The nimbus and halo stream from or surround the head, and the aureola emanates from the whole body. The glory is an intensified form of the whole-body glow – a veritable flooding of light. Theosophists speak of five: the health aura, the vital aura, the Karmic aura, the aura of character and the aura of spiritual nature. Different colours indicate emotional state or character. Brilliant red means anger and force; dirty red, passion and sensuality; brown, avarice; rose, affection; yellow, high intellectual activity; purple, spirituality; blue, religious devotion; green, deceit and jealousy or, in a deeper shade, sympathy. The medium Stephan Ossowiecki, in the early 1900s, occasionally saw a kind of dark aura that indicated the approach of unexpected death.

'Natural flames'
We are all familiar with the Christian representation of the halo. Less known is that the original purpose of the crowns and distinctive headdresses worn by kings and priests was to symbolise the halo. Representations of the aureola around the great teachers and the holy are found in virtually every culture: for example, in Peru, Mexico, Egypt, Sri Lanka, India and Japan.

Pope Benedict XIV in his great treatise on beatification and canonisation wrote:

It seems to be a fact that there are natural flames which at times visibly encircle the human head, and also that from a man's whole person fire may on occasion radiate naturally, not, however, like a flame which streams upwards, but rather in the form of sparks which are given off all round; further, that some people become resplendent with a blaze of light, though this is not inherent in themselves, but attaches rather to their clothes, or to the staff or to the spear they are carrying.

Stories are legion in the hagiographical records of priests lighting up dark cells and chapels with the light that emanated from them or, conversely, streamed upon them from some mysterious external source. When the 14th-century Carthusian monk John Tornerius failed to appear in time to celebrate the first mass, the sacristan who went to fetch him found his cell radiant with light. This light seemed to be diffused all round the priest like the midday Sun. In the process of beatification of the holy Franciscan Observant, Blessed Thomas of Cori, witnesses stated that on a dark morning the

The human enigma

whole church had been lit up by the radiance that glowed in his face. In what is apparently the earliest account of Blessed Giles of Assisi, we are told that on one occasion in the night time: 'so great a light shone round him that the light of the moon was wholly eclipsed thereby.'

The house of Blessed Aleidis of Scarbeke seemed to be on fire when she was praying within, the brightness coming from her radiant countenance. The cell of St Louis Bertran 'appeared as if the whole room was illuminated with the most powerful lamps'. Thomas à Kempis says of St Lydwina:

> And although she always lay in darkness, and material light was unbearable to her eyes, nevertheless the divine light was very agreeable to her, whereby her cell was often so wondrously flooded by night that to the beholders the cell itself appeared full of material lamps or fires. Nor is it strange if she overflowed even in the body with divine brightness.

Father Herbert Thurston in his highly regarded book, *The physical phenomena of mysticism* (1952), says of these records of saintly luminescence:

> Although a great number of these rest upon quite insufficient testimony, there are others which cannot lightly be set aside . . . . There can, therefore, be no adequate reason for refusing credence to the report of similar phenomena when they are recorded of those whose eminent holiness and marvellous gifts of grace are universally recognised.

Father Thurston cites two striking cases from the 17th century concerning the

Left: the crown of Rudolf II, Holy Roman Emperor from 1576 to 1612. Crowns and other special headdresses worn by kings and priests developed as a symbol of the shining halo

Below: Pope Benedict XIV, who wrote an important treatise on beatification and canonisation in the 18th century. In it he gave attention to the 'fires' that can encircle a human head and body

Right: Stephan Ossowiecki, the Polish clairvoyant who was active in the early 1900s. He occasionally saw a dark aura around people, which indicated the approach of unexpected death

Blessed Bernardino Realini and Father Francisco Suárez.

The process leading to the beatification of Father Bernardino, who died in Lecce in Italy in 1616, was begun in Naples in 1621. Among the witnesses examined was Tobias da Ponte, a gentleman of rank and good standing. He testified that in about 1608 he had gone to consult the Father and noticed a powerful glow that streamed around the door, which was slightly ajar, and through chinks in the boards. Wondering what could have prompted the Father to light a fire at midday in April, he pushed the door a little farther open. He saw the Father kneeling, rapt in ecstasy and elevated about 2 feet (more than half a metre) above the floor. He was so dazed by the spectacle that he sat down for a while and then returned home without making himself known to the priest. Other people bore witness to the extraordinary radiance with which Father Bernardino's countenance was transformed at times. They had not seen him levitate, but some declared that they had seen sparks coming from all over his body like sparks from a fire, and others asserted that the

biographer, Father R. de Scorraille, records da Silva's account of the incident:

> I called the Father but he made no answer. As the curtain which shut off his working room was drawn, I saw, through the space between the jambs of the door and the curtain, a very great brightness. I pushed aside the curtain and entered the inner apartment. Then I noticed that the blinding light was coming from the crucifix, so intense that it was like the reflection of the sun from glass windows, and I felt that I could not have remained looking at it without being completely dazzled. This light streamed from the crucifix upon the face and breast of Father Suárez, and in the brightness I saw him in a kneeling position in front of the crucifix, his head uncovered, his hands joined, and his body in the air five palms [about 3 feet or 1 metre] above the floor on a level with the table on which the crucifix stood. On seeing this I withdrew . . . as it were beside myself . . . my hair standing on end. . . .

About a quarter of an hour later, Father

Mohammed (left) appears fully encircled by flames in this 16th-century painting from Turkey; Quetzalcoatl (below), the Aztec god, in his guise as the morning star is surrounded by fire on an ancient stele from Mexico; the great Buddhist teacher Padmasambhava (below right), is haloed in an 18th-century painting from Tibet; the four kings of hell (bottom), on a Chinese hanging scroll, have crowned heads encircled by light

dazzling glow from his face on one or two occasions was such that they could not rightly distinguish his features, but had to turn their eyes away.

Father Francisco Suárez, the subject of Father Thurston's second example, was a Spanish theologian who from 1597 to 1617 taught at the Jesuit College at Coimbra in Portugal. One day at about 2 p.m., an elderly lay-brother, Jerome da Silva, came to tell the Father of the arrival of a visitor. A stick placed across the door indicated that the Father did not wish to be disturbed, but the lay-brother had received instructions to inform the Father at once, so he went in. He found the outer room in darkness, shuttered against the afternoon heat. Suárez's

Suárez came out and was surprised to see Brother da Silva waiting. The account continues: 'When the Father heard that I had entered the inner room, he seized me by the arm . . . then, clasping his hands and with his eyes full of tears, he implored me to say nothing of what I had seen . . . as long as he lived.'

They shared the same confessor, who suggested that da Silva write his account and seal it with the endorsement that it should not be opened and read until after the death of Father Suárez. That apparently was done. And the account provides us with a particularly compelling story of human luminescence – in this case, the glow of holiness.

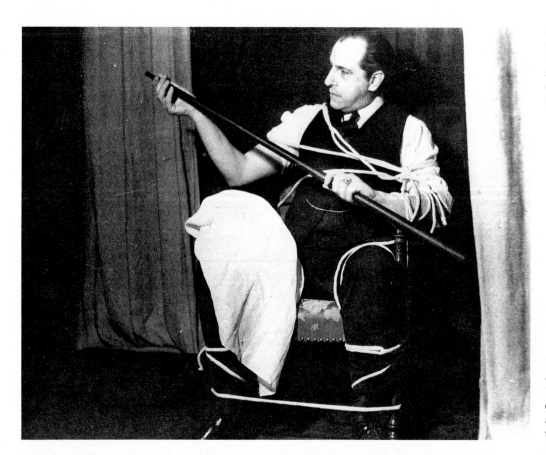

Switched on and shocking

There are people who can deliver an electric shock with their touch, make electrical appliances stop working, or attract objects to their bodies. How? This chapter examines the phenomenon of 'electric people'

IN 1938 MRS ANTOINE TIMMER went to New York with high hopes of winning a $10,000 prize offered for demonstrating a psychic phenomenon not reproducible by trickery. The demonstration was organised by the Universal Council for Psychic Research, headed by the famous stage magician Joseph Dunninger. Mrs Timmer, seeking to understand her singular ability herself, showed how spoons and other small objects stuck to her hands and could only be removed by a vigorous tug. Her claim was dismissed because Dunninger said that he could do what she did with a concealed thread. Nonetheless, there were no allegations of trickery against Antoine Timmer – and she no doubt went away as puzzled by her magnetic hands as when she came. On their part, the council missed a chance to explore a truly unexplained phenomenon.

People with unusual magnetic or electrical abilities are not all that rare. These 'human magnets' and 'human spark plugs' may attract objects to their body, create disturbances in electrical machines, shock other people with their touch. But whatever their

Above: Joseph Dunninger, the American stage magician who headed the Universal Council for Psychic Research. When in 1938 the organisation offered a prize for the demonstration of a psychic phenomenon 'not reproducible by trickery', they failed to recognise 'magnetic hands' as worthy of investigation

behaviour, 'electric people' make the news in the 20th century as they did in the 19th, when interest in all kinds of curiosities was particularly high.

For example, the *Daily Mirror* of 23 March 1967 told the story of Brian Clements, known to his friends as 'Flash Gordon'. Clements was so highly charged that he had to discharge his voltage into metal furniture before he touched anyone. The previous week the *Sunday Express* of 19 March 1967 reported the miserable life of Mrs Grace Charlesworth, who had been tormented by electric shocks in her house for two years after having lived there uneventfully for 40 years. She said: 'Sometimes they have swung me round bodily and in the night my head has started to shake as though I was using a pneumatic drill. One day sparks ran up the walls.' Curiously, it was only Mrs Charlesworth who was affected; her husband was aware only of an occasional humming noise.

Not surprisingly, many instances of electric people have been noticed or recorded by doctors. In January 1869, the doctor who delivered a baby in St Urbain, France, said the infant was charged up 'like a Leyden jar' (a type of electrostatic condenser). The baby shocked all who touched him, and luminous rays emanated from his fingers. This peculiarly endowed baby had a brief life, dying in his ninth month. Douglas Hunt records

the shock along 20 people holding hands in a line. The electrical phenomena lasted for several months and, once gone, never returned.

Thirdly, Gaddis mentions 16-year-old Louis Hamburger, who, in 1890, was a student in Maryland, USA. When the tips of his fingers were dry, he could pick up heavy objects simply by touching them. Pins would dangle from his open hand as though from a magnet, and needed a vigorous shake to send them flying. His favourite demonstration was to place his fingers against a glass beaker full of iron filings and pull the filings up the inside of the beaker by moving his fingers up the outer surface.

Both humans and animals have nervous systems that generate electricity, and some animals are able to store and use this potential. For example, electric eels – which are really fish – have an organ in their tails that produces an electric current. This current

two similar but non-fatal cases in *Prediction* magazine (January 1953). In the first instance, a doctor received a sharp shock while delivering a baby. The baby's 'electrification' lasted 24 hours, during which time he was actually used to charge a Leyden jar, and sparks issued from him. The second infant gave off a 'feeble white light' and caused 'vibrations' in small metal objects brought near his hands and feet.

Other 19th-century cases are even more spectacular. Vincent Gaddis mentions three in his book *Mysterious fires and lights* (1967). The first occurred in 1889 and concerned Frank McKinstry, of Joplin, Missouri, USA, a man with a reputation as a good dowser. He was plagued in a peculiar way: his charge was so strong in the early morning that he had to keep moving. If he stopped even for a second, he became fixed to the ground and had to wait until a helpful passer-by would pull one of his legs free. There would be a small faint flash and the grip would be broken – until the next time he stood still.

The second case cited by Gaddis concerned 17-year-old Caroline Clare of London, Ontario, Canada, who suffered from a strange undiagnosable debilitation in 1877. Her weight fell dramatically to about 6½ stone (40 kilograms), and she suffered spasms and trances. These passed after a year and a half – and then the electrical phenomena began. Metal objects would jump into her hand when she reached for them and, if she held one for any length of time, it stuck to her until someone pulled if off. She shocked those she touched, in one experiment passing

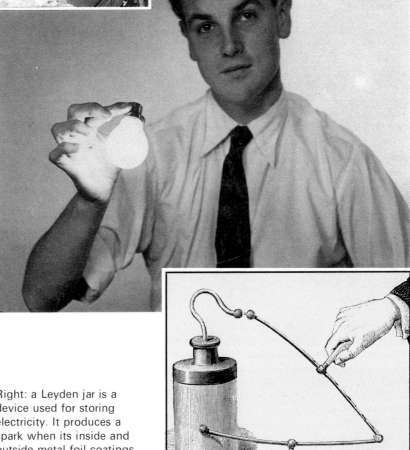

Right: a Leyden jar is a device used for storing electricity. It produces a spark when its inside and outside metal foil coatings are connected by a wire. One doctor has reported delivering a baby so 'electrified' that he was actually used to charge a Leyden jar

A highly-charged subject

In many respects electricity behaves like, and is described in terms of, a fluid. For example, we speak of an electric *current*. This is a *stream* of electrons that carry negative electric charge and are constituents of atoms. The rate of *flow* of the current is measured in amps. The 'pressure' that drives the current is electrical potential, measured in volts and more often simply called voltage. The quantity of electric charge is measured in coulombs, one coulomb being the amount of electric charge that flows when one amp passes for one second.

When electricity accumulates on the human body as a result of friction – say of a nylon shirt rubbing on car upholstery – it may be at a potential of thousands of volts. But the quantity of charge is tiny, so that it can do little harm when discharged. This can be compared to the jet of water from a water pistol – it is delivered at a high pressure, but in too small a quantity to do any damage. Dangerous shocks, such as those from electric mains, are caused by large currents flowing at a high voltage for a relatively long period.

Usually we are unaware of the electrical nature of matter because negative and positive charges exist in equal quantities around us, and their effects cancel out. Only when the two are separated are their effects seen.

Such effects include fleeting and small-scale examples of the phenomena exhibited by 'electric people'. Rub a plastic comb on a sleeve and it will take up electrons, which are negatively charged and can move about, from the cloth. It can then attract a small piece of paper. This is because the comb's negative electrons repel the paper's negative electrons in accordance with the fundamental electrical law that 'likes repel, unlikes attract'. The paper's negative electrons move away and leave the surface of the paper that is closest to the comb with a surplus of positive charge. The 'positive' paper is then attracted to the 'negative' comb. There is a similar effect when a balloon is rubbed on clothing: it will gain a charge that causes it to stick to things.

Angélique Cottin (bottom) was one of the most famous 'electric girls' of the 19th century. However, her powers seemed to wane when she was investigated by a hostile team appointed by the French Academy of Sciences and led by the physicist François Arago (below). But she was not accused of fraud

passes from the tail to the front and enables the fish to discharge a hefty shock of up to 500 volts, depending on the animal's size and health. The biggest jolt is delivered when the fish's head and tail touch well-separated parts of the victim's body, so allowing the current to travel some distance. The human body can accumulate about 10,000 volts when a person walks across a thick carpet but, unlike the electric eel's shock, any jolt given is harmless. This is because the body can develop only a small electrical charge, which means in turn that the current discharged is small. In contrast to this, the 'electric people' seem to be able to utilise their electrical potential, although they may not even want to. Their physiological state appears to have something to do with it, just as the electric eel's health influences its electrical power.

For example, disease may play a part – not in itself, but in its alterations of the metabolism and other physiological functions. An astonishing report was made in 1920 by Dr Julius Ransom, chief physician at a state prison in New York, after 34 inmates developed botulinus poisoning. During convalescence, one of them screwed up a piece of paper and tried to throw it away, but the paper stuck fast to his hand. Investigation showed that the man was carrying a high static charge, and so were all of his fellow sufferers. They could deflect compass needles and make a suspended steel tape sway by moving their hands towards and away from

it. The phenomena ceased when the men recovered.

There is also evidence that atmospheric and geomagnetic conditions may play a part in the strange phenomenon of electric people. Consider the case of 'a lady of great respectability', reported in the *American Journal of Science* (1838) by her physician Dr Willard Hosford. She was aged 30, of a nervous temperament and sedentary habits, and the wife of a prominent man in Orford, New Hampshire. For two years she had suffered from acute rheumatism and an unknown ailment called 'unseated neuralgia'. The electrical phenomena began on the evening of 25 January 1837 when she was feeling strange. She happened to pass her hand over her brother's face and, as she did so, vivid sparks shot from her fingers, to the astonishment of both. When she stood on a thick carpet, the sparks could be seen and heard discharging into objects near her hands – they were brilliant and shocking, felt by the woman and anyone she touched. The conditions favourable to bringing on the phenomena included hot weather with temperatures of about 80°F (20°C). Then the sparks would be about 1½ inches (4 centimetres) long, coming at the rate of four a minute.

Thinking the woman's silk clothes were generating the charges, Dr Hosford had her wear all cotton apparel. As a control, her sister wore silk. The woman's electricity was not reduced, and her sister remained normal. The electric charges, which caused her much discomfort, lasted for about six weeks, after which she was 'relieved of most of her neuralgia and other corporeal infirmities, and was in better health than she had been for many years'.

The atmospheric aspect was raised by Dr Hosford when he observed that 'a crimson aurora of uncommon splendour' was lighting the heavens and exciting scientific interest at the time of the Orford woman's strange attack. Her charges began on the same evening as this heavenly display of electricity, and Dr Hosford felt it was no mere coincidence. One is strongly reminded of the theory, put forward by Livingston

Below: her hair standing on end, science teacher Anthea Sothcott demonstrates the phenomenon of static electricity to her students. The Van der Graaf generator she touches is producing 500,000 volts; but she is standing on a deep pad of insulation, which cuts the current so drastically that no damage is done

Gearhart in the Fortean journal *Pursuit*, that relates instances of spontaneous human combustion to moments of change in the intensity of the Earth's magnetic field.

Perhaps the most famous 19th-century 'electric girl' was Annie May Abbott, who toured the world as 'The Little Georgia Magnet' in the late 1880s and early 1890s. On the stage in London in 1891, she raised a chair with a heavy man seated in it merely by touching it with the palm of her hand. Though she weighed only 7 stone (45 kilograms), groups of men could not lift her in a chair when she resisted it. In Japan she overcame the attempts of the huge and skilful Sumo wrestlers to budge her from where she stood, just as she could 'neutralise' their strenuous efforts to lift any small object upon which she had lightly rested her fingers. Another 'immovable' was Mary Richardson, who gave performances in Liverpool in September 1921. She was easily lifted one minute, and then six men would fail to move her even slightly. Her touch could knock men across the stage. A.C. Holms, the Scottish psychical researcher, put his hand on

Mary's shoulder while a line of 13 men pushed against her and his hand, and he felt no pressure at all from their push. He was convinced that somehow the force exerted against her was neutralised or shunted, perhaps into another dimension.

The classic 'electric girl' must be Angélique Cottin, a 14-year-old French girl from Normandy. Her ordeal began on 15 January 1846 and lasted 10 weeks. The first manifestation was when the weaving frame on which she and three other girls were making gloves twisted and rocked. Within a short time the girl's parents exhibited her in Paris, where she came to the attention of a Dr Tanchou. Dr Tanchou reported to the Academy of Sciences that the girl could identify the poles of a magnet, agitate a compass and alternately attract and repel small objects like a magnet. He also said that he could feel a sensation 'like a cold wind' in her vicinity during these activities – such a wind being reminiscent of the breeze that blows away from a highly charged object. Objects were violently propelled away from her at her slightest touch; her bed rocked violently; chairs twisted away from under her when she tried to sit down; and a 60-pound (25-kilogram) table rose into the air when her apron brushed against it.

An empty performance

The academy appointed a research team, led by the famous physicist François Arago. Although Angélique performed as best she could, her phenomena seemed to have deserted her, which also happens when modern poltergeist children and 'spoon-benders' face a sceptical enquirer or the starkness of a laboratory. The committee had ignored Dr Tanchou's observations that the girl performed best when she was relaxed. Poor Angélique was extremely frightened by the situation and the manifestations that did occur, and frequently left the room. The committee reported that they could not corroborate any claims made for Angélique, but drew back from calling her a fraud.

An electric force

Dr Tanchou had found that Angélique's force was strongest in the evening, especially after a meal, and that it radiated from her left wrist, inner left elbow and spine. From his experiments Dr Tanchou believed the cause was an undiscovered form of electricity. But Arago's team was not convinced. Besides, the academy was waging a 'holy war' against mesmerism at the time and could not accept phenomena so similar to those claimed by the detested practitioners and advocates of 'animal magnetism'. Arago recommended that the academy treat the case of Angélique Cottin 'as never having been sent in' – and another chance for the scientific world to discover what caused electrical phenomena in people slipped away.

Mind and magic

A belief in magic rituals and the power of potions, incantations, jinxes and curses is largely ridiculed in our sophisticated society, yet people continue to be profoundly affected by them. The symbolic power of magic is more widely acknowledged in other parts of the world. Do such beliefs indicate the existence of forces beyond our experience and at the control of a select few?

For centuries, scholars have been trying to unlock the secrets of a small book known as the Voynich manuscript which, they believe, presages the findings of modern science.

LATE IN 1912, a New York antique book-seller named Wilfred M. Voynich arrived back in his native city from a visit to Europe with a small, carefully wrapped manuscript in his possession. It had thick vellum covers that had broken away from the 204 vellum leaves at the spine – although Voynich calculated that originally it had held 28 extra pages, now missing. Its size was large quarto, measuring about 6 inches by 9 inches (15 centimetres by 22 centimetres), and the text, closely written in flowing black ink script, was illustrated by over 400 minute drawings in blood red, blue, yellow, brown and violent green.

The illustrations showed curious whorls and intestine-like tubes, naked female figures, stars and constellations, and hundreds of strange-looking plants. The vellum, style of script and known history of the manuscript indicated to Voynich that it was medieval in origin, and the many botanical

Below: two pages from what has been described as 'the most mysterious manuscript in the world'. Ever since 1912, when New York antique book dealer Wilfred M. Voynich (right) acquired the volume, experts have been using the methods of modern cryptology to try to unravel its secrets – with no success

A script full of secrets

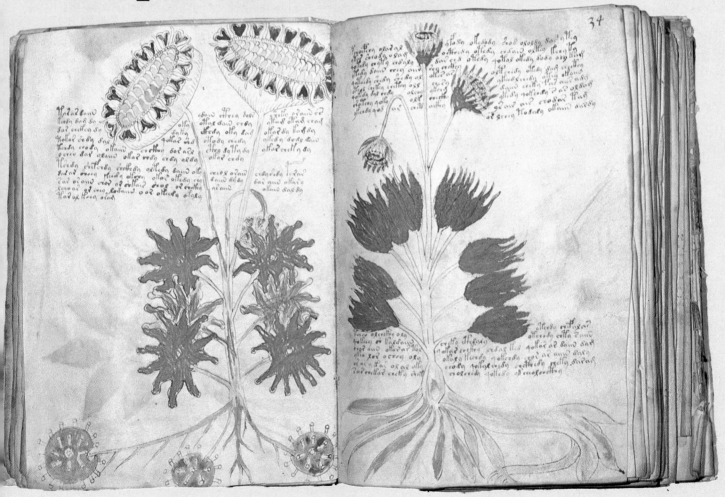

Mind and magic

specimens indicated it might be an herbal – a text-book, part scientific, part magical, showing the medical and mystical qualities of plants and their preparation. But this was simply conjecture, for the script was written in a language that Voynich could not recognise: although the text could clearly be broken down into 'words' whose characters were half familiar, it made no sense. Voynich could only assume that they were written either in a little-known language or dialect, or in code.

Practising black magic

Although Voynich was not a cryptologist, he did know something, in an oblique way, of symbolism. His father-in-law had been Professor George Boole, the English mathematician who had been one of the first to use mathematical symbolism to express logical processes, and had been elected a Fellow of the Royal Society for his work on modern symbolic logic. Voynich also knew that there was strong circumstantial evidence suggesting that the author of the bizarre work in his possession had been Roger Bacon, a 13th-century Franciscan monk who had combined the study of philosophy, mathematics and practical physics with alchemy. Perhaps Bacon had, 600 years before Boole, succeeded in inventing a system of symbolic logic; or perhaps he had simply devised a cipher in order to cover up his researches into the Philosopher's Stone and the Elixir of Life – thus avoiding a charge of practising black magic which, in medieval times, often led to death.

With these intriguing speculations in mind, Voynich began to sound out the academic world for a solution, having dozens of copies made of the document and circulating them to any specialist who felt that he could help. With each copy, Voynich sent an account of what he knew of the manuscript.

He had bought it, for an undisclosed sum,

Right: the 19th-century mathematician George Boole. He invented a system of symbolic logic (below right) that, some experts thought, might be similar to that employed in the Voynich manuscript

Below: Roger Bacon (1214–1294) who, it has been suggested, was the author of the Voynich manuscript

THE MATHEMATICAL ANALYSIS

OF LOGIC,

BEING AN ESSAY TOWARDS A CALCULUS
OF DEDUCTIVE REASONING.

BY GEORGE BOOLE.

CAMBRIDGE:
MACMILLAN, BARCLAY, & MACMILLAN;
LONDON: GEORGE BELL.

1847

Below: the Jesuit Collegium Romanum in Rome, where the Voynich manuscript lay undisturbed for two and a half centuries before being transferred to the library of Mondragone College

early in 1912, after coming across it in the library of Mondragone College, a Jesuit establishment in Frascati, Italy. Before arriving there, it had lain in the Jesuit Collegium Romanum for about 250 years, in the archives in which it had been lodged by a celebrated 17th-century Jesuit scholar and cryptologer named Athanasius Kircher, who had tried but failed to unlock its secrets.

According to a letter dated 19 August 1666, Kircher had received the book from his former pupil Joannes Marcus Marci, rector of the University of Prague, and it had formed part of the library of the Holy Roman Emperor Rudolf II until his death in 1612. Rudolf had, to all intents and purposes, allowed the Jesuits to rule his kingdoms of Hungary, Austria, Bohemia and Moravia, preferring to devote his time to the patronage of the sciences and pseudo-sciences. His particular interests were botany and astronomy, and he created an elaborate botanical garden and built an observatory at Benatky, near Prague, for the exiled Danish astronomer Tycho Brahe and his then assistant Johannes Kepler, who was later to name his 'Rudolphine Tables' after his former patron.

But Rudolf's own interests lay in the direction of alchemy, and he spent a great

deal of time and money in setting up an alchemical laboratory to which he invited alchemists from all over Europe; one of them, Johannes de Tepenecz, was later discovered to have signed his name on a margin of Voynich's manuscript. Another, more famous, was Dr John Dee, who spent the years between 1584 and 1588 at Rudolf's court as a secret agent of Queen Elizabeth I. It seemed possible that it was Dee who first brought the manuscript to Prague.

Dee had survived imprisonment at the hands of Queen Mary in 1555, charged with witchcraft, to become a favourite of her half-sister Elizabeth. The necromantic experiments he conducted with his assistant Edward Kelley smack of chicanery, but he had a deep and genuine knowledge of alchemical theory and practice, as well as astrology, astronomy, mathematics, geography and celestial navigation – one of his obsessions was with finding the North-West Passage to India – but above all else, he was a cloak-and-dagger spy. He had experimented with the invention of ciphers, and had studied existing codes on behalf of his chief, Lord Burghley.

Dee also deeply admired the work of Roger Bacon and collected many of his manuscripts. He had many things in common with the Franciscan monk; both men were, for example, intrigued by secret writing. In any event, it appears that it was Dr Dee who presented Rudolf II with the Voynich manuscript, telling him that it was Roger Bacon's work. Sir Thomas Browne – inventor of the English word 'cryptography'

Where did the Voynich manuscript come from? When scholars traced its history, it appeared that a well-known Jesuit scholar named Athanasius Kircher (above) had tried – but failed – to unlock its secrets during the 17th century. Kircher had received the manuscript from a former pupil of his, who was then rector of the University of Prague – and before that, the book had been in the library of the Holy Roman Emperor Rudolf II (above right) until his death in 1612

– claimed that Dr Dee's son Arthur had spoken to him about a 'book containing nothing but hieroglyphicks, which book his father bestowed much time upon, but I could not hear that he could make it out'.

This, then, was the background to the problem that Voynich presented to the academic world in 1912 – one that was destined to throw many a European and American high table into uproar, for though the groups of letters and 'words' looked at first glance tantalisingly simple, 'like old friends whose names are on the tip of one's tongue', as one writer put it, they were not. Philologists

Right: one of the intricate – and extraordinarily confusing – pages of the Voynich manuscript

sought in vain for any trace of a known language, and then carried out all the known methods used for reading lost languages – without result. Cryptanalysts, including a specialist from the Bibliothèque Nationale who had worked with 15th-century alchemical ciphers, struggled and gave up. In 1917 the manuscript even captured the attention of the cryptological section of the United States Military Intelligence Division – MI-8.

MI-8 was headed by a brilliant young director, Herbert Osborne Yardley, who was later to become a legend in the world of codebreaking, and his equally brilliant assistant, Captain John M. Manly, Ph.D., who had been, before the war, head of the department of English at Chicago University. In 1917 Manly was working on the so-called Witzke cryptogram, a 424-letter code that he cracked in three days to reveal the identity of Lothar Witzke, a German secret agent operating from Mexico. But after a long struggle with the Voynich manuscript, he too gave up, along with his boss Yardley, referring to the text as 'the most mysterious manuscript in the world'.

The pictures accompanying the text were equally baffling. One obvious procedure seemed to be for botanists to identify the plants depicted and then use their names to decode the captions accompanying them; the trouble was that most of the plants and shrubs were invented, and the names of those that were not made no sense cryptographically. Astronomers thought that they recognised such celestial signposts as Aldebaran, the Andromeda nebula, and the Hyades, but then lost their way again in a whirl of imaginary galaxies. Bacon authorities studied the manuscript with an eye to

Right: Dr John Dee (1527–1608), mathematician and astrologer who, in addition to more orthodox scientific activities, conducted necromantic experiments with the occultist and alchemist Edward Kelley (above). Dee spent four years at the court of Rudolf II, as a secret agent for Elizabeth I. Given his interest in the occult and the curious, it seems possible that Dee brought the Voynich script to Rudolf's court

Below: another page from the Voynich manuscript, showing mysterious star maps and zodiacs

concurrences, while the professor of anatomy at Harvard tried to make sense of the apparent physiological diagrams – all to no avail.

For one man, however, the Voynich manuscript had become an obsession. Professor William Romaine Newbold, a specialist in philosophy and medieval history at the University of Pennsylvania – a linguist and, like Manly, a cryptographer who lent his services to the US Navy Department – began work on the text in 1919. His processes were hugely complex; beginning by examining the writing under a magnifying glass, he found a secondary, microscopic text embodied in the characters – a form, he thought, of shorthand. Using code-breaking techniques, he

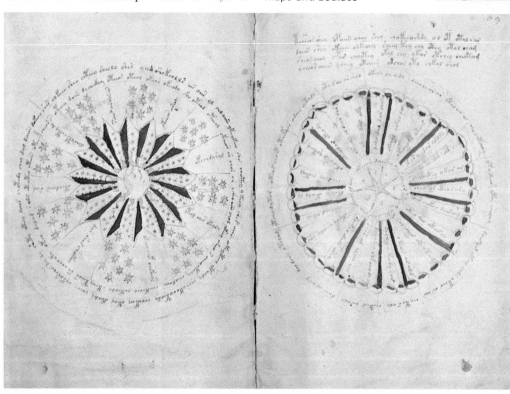

Right: this illustration, which appears to show women bathing in green ink, is typical of the manuscript's mysterious drawings

Below: an example of the script in which the Voynich manuscript is written. At first glance, the letters and 'words' seem familiar – 'like old friends whose names are on the tip of one's tongue', as one writer commented. So far, however, they have resisted all attempts at decipherment

Below: Professor William Romaine Newbold, a specialist in philosophy and medieval history who, in 1921, made the startling announcement that he had succeeded in breaking the code of the Voynich manuscript

was able to reduce this to a 17-letter Roman key, and with this worked his way through six different 'translations' each leading on to the other. He then 'anagrammed' the sixth text to produce a final 'plaintext' – the solution – in Latin.

In April 1921 he called a meeting of the American Philosophical Society in Philadelphia and announced his interim findings to an astonished and finally impressed audience. In his opinion the work was indeed that of Roger Bacon, who had encoded it to avoid the charge of 'novelty' in his thinking. Bacon was known to have been the inventor of the magnifying glass, and had speculated on the possibility of microscopes and telescopes long before they were invented. But, claimed Professor Newbold, the Voynich manuscript proved that Bacon had actually constructed a compound microscope, and had used it to study and describe germ cells, ova, spermatozoa, and organic life in general. Not only that, but he had also built a powerful reflecting telescope with which he had studied star systems unknown in his day.

Professor Newbold was a man of considerable reputation and, sensational though

they were, his findings seemed sound. Only a small number of the academics who gathered to listen to him had any grasp of cryptology, but the 'discoveries' he had made appeared to make sense; for instance, a leading physiologist considered that one drawing and its caption described the epithelial cells and their cilia – cells that line the bronchial and Fallopian tubes to assist the passage of mucus and eggs – to a magnification of 75. John Manly, out of his major's uniform and back at his chair at Chicago University, preferred to keep an open mind but wrote a review for *Harper's Magazine* that was, if anything, favourable to Newbold. There were very few dissenting voices after this first exposition.

For a further five years, until his death in 1926, Newbold continued his cryptanalysis of the Voynich manuscript, working closely with a friend and colleague Roland Grubb Kent, and it was Professor Kent who edited Newbold's findings into final form in 1928 under the title *The cipher of Roger Bacon*.

John Manly had, of course, kept a constant interest in the work in progress, and with the publication he was able to see Newbold's working methods at first hand and test them for himself. A genuine admirer of Newbold, he was deeply dismayed at what he found and, after checking his own results with, among other people, former colleagues at MI-8, he published a 47-page article in a 1931 edition of *Speculum* magazine – a closely reasoned analysis that made the dead professor's work seem completely worthless.

The uncrackable code

Who was the author of the tantalising Voynich manuscript? What was the message encoded in its cryptic text? In the 1920s it seemed the solution had been found – but had the script really given up its secrets?

FEW DOUBTED PROFESSOR NEWBOLD when, in 1921, he announced that the mysterious Voynich manuscript was a treatise written by the 13th-century philosopher-scientist Roger Bacon, containing advanced scientific information concealed by a complex code that Newbold claimed he had cracked. But, 10 years later, his former colleague Professor John Manly published a criticism that showed that his conclusions could not possibly have been correct.

Manly's first objection – in retrospect, an obvious one – was to the 'anagramming' process by which Newbold had arrived at his final Latin text. He pointed out that several anagrams could be built from any given line, making several meanings possible – thus breaking the cardinal rule that only one solution should be admissible for any given code passage. Constructing anagrams is an ancient pastime; for example, the salutation of the angel to the Virgin Mary at the Annunciation – *Ave Maria, gratia plena, Dominus tecum* – had long afforded a sort of devout game to scholars as a source of anagrams. Containing only 31 letters, the line had yielded 3100 anagrams in prose and an acrostic poem to one experimenter, while another had turned out 1500 pentameters

In 1931, Professor John Manly (right) published an analysis of Professor William Newbold's work that threw open, once again, the question of the authorship and meaning of the Voynich manuscript (below: two pages from the script, illustrating some of the many unidentified botanical specimens). Newbold had attributed the script to the 13th-century philosopher-scientist Roger Bacon but, said Manly, his method was 'open to objections of so grave a character as to make it impossible to accept the results' and, he added, these results threatened 'to falsify, to no unimportant degree, the history of human thought'

and hexameters, and a third had produced a 27-anagram life of the Virgin.

By comparison, Newbold had 'anagrammed' Bacon's alleged writing in blocks of 55 or 110 letters – rendering thousands of translations possible. But, asked Manly, was Newbold on the right track at all? His examination of the text under a magnifying glass had failed to turn up the secondary, 'shorthand' script that Newbold had seen; all he found was that the vellum had cracked and distorted with age, breaking up the original inked characters to give the appearance of minute lines and squiggles beneath them.

What of such pieces of evidence as the Andromeda nebula, of which Newbold had claimed to know nothing before he read the Voynich text? Without questioning the

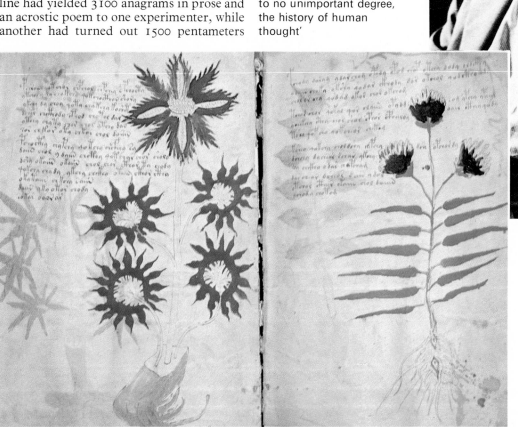

Professor's integrity, Manly suggested that, with his vast reading, he must have come across the facts before; 'he was a victim of his own intense enthusiasm and his learned and ingenious subconscious.'

The essay ended firmly. 'We do not, in fact, know when the manuscript was written, or where, or what language lies at the basis of the encipherment,' wrote Manly. 'When the correct hypotheses are applied, the cipher will perhaps reveal itself as simple and easy.'

The greatest challenge

There was silence for several years after the echoes of Manly's clinical denunciation had died. Although many cryptanalysts still worked away at the manuscript, which they justifiably looked upon as the greatest challenge ever to face them, they did so in private. In 1943 a New York lawyer was rash enough to produce his solution, a garbled Latin text that amounted to little more than gibberish. Two years later a leading cancer specialist, Dr Leonell C. Strong, perhaps feeling that his reputation in his chosen field was secure enough to withstand most academic brickbats, claimed he had successfully transcribed certain medical passages.

They were the work, he announced, not of Bacon but of Roger Ascham, a near contemporary of Dr John Dee who had been tutor and private secretary to the young Queen Elizabeth I. Like many scholars of his age, Ascham was a man of many interests, who had published several translations of

Roger Ascham, 16th-century English scholar and writer who, according to Dr Leonell Strong, was the author of the manuscript. Dr Strong, a highly respected cancer research specialist, made this claim in 1945 after allegedly transcribing certain medical passages in the script, including an effective contraceptive formula. However, linguistics experts did not support his theory and, since Dr Strong has failed to explain satisfactorily his method of cryptanalysis, it remains unproved

The use of ciphers was widespread in past centuries, and not always for reasons of military or diplomatic secrecy. The Voynich manuscript may have been written in code in order to avoid charges of witchcraft for the advanced scientific knowledge it may contain. But perhaps the most famous example of such a cryptic manuscript is one that was written in code for quite different reasons – the diaries of the 17th-century English man of letters and naval administrator Samuel Pepys.

In 1724, in accordance with Pepys's will, the diaries were given to his old Cambridge college – and there they remained, undeciphered, until their rediscovery in 1818. The task of translating them was given to an undergraduate of the college, one John Smith. He spent three years on the task of breaking the code and transcribing the manuscript, often working 12 or 14 hours a day. The result was published, at last, in 1825 – revealing a colourful and scandalous account of life in London at the time of the Restoration.

The last laugh, however, was on poor John Smith. When a new edition of the diaries was being prepared in the 1870s,

For your eyes only

it was discovered that, had he known the library in which he worked better, the solution would have been available to him all the time. For Pepys had used no abstruse code, but a well-known system of shorthand whose key formed part of the very same library that had held the Pepys diaries for so long.

Mind and magic

classical works, a treatise on education and a handbook explaining and defending the dying practice of archery.

According to Dr Strong, one of Ascham's passages in the Voynich manuscript described a contraceptive formula that, as Dr Strong demonstrated, worked, though the doctor did not explain his cryptological methods beyond saying that they were 'a double reverse system of arithmetical progressions by means of a multiple alphabet'. Nor did he explain why Ascham, a devout and discreet scholar, should have concerned himself with contraceptives. In any case, several of Dr Strong's assertions about Ascham's alleged linguistic style failed to stand up to expert scrutiny.

An extra dimension

What was perhaps the most promising effort to find the solution began in 1944, instigated by an old colleague of Professor Manly named Captain William F. Friedman, of the Army Signal Corps, who had helped demolish the Newbold theory. Captain Friedman assigned part of his huge team of experts then based in Washington to breaking the ancient mystery. Working after hours, they managed to reduce the text to a series of symbols that could be handled by tabulating machines – but they abandoned their task, leaving it unfinished, after the war. One curious result, however, was that Friedman's team showed that the words and phrases of the manuscript were repeated more often than those of an ordinary language: this gave it an extra, and unique, dimension, for all known cipher systems strive for the opposite effect.

A theory that sought to account for this was that the book was an herbal, as had been first suggested, and that the repetitions were of chemical formulae – repeated often, as they tend to be in modern medical textbooks.

When Wilfred Voynich died in 1930, his principal legatee was his wife Ethel Lillian. Ethel L. Voynich was a strong minded and

Antiquarian bookseller Hans Kraus (above) bought the manuscript on the death of Ethel L. Voynich (below left) in 1960 and, in 1969, presented it to Yale University Library. He believed that, when transcribed, the script would provide new insights into Man's history; others are of the opinion that it will tell nothing new – that it is, after all, nothing more than an elaborate herbal. But no one yet knows – the mystery remains

independent woman, as she could afford to be; in 1897 she had published a romantic novel about the Young Italy movement, entitled *The gadfly*, which became a world best-seller, particularly in post-revolutionary Russia. Before her death it had sold over 2,500,000 copies there, putting her in the same Soviet league as Shakespeare, Dickens and Robert Burns. She was not really interested in the entanglements of the 'Voynich controversy' and placed the manuscript in her safe deposit box at the Guaranty Trust Company, New York. When she died at the age of 96 in 1960, her estate put her effects up for auction and the manuscript was bought by another New York antiquarian bookdealer named Hans P. Kraus. Two years later, Kraus offered the book for sale at 160,000 dollars.

At the time he told the press that he had originally bought it in the belief that 'the manuscript contains information that could provide new insights into the record of man. The moment someone can read it, this book is worth a million dollars.'

Perhaps it does, perhaps it is, was the essence of the response of various American literary and academic foundations; on the other hand, perhaps it really was written as a simple 'herbal' – the work of some late medieval scribbler who did not quite know what he was doing and devised a secret code that he himself lost track of. Hans Kraus gave the book to Yale University Library in 1969 – and there it remains, guarding its secret.

Rites and wrongs

Magical rituals have been performed since time immemorial and are still used today – and not just in primitive tribes. Do these rites have the power to fulfil our wishes – for good or for evil?

THE PERFORMING OF RITES, that is to say, ceremonial observances, plays a bigger part in our lives than most of us realise. Even people who have never, for example, been present at a barmitzvah, the Jewish 'rite of passage' that marks the transition from boyhood to manhood, or witnessed a celebration of the Christian Eucharist, have probably attended a twenty-first birthday party – the 'ceremonial observance' of the attainment of

Young girls of the Caraya tribe of Peru perform a dance for the Sun to mark the onset of puberty; if they did not take part in this age-old ritual they would not be considered to be truly adult

an adulthood that, in purely legal terms, is reached some three years earlier.

When we throw a pinch of spilt salt over our shoulders, mutter 'Bless you' when a friend sneezes, or perform some other rite, however simple, we are following a pattern of behaviour that is probably almost as old as humanity itself. From prehistoric graves it is clear that our Stone Age ancestors carried out elaborate funeral rituals and most of the primitive communities that have survived into modern times seem to practise highly formalised and complex ceremonies to mark birth, puberty and death.

While it is impossible for us to know exactly what beliefs our prehistoric forbears

Aubrey Beardsley's illustration for the text of Oscar Wilde's play *Salome*, which inspired Aleister Crowley to perform one of his more repulsive and risible ceremonies. He solemnly baptised a cockerel with the name of John the Baptist and then beheaded it, in a manner loosely based on the relevant scene in Wilde's play. This ceremony was supposed to undermine the influence of Christianity, but Crowley's very act showed that he, at least, was obsessed with the subject

world. However, along with a similar Crowleyan unpleasantness, the crucifixion of a toad that he had baptised 'Jesus of Nazareth', the rite seems to have been singularly ineffective.

If a clay doll, a wax image, or – as in the two strange Crowleyan rites mentioned above – an animal, is supposedly given the inner qualities of a particular living being by means of baptism or some other ceremonial observance, it is believed that a 'magical link' is established between the image and the living being. In some way they have become mystically identified with one another, and anything that affects the image or animal will, so it is argued, affect its 'psychic twin' in a similar way.

If a peasant wanted to kill an enemy he would make a realistic image of him and baptise it with the enemy's name. To make the psychic identification of image and enemy as close as possible he would endeavour to obtain some hair and/or nail clippings of his intended victim and incorporate them with the clay or wax from which he moulded his image. Then he would perhaps hammer nails or pins into the image

held, it is likely that from the very beginnings of ritual they associated it with magic and the supernatural. A proper ceremony not only *marked* a particular event in life but in some way *produced* that event. If, for example, a man or woman had not undergone the appropriate rituals associated with the attainment of adulthood he or she was not considered a 'real adult' in spite of all appearances to the contrary.

It was only a short mental step from thinking that sexually mature individuals were not adult humans because they had not been *made* adults by the appropriate rite to thinking that the proper ceremonies would turn some non-human entity or thing (a tree or a clay image, for example) into a sort of honorary human being.

The taste of deception
Strange as such a mode of thinking may appear it has persisted throughout history and has even survived into historically recent times. In the late medieval period an abbot who yearned to eat meat during Lent was accused of adopting the ingenious device of baptising a sheep with the name of 'Carp', butchering it, and then eating it during the fast under the pleasant conviction that, whatever appeared to be on his plate, it was in substance fish, not mutton.

As recently as the 1930s the fanatically anti-Christian occultist and magician Aleister Crowley employed baptism in much the same way. He had a cockerel baptised with the name of John (the Baptist) and then solemnly beheaded in an elaborate ceremony based on Oscar Wilde's play *Salome*. This was supposed to destroy, in some mysterious way, the influence of Christianity upon the

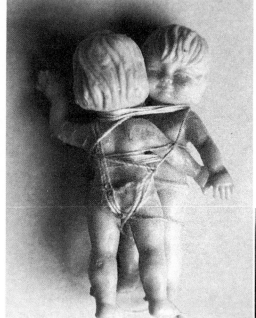

Dolls, or wax effigies, have long been used as magical aids. A male and a female doll (above), bound together as if making love, are traditionally used to secure a lover. But darker thoughts inspired this doll (right), bound tightly and stabbed with pins and placed face down, with a photograph and strands of hair of the intended victim. A sick mind may have devised it, but there is evidence that such 'games' can be deadly

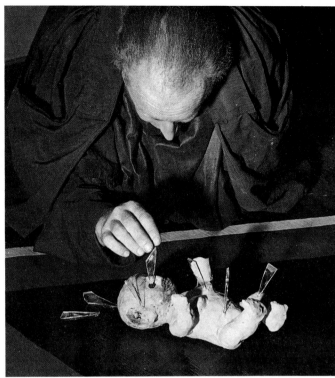

or slowly destroy it – melting it over a slow fire if it was made of wax, or putting it in a wet place if it was made of clay. As the fire or water wasted away the image, so the body of the enemy would also waste away.

A similar, if more kindly intentioned, process was often employed for sexual ends. A girl who desired a man would make images of herself and her beloved, incorporating, when possible, hair, nails, and bodily secretions in the images and endowing them with prominent genitals in a state of sexual excitement. The images would be baptised with the appropriate names and then tied together with thread (usually red – a colour psychologically associated with sexual excitement) as though energetically copulating. Soon the man's sexual desires would be directed towards the sorceress who, by this simple magical rite, had captured his love – or so it was believed.

Were such magic rites effective? Sometimes, so it would seem, for there are well-authenticated cases even in modern times of the mysterious and medically inexplicable deaths of those who have been attacked by ritual magic involving the use of images. Exactly why these victims die is uncertain. It may be that there really is some 'magical link', created by ritual, between image and victim. Or it may be that the concentrated hate that the sorcerer pours out upon the image of his enemy telepathically exerts a destructive influence. More probably the victim is aware, or very strongly suspects, that ritual magic is being used by an enemy and kills himself by autosuggestion – dying, quite literally, of fright.

Two stories from the 1930s that give support to the latter idea, although they

A woman who sent a curse in the form of a letter to the 'Witches' Kitchen' coven at Castletown, Isle of Man, provoked Cecil Williamson, the group's leader, to respond with all his painstaking art. First, he made a 'poppet' to represent the woman who had cursed the coven, then he appealed to the spirits for power. Next he breathed 'life' into the doll through a straw in its mouth (above left). Symbolically and, magicians believe, in some way *actually*, the doll had become the woman. Then Williamson inserted glass splinters into various parts of her body (above right); as long as the candles burned she would 'feel torment sharper than the sting of needles'. In ritual magic, it is often the person with the greater hate – and ingenuity – who wins the psychic battle

involved injury rather than death, were told by the American journalist William Seabrook. The first concerned a certain French concert pianist – Seabrook called him Jean Dupuis to disguise his real identity. A student of Rosicrucianism, astrology and other aspects of occultism, he had become involved with a dubious 'esoteric group' with which he had subsequently quarrelled. The group, angry at the musician's defection, decided to ruin him by using a combination of ritual image magic and applied psychology in order to destroy his ability to play.

Five-finger exercise

The magic came first. A doll was made in the image of Dupuis, baptised with his name and clad in miniature evening dress such as he wore on the concert platform. Then its hands were placed in a vice that was slowly tightened each day.

The psychology followed. Supposed friends of the victim, but in actuality members of the group that was working against him, began to make comments and ask questions. His finger-work seemed less dextrous than usual, they remarked. Perhaps he was in need of a few days rest? Had he sprained his wrist, they enquired, or was he suffering from neuritis?

Within a week or two the sly suggestions began to take effect. Jean Dupuis became excessively aware of his fingers. His playing began to degenerate. Then, a few days before a concert appearance, he received an anonymous note, beginning 'I can tell you what is wrong with your hands, but it is so frightful that I am almost afraid to tell you.' The letter then proceeded to go into occult theories about magical links between images and men

Mind and magic

– matters that the writer knew the pianist had studied – and concluded by giving details of the doll with its hands held in a vice. On the night of the concert a second note arrived: 'The handle of the vice will be slowly turned tonight, until your hands are crushed.'

The concert was a disaster: 'a false note, then a succession of jangling chords, followed by worse fumbling . . . whispers and hisses from the outraged audience . . . the young man half turned to the audience, resumed desperately, and, after a ghastly parody of the next few bars . . . fled from the stage in shame and confusion.'

Sinister rites
In this case the victim was a student of the occult, a believer in ritual magic and its powers to hurt or kill. The other story told by Seabrook does, however, illustrate the fact that such sinister rites may sometimes exert an influence upon even those who do not consciously believe in their efficacy.

In this instance the victim was Louis, a French motor mechanic, the lover of a young girl whose peasant grandmother, a woman locally reputed to dabble in witchcraft, took an intense and unreasoning dislike to him. One day Louis and the old woman quarrelled violently and almost came to blows. As the two parted, Louis to set off along a well-marked mountain path, the grandmother to return to her nearby cottage, the supposed witch chanted an incantation:
Tangled mind will twist and turn,
And tangled foot will follow . . .
So tangle, tangle, twist and turn,
For tangling webs are woven.
By nightfall Louis had not returned from his walk and a search party was sent out. He was found some distance from the path, entangled in briars, unable to walk, his legs paralysed although physically uninjured. He said that he had wandered off the path, became dizzy and increasingly confused, and suffered some sort of stroke that had paralysed him. He was ill, he asserted, and so he

Above: William B. Seabrook with the Ivory Coast forest people, including a young witch called Wamba, in the 1920s. Seabrook travelled widely and discovered the universality of magical rites. One of the most striking cases of magical ill-wishing he recorded took place in France. A young man called Louis fell foul of his girlfriend's grandmother – and was found lying in a briar patch, paralysed. Later, Seabrook found a doll tangled in briars in the old woman's cellar

Below: a medieval magical incantation, according to the 'Key of Solomon' – one of the most important of all grimoires

continued to assert even after the local doctor had been unable to find any physical injury to account for his condition.

Eventually Seabrook, convinced that ritual magic was responsible for Louis's condition, raided the old wine cellar in which the grandmother practised her witchcraft. On the floor was laid out a miniature landscape, 'a tangled labyrinth of thorns and briars'. In its midst lay an image of Louis, its eyes bandaged, its feet tied and enmeshed in thorns and brambles.

Powerless and paralysed
Seabrook took the doll and showed it to Louis, who was annoyed that the old woman had attempted to harm him but still refused to accept that her activities had in any way been responsible for his paralysed state. 'I don't believe any of it,' he said, 'I've had a stroke.' He lay there, victim of his own unconscious imagination, yet his conscious mind, paradoxically enough, was lacking in the imaginative ability to understand the real cause of his paralysis. If he had been able to understand that primitive beliefs in sorcery and the supernatural lurked in the hidden depths of his own mind, he would once again have been able to walk.

These two cases represent only the most primitive strand in ritual magic, for the rites employed were extremely simple. As long ago as classical times, however, far more complex forms of ritual magic were evolved. The formulae, techniques, and other secrets of such elaborate occult systems are enshrined in the *grimoires* – text books of ceremonial magic.

Exactly when and where the first grimoires were compiled is uncertain. But something very like them existed in ancient Egypt, while magical works, many of them of Jewish origin, were circulated widely in the later centuries of the Roman Empire. It is probable that the European grimoires of the

SALOMONIS
(CITATIO)
(ܗܒܪܫܝܗܢܐܝܩܝܗܢܩܝܗܢܩܗܢ)

XYWOLEH.VAY.BAREC
HET.VAY.YOMAR.HA.ELOHE
ELOHIM.ASCHER.TYWOHE
HYTHALE.CHUABOTAY.LEP
HA.NAWABRA.HAMVEYS.HA
HAKLA.ELOHIM.HARO.HE
OTYMEO.DY.ADDHAYON
HAZZE.HAMALECH.HAGO

ELOTYMYCCOL.RAH.YEBA
RECH.ETHANEA.TYM.VEI
KA.REBA.HEM.SCHEMVE.EEL
SCHEMABO.TAY.ABRAHAM
VEY.SCHAK.VEYYD.GULA
ROBBE.KEREBHAARETZ.
(ܩܒܫܗܪܗܫܒܩ)(ܫܩܫܡܗܩܫܘܫ)
(ܩܫܝܫܚܩܫܝ)

CHAY.SEWAH.ANOCHY.YA
HEL.PARYM.BEWO.WYKAR

HIER NENNE DER GEISTER NAHMEN MIT IHREN (HEBRÆ) RUF, DIE DU HABEN WILLST, ZU DIENSTEN, AUS (DENEN)(NB) AMULETEN, UND NIMM IHR AMULET, LEGE ES VOR DICH HIN AUF DIE ERDE.

medieval period were derived from the latter, for they show much evidence of Jewish influence. The authorship of many of them was attributed to King Solomon, who, according to legend, was such a master of magic that he had dominion over men, demons, and even the angels of heaven.

The *Clavicula Salomonis* and other magical works attributed to the great Jewish King display, like almost all the grimoires, a notable moral ambivalence. The hard core of the ritual magic of these works is the 'raising to visible appearance' of spirits, good and bad, with the object of obtaining benefits of one sort or another – usually wealth, power or knowledge – from these beings.

The processes used for these rites fall into three stages. First, the preparation of the materials and implements to be used in the ceremony; secondly, the preparation of the

Right: a common, if melodramatic, image of the ritual magician, summoning demons while standing in his magic circle, grimoire at his feet and loathsome 'familiars' cavorting around. Yet essentially the image is correct; a devoted magician will use ancient texts to summon up spirits and stand, often for hours, inside a magic circle. And he may indeed succeed in producing some entity – but it may be only an hallucination, owing its appearance more to the result of his long fast and meditation than to the use of 'the words of power'

Left: one of the images carved on the wall of a house at Bunbury, Cheshire, by a poacher who had been deported by the squire. On his return the poacher carved three images – to represent the squire and his two henchmen – and cursed them daily, as witches do with dolls. The three men soon died. There are very few cases recorded in which a person died without any knowledge of being cursed; the realisation that psychic venom is being concentrated upon one must be a major subconscious factor in such 'magical' deaths

magician's own mind and body; and, thirdly, the actual performance of the rite.

The first of these stages must have been found difficult by many magicians past and present. It involves the experimenter compounding incense, moulding candles, and first manufacturing and then consecrating a variety of 'magical weapons', including a wand, a sword, and even a sickle. These processes are often extremely complex. One grimoire, for example, instructs the magician to forge his sickle one hour after sunrise on a Wednesday, thrice bring it to a red heat and immerse it in a mixture of herbal extracts and the blood of a magpie.

The preparations enjoined upon the magician are sometimes almost as burdensome. One text tells the experimenter to build a stone altar on a river bank before dawn, behead a white cockerel at the moment of sunrise, throw its head in the river, drink its blood and burn its body. He must then jump into the river, climb out backwards, don new clothing and return to his dwelling.

The first two stages successfully accomplished, the magician can proceed to the ritual itself. He stands within a circle inscribed with names and symbols designed to protect him from demons who might wish to destroy him, He burns incenses, brandishes his magical implements, and chants the lengthy and sonorous incantations given in the grimoires. Eventually the spirit appears and gives the magician the things he desires. Or so some occultists believe.

On the face of it many of the processes involved in the ritual magic of the grimoires are so absurd – and often so repellent – that no normal person would wish to carry them out. This has led some modern occultists to deny that the texts of the grimoires are to be taken literally. These works, so it is argued, are written in a code only fully understandable by initiates. Thus, for example, one grimoire teaches a method of giving someone a sleepless night: 'Pick a June lily under a waning moon, soak it in laurel juice and bury it in dung. Worms will breed therein. Dry them and scatter on your enemy's pillow.' This means, say those who believe the grimoires to be written in code, invoke the demons Lilith (the June lily) and Q'areb Zareg (the laurel), both of whom are reputed to give bad dreams.

Similar interpretations are employed by modern practitioners of ritual magic – and there are a surprising number of these.

Although the practice of ritual magic declined towards the end of the 17th century it was by no means abandoned. The emphasis changed however, from conjuring up spirits to harnessing hidden forces

unsatisfactory science, for 'there was nothing in it which tended to mathematical demonstration'.

One day the Reverend Bedford, at the time the curate of Bristol's Temple parish, was approached by Parkes with a theological question. Was it lawful for a Christian, he asked, to raise spirits to visible appearance and converse with them? It was not, answered the clergyman.

Parkes then admitted that, using the processes outlined in a grimoire, the *Fourth book of Agrippa*, he had been doing that very thing. He would go, he said, in the dead of night to a causeway where he drew a circle with consecrated chalk. Then, standing within the circle, 'which no spirit had power to enter', he would invoke the spirits – and they would duly appear. These manifested themselves:

> in the shape of little girls, about a foot and a half [46 centimetres] high, and played about the circle. At first he was affrighted, but after some small acquaintance this antipathy in nature wore off, and he became pleased with their company . . . they spoke with a shrill voice, like an ancient woman.

At first the Rev. Bedford doubted Parkes's sanity but, after the latter had demonstrated mathematically the astronomical projection of a sphere, in order to prove himself free 'of the least tincture of madness', he felt compelled to accept the truth of the story. Nevertheless, he refused Parkes's offer to take him on one of his nocturnal expeditions and sternly advised the abandonment of ritual magic.

Symbols, signs and ceremonies

THE 200 YEARS from 1480 to 1680 marked the high tide of concern with the type of ritual magic which was taught in the sinister grimoires. After the latter date there seems to have been a general decline of interest in occult ceremony and by 1800 practitioners of magic rites were few and far between. Nevertheless, a few isolated individuals continued to experiment with the methods they had learned from printed and manuscript grimoires – sometimes with surprising and unfortunate results. Typical of these was Thomas Parkes of Bristol, who died soon after the year 1690 and whose occult misadventures were recorded in manuscript by the Reverend Arthur Bedford, a clergyman who knew Parkes well.

By trade Parkes was a gunsmith, but he was also 'well skilled in the mathematical studies', in astronomy, and in astrology. By the latter art he would cast horoscopes for his friends and acquaintances. The prophecies he derived from these often proved accurate, but, nevertheless, Parkes found astrology an

Up to the end of the 17th century necromancy relied heavily on rituals laid down in the grimoires, the medieval textbooks of magic. The magician stood in a circle inscribed with names and symbols designed to protect him from evil demons. He brandished his magic wand and chanted an incantation, hoping a spirit would appear to give him wealth, power or wisdom. But things could go badly wrong, as in the case of Thomas Parkes (above), whose conjurations produced terrifying supernatural creatures he could not control, or Dr Faustus (right), who was persuaded to sell his eternal soul to the Devil

The Tragicall Historie of the Life and Death of Doctor Faustus.

With new Additions.

Written by CH. MAR.

Some three months or so later Parkes once again approached the clergyman, saying he wished he had taken the latter's advice, 'for he thought he had done that which would cost him his life'. He had decided, he said, to acquire a familiar spirit – an otherworldly being that would be continually at his service – by following the instructions given in his grimoire.

His first step had been to prepare a parchment book; he then went to a cross-roads and invoked the spirit that was to be his familiar. The spirit duly appeared, said Parkes, and signed its name in the book. But then other, unwanted and uninvoked, spirits appeared, taking shapes – bears, lions, and serpents – that terrified the unhappy magician. His fears increased as he found it beyond his powers to control these super-natural creatures. Eventually the spirits vanished, leaving Parkes 'in a great sweat'. The rest of the story is best told in the words of the clergyman's manuscript:

> . . . from that time he was never well so long as he lived . . . he expressed a hearty repentance for, and detestation of, his sins; so that though these matters cost him his life, yet I have room to believe him happy in the other world.

At the beginning of the 19th century there were signs of a small revival of interest in ritual magic. In 1801 Francis Barrett published a curious magical textbook entitled *The magus*, which, although Barrett claimed authorship, was largely a compilation derived from the grimoires. Barrett, who lived in what was then the London suburb of St Marylebone, was sufficiently confident of his

In succeeding generations attitudes to the traditional magician and his apparitions underwent a gradual change. By the 19th century magicians had become figures from a realm of imaginative fantasy, as shown in the illustrations (right) of necromancers and their conjurations found in *The monastery*, a German collection of tales of the occult published in 1846. Practitioners of magic rites might take to the stage, like master magician De Philipsthal (below), shown performing at the London Lyceum theatre in 1803

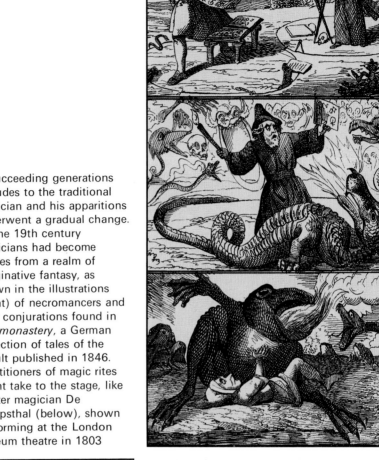

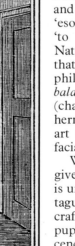

PHANTASMAGORIA
THIS and every EVENING,
AT THE
LYCEUM, STRAND.

own occult abilities to advertise for pupils, and to announce the setting up of a small 'esoteric academy', the purpose of which was 'to investigate the hidden treasures of Nature'. Barrett assured prospective pupils that they would learn the secrets of natural philosophy, natural magic, the mystical *qabalah*, chemistry, the art of making talismans (charms intended to ensure good fortune), hermetic philosophy, astrology and even the art of interpreting human character from facial appearance.

Whether Barrett was really competent to give practical instruction on all these subjects is uncertain, but according to the late Montague Summers, who wrote widely on witch-craft and black magic, some of Barrett's pupils 'advanced far upon the paths of trans-cendental wisdom'. One of them, added Montague Summers, was associated with the University of Cambridge, and the Barrett tradition was maintained – perhaps un-broken – at Cambridge, his occult teachings being handed on to promising subjects.

Throughout the course of the 19th century small groups of English occultists studied Barrett's book and experimented with ritual magic in accordance with his instructions. One such, for example, was grouped around Frederick Hockley, a tea merchant who experimented with crystal gazing and amassed a large library of occult books and manuscripts, many of them dealing with ritual magic. By the 1870s interest in ritual magic had revived sufficiently for a London bookseller to find it worthwhile to issue a reprint of *The magus*, and at around the same time a tiny band of English students of the paranormal began to take an interest in the writings and ideas of the French occultist Eliphas Levi. Notable among these was Kenneth R.H. Mackenzie, an active freemason who claimed to have been admitted into a secret (allegedly Rosicrucian) society. Mackenzie spent much time in France and Germany, and was on terms of friendship with several of the earliest members of the Golden Dawn, an organisation that taught a system of ritual magic that is still employed by many occult practitioners today.

The Golden Dawn, a secret society whose members received successive initiations, conferred by ceremonies bearing some resemblance to those of freemasonry, was founded in 1888 by three masonic occultists. Of these the most notable was S.L. MacGregor Mathers who, while at first subservient to the other two – Dr William Wynn Westcott and Dr Robert Woodman – came to

Above right: S.L. MacGregor Mathers in the ceremonial robes of the Order of the Golden Dawn, the late 19th-century occult society of which he was head. The revival of interest in magic was sparked off in 1801 by the publication of *The magus*, a textbook of occult practices by Francis Barrett (right)

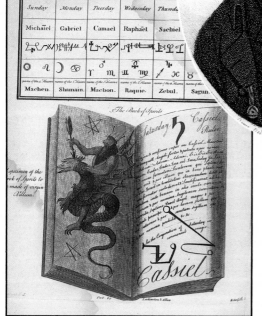

Left: a sample page from Barrett's magical textbook *The magus, or celestial influencer*, showing a table of the days of the week with their governing angels and associated planets and signs. Beneath it appears a spread from the 'Book of Spirits', giving an invocation to Cassiel, the chief spirit

dominate them by the sheer strength of his flamboyant personality.

At first the Golden Dawn was no more than a quasi-masonic society and the techniques of ritual magic were not taught to its members. Nor, indeed, was any occult teaching imparted to them save what was to be found in easily accessible books. In spite of this, newly admitted members were assured that 'the Order of the Golden Dawn, of which you have now become a member, can show you the way to much secret knowledge and spiritual progress, it can . . . lead . . . to . . . True Wisdom and Perfect Happiness.'

In actuality members were far from happy and began to grumble. They wanted to practise the occult arts, particularly ritual magic, rather than just talk about them.

Spiritual supermen

In 1892 Mathers decided to meet their wishes, producing a large and constantly growing body of instructional material that outlined a complex and – so it is claimed by those who have experimented with it – effective system of ritual magic. According to Mathers and his wife Moina, sister of the French philosopher Henri Bergson, this system was derived from the 'Secret Chiefs', superhuman beings of the same variety as the Mahatmas (or Masters) whom the Russian mystic Madame Blavatsky claimed to represent. Mathers said he had rarely met these beings in their physical bodies, but had done so on occasion, the appointments with them being made 'astrally' – presumably they either appeared to him in dreams, as disembodied spirits, or perhaps he received messages telepathically from them.

The meetings, when they did take place, exhausted Mathers. After they were over he felt he had been in contact with a 'terrible force', found such difficulty in breathing that he compared it to being half-strangled by the fumes of ether, and on some occasions suffered violent bleeding from his nose, mouth and ears.

There is no reason to think that Mathers invented all this – nor is there any reason to believe it to have been the literal truth. According to the poet W.B. Yeats, for many years a member of the Golden Dawn and on terms of friendship with Mathers, the latter was quite unable to distinguish fantasy from reality. Mathers believed, said Yeats, so fervently in angels, demons and Secret Chiefs, and his mind created such powerful images of them, that he became convinced that he saw and held conversation with them.

But whether Mathers's Masters were real or imaginary, there is no doubt that the system of magical practice attributed to their teachings is intellectually coherent and, in its way, impressive. The theories behind the techniques of ritual magic taught are not only more fully developed and better expressed than they are in the writings of Eliphas Levi, but the practice of the art is taught in a much

Left: a typical modern Golden Dawn initiation ceremony. Originally the society required that as a novice's knowledge of the occult increased he should pass through successive initiations based on the progression of the soul up the Tree of Life (below)

Below left: the top of the magic wand belonging to Aleister Crowley ('the Beast'), representing the head of Janus topped by a triple flame

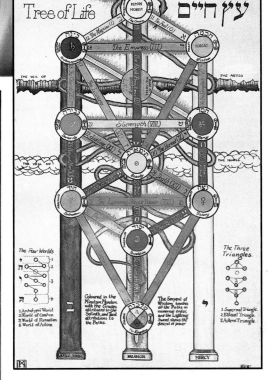

were ceremonially consecrated in accordance with rites supplied by Mathers.

The magician then began to devise his own ceremonies on the basis of his occult knowledge. Sometimes these were comparatively simple. Thus, for example, when a certain J.W. Brodie-Innes came to believe (on no very good grounds) that a 'vampirising entity' was obsessing himself and his wife he burned incense on a coal from his fire and drew a pentagram in the air with his right hand while resonantly chanting 'the Name of Power Adonai ha-Aretz'. At once there materialised before him 'a vague blot', rather like a scrap of London fog. The blot became more dense and formed itself into a terrifying apparition, a foul shape between that of 'a big bellied toad and a malicious ape'. Using the visualisation process outlined in one of Mathers's manuscripts the magician astrally projected – that is to say he visualised something so strongly that it was almost perceptible to his physical sight – a glowing ball of fiery force against the obsessing entity. There was 'a slight shock, a foul smell, a momentary dimness, and then the thing was gone'.

Power of symbols

Rather more elaborate rituals – those, for example, for raising spirits and the 'making of an astral shroud of darkness' (that is, obtaining invisibility) – were also undertaken. The basic form of these was taken from the grimoires, but the ceremonies were enriched by the incorporation into them of much additional material derived from the symbol system of correspondences that Mathers claimed to have derived from his teachers. A snake, for example, was said to correspond to both the god and the planet Mercury; so, if a Golden Dawn magician were evoking spirits whose nature was mercurial, he might incorporate snake fat into the candles employed in the ceremony.

The Golden Dawn eventually collapsed into a number of competing schisms. Personality differences in time destroyed even these, but the ritual magic of the Golden Dawn survived. Aleister Crowley incorporated whole sections of it into his evil and fanatical 'magick'. From his writings, and even more from those of his one-time secretary, Dr F.I. Regardie, anyone can learn enough about the system to experiment cautiously with it. At the present day, in both the UK and North America, groups and isolated individuals practising Golden Dawn magic are to be found in almost every large city.

But, it has been suggested by some students of the matter, it is not only occultists who have used ritual magic in modern times. Politicians, pop-singers and many others, it is said, may be unconsciously practising this strange art.

simpler way than in the grimoires – no ritual sacrifices of virgin rams at the dark of the Moon, for example.

The Golden Dawn initiate who had reached the stage at which he or she received access to Mathers's instructional material began by making a set of magical implements. These, mostly made from wood, cardboard and coloured paper, included a 'Lotus Wand', signifying the 12 signs of the zodiac and the triumph of spirit over matter, a ceremonial cup – this was usually a wine glass decorated with mystic symbols – a wooden disc, symbolic of matter, and a sword, emblem of the strength and power of Mars. After manufacture the implements

Ritual magic is not the exclusive province of the solitary magician. Elaborate rites, with no less magical intent, have been used to devastating effect by politicians and pop singers.

Method in their madness

appropriate to every type of magical rite are included.

Many modern magicians appear to live ordinary enough lives. They have jobs and families, they mow their lawns, go on their holidays, and pay their taxes just like their neighbours. But there is no denying that their private beliefs are odd to the point of eccentricity. They see the Universe as a living being, its visible appearance veiling its real nature; they regard symbol and allegory, dream and vision as more truly conveying ultimate reality than all the equations of the mathematician and the astrophysicist.

Amid circles and symbols

The various physical and psychological techniques employed by magicians are quite as strange as the beliefs that inspire them. The modern magician will hold his body in painful and unlikely postures for long periods of time. He will spend weeks in the visualisation of, and the meditation upon, some simple coloured symbol – perhaps a red triangle or a yellow square. He will half-choke himself with the smoke of exotic incenses, he will whirl like a spinning top until he falls senseless to the ground, he will clad himself in strange robes and stand, amid circles and symbols, chanting the barbarous words of

RITUAL MAGIC – defined by some of its contemporary devotees as 'the art of creating changes in consciousness in accordance with will' – is today practised in every great city of the Western world. A body of theory and practice that the confident mid-Victorian materialist regarded as a sad relic of the irrational past, doomed to be swept into the dustbin of history, has in fact survived and flourished. It is impossible to be sure just how many men and women regularly engage in ritual magic, but there is obviously a fair number, for several thriving businesses exist to supply their needs. In England, for example, the mail order firm of Sorcerer's Apprentice issues a catalogue containing details of a large selection of magical paraphernalia available to its customers – swords, daggers, ceremonial candles and incenses

evocation that, so he believes, will bring the gods down to earth.

It has been suggested, however, that many others besides an occult minority have practised ritual magic in the 20th century. Politicians and clergymen, speakers at protest meetings and strike leaders, all, so it is argued, unconsciously employ magical techniques. They have learned from others, or have themselves developed on the basis of experience, the same methods of altering consciousness employed by modern magicians – but while the magician is usually concerned only with altering the state of consciousness of himself and/or a few close associates, the politician or the priest is intent on altering the feelings and actions of hundreds, thousands, or, in the case of such revolutionaries as Adolf Hitler and Eva Peron, millions of people.

A magical performance

Ritual magicians employ light, colour, sound and highly theatrical spectacle to achieve what some have called 'one-pointedness', in other words, the directing of one's mind towards one particular idea, one universal factor. If, for example, a contemporary magician wants to concentrate his consciousness upon, to flood his mind and spirit with, the ideal of benevolent power, he will 'invoke Jupiter'. In other words, he will either play the chief part or be the only actor in a 'mystery play' in which he identifies himself with Jupiter and surrounds himself with theatrical 'props' traditionally associated with that deity and his attributes.

Inside his magic circle he will outline a square or a four-pointed star – four is the number sacred to Jupiter – with chalks or paints of the 'Jupiterian colours'; that is, violet, purple and shades of blue. He will decorate his 'temple', the room in which he carries out his ceremonial workings, with sprays of oak and poplar leaves, associated with the god since classical times. In his censer, or incense burner, cedar wood and saffron, the 'perfumes of Jupiter', will smoulder on a bed of glowing charcoal. If he is one of that small minority of ritualists who employ mind-altering drugs, some opium will also have been placed in the censer or he will have smoked opium before beginning the operation.

The setting for the Jupiterian mystery play having been prepared, the magician will act out his role, identifying himself with the god in exactly the same way that a 'method' actor identifies himself with the character he is portraying. Every word the magician will say during his performance, every act he will carry out, every 'Name of Power' he chants, will be associated with the Jupiterian principle of benevolent power. By the end of the rite the magician's mind will – if he has been successful – be filled with that principle to the exclusion of all else.

Exactly the same system, that of using

ceremony to alter emotions and consciousness, is employed by politicians and statesmen. Take, for example, a May Day procession in any communist country. The fluttering red flags, the pictures of revolutionary heroes and martyrs borne aloft, the thousands of clenched fists and stamping feet, and the dais upon which stand the party leaders beneath vast romanticised portraits of Marx, Engels and Lenin – all are the political equivalents of the furnishings and decorations of the magician's temple. There is no doubt that the consciousness of the onlookers and participants in the revolutionary ceremony is changed. Their drab working lives, their inadequate housing and food, their fears for the future are all forgotten. Instead they feel themselves to be part of a great marching army, a rushing tide of progress destined, by the laws of history, to smash down all that stands in its way, to create a new and better world.

The great masters of this 'political ritual magic' were the leaders of the Nazi Party. Indeed, some occultists have gone so far as to suggest that Adolf Hitler and his closest associates had studied the techniques of occult ceremony and deliberately applied them to political purposes. There is no evidence of this, however, that will bear

Few political or military movements in modern times have used 'special effects' such as lights, music and stirring speech in order to manipulate the minds of the masses as successfully as the Nazis (left). In effect, they were using all the trappings of ritual magic to invoke the god Mars. No detail was overlooked; the 'blood banner' that had been carried by Hitler in the putsch of 1923 was used in every ceremony consecrating new swastika banners (far left). Yet this total concentration on blood and death was to backfire on them – their vision of martial glory ending in the snows of Stalingrad (below left) and the ruins of Berlin. Some dictators achieved a personal glamour through their ritual 'stage management'; Eva Peron even inspired the hit musical *Evita* (right, with Elaine Page in the title role). Yet many familiar rituals today have no such sinister purpose, such as the Catholic mass (below)

Mind and magic

Above: a May Day celebration in Moscow. The giant idealised portraits of the USSR's officially approved heroes and the preponderance of red in the banners serve to direct the minds of the participants towards a single goal: the furtherance of the Communist state

scrutiny, although at one period of his early life the future Führer undoubtedly read a great deal of occult literature. What does seen certain, however, is that the Nazi's Nuremberg Rallies were extremely formalised, elaborately staged ceremonies designed to exert a particular effect upon the minds both of the participants and of those who later saw films of the rallies – such as *Triumph of the will* – in their local cinemas.

The fanfares from assembled trumpeters in traditional costume or the theatrical black and silver uniforms of the ss, the stirring military marches played to the gathering crowds and the concerts of Wagner's music that usually preceded each rally, began to evoke into consciousness, *and to cause mental associations with*, the ideas of Germanic myth and tradition, military glory and National Socialism (Nazism). At the rally itself the massed swastika banners, black, white and red, traditionally a colour combination associated with war, terror and death, brought into the consciousness of the participants the entire Nazi ideology. The choreographed precision of the movements of the brown- and black-shirted cohorts of the SA and the SS, all acting in unison as though controlled by some group-mind, evoked from the unconscious those archetypes of violence and strength that to the ancients symbolised the war gods Mars and Ares. The high point and prime ritual of the rallies – Hitler ceremonially consecrating new swastika banners by clasping them to the 'blood banner' that had been carried by him and others in the unsuccessful Munich putsch of 1923 – was the most potent element in the Nazis' loathsome 'mystery play'. The emotions conveyed by it were such that the minds of living Nazis were, in a sense, linked up with the thoughts and actions of dead National Socialist martyrs. This was almost a sacrament.

The magical and quasi-religious aspects of these rallies were emphasised by the fact

that their climax always came after darkness had fallen and took place in what Albert Speer, the brilliant Nazi technocrat, described as 'a cathedral of light' – an open space surrounded by upright beams of light, reminiscent of the pillars of Gothic architecture, emanating from anti-aircraft searchlights pointed directly up towards the sky.

The Nuremburg Rallies achieved their intended effects. The overwhelming majority of those who either witnessed or participated in them found their minds overflowing with the ideas of glory, military struggle and self-sacrifice for the good of the (non-existent) Aryan race. If an occultist of great expertise had spent years in devising a ritual to 'invoke Mars' he would have been unlikely to have come up with anything more effective than the ceremonies employed at Nuremberg.

Destroyed by the gods

Some occultists claim that those who raise the old gods from the depths of the unconscious run the risk of being destroyed by them. Certainly many of the young men who invoked Mars at Nuremberg eventually fell as sacrifices to that dreaded god – at Stalingrad, at Kursk and in the fire and smoke of besieged Berlin.

At the present day no statesman or politician conducts, consciously or otherwise, 'magical' ceremonies either as impressive or as sinister as those performed at Nuremberg. But the same use of light, colour and sound to alter the thought and feelings of an audience can be discerned in other aspects of contemporary life, in religious celebrations, and even in rock concerts. Anyone who saw the late Janis Joplin in action witnessed a ritual evocation of the spirit of Venus quite as effective as any carried out by magicians, past or present.

Right: the late Janis Joplin, whose electric stage performances embodied – unknowingly perhaps – all the elements of an invocation of Venus

Nothing but trouble

Curses have always been feared — with justice it seems, for disease, loss of loved ones and death have often befallen the victims. But is this coincidence, or could it be the direct result of knowing — and fearing — that one is cursed?

A CURSE IS AN INVOCATION of destruction or evil, part of the accustomed armoury of the priest, magician, shaman or ill-wisher. But do curses work and, if so, how? Swearing at someone gives vent to pent-up feelings; most psychologists would say that ritual curses do nothing more, *unless the victim is expecting trouble*. Sandford Cohen, a psychologist at Boston University, USA, is convinced from field research that curses can be lethal, because of the feeling of utter helplessness they can inspire. He sees a striking similarity between western Man dying from a fear of some disease generally believed to be fatal, and primitive Man dying from a witch doctor's curse.

Another explanation involves the 'tape recording' theory – that a thought can imprint itself on an object or person, and can be transferred to others. If the thought is malevolent, so is the effect. There do seem to be numerous cases of curse victims being totally sceptical of supernatural 'mumbo-jumbo', which nevertheless does nothing to save them from the effects.

Take the case of Robert Heinl junior, a retired colonel in the US Marine Corps. From 1958 to 1963 he served on Haiti as chief of the US naval mission, while his wife studied the voodoo religion. Afterwards, back in the United States, they wrote *Written in blood*, a history of Haiti that was openly critical of the ruling dynasty of François 'Papa Doc' Duvalier. Then they learned from a newspaper published by Haitian exiles that a curse had been placed on the book, probably after Papa Doc's death in 1971 by his widow, Simone.

At first, the Heinls were flattered that their book was thought to be worth cursing, but amusement soon turned to fear. First, the manuscript was lost on the way to the publishers, then it turned up four months later in a room the publishers never used. Meanwhile, the Heinls prepared another copy of the manuscript and sent it off for binding and stitching. The machine immediately broke down. A *Washington Post* reporter who was preparing to interview the authors was struck down with acute appendicitis. The colonel fell through a stage when he was delivering a speech, injuring his leg. And while walking near his home he was suddenly and severely bitten by a dog

A Mycenaean funeral mask representing Agamemnon – one of the many sufferers from the ancient curse on the House of Atreus by Hermes. Agamemnon, the grandson of Atreus, was killed by his wife and her lover as a direct result

The omens continued, two involving the number 22, which Papa Doc considered a magic number. Finally, on 5 May 1979, the Heinls were on holiday on St Barthelemy Island, near Haiti, when the colonel dropped dead from a heart attack. His widow mused 'There is a belief that the closer you get to Haiti, the more powerful the magic becomes.'

In Royal David's city

Curses, precisely laid down in many rituals, are still cast by priests in the major religions. In September 1981 Rabbi Moshe Hirsch, leader of the Neturei Karta, an orthodox Jewish sect, was threatening to invoke the 'Rod of Light' against the Israeli archaeologist Yigal Shilo if he persisted in excavating the biblical city of David, which the rabbi maintained involved desecrating a medieval Jewish cemetery. The archaeologists denied the existence of such a cemetery.

The Rod of Light ceremony involves the reading of a text based on *qabalistic* writings. The participants burn black candles, sound a ram's horn and invoke the name of the cursed man's mother. 'This ceremony is an absolute last resort,' said the rabbi. 'It has only been invoked twice in the last 30 years, both times with horrible consequences. There are many ways of dying, some less pleasant than others.' But unfortunately the

Left: Robert and Nancy Heinl, who fell foul of the Haitian dictator François 'Papa Doc' Duvalier and his wife Simone (below) while researching their book *Written in blood* – which was openly critical of Duvalier's regime – in the 1960s. The Heinls discovered that Simone Duvalier had cursed them and an extraordinary chain of events, culminating in the sudden death of Robert Heinl, followed. Coincidence? Nancy Heinl was in no doubt that the curse was responsible for their bad luck

by angry monks (see box).

There is a widespread ancient belief that no good will come from disturbing old stones or buried treasure – folklore worldwide is full of such tales. We can see the theme continuing in the enduring popularity of the idea of a mummy's curse in newspapers and films. Some researchers believe that such deep-seated and widespread beliefs, as part of the collective unconscious, can exert a material influence, thus bringing myths to life – and perpetually reinforcing them.

A heart of stone

The old castle of Syrie in Aberdeenshire, Scotland, has a legendary curse on it. A group of stones in the river there is known as the Weeping Stones, one of which is missing. It is said that no heir to Syrie will ever succeed until the missing stone is found.

In 1944 a 2-tonne 'Witch's Stone' was shifted from a crossroads at Scrapfaggot Green, Great Leighs, Essex, England, to widen the road. Psychic havoc broke out. A great boulder was found outside the local pub, chickens were found locked up in rabbit hutches, rabbits were loose in the garden, the church bells chimed irregularly, 30 sheep and two horses were found dead in a field, and a village builder found his scaffold poles tumbled about 'like matchsticks'. The 'Witch's Stone' was replaced and peace was restored.

In 1980 a 30-tonne boulder was removed from the Devil's Marbles to a park in Tennant Creek, an isolated copper mining town in the Australian outback. Aborigines of the Warramungu tribe believe the Marbles are a relic from the 'Dream Time' – when ancestral spirits created the world – and any interference with such relics will lead to sickness and death. After the boulder's removal, a number of Aboriginal children fell ill

rabbi claims he failed to discover Shilo's mother's name.

Even in the calm glade of the Church of England, spiritual contracts are occasionally put out on church thieves. Since the 1970s in Gloucestershire alone, two vicars have performed the commination service: the Reverend Harold Cheales of Wych Rissington in 1973, and the Reverend Robert Nesham of Down Ampney in 1981. The commination service contains 12 curses and leaves room for extemporisation. It first appeared in the 1662 Book of Common Prayer, but in the 1928 revision 'curse' was replaced by 'God's anger and judgement'. It was traditionally used against enemies of the Church on the first day of Lent, or whenever a church or churchyard had been desecrated. Christian curses seem to be, on occasion, just as effective as demonic ones: the old abbeys that Henry VIII seized from the monks after the dissolution of the monasteries in the early 16th century often bedevilled their new owners over generations with the curses laid

By fire and water

Battle Abbey in Sussex (below) was the scene of a grim curse laid on the descendants of Sir Anthony Browne, 'Esquire to the Body of Henry VIII, Master of the Horse and Justice in Eyre', in 1538.

with sores on their legs, and a tribal elder, Mick Taylor, warned that 'someone would get killed' if the stone were not returned. In March 1981 Mick Taylor died from meningitis at the age of 50. The town then agreed to return the boulder.

In late 1981 councillors in King's Lynn, Norfolk, England, refused to move an 18th-century obelisk that was in danger from vandals. A Latin inscription reads: 'Whoever shall remove or have removed this monument let him die the last of his line.'

Rocks of wrath

During the summer of 1977 airline vice-president Ralph Loffert, of Buffalo, New York state, USA, his wife and four children visited the Hawaiian volcano Mauna Loa. While there they collected some stones from the volcano despite a warning from the locals that this would anger the volcano goddess, Pele. Some claim to have seen Pele, who traditionally appears to warn of imminent eruptions. Shortly after they returned home, Mauna Loa erupted. Within a few months one of the Loffert boys, Todd, developed appendicitis, had knee surgery and broke his wrist; another son, Mark, sprained an ankle and broke his arm; another son, Dan, caught an eye infection and had to wear glasses; and the daughter, Rebecca, lost two front teeth in a fall. In July 1978, the Lofferts sent the stones to a friend in Hawaii who was asked to return them to the volcano. But the disasters continued – Mark hurt his knee, Rebecca broke three more teeth, Dan fractured a hand bone, while Todd dislocated an elbow and fractured his wrist again. Mark then confessed that he still had three stones. They were returned – and the trouble ceased.

Mrs Allison Raymond of Ontario, Canada, and her family also took some stones away from the volcano. She told reporters:

According to tradition, Sir Anthony was cursed at the feast held to celebrate his ownership of the abbey by a monk who was angry at the seizure of Church lands during the Reformation.

The curse was specific: the family would die 'by fire or water'. It seems, however, that the curse went awry: Sir Anthony's other property, Cowdray Park – which he had inherited from his half-cousin, the Earl of Southampton – was burned down; but this was much later, in 1793, after the property had passed into the hands of another family.

Antony Hippisley Coxe, compiler of *Haunted Britain* (1974), records that the curse came unstuck yet again, in 1907, when the Duchess of Cleveland – who had rented Battle Abbey briefly – drowned in its grounds on her way to church, but her daughter, who was with her, survived.

Above: a 788-year-old curse is ritually lifted by the Chief Rabbi at the consecration of Clifford's Tower in York on 31 October 1978. On the night of 16 March 1190, 150 Jews fled to the tower where they died by their own hand rather than fall into a mob's hands. The last to die was the Chief Rabbi, whose final act was to curse the city of York. Until well into the 20th century York was avoided by Jews – even though nearby Leeds has always had a thriving Jewish community

Right: 'The curse has come upon me, cried the Lady of Shallott' – Tennyson's doomed heroine prepares to meet her fate

Jon Erickson, a naturalist at the Volcanoes National Park in Hawaii, said he receives up to 40 packages of rock a day from frightened tourists who have returned home.

Lieutenant Commander 'Buster' Crabbe dived with Royal Navy men in 1950 in Tobermory Bay, Isle of Mull, in search of the *Duque de Florencia*, a payship of the Spanish Armada, which had been sunk in 1588 with a reputed 30 million pounds of gold on board. One of the trophies with which he surfaced was a skull that medical experts said had belonged to a North African woman. Crabbe disappeared, some maintain mysteriously, while on an underwater mission near Russian warships in Portsmouth harbour in 1956. The following year a coroner decided that the headless body of a frogman washed up at Chichester, Sussex, was that of Crabbe.

The skull that had been found on the

My husband was killed in a head-on car crash and my mother died of cancer. My younger son was rushed to hospital with a pancreas condition that's slowly getting worse. Then he broke his leg. My daughter's marriage nearly broke up and it was only when I posted the rocks back that our luck improved.

Despite warnings, Nixon Morris, a hardwood dealer from El Paso, Texas, took a Mauna Loa stone home in 1979. After returning home he fell off his roof, lightning struck an aerial and ruined several home appliances, and his wife fell ill with a mysterious infection that left her knee swollen.

Then Morris broke a hip and thigh when he fought with a burglar in their house. The family cat was sleeping under the bonnet of his wife's car when she started the engine and was stripped of its fur down one side. Then Morris's grand-daughter fell and broke her arm in two places.

Morris said he had broken the rock in two and given a piece to a friend, adding: 'He brought the rock back to me after he wrecked four cars in less than two years, and he'd never before had a wreck in his life.' In March 1981 Morris sent the rocks back.

Above: the Devil's Marbles, Australia, a sacred Aboriginal site. In 1980 one of the boulders was removed; Mick Taylor, a tribal elder, warned that the removal would lead to sickness and death. Several children fell ill – and he died the next year, at the age of 50

Below: the Mauna Loa volcano of Hawaii. In 1977 the Loffert family, on holiday from the USA, picked up some stones from the volcano – despite a warning that this would anger the local deity, the goddess Pele. A series of disasters struck the family, ceasing only when the last stone had been sent back to Hawaii. Other tourists have reported similar runs of bad luck after taking stones away

wreck was kept in the Western Isles Hotel, Tobermory, Scotland, where one day the barman accidentally caused it to fall and break. The same day he crashed his motor scooter and cracked *his* skull. He never returned to the island. The hotel owner, Donald Maclean, stored the skull away in a cupboard. In 1970 Richard Forrester, the new English owner of the hotel, drilled a hole in the skull so that he could hang it up in his cocktail bar:

I was using an ordinary electric drill. The first odd thing that happened was that the metal bit of the drill, after piercing the bone, bent inside at an angle of 45 degrees. I found this surprising but thought nothing more about it. Two hours later I was struck

The curse of the Pharaohs

Archaeologists can be said to be modern grave robbers – and as such seem to have paid the price, for many ancient Egyptian tombs apparently carry curses for any who dare to desecrate them.

According to the American journalist Webb Garrison, Professor S. Resden opened an Egyptian tomb in the 1890s that was thus inscribed: 'Whosoever desecrates the tomb of Prince Sennar will be overtaken by the sands and destroyed.' Resden knew he was doomed, it is said. He left Egypt by ship – and died on board, a victim of suffocation with no discernible cause. Small

amounts of sand were found clutched in his hands.

The poetic neatness of this story is, it must be said, rather suspicious and should perhaps be taken with a pinch of salt – or sand.

But the 'curse of the pharaoh' continues. In September 1979, George LaBrash had a stroke while guarding the Tutankhamun mask (left) in San Francisco. In January 1982 he sued the city authorities for disability pay, claiming that the stroke was a job-related injury caused by the alleged curse on the tomb's desecration. The case was dismissed. Was this in itself a refinement of the curse? Has the curse of the boy king moved into legal circles?

Above: the appalling crash that killed film star Jayne Mansfield on 29 June 1967. This was widely rumoured as being no *accident* – Jayne had been cursed by her former friend, Anton la Vey, head of the Church of Satan

Above right: Lance Sieveking, broadcaster and father of author Paul Sieveking. He demonstrated an unusual immunity to a curse laid by black magician Aleister Crowley by living 30 years longer than the curse allowed

by excruciating pain in the back of the head. I was completely incapacitated for two days. Since then I have been taking prescribed pills but the searing pain continues and never leaves.

And the only other person to handle the skull since the drilling had also experienced searing headaches.

The notion of a curse affecting a whole family is at least as old as civilisation. The ancient Greeks were firm believers in the efficacy of curses – the most celebrated curse affecting the house of Atreus: Atreus killed the son of the god Hermes in a love contest, and Hermes put a curse on the murderer 'and all his house'. Atreus killed his own son by mistake; his grandson, the Homeric hero Agamemnon, was killed by his wife and her lover; and she in turn was murdered by her son and daughter.

In Moorish Spain, a curse was believed to hang over the great Abencerrage family – 'the Flower of Granada'. Many died in war and vendettas before the whole family was wiped out by King Muley Hassan on one of the patios of the Alhambra palace during the 15th century.

Relatively speaking

In Britain, several aristocratic families are believed to be afflicted by family curses. In the 18th century the Scottish Earl of Breadaulbin moved a graveyard to build the castle of Taynmouth. According to tradition a lady whose grave was disturbed laid a curse on the family whereby no two earls of the same line would succeed each other. The prophecy apparently came true.

Even writing about curses might be considered a hazardous business, but this author draws a certain comfort from the apparent immunity of his father. In 1928 the magician Aleister Crowley ('The Beast'), recently expelled from Sicily, met the young radio producer Lance Sieveking in Cassis on the French Riviera. They spent many hours in conversation, and Crowley subsequently

cast Sieveking's horoscope. It contained a number of predictions that were later fulfilled. One, however, was not. Crowley wrote: 'By the way, you will oblige me personally by dying at the age of forty-five.' Sieveking was then 32 but he disobligingly lived to be 75.

Crowley's curses, however, often successfully claimed their victims. The last to go was young Dr William Brown Thompson, who withheld the addicted Beast's supply of morphia. In a rage, Crowley put a curse on him, saying that when he died he would take the doctor with him. And so it came to pass. Crowley died on 1 December 1947, aged 72. Thompson was dead within 24 hours.

No hiding place

Bad luck appears to attach itself to some people with a single-mindedness that seems to imply an organising intelligence. This chapter describes the appalling progress of some of the world's worst jinxes

WHILE A CURSE is a conscious invocation of misfortune against others, a jinx is merely a bringer of bad luck – why it starts is anybody's guess. Jinxes may be curses in disguise, unknown to the victims. It could even be that someone who suffers a series of inexplicable misfortunes comes to believe himself to be jinxed – and so unconsciously brings about further disasters.

For 400 years the Haanappel family of Doesburg in Holland have had the palms of their hands turn black six months after they are born. Doctors say this is the result of a gene mutation, but local folklore maintains that a Haanappel saved a church from fire by ringing the bells, burning his hands as he slid down the bell rope. The Devil, in his anger, cursed him and his heirs forever.

No one has come up with an explanation for the misfortunes of the Guinness brewery family. In 1978 they suffered four deaths in as many months: in May Lady Henrietta Guinness plunged to her death from an aqueduct in Spoleto, Italy; in June another Guinness heiress drowned in a bath while trying to inject herself with heroin. Also in June, Major Dennys Guinness was found dead in Hampshire with an empty pill bottle by his side. In August, John Guinness, then an aide to British Prime Minister James Callaghan, survived a head-on collision in Norfolk, but his four-year-old son was killed and another son seriously injured. Lady Henrietta's cousin, Tara Browne, had died in a car crash in Chelsea in 1966.

Jinxes can perform to the most exacting timetables. The Milli family, from a lonely mountain village in central Italy, seem to

Below: the death of 21-year old Tara Browne – heir to the Guinness family fortune – in 1966 was only one tragedy in the long history of the family jinx. Fatal crashes and inexplicable suicides, death plunges and drug accidents have bedevilled the Guinness family

have such a jinx. On 17 January 1949 a woman in the family died, as happened on the same day in 1959 and 1969. On 17 January 1978, misfortune struck a year early when Giuseppina Milli, aged 72, died of a heart attack. On 17 January 1989 the remaining family members plan to stay in hospital, taking no chances.

Black Tuesday

This patterning effect sometimes emerges around specific days of the week as well. The Marquis of Chaumont hated Tuesday so much that he had the word cut out of all his books and papers. He was ill every Tuesday for 79 years and died on a Tuesday in 1780.

One famous periodical jinx hangs over the American presidency. Since 1840 no president elected in a year ending with a zero has survived his term of office. Pneumonia took off William H. Harrison (elected in 1840). Lincoln (1860), Garfield (1880), McKinley (whose second term began in 1900) and Kennedy (1960) were all assassinated while still in office. Harding (1920) had a heart attack; Roosevelt (1940) died of polio. And there has already been one assassination attempt on Reagan (1980).

There is a jinxed aria in Halévy's opera *Charles VI*, which was premiered at the Opéra Comique in Paris in 1852. As the celebrated tenor Maffiani sang 'Oh God, smash him', meaning the traitorous villain, he lifted his eyes to the ceiling. One of the stage hands immediately toppled to his death from a perch aloft. Maffiani was inconsolable, and the following morning the newspapers were calling it the 'Curse Aria'. On the next night when he sang it he fixed his eyes on an empty box. Suddenly, the curtains of the box parted and a man taking his seat swayed and toppled to his death. On the third night the tenor sang the aria staring at the floor, but a musician in the orchestra pit

One of the most famous periodical jinxes hangs over American presidents who are elected in years ending with a zero. Abraham Lincoln (left, centre), who came to office in 1860, McKinley (left), who was elected in 1900 for the second time, Roosevelt (bottom centre), whose third term as president began in 1940, and John F. Kennedy (below), who was elected in 1960, all died during their terms of office. And there has already been one attempt on the life of Ronald Reagan (bottom), who was elected in 1980

played off-key. Maffiani glared at him and he died of a heart attack.

Further performances were cancelled, but in 1858 Napoleon III asked Halévy to stage *Charles VI* for him. On the night before the performance Napoleon and Eugénie narrowly escaped bombs hurled by Italian revolutionaries. The opera was cancelled and has never been staged since.

Various stretches of railway and road appear to have jinxes on them. The railway line between Acklington and Belford in Northumberland, a distance of 21 miles (34 kilometres), has been dubbed the 'hoodoo line'. Passengers just fall out of 'secure' doors on London to Edinburgh expresses. Two lives were lost within 18 days in August 1980, exactly a year after an identical death fall. A young sailor had also died on the same stretch in 1978. British Rail remain mystified.

A 100-yard (90-metre) section of the M4 motorway between Swindon and Chippenham in Wiltshire claimed four lives within a week in the spring of 1979. Traffic experts could find no obvious cause. Equally baffling were a string of fatal 'carbon-copy' accidents at night on a stretch of the Sevenoaks bypass between Gracious Lane Bridge and Chipstead flyover in Kent. In each case the driver swerved inexplicably across the grass verge separating the two carriageways.

In the first crash in November 1977, three people lost their lives. Then in May 1978 three young men died 100 yards (90 metres) away. In the following August another young man in a car swerved to his death, and in February 1979 a mother and her son heading for Tonbridge were killed when another car left the northbound carriageway and hit them head-on.

Road to dusty death

A possible clue lies in the unnerving experience of Mrs Babs Davidson, an employee of British Telecom. She was driving home in winter moonlight along the jinxed road around the time of the last-mentioned crash. She knew the road well, but suddenly the way ahead was no longer familiar. Part of it was blacked out and a road she had never seen before forked mistily away to her right. 'I felt a tremendous compulsion to take it,' she recalled, 'but forced myself to go on. I was very relieved when I found I had done the right thing and was still heading north on the carriageway.' The appearance of a ghost road could easily be dismissed as an hallucination due to fatigue, but Mrs Davidson claims to have seen it on two subsequent occasions, although she is unable to identify the spot exactly. And usually her claims have been taken seriously by Department of Transport investigators looking for the cause of the crashes.

Many jinxes seem to be analogous to an outbreak of disease that infects a few victims and then peters out. Behavioural syndromes

Left: the jinxed stretch of the Sevenoaks bypass in Kent, between Gracious Lane Bridge and Chipstead flyover, where several fatal 'carbon copy' accidents took place in the late 1970s. One driver who avoided disaster was Mrs Babs Davidson who, on three occasions, claims to have seen a 'ghost' road branching off the main carriageway. She felt an overwhelming urge to follow it, but managed to continue on her route. Had the other drivers succumbed and taken the ghost road – to their deaths?

such as mass faintings and the spread of rumours and panic also seem to fit this pattern.

Films about the occult often seem to engender such an outbreak, their productions plagued with accidents, illness and death. *The omen I* was typical. Star Gregory Peck's aeroplane was struck by lightning, as was one carrying author David Seltzer and Robert Munger, who devised the film. Director Richard Donner had a rough flight too and was later hit by a car. Lightning struck the building next to his Rome hotel. Special effects man John Richardson was in a car accident with a lorry in Holland, and his passenger was killed. When he regained consciousness, he saw a milestone for the town of Ommen. A pack of dogs ran amok and injured two stuntmen, and a zoo keeper was killed by a tiger the day the film crew left the zoo.

Casualties of curses?

We all know, or have read about, accident-prone people. Whether they suffer from some elusive behavioural 'infection' or had a curse put on them at an early age by some ill-disposed person, it is impossible to say. Perhaps someone (or something) 'up there' (or wherever) is trying to get a message through to the hapless victims.

Brian Challender, a bricklayer from Bournemouth, Dorset, was born on a Friday the 13th, which he believes accounts for his run of misfortune. As a boy he had a bad bicycle accident, was knocked out by a golf club and attacked by a man with an axe. He was stabbed at a fairground, pinned down by a 55-tonne motorway earth mover, trapped under a garage door, stunned by falling metal on a building site (he had removed his hard hat in the heat to cool down), scarred for life by steam and rammed by a rowing boat off Bournemouth pier. His last recorded disaster was when he was bending down to pick up a pin for good luck – he was knocked unconscious by a falling brick.

Besides the accident-prone, there are the

'Jonahs', those people who always seem to be around to witness the misfortune of others. A certain Mrs Murray was a passenger on the final journeys of three doomed ships: the *Titanic*, the *Lusitania* and the *Celtic*, which was rammed by the *Anaconda* in 1927. It happens on land too. Dr Max Benis, a specialist in allergies, has been on hand at least 19 times to help people in distress. Wherever he goes people touch live wires, choke on their food, begin to drown or fall off high rocks. Said the *Daily Mail* of 6 December 1977, 'not many of the victims seem particularly grateful to Dr Max.'

Also within this category are people who seem to trigger illness in others in some unfathomable way. The classic example is 'Typhoid Mary', a cook in New York in 1906. Several people contracted typhoid and she was detained in hospital for three years, even though she was not suffering from typhoid herself. After her release she returned to work as a cook under various aliases. About five years later, 25 people in the Sloane Maternity Hospital, New York, went down with the disease and two died. Mary was cooking at the hospital and was detained again.

Below: the *Lusitania*, which sank in 1915. A certain Mrs Murray survived not only the wreck of this ship but also that of the *Titanic*, in 1912, and that of the *Celtic*, in 1927. Jinx, curse – or some kind of *good* luck?

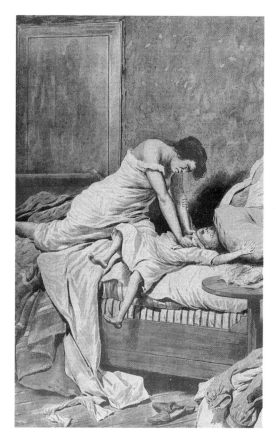

Below: Wesley MacIntire is carried from the wreck of the Sunshine Skyway Bridge in Florida, USA, which was rammed by a freighter in May 1980 (bottom). He was the sole survivor of this disaster and has emerged unscathed from many others. He devoutly hopes that his life is not being preserved by Providence just for one final accident

encephalitis, an inflammation of the brain. A few days later, another nearly died of meningitis. In February 1981, after Christine had moved to Lakeland, Florida, two young brothers in her care went into convulsions, but recovered after emergency treatment. A few days later, on 23 February, Christine was looking after another boy when he died of myocarditis, an inflammation of the heart muscle. Three days later, the same disease killed another of her charges. Finally, on 14 July 1981, a little girl died in her arms after being inoculated against diphtheria, whooping cough and tetanus. Extensive medical tests showed that Christine was not carrying any communicable diseases. She told the Florida newspaper *Sentinel Star*: 'Sometimes I wonder if I don't have some kind of spell over me when I get around young'uns.'

Another category of jinxed folk are those who constantly emerge unscathed from accidents. The life story of Wesley MacIntire illustrates this rather well. On 9 May 1980 a freighter rammed the Sunshine Skyway Bridge in Florida, USA. Thirty-five people were killed, and the sole survivor was MacIntire, who swam to the surface when his pick-up truck plunged into the river.

During the Second World War when he was in the navy he had dived off the side of his

The case of Jeanne Weber, known throughout France as 'the Ogress', is featured in this author's book *Man bites man* (1981). In 1906 she was accused of murdering two of her children and two of her nephews. The children had died after being alone with her, but the deaths were proved to be natural and she was acquitted. The following year she was staying in the house of a woodcutter when a small child died of convulsions while sitting on her knee. After two further trials she was acquitted.

More recently, four children died and three narrowly escaped death while being watched over by an 18-year-old epileptic, Christine Fallings of Blountstown, Florida, USA. In February 1980, the first died of

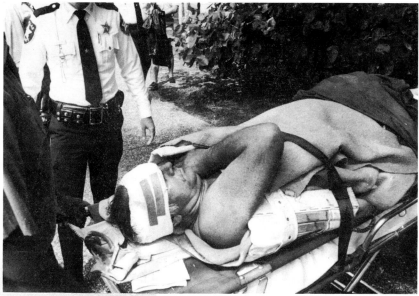

ship seconds before it was bombed. Later, as a lorry driver, he drove a 20-tonne load of gravel 1½ miles (2.5 kilometres) down a mountainside after his brakes failed, and managed to spin the lorry round and round in a parking lot until it stopped. In 1959 he crashed a container lorry loaded with explosive gases. It did not explode. Then an air tank in another lorry he was driving did explode, but MacIntire was saved by his mattress. There were many other accidents that he managed to survive. 'The only thing I can think of,' he said, 'is that the Good Lord must really be saving me up for something. I hope it's not another accident.'

Creatures of the impossible

Can a toad stay alive inside a rock for hundreds of years? Do mermaids really exist? How does a new pond become instantly and mysteriously stocked with fresh fish? Science cannot as yet provide satisfactory explanations of the bizarre puzzles of the natural world to be found in the animal kingdom.

The great toad mystery

In the 19th century numerous toads were found encased in rock and – inexplicably – alive. How did they get there, and how did they survive? The resulting controversy threw Victorian scientists into disarray

IN THE WINTER of 1856, French workmen were blasting a tunnel to carry the railway line from Saint-Dizier to Nancy when they came across a 'monstrous form' in the darkness. They had just split open a huge boulder of 'lias', or Jurassic limestone, when the thing staggered from a cavity within the rock, rattled its wings, gave a hoarse cry, and died without further ado.

It was the size and shape of a large goose, though its head was 'hideous' and its mouth contained sharp teeth. Four long legs ended in hooked talons and were joined by a bat-like membrane, and the skin itself was black, leathery, thick and oily.

Somewhat gingerly, the workmen carried the carcase to the nearby town of Gray where, according to a report in the *Illustrated London News* of 9 February 1856, 'a naturalist, versed in palaeontology, immediately

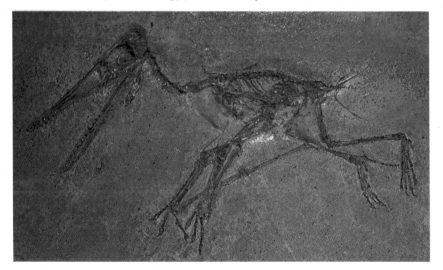

A fossilised pterodactyl, more than 100 million years old. In France in 1856 one was reported to have stumbled from the middle of a boulder – alive

recognised it as belonging to the genus (*sic*) *Pterodactylus anas*.'

The rock strata from which it had come tallied with the era in which pterodactyls flourished, and it was noted that the cavity whence it had emerged formed an 'exact hollow mould of its body, which indicates that it was completely enveloped with the sedimentary deposit.'

The story of the French pterodactyl was perhaps the most dramatic of a series of accounts concerning living creatures immured for thousands of years in solid rock that set the fringe of Victorian science in quiet disarray and caused more entrenched taking of sides than, for instance, even physicist William Crookes's experiments with psychical research. Its nearest modern equivalent is the UFO question and, like this, it simmered for decades without any satisfactory conclusion being reached.

The foundations of the 'suspended animation' controversy were laid in 1761 with the publication of the *Annual Register*, which that year devoted its pages to accounts – some from antiquity, some from more recent times – of living creatures, usually small reptiles or shellfish, having been found sealed in stone. Among other things, it reported that the stones used for paving Toulon harbour were often broken open to yield up living shellfish of 'exquisite taste', and quoted the writings of such as Francis Bacon, Baptist Fulgosa, Agricola and Horstius in seeking to show that snakes, crabs, lobsters, toads and frogs could all live indefinitely while apparently deprived of food, air, light and moisture.

It also retailed the first known personal observation on the subject, by Ambroise Paré, who was principal surgeon to Henry III. Paré stated that, in the late 16th century, while at his house in Meudon, he was watching a quarryman break 'some very large and hard stones, in the middle of one we found a huge toad, full of life and without any visible

Creatures of the impossible

aperture by which it could get there . . . .'

With only minor alterations, Paré's story was to be echoed over and over again during the Victorian era – sometimes well documented, sometimes not, but always rather impressively consistent in detail.

There can have been few more academically respectable accounts, for example, than that given by the geologist Dr E. D. Clarke during a lecture at Caius College, Cambridge, in February 1818. Dr Clarke had been supervising the digging out of a chalk pit in the hope of finding fossils, and at a depth of 45 fathoms had uncovered a layer of fossilised sea urchins and newts. Three of the latter appeared to be in perfect condition, and Dr Clarke carefully excavated them and placed them on a piece of paper in the sunlight. To his astonishment, they moved. Although two of them died shortly afterwards, the third was placed in pond water and 'skipped and twisted about, as well as if it had never been torpid' and became so active that it escaped. Dr Clarke immediately began collecting examples of all the live newts in the area in the hope of matching them with the disinterred bodies, but none resembled the long-buried ones. The Reverend Richard Cobbold, who attended the lecture and saw the newts, said 'They are of an entirely extinct species, never before known.'

On 31 October 1862 a paragraph in the *Stamford Mercury* anticipated criticism when it told of a living toad found 7 feet (2 metres) down in bedrock during the excavation of a cellar in Spittlegate, Stamford. 'No fact,' insisted the anonymous reporter sternly, 'can be more fully or certainly established by human evidence, let the sceptics on this subject say what they will.'

The toad that barked

Three years later, on 8 April 1865, the august and sober *Leeds Mercury* was careful to go into meticulous detail when it reported the finding of a living, embedded toad during the excavation of Hartlepool Waterworks. Quarrymen, under their foreman Mr James Yeal, found the creature in a block of magnesian limestone 'at a depth of twenty five feet [8 metres] from the surface of the earth and eight feet [2.5 metres] from any spring water vein.'

As in many similar instances, the toad's body had been perfectly moulded into the rock, 'and presented the appearance of being a cast of it. The toad's eyes shone with unusual brilliancy, and it was full of vivacity on its liberation. It appeared when first discovered, desirous to perform the process of respiration, but evidently experienced some difficulty, and the only sign of success consisted of a "barking" noise . . . .'

This was not surprising, as its mouth proved to be completely closed and the 'barking' came from its nostrils. The paper reported that though at first it had been as

Top: this mummified toad in a flint nodule was discovered by workmen in Lewes, Sussex. It is probably the only existing example of the phenomenon and is now preserved in the Brighton Museum, England

Above: Dr Edward Clarke, who in 1818 discovered three 'fossilised', but living, newts

Right: one of the numerous letters written to *The Times* in 1862 on the toad controversy

pale as the stone from which it came, it later changed colour to a fine olive brown. Apart from these facts, and the 'extraordinary length' of its hind claws, it was quite normal. The Rev. Robert Taylor, vicar of St Hilda's and a local geologist of renown, estimated that the magnesian limestone in which it was found was at least 200 million years old. Yet the toad stayed alive for some days.

Several reports came in from the United States, via such respected scientific journals as *American Naturalist* and *Scientific American*. A typical story, from the latter, told how a silver miner named Moses Gaines was chipping away at a boulder 2 feet (60 centimetres) square when it broke open to reveal a toad; again, the toad's body fitted its crevice precisely. The animal was 'three inches [7.5 centimetres] long and very plump and fat . . . its eyes were about the size of a silver cent piece, being much larger than those of

TOAD IN COAL.

TO THE EDITOR OF THE TIMES.

Sir,—The controversy in your columns on the above subject reminds me of what I heard when resident in Northumberland, as having occurred at Chillingham Castle, the seat of the Earl of Tankerville.

A slab of marble, forming one side of the chimneypiece, in either the dining-room or drawing-room, was observed to be always damp and somewhat discoloured, and partly from curiosity, and partly because the chimneypiece was injured in appearance at that part, it was determined to examine the place carefully. The slab was removed, and, I believe, was cut by a saw near the part where the unusual appearance existed, and a toad was discovered, alive, in the marble at this spot, and in the marble was found a recess of the size of the toad, and in which it exactly fitted.

I give you the story exactly as I heard it in the immediate neighbourhood of Chillingham Castle, and a single line from the Earl of Tankerville would confirm or disprove the above statement, as its truth or want of foundation must be perfectly well known to his Lordship, and to those resident thereabouts.

If the story is substantially true, I suppose that it is not more astonishing that a toad should be found in coal than in marble.   Your obedient servant,

GODFREY SINCLAIR.

Ormsary, Lochgilphead, North Britain, Sept. 18.

toads of the same size such as we see every day.' Although alive, Gaine's toad was lethargic: 'They tried to make him hop or jump by touching him with a stick, but he paid no attention . . . .'

These and similar stories, although delighting the sensation-hungry general public, upset the scientific flock no end.

There was no question in the mind of one Captain Buckland, who wrote sternly to the directors of the Great Exhibition of 1862 via *The Times*. Toads in rocks were 'a gross imposition', he declared, and demanded that an example from a coalmine in Newport, Monmouthshire, should be 'expelled' from the show. To be fair, the Captain had some claim to prior knowledge of the subject, for his father Dr Frank Buckland, late Dean of Westminster, had experimented with the burial of toads in 1825. He had taken two blocks of stone, one limestone, the other sandstone, and had cut six small cells in each,

Below: Dr Frank Buckland, whose experiments led him to surmise that toads could not live incarcerated in rocks

Centre: common frogs (*Rana temporaria*) can survive for months buried in mud

into which he placed live toads, sealing them in with a sheet of glass and slate, and burying them 3 feet (1 metre) down in his garden. A year later he dug up the blocks. All the toads in the sandstone appeared to have been dead for some time, though some of those in the limestone were alive, and two had actually put on weight. Unfortunately the glass had cracked, and it was possible that small insects had got in and inadvertently provided food for the entombed creatures. When Dr Buckland tried the experiment again, this time sealing the toads securely, all of them died.

For most scientists, Dr Buckland's experiments marked an end to the matter, and yet there remained a dissident group to support the possibility of survival.

One of its spokesmen, William Howitt, commented on the question in his *History of the supernatural* (1863). He pointed out that all naturalists were familiar with the fact that frogs and toads sink themselves into the mud at the bottom of ponds to pass the winter. He

Above: Gilbert White, the great 18th century naturalist, claimed to have found a mummified frog inside a stone

recalled an occasion at Farnsfield, Nottinghamshire, when, during the digging out of a ditch, he had seen a 'regular stratum of frogs' in a foot of mud, 'as stiff as butter. Scores of frogs speedily woke up and hopped away to seek fresh quarters. If these frogs could live six months in this nearly solid casing of viscous mud, why not six or any number of years?'

In time, of course, the mud would become rock; but the great question remained: could frogs and toads survive the enormous pressure involved, let alone the vast geological time spans, before such a metamorphosis could take place?

The answer to the first point seemed to be that the frail bodies could indeed survive; the great 18th-century naturalist Gilbert White, among others, had recorded finding a mummified frog in a stone – mummified, not fossilised. And this question of surviving the pressure, as opponents of the Buckland faction pointed out, seemed to depend on the fact that the rock, in its plastic state, was moulded to the body of the frog or toad as neatly as a nutshell to the kernel. Buckland had failed because his 'cells' did not fit the bodies of his subjects, whereas a Monsieur Seguin of France, according to *The Times* of 23 September 1862, had encased 20 toads in a block of plaster of Paris, which was then allowed to set and was buried. After 12 years, four were still alive.

Worthen's limestone theory

A further theory was put forward by A. H. Worthen in the *American Naturalist* of 1871. Examining a toad found alive in limestone near St Louis, Worthen found that the original Warsaw limestone had been coated with a deposit of calcium carbonate to a depth of over an inch. Supposing, he reasoned, that the toad had hibernated in a crevice of the mother rock, and had been sealed in by the dripping of water that held carbonate of lime in solution? To the uninitiated, the entire mass would be solid limestone, with no difference between the old rock and the new deposit. At best, Worthen's theory went some way towards explaining what might happen in *some* circumstances.

'Toad in the hole'

The vast majority of doubting scientists refused to look into the matter even so far, however; they fell back on the theory that the witnesses, many of them workmen, had been dishonest, credulous, or both. But why should a man such as Dr Clarke of Cambridge lay his reputation on the line, as it were, for the sake of sensation?

The pros and cons continued to be argued until the end of the century, when the issue finally all but died. It did leave behind one curious culinary legacy, that indigestible, but delicious concoction of sausage and batter that the Victorians dubbed 'toad in the hole'.

Curse of the Hexham heads

The discovery of two carved stone heads in a Hexham back garden seemed, at first, unremarkable enough. But when the heads apparently triggered paranormal phenomena and terrifying appearances of a wolf-man, the nightmare began

ONE AFTERNOON in February 1972, 11-year-old Colin Robson was weeding the garden of his family's council house in Rede Avenue, Hexham, a market town 20 miles (32 kilometres) west along the Tyne valley from Newcastle-upon-Tyne, when he uncovered what appeared to be a lump of stone about the size of a tennis ball, with a strange conical protrusion on one side. Clearing the earth from the object, he found that it was roughly carved with human features, and that the conical protrusion was actually a neck.

Excited by the find, he called to his younger brother Leslie, who was watching from an upstairs window. The boys continued to dig – and soon Leslie had uncovered a second head.

The stones, which soon became known as the Hexham heads, appeared to be representatives of two distinct types. The first

had a skull-like face, and seemed to everyone who saw it to be masculine; it was dubbed the 'boy'. It was of a greenish-grey colour, and glistened with crystals of quartz. It was very heavy – heavier than cement or concrete. The hair appeared to be in stripes running from the front to the back of the head. The other head – the 'girl' – resembled a witch, with wildly bulging eyes and hair that was combed backwards off the forehead in what was almost a bun. There were traces of a yellow or red pigment in her hair.

After the heads had been unearthed, the

The back garden of a council house in a small town in northern England hardly seems a likely place for a controversy about the paranormal to start. But it was in this garden in Hexham (below left) that, in 1971, two small boys unearthed a pair of crudely carved stone heads that apparently carried some ancient curse. A distinguished archaeologist suggested that they were around 1800 years old, and designed to play a part in Celtic head rituals – but Desmond Craigie (left) claims that he made them in the 1950s

boys took them inside the house. It was then that the strange happenings began. The heads would turn round spontaneously, objects were broken for no apparent reason – and when the mattress on the bed of one of the Robson daughters was showered with glass, both girls moved out of their room. Meanwhile, at the spot at which the heads were found, a strange flower bloomed at Christmas and an eerie light glowed.

It could be argued that the events in the Robson household had nothing to do with the appearance of the heads – that they were, instead, poltergeist phenomena triggered by the adolescent children of the Robson family. But the Robsons' next door neighbour, a Mrs Ellen Dodd, underwent a truly unnerving experience that could clearly not be explained away so easily:

> I had gone into the children's bedroom to sleep with one of them, who was ill. My ten-year-old son Brian kept telling me he felt something touching him. I told him not to be so silly. Then I saw this shape. It came towards me

and I definitely felt it touch me on the legs. Then, on all fours, it moved out of the room.

Mrs Dodd later described the creature that had touched her as 'half human, half sheep-like'. Mrs Robson recalled that she heard a sound like a crash and screams next door on the night in question. Her neighbour told her that the creature that made them was like a werewolf. And when Mrs Dodd went downstairs she found, disconcertingly, that her front door was open. Whatever caused the phenomenon, Mrs Dodd was terrified, and was rehoused by the local council after she had told them of her experience. Eventually the heads were removed from the Robsons' house, the house itself was exorcised, and all was quiet in Rede Avenue.

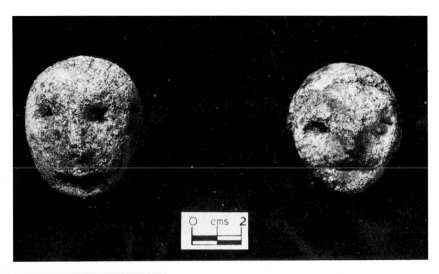

Top: this photograph of the Hexham heads is the best now available. A comparison with heads that are known to be modern reveals striking similarities (above). The head on the left was made by Desmond Craigie in an attempt to prove that he made the original heads; the one on the right, curiously enough, was made shortly before the discovery of the Hexham heads by one of the small boys who unearthed them

Left: the figure of the wolf-man, which appears in legends throughout the world. The mere presence of the Hexham heads was reportedly able to induce manifestations of such creatures

Meanwhile, however, a distinguished Celtic scholar, Dr Anne Ross, had become interested in the stones. In an article for *Folklore, myths and legends of Britain*, a book published by Reader's Digest, Dr Ross had claimed that the heads were around 1800 years old and had been designed to play a part in Celtic head rituals (see box). And, when the heads were banished from the Robsons' house, Dr Ross took charge of them. She recalls what happened next:

I didn't connect it with the heads then. We always keep the hall light on and the doors kept open because our small son is a bit frightened of the dark, so there's always a certain amount of light coming into our room, and I woke up and felt extremely frightened. In fact, panic-stricken and terribly, terribly cold. There was a sort of dreadful atmosphere of icy coldness all around me. Something made me look towards the door, and as I looked, I saw this thing going out of it.

It was about six feet [2 metres] high, slightly stooping, and it was black against the white door. It was half-animal and half-man. The upper part I would have said was wolf and the lower part was human. It was covered with a kind of black, very dark fur. It went out and I just saw it clearly and then it disappeared and something made me run after it – a thing I wouldn't normally have done, but I felt compelled to run after it. I got out of bed and I ran and I could hear it going down the stairs. Then it disappeared toward the back of the house. When I got to the bottom of the stairs I was terrified.

That, however, was not the end of the story. A few days later, Dr Ross and her husband arrived home from London one evening to find their teenage daughter in a state of shock. Dr Ross described her daughter's experience:

She had opened the front door and a black thing, which she described as near a were-wolf as anything, jumped over the bannister and landed with a kind of plop. It padded with heavy animal feet, and it rushed toward the back of the house and she felt compelled to follow it. It disappeared in the music room, right at the end of the corridor, and when she got there it had gone. Suddenly she was terrified.

The day the heads were removed from the house everybody, including my husband, said it's as if a cloud had lifted; and since then there hasn't been, really, a trace of it [the paranormal activity].

Before the heads were removed, however, there were a number of manifestations of the unwelcome 'lodger'. During those frightening months, Dr Ross insisted, the creature appeared to be very real. It was not something shadowy, or only glimpsed out of the corner of the eye. It was noisy, and everyone who came to the house commented on a definite presence of evil. While he never observed it directly, Dr Ross's archaeologist husband was fully aware of his unwelcome 'guest's' presence, although he is not usually sensitive to psychic phenomena. The phenomena eventually ceased after the heads had been removed and the house exorcised – but not before Dr Ross had disposed of her entire collection of Celtic heads.

What was the origin of the heads? Were

Below: the complex but ordered shape of copper sulphate crystals reflects the regularity of its subatomic structure. Dr Don Robins (below right), an inorganic chemist and one of the many people to experience the disquieting effect of the Hexham heads, believes that crystal structures can store information in the form of electrical energy. The Hexham heads contain a high proportion of quartz – a crystalline substance; and Robins explains their apparent ability to induce paranormal effects by suggesting that they derive from the place in which the heads were made

the previous year. One day, his daughter Nancy had asked him what he did for a living. At that time Mr Craigie worked with artificial cast stone, making objects such as concrete pillars. To explain to his daughter what he did at work, he made three heads for her in his lunch break, and took them home for her to play with.

'Nancy played with them as dolls,' he said. 'She would use the silver paper from Penguin chocolate biscuits as eyes. One got broken and I threw it in the bin. The others just got kicked around and must have landed up where the lads found them.'

Embarrassed by the publicity that his own handiwork had attracted, Desmond Craigie said he was concerned merely to set the record straight. Speaking of the heads, he said, 'To say that they were old would be conning people.' But Dr Ross was not entirely convinced. 'Mr Craigie's claim is an interesting story. . . . Unless Mr Craigie was familiar with genuine Celtic stone heads it would be extraordinary for him to make them like this. They are not crude by any means.' Scientific analysis has, surprisingly, been unable to determine the age of the heads.

Bearers of an ancient curse

If the heads are indeed Celtic it is easy to imagine that they may be the carriers of some ancient curse. But if they are not, why is it that they appear to provoke paranormal phenomena? The evidence that they do so is strengthened by the testimony of another scientist, an inorganic chemist named Dr Don Robins. Dr Robins was exploring the idea that mineral artefacts can store visual images of the people who made them. He suggests that places and objects can store information that causes specific phenomena to occur – an idea similar to archaeologist Tom Lethbridge's notion that events can be 'tape-recorded' into the surrounding in

they, as Dr Ross believed, Celtic – and somehow imbued with an ancient curse?

The story took on a new twist in 1972 when Desmond Craigie – then a truck driver – announced that the 'Celtic' heads were actually a mere 16 years old. They had not been fashioned as votive offerings by a head-hunting Celt – for, Mr Craigie claimed, he himself had made them as toys for his daughter Nancy.

He explained that he had lived in the house in Rede Avenue that was now the Robsons' home for around 30 years; indeed, his father had remained a tenant there until

Two heads are better?

Hundreds of stone heads have been found in the north of England, Scotland and in mainland Europe. Most of these primitively carved objects can be positively identified as dating from the pre-Roman Celtic period – but some of them are of more mysterious provenance.

The Celts of the kingdom of Brigantia, in north-east England, were among those who revered the human head both as a charm against evil and as a fertility symbol. They would set the severed heads of vanquished enemies over the doors of houses and barns. Historians believe that it is an echo of this gruesome cult that lies at the heart of the veneration of stone heads (left) practised by later Celts.

West Yorkshire is particularly rich in such heads. Many are mounted in the walls of buildings, by doorways or on gables, or close to wells, where they seem to be serving their original purpose of warding off evil. But the curious thing is that many of these relics of the Celts' grisly cult are no more than a century old. Consciously or unconsciously, Yorkshire men and women have been perpetuating a tradition that is more than two thousand years old.

which they take place. Robins believes, too, that certain minerals have a natural capacity to store information in the form of electrical energy encoded in the lattice structure of their crystals. Summing up the argument, Dr Robins states:

> The structure of a mineral can be seen as a fluctuating energy network with infinite possibilities of storage and transformation of electronic information. These new dimensions in physical structure may well point the way, eventually, to an understanding of kinetic imagery encoded in stone.

He was interested, too, in the reports of sounds that had allegedly accompanied the phenomena induced by the presence of the heads, and drew a tentative parallel with a creature from Norse mythology, called the wulver, powerful and dangerous, but well-disposed towards mankind unless provoked. There are several reports of sightings of this creature in the Shetlands in the 20th century.

Dr Robins's interest in the heads prompted him to agree to take charge of them. As he put them in his car to take them home, however, and turned on the ignition, all the dashboard electrics went dead. He looked at the heads, told them firmly to 'Stop it!' – and the car started!

Back at his own home, Dr Robins in his turn began to find the presence of the heads disquieting. He described his reactions:

> There was no doubt that any influence that the heads possessed came from the

girl. I felt most uncomfortable sitting there with them looking at me and eventually we turned them round. As we did so, I had the distinct impression that the girl's eyes 'slid round' watching me.

Perhaps disappointingly, however, Dr Robins did not witness any paranormal events that might be caused by the heads. There were, however, some disquieting moments. One day, leaving the house, he muttered to the heads 'Let's see something when I get back!' Moments later, he re-entered the house to collect a book he had forgotten. Outside it was fresh and blustery – but in his study the atmosphere seemed 'almost electric with a stifling, breathless quality'. Attributing the effect to the 'girl' head, he left hurriedly. He found nothing amiss on his return home.

The present whereabouts of the Hexham heads is not known. But there seems little reason to doubt that they really did produce phenomena similar to those classically attributed to poltergeists – that, somehow they acted as epicentres. But why? There remains the mystery of their age – are they Celtic, as Dr Ross maintains, or were they really made in 1956 by a Hexham man for his daughter? Dr Robins's theory is that the power of an artefact to produce poltergeist phenomena depends, not on the maker, but upon *where* it was made. This may eventually throw some light on the Hexham heads; but clearly, there remain many questions to be answered.

Half human and half fish, mermaids and mermen have appeared many times over the centuries. But are the merfolk merely colourful figments of our imagination – or do they really exist?

ACCORDING TO THE South African *Pretoria News* of 20 December 1977, a mermaid had been found in a storm sewer in the Limbala Stage III township, Lusaka. The reports are garbled and it is difficult to tell who saw what – and what exactly it was they saw – but it seems that the 'mermaid' was first seen by some children and, as the news spread, so a crowd gathered. One reporter was told that the creature appeared to be a 'European woman from the waist up, whilst the rest of her body was shaped like the back end of a fish, and covered with scales.'

Legends about mermaids and mermen stretch back into antiquity and can be found in the folklore of almost every nation in the world. Merfolk have been seen and vouched for down the ages by witnesses of attested integrity – and they continue to be seen today.

The earliest merman in recorded history is the fish-tailed god Ea, more familiarly known as Oannes, one of the three great gods of the Babylonians. He had dominion over

A fishy tale

the sea and was also the god of light and wisdom, and the bringer of civilisation to his people. Originally Oannes was the god of the Akkadians, a Semitic people of the northern part of Babylonia from whom the Babylonians derived their culture, and was worshipped in Akkad as early as 5000 BC.

Almost all we know about the cult of Oannes is derived from the surviving fragments of a three-volume history of Babylonia written by Berossus, a Chaldean priest of Bel in Babylon, in the third century BC. In the 19th century, Paul Emil Botta, the French vice-consul in Mosul, Iraq, and an enthusiastic archaeologist – albeit one whose primary concern was loot – discovered a remarkable sculpture of Oannes dating from the eighth century BC, in the palace of the Assyrian king Sargon II at Khorabad, near Mosul. The sculpture, along with a rich collection of carved slabs and cuneiform inscriptions, is now held in the Louvre in Paris.

Another early fish-tailed god was Dagon of the Philistines who is mentioned in the Bible: 1 Samuel 5:1–4. The Ark of the Covenant was placed next to a statue of Dagon in a temple dedicated to Dagon in Ashod, one of the five great Philistine city states. The following day the statue was found to have 'fallen upon his face to the earth before the ark of the Lord'. Amid much consternation

and, no doubt, great fear, the people of Ashod set the statue of Dagon in its place again, but the following day it was again found fallen before the Ark of the Covenant, this time the head and the hands having broken off.

It is also probable that the wife and daughters of Oannes were fish-tailed, but the surviving representations of them are vague and it is impossible to be sure. However, no doubts surround Atargatis, sometimes known as Derceto, a Semitic Moon goddess. In his *De dea Syria* the Greek writer Lucian (*c.* AD 120–*c.* 180) described her: 'Of this Derceto likewise I saw in Phoenicia a drawing in which she is represented in a curious form; for in the upper half she is a woman, but from the waist to the lower extremities runs in the tail of a fish.'

Fish-tailed deities can be found in almost every culture of the ancient world but by medieval times they had become humanoid sea-dwellers. One of the most important scientific influences on the Middle Ages was Pliny the Elder (AD 23–79), a Roman administrator and encyclopedic writer who died in the eruption of Vesuvius that destroyed Pompeii (and whose 15th-century statue outside Como Cathedral looks disconcertingly like Harpo Marx). As far as medieval scholars were concerned, if Pliny said that something was so then it was

Top left: the 'Fejee mermaid' that was the star attraction of Phineas T. Barnum's touring show in 1842. Barnum, a cynical American showman who coined the phrase 'every crowd has a silver lining', advertised the creature with posters depicting voluptuous mermaids, similar to the painting by Waterhouse (top). The 'mermaid' was perhaps a freak fish

undeniably so. Of mermaids, Pliny wrote:

I am able to bring forth for mine authors divers knights of Rome . . . who testifie that in the coast of the Spanish Ocean neere unto Gades, they have seen a Mere-man, in every respect resembling a man as perfectly in all parts of the bodie as might bee. . . .

Why, if the man so perfectly resembled a human, the 'divers knights of Rome' thought they had seen a *mer*man is not clear, but Pliny was convinced that merfolk were real and that they were seen regularly.

Tales of merfolk proliferated and were, oddly, encouraged by the Church, which found it politic to adapt ancient heathen legends to its own purpose. Mermaids were included in bestiaries, and carvings of them were featured in many churches and cathedrals. A fine example of a mermaid carving can

Above: the mermaid who is said to have abducted one Mathy Trewhella, carved for posterity on a pew in the church at Zennor, Cornwall. The carving is about 600 years old, but the legend may be considerably older

Left: mermaids, mermen and mer-children disport themselves in the turbulent sea

Below: the mermaid as erotic fantasy figure. She was widely believed to prey on drowning sailors, making them her sexual slaves

be seen in the church at Zennor, Cornwall, on a bench end. It is thought to be about 600 years old and is associated with the legend of Mathy Trewhella, the son of the churchwarden, who one day inexplicably disappeared. Years later a sea captain arrived at St Ives and told how he had anchored off Pendower Cave and seen a mermaid who had said to him: 'Your anchor is blocking our cave and Mathy and our children are trapped inside.' For the people of Zennor the mystery of Mathy's disappearance was explained.

On the whole, mermaids were not a sight to be relished. Their beautiful song, it was said, had captivated many a ship's crew and, like the fabled sirens, lured vessels to grief on dangerous rocks.

When mermaids surface

In the late Elizabethan, early Jacobean age belief in the mermaid waxed and waned. Men such as Frances Bacon and John Donne gave rational explanations for many natural phenomena, including the mermaid – yet it was also a time of blossoming maritime travel and some of the great seamen of the age told of personal encounters with merfolk. In 1608 Henry Hudson, the navigator and explorer (after whom the Hudson Bay territories are named), made the following matter-of-fact entry in his log:

This morning, one of our companie looking over boord saw a Mermaid, and calling up some of the companie to see her, one more came up, and by that time she was come close to the ship's side, looking earnestly on the men: a little after, a Sea came and overturned her: From the Navill upward, her back and breasts were like a womans (as they say that saw her) her body as big as one of us; her skin very white; and long haire hanging down behinde, of colour blacke; in her going downe they saw her tayle, which was like the tayle of a Porposse, and speckled like a Macrell. Their names that saw her were Thomas Hilles and Robert Raynar.

Hudson was a very experienced seaman who surely knew the calibre of his men and presumably would not have bothered to record a blatant hoax. Also, the report itself shows that his men were familiar with the creatures of the sea and were of the opinion that this creature was exceptional – which, if their description is accurate, indeed it was.

But the great age for mermaids was the 19th century. More mermaids were faked and displayed to awed crowds at fairs and exhibitions than at any other time. It was also the period in which several remarkable sightings were reported, including two of the best authenticated on record.

On 8 September 1809 *The Times* published the following letter from one William Munro:

About twelve years ago when I was Parochial Schoolmaster at Reay

Creatures of the impossible

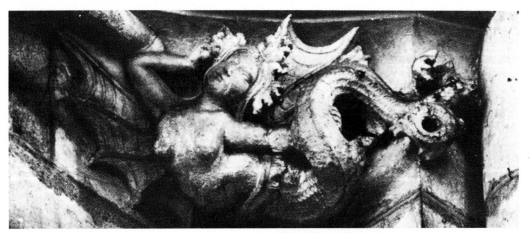

Left: a mermaid cornice decoration in Sens Cathedral, France

Below: the sirens attempt to lure Ulysses and his crew to their doom with their irresistible singing. Seen here as mermaids, they are more often thought of as half woman, half bird (below right)

Bottom: a predatory mermaid seizes a sailor and carries him off to her lair

[Scotland], in the course of my walking on the shore at Sandside Bay, being a fine warm day in summer, I was induced to extend my walk towards Sandside Head, when my attention was arrested by the appearance of a figure resembling an unclothed human female, sitting on a rock extending into the sea, and apparently in the action of combing its hair, which flowed around its shoulders, and of a light brown colour. The resemblance which the figure bore to its prototype in all its visible parts was so striking, that had not the rock on which it was sitting been dangerous for bathing, I would have been constrained to have regarded it as really a human form, and to an eye unaccustomed to the situation, it most undoubtedly appeared as such. The head was covered with hair of the colour above mentioned and shaded on the crown, the forehead round, the face plump, the cheeks ruddy, the eyes blue, the mouth and lips of natural form, resembling those of a man; the teeth I could not discover, as the mouth was shut; the breasts and abdomen, the arms and fingers of the size of a full-grown body of the human species, the fingers, from the action in which the hands were employed, did not appear to be webbed, but to this I am not positive. It remained on the rock three or four minutes after I observed it, and was exercised during that period in combing its hair, which was long and thick, and of which it appeared proud, and then dropped into the sea. . . .

Whatever it was that William Munro saw and described in such detail, he was not alone, for he adds that several people 'whose veracity I never heard disputed' had claimed to have seen the mermaid, but until he had seen it himself he 'was not disposed to credit their testimony'. But, as they say, seeing is believing.

In about 1830 inhabitants of Benbecula, in the Hebrides, saw a young mermaid playing happily in the sea. A few men tried to swim out and capture her, but she easily outswam

them. Then a little boy threw stones at her, one of which struck the mermaid and she swam away. A few days later, about 2 miles (3 kilometres) from where she was first seen, the corpse of the little mermaid was washed ashore. The tiny, forlorn body brought crowds to the beach and after the corpse had been subjected to a detailed examination it was said that:

the upper part of the creature was about the size of a well-fed child of three or four years of age; with an abnormally developed breast. The hair was long, dark and glossy; while the skin was white, soft and tender. The lower part of the body was like a salmon, but without scales.

Among the many people who viewed the tiny corpse was Duncan Shaw, factor (land agent) for Clanranald, baron-bailie and sheriff of the district. He ordered that a coffin and shroud be made for the mermaid and that she be peaceably laid to rest.

Of the many faked merfolk of this period, only one or two need be mentioned to

Below right: the Reverend Robert S. Hawker, who, in his youth, impersonated a mermaid off the shore of Bude, Cornwall. For several nights he draped himself over the rocks, with plaited seaweed for hair and oilskins wrapped round his legs, and sang off-key. The citizens of Bude flocked to see the 'mermaid' but, tiring of his joke, Hawker launched into *God save the King* and dived into the sea – his mermaid days over

illustrate the ingenuity of the fakes and the fakers. A famous example is recounted in *The vicar of Morwenstow* by Sabine Baring-Gould. The vicar in question was the eccentric Robert S. Hawker who, for reasons best known to himself, in July 1825 or 1826 impersonated a mermaid off the shore of Bude in Cornwall. When the Moon was full he swam or rowed to a rock not far from the shore and there donned a wig made from plaited seaweed, wrapped oilskins around his legs and, naked from the waist upwards, sang – far from melodiously – until observed from the shore. When the news of the mermaid spread throughout Bude people flocked to see it, and Hawker repeated his performance.

Mermaids have continued to be seen in more recent years. One was seen in 1947 by a fisherman on the Hebridean island of Muck. She was sitting on a floating herring box (used to preserve live lobsters) combing her hair. As soon as she realised she was being observed she plunged into the sea. Until his death in the late 1950s the fisherman could not be persuaded to believe that he had not seen a mermaid.

In 1978, a Filipino fisherman, 41-year-old Jacinto Fatalvero, not only saw a mermaid one moonlit night but was helped by her to secure a bountiful catch. Little more is known, however, because having told his story, Fatalvero became the butt of jokes, the

After several appearances Hawker, having tired of his joke – and his voice a little hoarse – gave an unmistakable rendition of *God save the King* and plunged into the sea – never to appear (as a mermaid) again.

Phineas T. Barnum (1810–1891), the great American showman to whom are attributed two telling statements – 'There's one [a sucker] born every minute' and 'Every crowd has a silver lining' – bought a mermaid that he had seen being shown at a shilling a time in Watson's Coffee House in London. It was a dreadful, shrivelled-up thing – probably a freak fish – but Barnum added it to the curiosities he had gathered for his 'Greatest Show on Earth'. His trick, however, was to hang up outside his 'mermaid' sideshow an eye-catching picture of three beautiful women frolicking in an underwater cavern; under this he had a notice that read: 'A Mermaid is added to the museum – no extra charge.' Drawn by the picture and the implication of what would be seen within, many thousands of people paid their admission fee and went to see this spectacle. As Barnum said, if the shrivelled-up 'mermaid' did not meet with their expectations, the rest of the exhibits were worth the money.

object of derision – and, inevitably, hounded by the media. Understandably he refused to say another word.

It is widely accepted that the mermaid legend sprang from the misidentification of two aquatic mammals, the manatee and dugong, and possibly seals. Obviously many reports can be thus explained, but does this explanation satisfactorily account for what was seen by Henry Hudson's sailors in 1608 or for the mermaid seen by the schoolmaster William Munro? Were these and other similar sightings sea-mammals or mermaids?

One suggestion, perhaps slightly tongue in cheek, is that the merfolk are real, the descendants of our distant ancestors who came ashore from the sea. The merfolk, of course, are descended from those ancestors who either stayed in the sea or chose to return to it. Human embryos have gills that usually disappear before birth, but some babies are born with them and they have to be removed surgically.

But, whatever she is, the mermaid has a long history of sightings and continues to be seen. For this we should be thankful; the romance and folklore of the sea would be all the poorer without her.

When fish pour down like rain

For centuries there have been incidents of fish falling from the sky, the latest occuring as recently as 1975. This strange phenomenon is one of the least explicable quirks of nature

ON 16 FEBRUARY 1861 a violent earthquake shook the island of Singapore. For the following six days, rain fell in torrents. Then, on the morning of the 22nd, after a last furious downpour, it stopped. François de Castelnau, a French naturalist staying on the island, reported what happened next to the Academy of Sciences in Paris, later that year.

At 10 a.m. the sun lifted, and from my window I saw a large number of Malays and Chinese filling baskets with fishes which they picked up in the pools of water which covered the ground. On being asked where the fishes came from they answered that they had fallen from the sky. Three days afterwards, when the pools had dried up, we found many dead fishes.

Although de Castelnau did not see the rain of fish himself, he was convinced that they had fallen from the sky. Dr A. D. Bajkov, an American marine scientist, was luckier. On 23 October 1947 he was having breakfast with his wife in a café in Marksville, Louisiana, USA, when shortly after a sudden shower of rain, he noticed fish lying in the streets: 'sunfish, goggle-eyed minnows and black bass up to 9 inches [23 centimetres] long.' More fish were found on rooftops, cold

Right: despite the fact that the phenomenon of fish falling from the sky has been the subject of discussion and eyewitness reports for centuries, no 'natural' explanation has yet been found. This illustration of falling fish comes from a book by Claus Magnus, *Historie de gentibus septentrionalibus* (1555), in which the author discusses falls of fish, frogs and other animals

Far right: one of the most reliably recorded incidents in Britain involved a timber yard worker, John Lewis, of Mountain Ash, Glamorganshire. On 9 February 1859 he was hit by falling fish, as illustrated in Charles Tomlinson's *Raincloud and snowstorm* (1864)

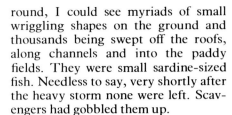

and dead, but nevertheless still fit to eat.

On their own, such accounts are not much to go on. Much of the evidence for fish falling from the sky is circumstantial – fish being found, usually after heavy rain, in places and on surfaces where no fish were before. But there are some eyewitness accounts.

One of the best attested cases to have occurred in Britain was at Mountain Ash, Glamorganshire, Wales, in 1859. In a paper published in the *Fortean Times* of Autumn 1979, Robert Schadwald established on the evidence of eyewitness accounts published at the time that it had happened on 9 February 1859. John Lewis, working in a timber yard at Mountain Ash, was startled at 11 a.m. by being suddenly struck by small objects falling out of the sky. One of the objects fell down the back of his neck.

On putting my hand down my neck I was surprised to find they were small fish. By this time I saw that the whole ground was covered with them. I took off my hat, the brim of which was full of them. They were jumping all about . . . The shed [pointing to a large workshop] was covered with them, and the shoots were quite full of them. My mates and I might have gathered bucketsful of them, scraping with our hands . . . There were two showers . . . It was not blowing very hard, but uncommon wet . . . They came down in the rain in 'a body like'.

A similar experience happened some 85 years later to Ron Spencer of Lancashire, while serving with the RAF at Kamilla, India, near the Burmese border. Speaking on BBC Radio 4 in April 1975, after another listener had described his experience of a fish fall, Ron said that he had loved going out into the monsoon rains to wash himself. On one occasion he was standing naked in the middle of this ritual when

Things started to hit me, and looking

round, I could see myriads of small wriggling shapes on the ground and thousands being swept off the roofs, along channels and into the paddy fields. They were small sardine-sized fish. Needless to say, very shortly after the heavy storm none were left. Scavengers had gobbled them up.

No one has yet discovered how often fish falls occur. The records are widely scattered and there is not a full study available that has collected *all* known cases. But it seems that only falls of frogs and toads are more abundant. For example, Dr E. W. Gudger, of the US Museum of Natural History, collected accounts for 40 years, and found only 78 reports spanning 2350 years. Seventeen of these occurred in the USA; 13 in India; 11 in Germany; 9 in Scotland; 7 in Australia; and 5 in England and Canada. But Gilbert Whitley, working from the records in the Australian Museum, lists over 50 fish falls in Australasia alone between 1879 and 1971.

One of the earliest references to a fish fall is to be found in the ancient Greek text the *Deipnosophistai*, compiled at the end of the second century AD by Athenaeus. These fragments, drawn from the records of nearly 800 writers, contain the report:

I know also that it rained fishes. At all events Phoenias, in the second book of his *Eresian magistrates*, says that in the Chersonesus it once rained fishes uninterruptedly for three days and Phylarchus in his fourth book says that the people had often seen it raining fish.

The earliest known case in England happened in Kent in 1666, and was reported in the *Philosophical Transactions* of 1698.

But despite the wealth of authenticated and reliable reports that fish falls have occurred, no one has yet produced a convincing account of *why* they happen. One of the most plausible explanations is that they are caused by tornadoes, waterspouts or whirlwinds lifting water containing fish high up into a cloud mass and carrying them inland.

Other explanations include the suggestion that the phenomenon is caused by fish 'migrating overland'; that fish-eating birds regurgitate or drop their food; that fish are left behind by ponds and streams overflowing; and that fish hibernating in mud are brought to life again by rain. But these do not account for the variety of eyewitness reports, the assortment of species found in the same place, the variety of terrain where fish have been found and the sheer number of fish involved in some cases. And even though there are well-documented cases of whirlwinds and waterspouts transporting fish, this explanation is inadequate to cover *all* cases.

Whirlwinds, tornadoes and waterspouts are very messy. They tend to pick up anything in their way and scatter it in every direction. This conflicts dramatically with the great majority of cases of fish falls. In the

Mountain Ash, for example, witnessed 'two showers, with an interval of ten minutes [between them] and each shower lasted about two minutes, or thereabouts.'

The length of time during which fish have been transported through the air seems, according to the evidence, to vary considerably. In many accounts, the fish are alive and thrashing when found on the ground; in other cases they have been found dead, but fresh and edible. It is difficult to believe that fish could be hurled against the ground and not be killed, but the evidence suggests that even those found dead were not killed by their fall. In his *History of Ceylon*, Sir James Tennant describes fish that were not injured by their fall onto gravel.

More puzzling still are the falls of dead fish. On two occasions in India, at Futtepoor in 1833 and at Allahabad in 1836, the fish that fell from the sky were not only dead, but dried. In the former case, the number of fish that fell was estimated to be between 3000 and 4000, all of one species. It is difficult to imagine how a whirlwind could keep so many fish in the air long enough for them to have dried out. But, despite widespread publicity in the Indian press at the time, no one came forward to report that a whirlwind *had* snatched up a valuable heap of dried fish! Perhaps even more extraordinary is the case from Essen, Germany, in 1896, where a Crucian carp fell out of the sky during a storm, encased in ice. Here, the fish must have been kept aloft by vertical currents long enough to become the nucleus of an egg-sized hailstone.

Sticklebacks from the sky

In the falls of other animals and insects there is a tendency for only one species to descend at any one time. But the evidence available concerning fish falls shows that they can be equally divided between falls of a single species and mixed falls. Up to six different species have been identified in a single fall, lending support to the idea that the phenomenon is caused by a waterspout scooping randomly from seas and lakes.

Falls of single species present many problems. The Mountain Ash fall in Glamorganshire, for example, was found to contain mostly sticklebacks with just a few minnows. Sticklebacks live in freshwater streams and do not congregate in shoals. How was it possible for a whirlwind to have scooped out such a vast quantity of sticklebacks together from a single source and deposit them all in one place? Similar questions apply to other cases of fish falls involving just one species. Another curious feature is the absence of all accompanying debris.

Objects caught up in the currents of a whirlwind might be expected to be hurled out at different times and distances according to their mass, size or shape. Contrary to this expectation, however, fish falls often involve many different sizes of fish. At Feridpoor,

Mountain Ash case, for example, the fall was restricted to an area 80 yards by 12 yards (73 metres by 11 metres). In the Kent case of 1666 it was claimed that the fish were dumped in one particular field and not in any of the surrounding ones. Most falls, in fact, seem to follow this localised pattern. Perhaps the most extreme example of this orderly fall of fish took place south of Calcutta on 20 September 1839. An eyewitness said: 'The most strange thing which ever struck me was that the fish did not fall helter-skelter . . . but in a straight line not more than one cubit [an ancient measurement deriving from the length of the forearm] in breadth.'

Whirlwinds move continuously. There is considerable evidence that fish falls have lasted much longer than the time possible for them to have been caused by a whirlwind. The torrent of many hundreds of sand eels on Hendon, a suburb of Sunderland, north-east England, on 24 August 1918 is a case in point. A. Meek, a marine biologist, reported seeing a fall, that lasted a full 10 minutes and was confined to one small area.

Even if whirlwinds do retrace their path, some fish falls have occurred in such a rapid succession that they could not have been caused by one whirlwind. John Lewis of

Above: one popular theory as to how fish could be transported overland and then 'dropped' from the sky is that water containing quantities of fish is gathered up by tornadoes. This tornado was photographed in Nebraska

India, for example, two species of fish fell in 1830, one larger and heavier than the other. Similarly, fish ranging in length from 6 to 12 inches (15 to 30 centimetres) fell in several gardens in Harlow, Essex, on 12 August 1968, according to next day's newspapers.

Charles Fort, who spent a lifetime collecting accounts of strange phenomena, suggested that fish falls are the result of what he called 'teleportation', a force that can transport objects from place to place without traversing the intervening distance. Such a force, Fort claimed, was once more active than it is now, and survives today as an erratic and feeble semblance of its former self. Through this agency fish are snatched away from a place of abundance to a point in the sky, from which they fall. Sometimes this point is not very high off the ground, which would account for the fact that the fish are often found alive. At other times the point is *very* close to the ground, accounting for the many observations of fish that seem to have appeared on the ground during a rainstorm.

Fort further suggested that fish falls might be the result of a new pond 'vibrating with its need for fish'. There is the case of Major Cox, for example, a well-known writer in England after the First World War. In an article published in the *Daily Mail* on 6 October 1921, Cox reported that the pond at his Sussex home had been drained and scraped of mud. The pond was then left dry for five months before refilling with water in November 1920. The following May, Cox was astonished to find it teeming with tench.

In 1941 the *American Journal of Science* published a story of a farm in Cambridge, Maryland, USA, where work on a new system of drains was halted because of rain. When work resumed, the ditch was found to be full of rainwater and hundreds of perch, of two different species, measuring between 4 and 7 inches (10 to 18 centimetres).

In neither case, however, was there time for aestivation. Overflows and migrating fish were ruled out because of the distance of both sites from any surrounding water. Fort also ruled out the possibility that the fish fell from the sky since they were found only in the new water. If they had fallen from the sky one would expect there to be some dead fish lying around. But none was found.

Most fish falls occur during heavy rains, so the whirlwind theory seems to be partially acceptable. A look at the range of reported cases, however, shows that a number of falls

Left: another drawing from Claus Magnus' *Historia de gentibus septentrionalibus* (1555) showing fish falling from the sky onto a town

Below: this woodcut showing a man struggling through a torrential shower of rain and fish was based on an 18th century incident in Transylvania

have occurred in cloudless skies and quite independently of any accompanying strong wind. But if teleportation seems too far-fetched – and it is difficult to believe that fish can disappear from one place and reappear in mid-air – what other explanation is there? At present the only rational explanation in terms of known causes seems to be the whirlwind theory. But this, as we have seen, cannot account for all cases. The fish fall remains one of the oddest, and least explicable, quirks of nature – if, indeed, it *is* nature, as we understand it, at work here.

Historical mysteries

*The course of history would almost
certainly have been different if the two
young princes in the Tower had not
mysteriously disappeared, or if King
William Rufus had not been killed
while out hunting. We will probably
never know the whole truth behind the
legends that have grown up around such
events, but the facts we do have make
fascinating reading.*

Who killed the king?

The ruthless, illiterate and homosexual tyrant William Rufus was mysteriously killed by an arrow in the New Forest after only 13 years on the throne. This homicide is still unsolved 900 years later

A STONE OBELISK standing in the leafy heart of the New Forest near Brockenhurst, Hampshire, England, has for hundreds of years been known as the 'Rufus Stone'. It supposedly marks the spot where William II of England was killed by an arrow on 2 August 1100 while he was out hunting.

According to the chroniclers of the day (all of whom were clerics) the King's death was divine retribution for his irreligious lifestyle, and had been clearly foretold in prophecies that he had chosen, fatally, to ignore. To later, less superstitious, historians his death was a happy accident that rid the throne of a wastrel monarch and brought his virtuous brother Henry to power. Only since the late 19th century has it been suggested that the 'Rufus Stone' commemorates one of the most ruthless and cunningly planned assassinations in history.

Second surviving son of William the Conqueror, William Rufus was born about 1060 in Normandy, France, and was brought to London soon after his father's coronation. He grew up to be an ebullient youth who loved drinking, hunting and horseplay; short, stocky and massively strong, he had yellow hair and a ruddy complexion, which earned him his nickname 'Rufus'.

On his death William the Conqueror left Normandy to his eldest son Duke Robert, the throne of England to William Rufus, and £5000 in silver to his youngest son Henry, adding enigmatically, according to *The ecclesiastical history* of the monk Ordericus Vitalis, that in due time Henry would succeed to everything, and 'surpass your brothers in wealth and power'. Although many of the Norman barons disapproved of dividing Normandy and England, and wanted Duke Robert to reign over the combined kingdom, William Rufus was nevertheless consecrated King of England at Westminster by Archbishop Lanfranc three days before Michaelmas day 1087.

Headstrong from the start

Even though Rufus owed his coronation to the willing co-operation of Archbishop Lanfranc, he seemed right from the outset of his 13-year reign deliberately to antagonise the Church and make bitter enemies of his bishops. At that time there were two claimants for the title of pope, and Rufus chose to recognise Clement III, the 'antipope', as the rightful pontiff, even though the Church and most other European monarchs elected to pay homage to Urban II, who ruled from the Lateran Palace in Rome. But even to Clement, Rufus's recognition amounted to no more than a nod of the head; anticipating

Historical mysteries

1089, Rufus left the see of Canterbury vacant for more than three years – a scandal that could not be allowed to continue. In 1093 the bishops urged him to appoint the 60-year-old monk Anselm Archbishop of Canterbury. Anselm was at that time abbot of the monastery of Bec in Normandy. He was very devout, and kept a monk beside him as his 'monitor', whose duties were to remind the Abbot of the virtue of obedience by telling him when to get up, when to go to bed, and when to eat. Anselm would even wake his monitor in the middle of the night, and humbly ask permission to turn over in bed. These irritating habits were reported to Rufus as evidence of Anselm's holiness, along with the assurance that 'He is a godly man, who has no earthly wish.'

'Indeed?' retorted Rufus. 'No earthly wish except, I suppose, to be made Archbishop of Canterbury.'

Henry VIII by about 450 years he argued that no pope had jurisdiction in the kingdom of England.

One of Rufus's innovations to increase his income was to allow livings that became vacant through the death of the incumbent to remain vacant – while the King collected the revenues. Or, instead of simply appointing a new cleric to the office, he would sell it to the highest bidder. He also had a reputation as a free thinker, and he actively encouraged the hated Jews to settle in his kingdom. On one occasion he set up a mock debate between the bishops of England and the Jewish rabbis on their faith. 'And by the Holy Face at Lucca,' he declared (according to William of Malmesbury), 'if the Jews have the best of the argument, I will myself turn Jew.'

None of these antics endeared him to the bishops. He was accused of being a member of the heretical Cathar sect (which was unlikely) and of being a homosexual (which was very likely). Nevertheless, he was popular with the people of London, and the practical achievements of his reign were considerable. He made a new survey of England to update his father's Domesday Book, defeated the invading Scots (under King Malcolm) at Alnwick, subdued the Welsh and crushed the conspiracy of the De Mowbray and De Lacy families against him. He gave financial support to his brother Robert's crusade to the Holy Land (which resulted in the capture of Jerusalem from the Saracens); he rebuilt the derelict township of Carlisle, transforming it into a handsome and prosperous city; he added to the Tower of London, and built the first stone bridge across the river Thames (the original London Bridge) and the great hall at Westminster, which remains his finest memorial.

After the death of Archbishop Lanfranc in

William the Conqueror (top), King of England from 1066 to 1087, was a man of austere moral character and punctilious in his religious observances. His ebullient son William Rufus (left) enjoyed life to the full and earned himself a reputation for being irreligious and decadent. On his death his brother Henry (below) succeeded to the throne, and has gone down in history as an upholder of law and order; curiously enough, several relatives of Rufus's supposed killer were given preferment at Henry's court

This story was told by Anselm's friend Eadmer, in his *History of modern times in England*. He also related how, reluctantly, Anselm accepted the appointment. To please his new archbishop, Rufus belatedly acknowledged Urban II as the rightful pope; yet despite this the King and Anselm remained at loggerheads for four years over the question of papal supremacy. Matters came to a head over the question of the *pallium*: Anselm wanted to go to Rome to receive this official badge of office from the hands of Urban II himself. Rufus refused to give him permission to go. Finally, in 1097, Anselm left England without permission, thus making it impossible for him to return. Rufus promptly seized all his estates. In Rome, Urban denounced Rufus for having 'expelled' Anselm; and two years later, at a Vatican Council, the Bishop of Lucca proclaimed Anselm a victim of tyranny: 'Robbed of his goods, cruelly treated, he has sought justice from the Holy See.'

Pope Urban promised that the matter should be looked into.

'The sooner the better,' exclaimed the

Despite Rufus's reputation as a wastrel, he left some solid achievements behind him. He rebuilt the derelict town of Carlisle, added to the Tower of London, built the first stone bridge across the Thames (the original London Bridge) and erected for his own glory the magnificent hall (above) at Westminster

Bishop, rapping on the floor with his pastoral staff. 'Think on divine judgement.'

From that time a series of menacing events began which ended with the King's death in the New Forest.

Throughout that summer of 1099, as William of Malmesbury records in *Deeds of the kings of the English*, supernatural happenings were reported up and down the kingdom:

the devil visibly appeared to men in woods and secret places, and spoke to them as they passed by. Moreover, at Finchampstead in Berkshire, a well flowed so freely with blood for 15 whole days that it discoloured a neighbouring pool.

In the north, the Sun and the Moon stood still for a time, while around the coast whole villages were deluged by tidal waves. Thunder, lightning and winds wreaked havoc on crops and destroyed the towers of several churches. These were all omens, the priests asserted, warning the King to mend his ways.

But Rufus laughed heartily when he heard the tale about the well flowing with blood, and pointed out, reasonably enough, that if God was destroying church towers, he was damaging his own property.

In the early summer of 1100 a message came from Serlo, Abbot of the convent of St Peter at Gloucester, which was famous as a centre of visions and prophecies. One of his monks had dreamed that he saw the Virgin Mary 'praying to the Lord to deliver England from the tyranny of William'. The Lord apparently replied, 'Be patient; in a little while you shall be avenged and redeemed.' This was scarcely a tactful vision to relay to a tyrant – yet no action was taken against the Abbot or his convent.

On 1 August Fulchered, Abbot of Shrewsbury, preached a remarkable sermon at Gloucester. England, he said, was smitten with 'leprosy' to the 'very crown of the head'. But the Lord was coming to avenge; there would be a 'sudden change; the bow of divine judgement is already bent, and the arrow is drawn from the quiver even now.'

On 2 August Rufus was due to go hunting in the New Forest. The previous night seems to have produced a plethora of prophetic dreams. The Prior of Dunstable dreamed

that the King's armourer presented Rufus with a quiver of five arrows, and that this boded ill. William of Malmesbury recorded that the King himself had dreamed 'he was let blood by a surgeon, and that the stream [of blood] reaching to heaven clouded the light and obscured the day.' A foreign monk at court dreamed that Rufus committed a 'gross outrage' to the crucifix, whereupon the figure of Christ kicked him in the mouth, causing him to fall on his back, and belch fire.

When this last dream was told to the King he burst into loud laughter and said, 'He is a monk and dreams for money. Give him a hundred shillings.'

Nevertheless, says William of Malmesbury, the King was 'not unmoved, and

hesitated a long time whether he should go out hunting as he had planned.' He put off the outing until after he had dined, and then set out into the forest with a small party consisting of his brother Henry, several barons, his armourer Ralph of Aix and 'Walter, surnamed Tirel'. The party were using arbalests, a form of crossbow.

Ralph of Aix offered the King a present of arrows; perhaps with the Prior of Dunstable's warning in mind, Rufus asked Ralph to carry them. What happened next was described by several contemporary chroniclers; all were agreed it was an 'accident' and that it was Walter Tyrell who shot the fatal arrow. According to Matthew Paris,

> When a great stag passed before him the King shouted to Walter Tyrel, a knight, 'Shoot, damn you.' The shaft flew, and glancing off a tree, pierced the King full in the heart, so that he instantly dropped dead.

William of Malmesbury's account said the headstrong and reckless Walter pierced the royal bosom with a fatal arrow. The smitten King uttered no sound, but breaking off as much of the shaft as stuck out of his body forthwith fell on his wound, and so hastened his death.

A further detail added by Gervase of Canterbury was that 'When he [the King] let fly an arrow at a stag which was against the sun, he himself, struck by an arrow, fell and died.'

Unceremonious haste

Rufus's body was placed in a charcoal-burner's cart and carried to Winchester, about 25 miles (40 kilometres) away, where it was buried hastily without ceremony under the cathedral tower. Henry, the King's younger brother, had apparently got separated from the main party and was not present at Rufus's death, but he certainly heard about it quickly enough. He arrived at Winchester before the body itself, stripped the royal apartments of their treasure, and hastened to Westminster, where he was crowned king just three days later.

Before his coronation Henry signed a document that had apparently been drawn up well in advance. It granted freedom to the 'Holy Church' and a pardon for all acts of murder committed prior to his coronation. The new King then invited Anselm to return to his see of Canterbury – and begged his pardon for being crowned before he arrived. Everything showed signs of being tidied up with unseemly haste.

Walter Tyrell fled immediately after the killing and crossed the Channel to Picardy; he was never to return. But although it was generally assumed that he was the one who had loosed the fatal arrow, he was never charged with murder, nor were his lands confiscated or his relatives harassed. And according to Suger, Abbot of St Denis, with whom he stayed for a time:

Rufus's rift with Archbishop Anselm (left, from a 16th-century engraving) precipitated the sequence of prophecies and portents that ended in his death. Apart from Rufus's own irreligious lifestyle, his court was condemned by the monkish chroniclers of the day for the 'vain and foppish' forms of attire adopted by the gilded youth of Norman England, who wore flowing garments and extravagantly pointed shoes, and let their hair grow long like women (above)

After Rufus was fatally struck down by an arrow in the forest, his body was placed on a charcoal burner's cart and taken as quickly as possible to Winchester. There it was buried in the cathedral (below) without any of the ceremony proper to a king. The tomb (bottom) marks Rufus's burial place under the cathedral tower. Only three days after Rufus's death his brother Henry was crowned king at Westminster; his suspiciously hasty coronation suggested that he was unnaturally anxious to consolidate his position

in Lyndon Johnson's administration.

But if Walter Tyrell did not kill Rufus, why did he flee? The obvious answer is that he was covering up for the real murderer.

Rufus had made the all-powerful Church his bitterest enemy. He had defied Archbishop Anselm, who had taken his complaints to Pope Urban II in Rome. Possibly a plot was hatched at the Vatican Council in 1099; certainly the tales of ill-omen that circulated in England that year seem, in retrospect, calculated to prepare the minds of ordinary people for some momentous happening.

Prophecies specifically threatening the life of the King followed. First Serlo's dream, then Fulchered's warning delivered the very day before the 'accident'. On the night before Rufus's death a number of people had prophetic dreams, including apparently Archbishop Anselm, who dreamt that St Alban received a flaming arrow from God, threw it down into hell, and cried, 'Take it, Satan, and take therewith this William the Tyrant into thy keeping.'

All the accounts of the death by the ecclesiastical chroniclers are remarkably consistent – as if they were all toeing a party line. But one account, by the 12th-century Anglo-Norman verse chronicler Wace, tells a different story. On the day Rufus died, Henry was hunting in another part of the forest. The string of his bow broke, and he sat down beside a cottage to mend it. An old peasant woman from the cottage asked an attendant who Henry was. When told he was the King's brother, she replied that the King's brother would soon be the king himself. 'My prophecies are never wrong,' she added.

Did the old woman know of a plot? Or was the story a belated attempt by Henry to establish an alibi? It is certainly strange that he rushed off in such haste to take possession of the royal treasure, and claim the crown his father had said would one day be his.

It was laid to the charge of a noble, Walter Tirel, that he had shot the King with an arrow; but I have often heard him . . . solemnly swear that on the day in question he was not in the part of the forest where the King was hunting. . . .
At the court of the new King, Tyrell's in-laws became favourites. Two of them were his wife's brothers, Gilbert and Roger de Clare, who had been present when Rufus was slain; another brother-in-law, Richard, was made Bishop of Ely in the first weeks of Henry's reign. William Giffard, another Tyrell relative, received the see of Winchester. In modern terms, it was as if the relatives of Lee Oswald, President Kennedy's supposed killer, had been given important posts

Dufferin: the fatal flaw

A brilliant diplomat saved from death by the intervention of supernatural forces – this spectacular story, in various guises, travelled the world in the late Victorian period. But how do the often repeated facts stand up to scrutiny?

FATE WAS KIND to the first Marquis of Dufferin and Ava: in 1893 he was saved – so his chroniclers tell us – by supernatural intervention from a violent death.

The story begins some 10 years earlier, when Lord Dufferin was enjoying a welcome break from the incessant bustle of diplomatic life. His distinguished career had already included six years as Governor General of Canada, and in 1883 he was completing a report on British government reorganisation in Egypt. A great house near Tullamore in County Offaly, Ireland, seemed to provide an ideal refuge for anyone seeking tranquillity. But one night, this peaceful idyll was shattered by a terrifying apparition.

Lord Dufferin was in bed when he suddenly found himself wide awake, sick with terror. He had been awoken by strange sounds from the grounds outside – terrifying sounds. However, Lord Dufferin was no coward; he climbed out of bed to investigate. Trembling in every limb and heart racing, he went to the French windows and peered out.

He could see the trim lawns, bathed in moonlight. Almost every section was in plain view, except for one spot, where tall trees cast long black shadows. And from these shadows came the sounds that had woken him – heartrending sobs, more animal than human.

Lord Dufferin began to fumble with the window latches – and, as he did so, a man staggered out of the shadows into the moonlight. He was bent double under the weight of a load on his back. At first sight it looked like a long linen-chest – but, as the man came closer, Dufferin suddenly became aware that the chest was, in fact, a coffin.

Lord Dufferin threw open the windows, ran across the lawn and shouted at the man to halt. Until then the man's face had been held down and hidden, but on hearing the shout

he lifted his head and turned it towards Lord Dufferin. And the moonlight fell on a face that was unforgettably loathsome – so contorted with hate that Lord Dufferin stopped dead in his tracks. Then, he drew on his reserves of courage, advanced on the man and walked – right through him!

At the same time the man disappeared – coffin and all. And with his disappearance the gloom lifted and the house and grounds became as calm and restful as ever.

Lord Dufferin returned to his bedroom shaken and puzzled. Then, after writing a complete account of the event in his diary, he managed to snatch some sleep.

At breakfast next morning he read out his account and appealed to his host and fellow guests for an explanation. But no one could help. The description of the man matched no one in the area, past or present. There wasn't even a local ghost to blame – and so the event remained an inexplicable mystery.

Over the years, the memory of that night stayed with Lord Dufferin – but it no longer troubled him. He grew to believe that it really might have been nothing more than an extraordinarily vivid nightmare. And that is how things stood for the next 10 years. Then, in 1893, the vision took on a new significance.

At the time, Lord Dufferin was the British Ambassador to France, and was obliged to attend a diplomatic reception at the Grand Hotel in Paris. When he entered the hotel foyer he found it jam-packed with impatient guests, for the lift was taking ages to make its trips to the reception area on the top floor. Together with his secretary, he joined the queue for the lift. Eventually he reached the head of the queue; the lift arrived, its door squealed open and the attendant waved the guests in.

A hideous double

Lord Dufferin turned pale, stood fast and refused to enter. He mumbled an excuse to the officials with him, then stepped backwards, pulling his secretary after him. Nothing would persuade him to use that lift, for the lift attendant was, in every feature, the double of that hideous man he had seen 10 years earlier in Ireland.

The other officials ignored the eccentric Englishman. They crowded into the lift and it began its laborious climb. Lord Dufferin, meanwhile, went hunting for the manager's office. He had to know who the lift attendant was and where he came from. But, before the Marquis reached the office there came a disaster. The lift's cable snapped and it plunged down the shaft to destruction. The passengers were killed outright – as was the ghastly lift attendant.

No one ever came forward to claim or identify the attendant's body. The hotel manager could answer no questions either, for the attendant was a casual worker taken on for the day. A man without documents or records. Lord Dufferin was baffled. But not

even his money and influence could turn up a single fact about the man. The one certainty was that his strange vision at Tullamore had saved Dufferin's life.

That, in its essentials, is the remarkable story of Lord Dufferin's escape. Published accounts often vary in detail, but no one ever questions the basic truth of the tale. On the contrary, it is always asserted that the facts have been fully researched and investigated. One writer, for example, states that 'The evidence is incontrovertible . . . the details of this story have been carefully investigated by the well-known French psychologist de Maratray, who brought them to the attention of the British Society for Psychical Research.' Another writer adds, 'the accident was reported in the Press . . . but neither the management of the hotel, nor the accident investigators could find any record of the man's name or background.' So, here we seem to have a case that cannot be challenged.

But in fact, the facts are not as watertight as they seem. To begin with, the case was never investigated by the Society for Psychical Research. The society was certainly in existence at the time of the alleged event, but its files prove that it had no record of the Dufferin case. And no newspaper carried reports of the accident – for very good reasons. In fact, the first written account of the Dufferin case did not emerge until 1920 – that is, 18 years after the death of Lord Dufferin and 26 years after the alleged lift crash.

This primary account was written by the French pyschologist Monsieur R. de Maratray on 18 July 1920. He gave it to the

Above: Frederick Temple Hamilton-Temple-Blackwood, first Marquis of Dufferin and Ava (1862–1902). Was he, as his chroniclers insist, saved from death in 1893 by the action of some supernatural power?

Left: the Grand Hotel in Paris. Legend has it that, at a diplomatic reception held here in 1893, a lift cable snapped, killing all the passengers. Lord Dufferin made a narrow escape by refusing to travel in the lift – and the story goes that he owed his life to a vision he had had 10 years earlier

Right: the French astronomer Camille Flammarion who, told the story of Lord Dufferin's miraculous escape, published it in his *Death and its mystery* – without, however, checking the facts

French astronomer Flammarion, who included it in his book *Death and its mystery*. De Maratray added force to his account by claiming that his wife was related to Lord Dufferin and his family had been kept informed of the events at the time. Flammarion made no attempt to check the story for himself. He even neglected to ask why de Maratray had kept quiet for so long. Instead, he simply took de Maratray's word for everything.

In fact, the fatal accident in the lift of the Grand Hotel took place in 1878 – some five years before the vision in Ireland, and 15 years before the date of Lord Dufferin's 'miraculous escape'. At the time of that genuine accident there was not a diplomatic reception at the hotel. In any case, Lord Dufferin was not even in Paris – but was serving in Canada as Governor-General. On top of that, in the real accident only one person, a young lady, died – not a lift full of people, certainly no unknown lift attendant!

Jettisoning logic

All the facts were established shortly after the publication of Flammarion's book. The intrepid investigator who nailed the story as a lie was Paul Heuze, a journalist with the Paris magazine *L'Opinion*. Heuze proved that, when it came to psychical research, Flammarion jettisoned all the logic and care that went into his astronomical work. As a result his books were crammed full of unsubstantiated stories and hearsay. To his discredit, Flammarion made no attempt to revise these books and the Dufferin story was given wide circulation and picked up by author after author.

But how did such a tale become linked with Lord Dufferin? The files of the Society for Psychical Research provide the answer. They show that in November 1949, a Mr Louis Wolfe of New York wrote to the SPR and asked for details of the society's 'Dufferin investigation'. The SPR replied that it had never been asked to check on the case. But, prompted by this enquiry, the society's secretary then wrote to Lord Dufferin's grand-daughter and asked for her help. In her reply Lady Dufferin stated that the tale did not apply to her grandfather. It was a new version of an old story he used to tell about *someone else*! In the original version, though, an unnamed man had taken his holiday in Scotland, at Glamis Castle. And the vision itself had involved a hearse driven by a man with an ugly and hateful face.

Further research showed that the yarn first appeared as an anonymous second-hand account in the spiritualist paper *Light* of 16 April 1892. *Light*'s editor at the time was the Reverend Stainton Moses and his behaviour paralleled that of Flammarion: he took the tale completely on trust. He wrote this about it: 'It has been communicated to me by a personal friend, and is both authentic and trustworthy.' The account by the Reverend

Moses's personal friend ran as follows: I have just heard from a friend of a remarkable dream. She thought she heard a loud knock on the door, and on looking out she saw that a hearse had stopped at the house. Being greatly surprised, she rushed downstairs and herself opened the hall door. A strange-looking man was on top of the hearse; on seeing her, he said, 'Are you not ready yet?' She said, 'Oh, no; certainly not.' And slammed the door. The sound seemed to have caused her to wake.

She was much puzzled to know what could be the significance of such a very unusual dream. The face of the man haunted her, and for weeks she could not get the remembrance out of her head. All her family and friends were told about the dream, and all the circumstances of it had been discussed.

Some weeks had passed when one day the young lady happened to be in a

Top: Lady Dufferin, grand-daughter of the first Marquis, pictured in 1958. It was she who finally cleared up the origin of the escape story: it was a version of a tale her grandfather used to tell about someone else – a man who had taken his holiday at Glamis Castle in Scotland (above). In Lord Dufferin's original version, however, the apparition had been of a man driving a hearse

large warehouse in the City, and was just going to step into the lift, when she looked at the man who had charge of it, and immediately drew back, having recognised the face of the man she had seen in her dream. When she drew back her consternation was added to by the exclamation from the man of the very words she had heard in her dream, 'What are you not ready yet, Miss?' Her determination not to ascend in the lift was confirmed, and she declined to go into it. It only reached to the next floor, when the machinery gave way, the lift being smashed to pieces and the man killed.

The lift tale travelled to the United States and Europe, being constantly altered and

The face of death

The weird blend of fact and fantasy that characterises the Dufferin tale reached another level of confusion with the release of the classic Ealing movie *Dead of night* in 1945. It was based on a short story by E.F. Benson, *The room in the tower* – itself based on a hearsay version of the Dufferin legend.

The film concerns a group of people at a party, each of whom tells a story about a mysterious happening – and one of the stories is strangely similar to the Dufferin tale. A racing driver dreams, not of a man carrying a coffin, but of the driver of a hearse. And later, the racing driver refuses to get into a bus when he recognises its conductor as the driver of the hearse. The bus subsequently plunges over an embankment.

added to in its passage. Nine years later, it returned to England in a new guise, now posing as an authentic American event! Ironically enough, it was promptly picked up and reprinted in the pages of *Light*. It seems the new editor and his staff had completely forgotten their earlier account furnished by a 'personal friend' of the Rev. Moses. And on 9 February 1907, it ran the following story under the heading 'Saved by a vision':

The Progressive Thinker gives an instance of a warning dream, as related by Miss Gray, 'A young woman prominent in educational work' in Washington State. While staying in Chicago, where she had planned to visit 'a new department store which had just been opened, whose elevators were death-traps,' she woke up in the middle of the night and saw an unknown face at the window, twenty feet [6 metres] above the ground. On going to the window she saw a hearse standing in the street below, with her nocturnal visitant occupying the driver's box; he looked her squarely in the face and beckoned to her. The next day she visited the store, and on going to one of the crowded elevators the man in charge beckoned to her and said that there was room for one more. His features were those of the man on the hearse in her dream or vision of the night before. She refused to enter the elevator, which 'started down, stuck, and dropped four storeys, killing two of its passengers and injuring everyone else in the car'.

In the meantime, another variation of the story had been incorporated in Lord Dufferin's bag of after-dinner yarns. One day he related it to a young impressionable nephew and gave it special treatment. Adult wiles were not fully appreciated. The twinkle

in Dufferin's eyes was missed. And when he spun out the tale as his very own real-life adventure, the boy was awe-struck and convinced. The boy grew up to become a distinguished diplomat and writer. Out of conviction he retold this 'true story' frequently to his friends – once, unfortunately, to the de Maratrays, who proved as gullible as he himself had been. The innocent culprit, the unwitting father of this tenacious myth was none other than Harold Nicolson.

Right: Harold Nicolson, diplomat and writer – and nephew of Lord Dufferin. Lord Dufferin told the schoolboy Nicolson of his 'escape' – and Nicolson believed it. In adult life he used often to retell the story, so beginning the extraordinarily tenacious myth that, in various guises, was soon known all over the world

The terror of London

Who was the frightening figure – a man known only as Spring-heeled Jack – who terrorised the people of London for decades in the 19th and early 20th century? A mysterious legend has built up around this bizarre character

THE LONELY LANES AND COMMONS of 19th-century suburban London were haunted by the weird and terrifying figure of Spring-heeled Jack, who pounced upon passers-by, sometimes wounded them severely, and bounded away in enormous leaps. Today the antics of Spring-heeled Jack are almost forgotten, or dismissed as a figment of the imagination – a mere character in Victorian horror literature, or a bogeyman used by mothers to warn errant children: 'Be good or Spring-heeled Jack will get you!' Some writers believe that Jack is a figure of popular folklore. Kellow Chesney in his book *The Victorian underworld* says that Jack is 'pure legend' – perhaps the invention of servants reluctant to admit negligence when thieves robbed their master's home.

But Jack was not a character in fiction, folklore or legend. He was real, and his appearances were widely reported in the local and national press.

Nobody seems certain when Jack first appeared. Many sources say that reports of a peculiar leaping man were in circulation as early as 1817, but it was not until 1838 that Spring-heeled Jack became a figure of considerable and widespread interest and speculation. On 9 January 1838 the Lord Mayor of London, Alderman Sir John Cowan, revealed, at a public session held in the Mansion House, the contents of a letter he had received several days earlier. He had withheld it, he said, in the hope of obtaining further information. The correspondent, who signed the letter 'a resident of Peckham', wrote that, as the result of a wager, a person of the highest rank had adopted several frightening guises and set out to scare 30 people to death. He had 'already succeeded in depriving seven ladies of their senses', two of whom 'were not likely to recover, but likely to become burdens to their families.' The resident of Peckham continued:

> The affair has now been going on for some time, and, strange to say, the papers are still silent on the subject. The writer has reason to believe that they have the whole history at their finger-ends but, through interested motives, are induced to remain silent.

We do not know why the Lord Mayor made

On the tombstone, with upraised arms and rage in every feature, towered the terrific form of Spring-Heeled Jack. Freezer and Links stood transfixed; their ghastly burden slipped slowly to the grass, but they remained gazing, terror-struck. Vengeance had fallen!

the contents of this letter public, nor can we judge the truth of the letter's allegation of a press 'cover-up', but from the quantity of letters that poured into the Mansion House it is clear that the activities of Spring-heeled Jack were common knowledge in suburban London.

Spring-heeled Jack had appeared as a milk-white bull, a white bear, and an enormous baboon; he had been seen dressed in a suit of shining brass armour, and on another occasion in one of burnished steel; once, in Hackney, he appeared as a lamplighter – who walked upon his hands and carried his ladder between his feet. His ability to make prodigious leaps was popularly ascribed to springs attached to his boots.

On Wednesday, 18 February 1838, 18-year-old Lucy Scales and her sister Margaret were returning home after visiting their brother, a butcher who lived in a respectable part of the district of Limehouse. Lucy, slightly ahead of her sister, was passing the

Above: Tod Slaughter as Spring-heeled Jack in the spine-chilling film *The curse of the Wraydons*, which was made in 1946

Left: 'Spring-heeled Jack parts the lovers', an illustration from a 19th-century 'penny dreadful'. Jack was the inspiration for several of these weekly serials: although usually portrayed as the villain of the piece, often terrorising young women (far left), he occasionally appeared as the hero, an avenger of crime and a punisher of wrong-doers (below left)

entrance to Green Dragon Alley when a figure leapt upon her from the shadows. The apparition breathed fire into Lucy's face and then bounded away as the girl fell to the ground, seized by violent fits.

Two days later, 18-year-old Jane Alsop replied to a violent ringing of the bell at the front gate of her parents' home in east London. Outside was an extremely agitated man who identified himself as a policeman. 'For God's sake bring me a light,' he cried, 'for we have caught Spring-heeled Jack in the lane!'

Blinded by fire

Jane fetched a candle, but when she handed it to the 'policeman', the man discarded his all-enveloping cloak. On his head was a large helmet, he wore a skin-tight suit of what looked like white oilskin, and in the light of the candle his protuberant eyes burned like coals. Without uttering a word, he vomited blue and white flames into Jane's face and grabbed the temporarily blinded and very frightened girl with talon-like fingers, which tore her dress and raked her skin. Attracted by her screams, Jane's sisters, Mary and Sarah, came to the girl's assistance. Somehow Sarah pulled Jane from the fiend's grasp, thrust her indoors and slammed the door in Jack's face.

A week later Jack tried the same deception but for some reason his intended victim was suspicious and Jack was forced to flee. A witness claimed that under his cloak Jack had been wearing an ornate crest and, in gold filigree, the letter 'w'.

After these attacks Jack's infamy grew. His exploits were reported in many newspapers and became the subject of no less than four 'penny dreadfuls' and melodramas performed in the cheap theatres that abounded at that time. But, perhaps as a result of the publicity, Jack's appearances became less frequent and occurred over a large area. It was not until 1843 that terror of Spring-heeled Jack again swept the country. Then he appeared in Northamptonshire, in Hampshire – where he was described as 'the very image of the Devil himself, with horns and eyes of flame' – and in East Anglia, where he took particular delight in frightening the drivers of mail coaches.

In 1845 reports came from Ealing and Hanwell, in west London, of a weird figure, leaping over hedges and walls and shrieking and groaning as it went. The perpetrator turned out to be a practical joker, a butcher from Brentford.

Later that year Jack was seen at Jacob's Island, Bermondsey, a disease-ridden slum of decaying houses linked by wooden galleries across stinking ditches. This area had been immortalised by Charles Dickens seven years earlier as the lair of Fagin and his motley band in *Oliver Twist*. Jack cornered a 13-year-old prostitute named Maria Davis on a bridge over Folly Ditch. He breathed fire into her face and hurled her into the stinking, muddy ditch below. The girl screamed terribly as the muddy waters claimed her. Witnesses reported the affair to the police, who dragged the ditch and recovered the poor girl's body. The verdict at the subsequent inquest was one of death by misadventure, but the inhabitants of the area branded Jack as a murderer.

There were isolated reports of Spring-heeled Jack over the next 27 years, none of them well-attested. Then, in November 1872, the *News of the World* reported that London was 'in a state of commotion owing to what is known as the Peckham Ghost . . . a mysterious figure, quite as alarming in appearance' as Spring-heeled Jack, 'who terrified a past generation.'

In 1877 Jack gave a virtuoso performance

at Aldershot Barracks. The terror began one night in early March. A sentry on duty at the North Camp peered into the darkness, his attention attracted by a peculiar figure bounding across the common towards him. The soldier issued a challenge, which went unheeded or unheard, and the figure disappeared from sight for a few moments. Then it was beside the guard and delivered several slaps to his face with a hand as cold and clammy as a corpse.

There were several more attacks on guards at Aldershot. Once a soldier shot at Jack; afterwards a rumour that Jack was invulnerable to bullets spread like wildfire. In fact the soldier had fired blanks at him.

Various theories were advanced at the time, but no real clues ever emerged. The identity of the miscreant and the purpose of his attacks remains unknown.

The final bow

It was 10 years before Jack's activities made further headlines, this time in Cheshire, where he frightened several young ladies. One was playing the piano in the drawing-room of her father's House in Oxton when a black-clad figure rushed into the room, swept every ornament off the mantelpiece and vanished as suddenly as he had appeared. According to a rather satirical article in the *Liverpool Citizen*, it was widely rumoured that a number of young 'swells . . . sons of well-known men and bearing historic names' had wagered £1000 that none of their number could impersonate the original Jack. The wager was accepted, and presumably won.

Spring-heeled Jack made his final bow in a sensational appearance in Everton, Liverpool, in 1904. According to the *News of the World* of 25 September, crowds of people gathered to watch Jack scampering up and down William Henry Street, where he executed tremendous leaps, some of which are

Left: Jacob's Island in east London, the scene of the murder of young Maria Davis. Witnesses stated that Spring-heeled Jack was the culprit, but that he bounded away before he could be apprehended. A verdict of death by misadventure was recorded at the inquest

Right: Jack outwits the peelers with one enormous leap – another illustration from a 'penny dreadful'

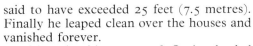

Left: the barracks at Aldershot, where Jack made one of his most sensational appearances in 1877. As in other reports, he was said to have worn a tight-fitting oilskin suit and a large helmet. When challenged by the sentries, he leaped right over them, breathing blue flames into their faces as he passed by

Below: Henry de la Poer Beresford, Marquis of Waterford. In his youth the Marquis was a notorious practical joker and his pranks were often reported in the press. Many people believed that he invented the disguise of Spring-heeled Jack

said to have exceeded 25 feet (7.5 metres). Finally he leaped clean over the houses and vanished forever.

Although this story of Spring-heeled Jack's final bow has been widely told and might seem to be one of the best-attested examples of his prowess, investigation has proved it to be untrue. Only four days before the report quoted above, the *Liverpool Echo* contained an article about a house in William Henry Street that was said to be haunted by a poltergeist. 'The story,' said the *Echo*, 'as it passed from mouth to mouth, reached sensational dimensions.' At about the same time further excitement was caused by a man suffering from religious mania who would climb upon the roof of his house and cry out that his wife was a devil or witch. The police or a fire-engine would attempt to bring the man down, but he would escape them by jumping from one roof to the next. From these incidents the spurious story of Spring-heeled Jack was born.

But who or what was the original Spring-heeled Jack? One suggestion is that he was an insane circus fire-eater or acrobat; other theories range from a kangaroo dressed up by a demented animal trainer to, more recently, the inevitable UFO occupant. But Jack was almost certainly a human being – or to be more precise more than one, for it is unlikely that the apparition that appeared at Aldershot in 1877 was the same as the one that spread terror in suburban London some 40 years earlier. And Jack is known to have had his imitators, such as the Brentford butcher

and, perhaps, the perpetrators of the Cheshire scare of 1887.

A very plausible candidate for the title of the Spring-heeled Jack behind the terror of 1837 to 1838 is Henry de la Poer Beresford, Marquis of Waterford. He had already been an inveterate and notorious prankster during his days at Eton and Oxford, where he was also an outstanding boxer and oarsman. He once proposed to a railway company that they should arrange for two locomotives to crash, at his expense, so that he could witness the spectacle. One night in 1837, having been to the races, he painted the town red – literally. His decorative activities included doors, windows and one of the town watchmen. He and his associates were each fined £100 for this escapade.

Later in that year the *Herald*, of Fife in Scotland, reported:

The Marquis of Waterford passed through this town the other day, on the top of a coach, with a few of his associates. In the course of the journey they amused themselves with the noble occupation of popping eggs from a basket at any individual who happened to be standing at the wayside.

The Times commented on this incident: 'This vivacious person is a long time sowing his "wild oats". He is nearly 27 years old.'

The activities of the Marquis were not always so entertaining. Once he evicted more than 30 tenant families from their homes on his estate at a moment's notice. He habitually treated people and animals with cruelty.

A brutal attack

The young Lord Waterford visited Blackheath Fair in October, 1837; on the same day Polly Adams, a 17-year-old serving-girl, was brutally attacked as she left the fair. Earlier she had been accosted by someone with 'pop eyes', whom she believed to be a nobleman. Waterford's eyes had always been noticeably protruberant. His family emblem fitted the description of a crest seen on the clothes of Jack in one attack. The whereabouts of the Marquis during this period are consistent with the locations of Jack's appearances.

Waterford's cruel and bullying exploits gradually ceased after this time, and he became a model of respectability after his marriage in 1842. He was killed in a fall from his horse in 1859. The idea that Waterford was Spring-heeled Jack was being treated virtually as established fact by newspapers later in the century.

Never caught, never positively identified, Spring-heeled Jack, together with his escapades, is all but forgotten today. Nobody remembers the 'penny dreadfuls', the melodramas, or the only film about Jack – *The curse of the Wraydons*, made in 1946 and starring Tod Slaughter. And the names of new bogeymen come to the lips of mothers who a century ago would have cried: 'Be good or Spring-heeled Jack will get you!'

Murder most foul?

In 1483 the two young sons of Edward IV were murdered in the Tower of London by their wicked uncle Richard of Gloucester – or were they? This chapter examines the facts in the light of the latest evidence

ON THE MORNING of 22 May 1455 two armed forces converged on St Albans, north-west of London. One was led by the former Lord Protector of the Realm, Richard, Duke of York, and the other by the mentally unstable Lancastrian king, Henry VI, with his powerful minister, the Duke of Somerset. The encounter was short and fierce: within an hour, Somerset was dead, and the King taken prisoner.

The first battle of St Albans marked the beginning of a bitter and bloody dynastic

The Princes in the Tower, in a painting by John Millais (1829–1896). Edward was 12 and Richard 10 when they were last seen in July 1483 playing together in the Tower of London. They disappeared without trace – presumed murdered

struggle that was to last for 30 years. Dubbed the 'Wars of the Roses' by later historians, because the opposing factions supposedly adopted a red and white rose as their respective emblems, this period was one of the most brutal in English history, as well as being a prelude to its greatest mystery.

The protagonists were the mighty families of Lancaster and York, both descended from Edward III who had died three quarters of a century earlier. The Lancastrians had been in power since 1399, when Henry Bolingbroke, son of John of Gaunt, had seized the crown from Richard II. The house of York might have remained content with their status as the second most powerful family in the land, had not Henry V died young, leaving an eight-month-old son as his heir. The reign of Henry VI was a disaster. With a minor as king, the arrogance of the powerful nobles increased; and when, at the age of 15, Henry began to rule in his own right, he proved to be weak, ineffectual and mentally unstable. Nor was his young French wife, Margaret of Anjou, particularly popular. In gratitude to the nobles who had helped arrange her marriage she appointed many of them ministers; they proceeded to give away England's possessions in France.

King in name only

Matters came to a head in 1453, when Henry's first bout of insanity occurred. Richard, Duke of York, backed by the influential Earl of Warwick, was appointed lord protector, a position that made him virtual king. When Henry's sanity returned two years later York was unwilling to relinquish power, and the parties fought it out at the first battle of St Albans. The captured Henry continued as titular king, but with York as the power behind the throne; three decades of intermittent civil war followed.

After York was killed at the battle of Wakefield in December 1460, his son Edward roundly defeated the Lancastrians at Towton the following March and was crowned Edward IV. But the struggle was not over. Henry was restored in 1470; the following spring the Lancastrian forces were defeated by Edward, first at Barnet and then at Tewkesbury, where Henry's son, the Prince of Wales, was killed. Edward followed through by having Henry murdered in the Tower of London on the night of 21 May 1471. He then reigned as a popular and energetic monarch for over 10 years, until his health collapsed and he died suddenly, at the age of 40, on 9 April 1483.

It was a severe blow to the Yorkist cause. His eldest son, also Edward, was a mere lad of 12, and it seemed that another prolonged regency lay ahead, with all its attendant

The seeds of the Wars of the Roses between York and Lancaster had been sown when Henry V (left, from an effigy in Westminster Abbey, London) died at the age of 35 leaving an eight-month-old son as his heir. Henry VI grew up to be a recluse, of uncertain mental stability; he was unable to make decisions and left state affairs to his ministers and Queen. Below: Henry VI during the battle of Towton (1461), in a painting by William Dyce (1806–1864)

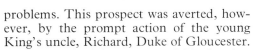

with her younger son in the Palace of Westminster.

June was a month of decisive action for Richard. Hastings, his brother Edward's chief adviser, was charged with treason and summarily beheaded. Rivers and other leading members of the Woodville faction were executed. The Queen was persuaded to give up her younger son, the 10-year-old Richard of York, who was taken to join his brother in the Tower. On 22 June a cleric, one Dr Ralph Shaw, preached a sermon at St Paul's Cross proclaiming both the Princes bastards, on the grounds that Edward IV's marriage to Elizabeth Woodville was invalid; on 26 June Richard had himself proclaimed king, and on 6 July he was crowned. All this time, the Princes remained in their lodgings in the Tower of London.

What happened to the Princes?

The bewildering speed with which Richard had achieved his objective worried many of his subjects. It is true that he had avoided the risk of civil war; but few people believed that Edward's sons were indeed illegitimate. Richard's actions were those of a usurper. In September a fully fledged revolt broke out, led by the Duke of Buckingham; its objectives were to crown Henry Tudor, Earl of Richmond, who was a Lancastrian with a tenuous claim to the throne. The rebellion fizzled out, and Buckingham was beheaded. Significantly, when the rebels first began to march, they demanded the reinstatement of Edward V; later, to justify their uprising, they claimed that both Edward and Richard were dead, and that Richard III had murdered them.

Was this true? Certainly it seems that Sir Thomas More thought so. Writing in about 1513, he described in his *History of the reign of Richard III* how Richard sent a messenger

problems. This prospect was averted, however, by the prompt action of the young King's uncle, Richard, Duke of Gloucester.

Richard had been one of his brother Edward's staunchest supporters, and had fought fiercely at his side at Barnet and Tewkesbury. His prestige was enormous, and he had been named by the late King as lord protector and guardian of his son.

The young Edward had been brought up at Ludlow castle, on the Welsh Marches, surrounded by members of the powerful Woodville family, relations of his mother Elizabeth Woodville. On 24 April he set out to ride to London, accompanied by his maternal uncle Lord Rivers and a troop of 2000 armed men. In an extremely effective *coup d'état*, Richard, accompanied by the Duke of Buckingham, intercepted the party on the road on 30 April, arrested Lord Rivers, and brought the young King under escort to London, where he was eventually lodged in the Tower. His mother, hearing news of the *coup*, promptly took sanctuary

shortly after his coronation to the Keeper of the Tower, Sir Robert Brackenbury, ordering him to kill the Princes. Brackenbury refused. Richard then sent an enthusiastic protégé, Sir James Tyrell, who persuaded Brackenbury to hand over the keys to the rooms where the Princes were lodged 'for one night'. More describes what followed with shocked relish:

> Sir James Tyrell devised that they should be murdered in their beds. To the execution whereof, he appointed Miles Forest, one of the four that kept them, a fellow fleshed in murder beforetime. To him he joined one John Dighton, his own horsekeeper, a big, broad, square, strong knave. Then, all

Right: this simplified family tree shows how the two factions of York and Lancaster were both descended from Edward III. Richard of Gloucester (above right) claimed that his brother Edward IV had entered into a contract of marriage with one Dame Eleanor Butler prior to marrying the beautiful Elizabeth Woodville when he was 22. This meant that the young Princes were illegitimate, and Richard was therefore perfectly entitled to the crown. Henry Tudor (above) had a very tenuous claim, being descended from John of Gaunt on his mother's side through an illegitimate line. He had strong motives for despatching the Princes

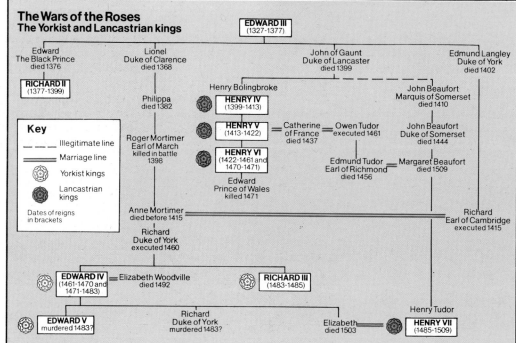

The Wars of the Roses
The Yorkist and Lancastrian kings

EDWARD III (1327-1377)

Edward The Black Prince died 1376

RICHARD II (1377-1399)

Lionel Duke of Clarence died 1368

John of Gaunt Duke of Lancaster died 1399

Edmund Langley Duke of York died 1402

Henry Bolingbroke

HENRY IV (1399-1413)

Philippa died 1382

John Beaufort Marquis of Somerset died 1410

Key
- - - Illegitimate line
═══ Marriage line
⚪ Yorkist kings
⚫ Lancastrian kings
Dates of reigns in brackets

Roger Mortimer Earl of March killed in battle 1398

HENRY V (1413-1422) = Catherine of France died 1437 = Owen Tudor executed 1461

John Beaufort Duke of Somerset died 1444

HENRY VI (1422-1461 and 1470-1471)

Edmund Tudor Earl of Richmond died 1456

Margaret Beaufort died 1509

Edward Prince of Wales killed 1471

Anne Mortimer died before 1415

Richard Earl of Cambridge executed 1415

Richard Duke of York executed 1460

EDWARD IV (1461-1470 and 1471-1483) = Elizabeth Woodville died 1492

RICHARD III (1483-1485)

Henry Tudor

EDWARD V murdered 1483?

Richard Duke of York murdered 1483?

Elizabeth died 1503

HENRY VII (1485-1509)

Previous page: Prince Edward's uncle, Anthony Woodville, Earl Rivers (kneeling), presenting a volume to his brother-in-law Edward IV. Edward IV's Queen, Elizabeth Woodville, sits behind him, and his son Edward, Prince of Wales (at the time about seven years old) stands in front of his parents. The Prince of Wales had his own separate household, composed mainly of his mother's relations, at Ludlow castle, and scarcely knew his father's brother, Richard of Gloucester. When his father died, Richard 'kidnapped' him from the Woodville faction

the others being removed from them, this Miles Forest and John Dighton about midnight (the . . . children lying in their beds) came into the chamber and suddenly lapped them up among the clothes, so bewrapped and entangled them, keeping down by force the featherbed and pillows hard unto their mouths, that within a while, smothered and stifled, their breath failing, they gave up to God their innocent souls into the joys of heaven, leaving to their tormentors their bodies dead in the bed.

To dispose of the bodies, More adds, Tyrell caused the murderers to bury them 'at the foot of the stair, under a great heap of stones'.

It is a vivid account, based, More claimed, on a confession made by Tyrell before his execution for treason in 1502. But More was writing 30 years after the events supposedly took place and, as an upholder of the Tudor state, was intent on blackening the reputation of the man Henry Tudor had deposed.

It was More who claimed that Richard III was 'ill-featured' and 'crook-backed', although no contemporary portrait of him suggests he was either ugly or deformed.

If More's account is suspect, what other evidence is there that the Princes were murdered? *The great chronicle of London* (c. 1500) records that during the time Sir Edmund Shaw was mayor of London (that is, before the end of October 1483) 'the children of King Edward were seen shooting and playing in the garden of the Tower by sundry times.' And an Italian, Dominic Mancini, who was visiting London, wrote in December 1483 in his *Usurpation of Richard III*:

> He and his brother were withdrawn into the inner apartments of the Tower proper, and day by day began to be seen more rarely behind the bars and windows, till at length they ceased to appear altogether. A Strasbourg doctor, the last of his attendants whose services the King [Edward] enjoyed, reported that the young King, like a

a painting by Hans Holbein of Sir Thomas More and his family contained evidence that the Princes survived, and were raised under false names.

Another theory is that the Princes succumbed to illness and died in prison. But if this were so, why was the fact not announced? And what became of the bodies?

If we assume that the boys were indeed murdered, who else is suspect apart from Richard? One likely candidate is the Duke of Buckingham. He had been a prime mover in Richard's *coup* early in the year, and was both ambitious and ruthless. He might have killed the Princes some time before his revolt in the autumn of 1483, either to curry favour with Richard (before the rupture in their relations) or to strengthen the claim of his own candidate for the throne, Henry Tudor. Yet

victim prepared for the sacrifice, sought remission of his sins by daily confession and penance, because he believed that death was facing him. . . . And already there was a suspicion that he had been done away with.

Mancini left England in July 1483, and it is generally assumed that that was the last time the Princes were seen alive. His was the first written account to voice the suspicion that something dire had befallen them – although the fear was widespread at the time of Buckingham's revolt in September.

The case against Richard III rests chiefly on his failure to comment on the Princes' fate. He had both motive and opportunity to kill them; and there is no record that he ever suggested anyone else had done so. It is unlikely that the Princes could have remained alive in the Tower in secret; the Tower was a bustling community inhabited by hundreds of soldiers, servants and residents, and visited daily by merchants and workmen. The fact that the disappearance of the Princes coincided with the first rumours of their deaths is significant.

Could they have been smuggled out of the Tower and then lost to history? In March 1484 Elizabeth Woodville agreed to allow her daughters to leave sanctuary and go to Richard's court; it is almost inconceivable that she would have allowed her daughters to be brought up by their brothers' murderer. Some historians have suggested that she herself left sanctuary at this time and went to live in retirement in the country, possibly with her two sons in her keeping. In March 1983 it was suggested by Mr Jack Leslau that

This scene of the two Princes being parted from their mother by Richard of Gloucester (top, after a 19th-century painting by N. Gosse) probably never took place. After his father's death Edward V rode direct from Ludlow castle (above right) to London, and was met on the road by his uncle Richard, who escorted him the rest of the way and lodged him in the Tower of London (above). Richard later persuaded Elizabeth Woodville to allow her younger son to join his brother in the Tower

it seems unlikely that he could have masterminded the Princes' death in the Tower without Richard's complicity. And if he had killed them, why did Richard not denounce him when he rebelled?

In fact Henry Tudor seems to have had the strongest motive of all to despatch the Princes. While they remained alive, assuming they were legitimate, they invalidated his claim to the throne. And if they were illegitimate, as Richard had proclaimed, then so was their sister, Elizabeth of York, whom Henry subsequently married to strengthen his claim. When he succeeded to the throne, after defeating Richard at Bosworth on 22 August 1485, he kept very quiet about the Princes until he allegedly produced a confession from Sir James Tyrell (who died in 1502); it may be that Tyrell killed them on

Historical mysteries

Henry's account, not Richard's.

Yet another theory has it that, far from murdering the Princes, Tyrell removed them from the Tower at Richard's behest and had them brought up secretly, with their mother, at his house, Gipping Hall, in Suffolk. Only in 1513 did Henry feel it expedient to publish the story of the Princes' murder – after Tyrell and the boys' mother and sister (Henry's Queen) were all dead.

Bones discovered

Speculation about the fate of the young Princes was revived in Charles II's reign when, in 1674, workmen demolishing a staircase in the Tower of London's White Tower (where the Princes had been lodged) found a wooden chest buried some 10 feet (3 metres) deep. It contained the skeletons of two

severe infection of the lower jaw. It was concluded that the remains were probably those of Edward V and his brother Richard of York.

Even though it has not been possible to examine the bones again in the light of today's improved dating techniques, it still seems possible that they are those of the Princes in the Tower. But because the children were below the age of puberty it was not possible to identify the sex of the remains. Nor was it possible to date the bones accurately – they could belong to a much earlier period than the 15th century. Yet it seems a strange coincidence that they should be found buried beneath the stair just as Sir Thomas More described. Richard III continues to stare enigmatically from his portraits, his silence as incriminating as ever.

Left: the two young Princes fearfully await their murderers in the Tower (in a 19th-century painting by Paul Delaroche). However, perhaps they were not murdered, but smuggled out of the Tower and brought up under assumed names: it has been suggested that in the painting by Hans Holbein (below) of Sir Thomas More and his family, the young man leaning on the door (extreme right) is the younger prince, Richard of York, as an adult

children, the taller lying on its back, the other lying across it, face down. Charles had them examined, and concluded that they were the remains of the Princes. He had them re-interred in Westminster Abbey, in a white marble tomb designed by Christopher Wren.

In 1933 permission was given for the bones to be exhumed and examined by a team headed by Professor William Wright, a pathologist, and Dr George Northcroft, a dental surgeon. Although it was found that the skeletons were incomplete (some bones had apparently been lost, and some may have been stolen by souvenir hunters in the 17th century) it was possible to identify them as the remains of two children, one about 10 years of age, the other about 12. It was even possible to deduce from the jaw bones that the elder child had been suffering from a

The Cottingley fairytale

In 1917 two little girls claimed they saw fairies – and, what is more, that they could take pictures of them. These photographs bore none of the hallmarks of forgery, and the controversy they aroused involved eminent figures such as Sir Arthur Conan Doyle. It has taken until the present for the true facts to emerge.

The case of the Cottingley fairies

All of us, when we were children, believed in fairies. These chapters tell the extraordinary story of two little girls who not only believed in fairies, but made friends with them – and even captured them on film

IN THE WEEK BEFORE the end of the First World War, 11-year-old Frances Griffiths sent a letter to a friend in South Africa, where she had lived most of her life. Dated 9 November 1918, it ran:

Dear Joe [Johanna],

I hope you are quite well. I wrote a letter before, only I lost it or it got mislaid. Do you play with Elsie and Nora Biddles? I am learning French, Geometry, Cookery and Algebra at school now. Dad came home from France the other week after being there ten months, and we all think the war will be over in a few days. We are going to get our flags to hang upstairs in our bedroom. I am sending two photos, both of me, one of me in a bathing costume in our back yard, Uncle Arthur took that, while the other is me with some fairies up the beck, Elsie took that one. Rosebud is as

Above: a sharpened version of the first photograph (right), which shows Frances Griffiths behind a group of dancing fairies. Photographic experts examined the negative and the print but could find no trace of trickery

fat as ever and I have made her some new clothes. How are Teddy and dolly?

An ordinary and matter-of-fact letter from a schoolgirl to her friend, one might say, apart from the rather startling reference to fairies. But, as both Frances and her cousin Elsie Wright have since pointed out (they are now grandmothers), they were not particularly surprised by seeing fairies; they seemed a natural part of the rural countryside around the 'beck' (stream) at the bottom of the long garden in Cottingley, near Bradford, in West Yorkshire.

The photograph enclosed by Frances – the famous one, which has since been reproduced thousands of times around the world, albeit in an improved and sharpened version – showed a little girl staring firmly at a camera, since fairies were frequently to be seen, but she herself was photographed not so often! On the back of the snap was scrawled in untidy schoolgirl writing:

> Elsie and I are very friendly with the beck Fairies. It is funny I never used to see them in Africa. It must be too hot for them there.

Elsie had borrowed her father's camera – a Midg quarter-plate – one Saturday afternoon in July 1917 in order to take Frances's photo and cheer her up (for her cousin had fallen in the beck and been scolded for wetting her clothes). They were away for about half an hour and Mr Wright developed the plate later in the afternoon. He was surprised to see strange white shapes coming up, imagining them to be first birds and then sandwich papers left lying around; in vain Elsie behind him in the dark-room said they were fairies.

In August it was Frances who had the camera, when she and Elsie scaled the sides of the beck and went up to the old oaks. There she took a photograph of Elsie with a gnome. The print was under-exposed and unclear, as might be expected when taken by a young lady rising 10 years old. The plate was again developed by Elsie's father, Arthur, who suspected that the girls had been playing tricks and refused to lend his camera to them any more.

Parents turn sleuth

Both Arthur and his wife, Polly, searched the girls' bedroom and waste-paper basket for any scraps of pictures or cut-outs, and also went down to the beck in search of evidence of fakery. They found nothing, and the girls stuck to their story – that they had seen fairies and photographed them. Prints of the pictures were circulated among friends and neighbours, but then interest in the odd affair gradually petered out.

The matter first became public in the summer of 1919 when Polly Wright went to a meeting at the Theosophical Society in Bradford. She was interested in the occult, having had some experiences of astral projection and memories of past lives herself. The lecture that night was on 'fairy life', and Polly mentioned to the person sitting next to her that fairy prints had been taken by her daughter and niece. The result of this conversation was that two 'rough prints' (as they were later called) came to the notice of Theosophists at the Harrogate conference in the autumn, and thence to a leading Theosophist, Edward Gardner, by early 1920.

Mr Gardner was a precise, particular man. Even a look at his photograph conveys this precision, which is also suggested by the neat copies he kept of his letters. Gardner's immediate impulse after seeing the fairy pictures was to clarify the prints and, in a letter to a photographic expert, Fred Barlow, he describes the instructions he gave to his assistants:

> Then I told them to make new negatives (from the positives of the originals) and do the very best with them

Above: Sir Arthur Conan Doyle, who used sharpened prints of the first two Cottingley photographs to illustrate his article on fairies, which was published in the Christmas 1920 issue of the *Strand Magazine*

Above: Elsie Wright and her cousin Frances (above right). The girls were close companions and spent hours playing together near the beck where the fairy photographs were taken

Below: Polly Wright, Elsie's mother, began to take the photographs seriously after she had attended a Theosophical Society lecture on 'fairy life'

short of altering anything mechanically. The result was that they turned out two first class negatives which . . . are the same in every respect as the originals except that they are sharp cut and clear and far finer for printing purposes . . .

It seems incredible to us today that he could be so naïve, not anticipating the inevitable questions from critics as to shutter speed, figure definition, the suspicious resemblance of the fairies' clothes and hairstyles to the latest fashions . . . But Gardner only wanted the clearest pictures – as a Theosophist he had been studying fairy lore for years and had heard many accounts of fairy sightings, so the possible reactions of sceptics never entered his head.

By a striking coincidence, Sir Arthur Conan Doyle (creator of Sherlock Holmes and fanatical Spiritualist) had been commissioned by the *Strand Magazine* to write an article on fairies for their Christmas issue, to be published at the end of November 1920. He was preparing this in June when he heard of the two fairy prints in circulation and eventually made contact with Gardner and borrowed copies.

From the beginning, contrary to the impression the public later gained of him, Conan Doyle was on his guard. He showed the prints to Sir Oliver Lodge, a pioneer psychical researcher, who thought them fakes – perhaps involving a troupe of dancers masquerading as fairies. One fairy authority told him that the hairstyles of the sprites were too 'Parisienne' for his liking. Lodge also passed them on to a clairvoyant for psychometric impressions – Gardner's photoprinter, Mr Snelling (who had prepared the second batch of prints from the originals) was described accurately.

What seems rather mysterious to us today is that no one was over-anxious to examine the original photographs, but seemed content to analyse prints. Snelling (of whom it had been said 'What Snelling doesn't know about faked photography isn't worth knowing') said in his first report to Gardner on the

Cottingley fairies

Above: a sharpened print of 'Elsie and the gnome', the second fairy photograph, which was taken by Frances in August 1917. The original was examined by experts in the same way as the first – again no evidence of fakery could be found

Below: Arthur Wright, Elsie's father, whose camera – a Midg quarter-plate – was used to take the photographs

'rough' print that he could detect movement in all the fairy figures. Kodak, by contrast, stated that an experienced photographer may have been involved – which suggests that the prints that they had been examining may have been sharpened ones.

A possible explanation is that Conan Doyle and Gardner may have wished to avoid any mention of improving the originals at that stage; perhaps they did not consider the matter important. What was vital to them was the propagation of Theosophical and Spiritualist doctrines. As far as they were concerned, clear prints showing recognisable fairies and a gnome would provide the long-sought firm evidence for 'dwellers at the border' (as Conan Doyle was later to term nature spirits).

Conan Doyle despatched his 'Watson' – in this real-life case, Gardner – to Cottingley in July. Gardner reported that the whole Wright family seemed honest and totally respectable. Conan Doyle and Gardner decided that if further fairy photographs were taken then the matter would be put firmly beyond question. Gardner journeyed north in August with cameras and 20 photographic plates to leave with Elsie and Frances hoping to persuade them to take more photographs. Only in this way, he felt, could it be proved that the fairies were genuine.

Meanwhile, the *Strand* article was completed, featuring the two sharpened prints, and Conan Doyle sailed for Australia and a lecture tour to spread the gospel of Spiritualism. He left his colleagues to face the public reactions to the fairy business.

Newspaper sensation

That issue of the *Strand* sold out within days of publication at the end of November. Reaction was vigorous – especially from critics. The leading voice among them was that of one Major Hall-Edwards, a radium expert. He declared:

> On the evidence I have no hesitation in saying that these photographs could have been 'faked'. I criticise the attitude of those who declared there is something supernatural in the circumstances attending to the taking of these pictures because, as a medical man, I believe that the inculcation of such absurd ideas into the minds of children will result in later life in manifestations and nervous disorder and mental disturbances . . .

Newspaper comments were varied. On 5 January 1921 *Truth* declared: 'For the true explanation of these fairy photographs what is wanted is not a knowledge of occult phenomena but a knowledge of children.' On the other hand the *South Wales Argus* of 27 November 1920 took a more whimsical and tolerant view: 'The day we kill our Santa Claus with our statistics we shall have plunged a glorious world into deepest darkness'. The Day's Thought underneath was a Welsh proverb: ''Tis true as the fairy tales told in books.' *City News*, on 29 January, said straightforwardly: 'It seems at this point that we must either believe in the almost incredible mystery of the fairy or in the almost incredible wonders of faked photographs.'

The *Westminster Gazette* broke the aliases used by Conan Doyle to protect Frances and Elsie – and a reporter went north. However, nothing sensational, or even new, was added to the story by his investigation. He found out that Elsie had borrowed her father's camera to take the first picture, and that Frances had taken a picture of Elsie and a gnome. In fact there was nothing he could add to the facts listed by Conan Doyle in his article 'Fairies photographed – an epoch-making event'. The reporter considered Polly and Arthur Wright to be honest enough folk – and he returned a verdict of 'unexplained' to his paper in London.

The case might well have faded away with the coming of spring in 1921, had not the unexpected happened: Elsie and Frances took three more fairy photographs.

The reappearance of the fairies

The Cottingley 'fairy' pictures provoked heated argument. To Sir Arthur Conan Doyle they were the long-awaited proof of the existence of spirits – but to many people they were just clever fakes. Reactions to the second set of fairy photographs taken in the 1920s were equally varied

IN THE SCHOOL HOLIDAYS of August 1920, Frances Griffiths was asked to come by train to Cottingley from Scarborough, where she had gone to live with her mother and father after the First World War. Aunt Polly had written to say that Edward Gardner would be travelling up from London, with new cameras, so that the cousins might have further opportunities of taking fairy photographs to add to the two they took in 1917.

Frances was a month away from her 14th birthday and had won a scholarship to go to grammar school, being both industrious and intelligent. Elsie, by contrast, had thankfully left school at the age of 13.

Edward Gardner came from London to Bradford by train and took the tram out to Cottingley Bar, three miles (5 kilometres) away. He had brought with him two cameras and two dozen secretly marked photographic plates. He described the briefing of the girls thus in his book *Fairies: a book of real fairies* published in 1945:

> I went off, too, to Cottingley again, taking the two cameras and plates from London, and met the family and explained to the two girls the simple working of the cameras, giving one each to keep. The cameras were loaded, and my final advice was that they need go up to the glen only on fine days as they had been accustomed to do before and tice the fairies, as they called their way of attracting them, and see what they could get. I suggested only the most obvious and easy precautions about lighting and distance, for I knew it was essential they should feel free and unhampered and have no burden of responsibility. If nothing came of it all, I told them, they were not to mind a bit.

Only two more fairies

One might imagine the scene in the parlour of the Wright household. Beautiful Polly, listening intently, gangly 19-year-old Elsie with her auburn gold hair and gentle blue eyes, and sharp Frances, her energies suppressed for the occasion. ('Pity anyone with corns who is around when Frances gets excited,' Polly had written wryly on one occasion.) And solemn Edward Gardner, bearded and perhaps sporting a bow tie as usual, eager to engender some sort of scientific atmosphere but, in his heart, really not hoping for very much, in spite of the new cameras and carefully marked plates. So he returned to London, hoping for fine weather at least.

Alas, it rained for two weeks. They had little opportunity of adding anything to fairy history, and the first record of anything happening is in a letter to Gardner from

Previous page: a fairy offering flowers to Elsie, 1920. She said the flowers were tiny harebells, and that the colours of the fairy's dress were pastel shades of mauve and yellow. This particular Cottingley photograph prompted widespread criticism: the fairy has a suspiciously contemporary appearance, with its bobbed hair and fashionable dress

Above: Frances and the leaping fairy, taken by Elsie from a distance of about 3 feet (1 metre). The fairy was said to be leaping, not flying, as it appears to be. It bounded up in the air four times before Elsie took the picture. The fifth leap was so vigorous that Frances thought it was jumping at her face and flung her head back; the movement can be seen in the print

Polly, which is truly astounding in its modesty. She wrote about the events of Thursday, 19 August 1920:

The morning was dull and misty so they did not take any photos until after dinner when the mist had cleared away and it was sunny. I went to my sister's for tea and left them to it. When I got back they had only managed two with fairies, I was disappointed.

and about those of two days after:

They went up again on Saturday afternoon and took several photos but there was only one with anything on and it's a queer one, we can't make it out. Elsie put the plates in this time and Arthur developed them next day.

and what must rank as one of the most charming postscripts ever: 'P.S. She did not take one flying after all.'

So the plates were returned to London. Elsie remembers the care with which they were packed in cotton wool by her father, who was puzzled – about the whole affair. He never understood it until the end of his days (he died in 1926) and Conan Doyle went down in his estimation. Before the great man had shown an interest in fairies, Arthur held him in high regard; afterwards he found it hard to believe that so intelligent a man could be bamboozled 'by our Elsie, and her at the bottom of the class!' But whereas Arthur could not bring himself to believe in fairies, Polly, as the tone of her letter suggests, supported her daughter and acknowledged the existence of nature spirits.

Gardner was elated to receive the secretly marked plates that bore such intriguing fairy photographs, and telegrams were sent off to Conan Doyle who was on his Australian lecture tour, currently in Melbourne. Conan Doyle wrote back:

My heart was gladdened when out here in far Australia I had your note and the

brought the benefits of public baths to the slum children of Bradford), waxed fulsome about the Cottingley incidents: 'How wonderful that to these dear children such a wonderful gift has been vouchsafed.'

Another eminent personality of the day, the novelist Henry de Vere Stacpoole, decided to take the fairy photographs – and the girls – at face value. He accepted intuitively that both girls and pictures were genuine. In a letter to Gardner he said:

> Look at Alice's face. Look at Iris's face. There is an extraordinary thing called TRUTH which has 10 million faces and forms – it is God's currency and the cleverest coiner or forger can't imitate it . . .

(The aliases 'Alice' and 'Iris' first used by Conan Doyle to protect the anonymity of the girls were deliberately preserved by Stacpoole.)

'Fed up with fairies!'
The fifth, and last, fairy photograph is often believed to be the most striking. Nobody has ever been able to give a satisfactory explanation as to what seems to be happening in the picture. However, Conan Doyle, in his *The coming of the fairies* advances a detailed, if somewhat over-elaborate, view of the pictured proceedings:

> Seated on the upper left hand edge with wing well displayed is an undraped fairy apparently considering whether it is time to get up. An earlier riser of more mature age is seen on the right possessing abundant hair and wonderful wings. Her slightly denser body can be glimpsed within her fairy dress.

This piece of whimsy from the creator of that most unsentimental and coldly logical character in English fiction – Sherlock Holmes – provided the 'Conan Doyle's going soft' school with formidable ammunition. It is perhaps unfortunate that his ardent interest in Spiritualism should coincide with his

three wonderful pictures which are confirmatory of our published results. When our fairies are admitted other psychic phenomena will find a more ready acceptance . . . we have had continued messages at seances for some time that a visible sign was coming through . . .

Both Conan Doyle and Edward Gardner were primarily interested in spreading their own ideas of the infinite to what they considered to be a far from receptive public. Conan Doyle saw the Cottingley fairies incident as (perhaps literally) a gift from the gods, paving the way for more profound truths that may gradually become acceptable to a materialistic world. He used the last three photographs to illustrate a second article in the *Strand Magazine* in 1921. It described other accounts of alleged fairy sightings and served as the foundation for his later book entitled *The coming of the fairies*, published in 1922.

Reactions to the new fairy photographs were, as before, varied. The most common criticism was that the fairies looked suspiciously like the traditional fairies of nursery tales and that they had very fashionable hairstyles. It was also pointed out that the pictures were particularly sharply defined, as if some improvement had been made by an expert photographer.

However, some public figures were sympathetic – sometimes embarrassingly so. Margaret McMillan, the educational and social reformer (who, among other reforms,

Above: the 'fairy bower' long believed by some fairylorists to exist, but, as Conan Doyle exclaimed, 'Never before, or other where [*sic*], has a fairy's bower been photographed!' The cocoon-like structure is said to be used by fairies to bathe in after long spells of dull and misty weather

Below: Cottingley as it was in the 1920s

Cottingley fairies

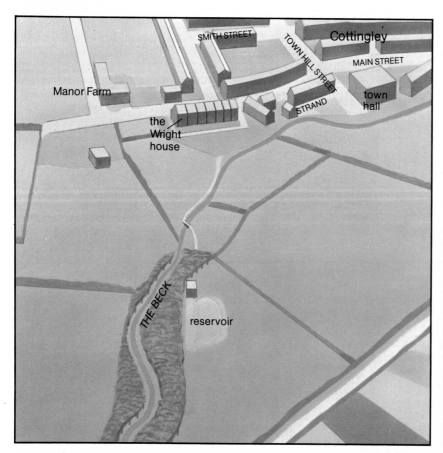

later years, especially in an age when anyone in his or her sixties was very much considered 'past their best'. His championship of the Cottingley fairies did little to dispel the growing image of him as a gullible old man. However, he was by no means the only believer in elemental spirits.

As can be seen from a map of Cottingley, it is virtually on the outskirts of populous Bradford, and is not, as many imagine, an isolated village. There is a reservoir and an old water bridge over the 'beck' – key markers for the fairy photographs. Traditionally nature spirits inhabit wooded and watery places and there are many stories of nature spirits being observed in such secluded spots. Also, the oak, ash and thorn are traditionally associated with fairies and these varieties of tree are found around the beck.

In August 1921, a last expedition was made to Cottingley – this time the clairvoyant Geoffrey Hodson was brought along to verify any fairy sightings. (The feeling being that if anyone, apart from the girls, could see the fairies, Hodson could.) Alas, the fairies refused to be photographed – although they were seen both by Hodson and by Elsie.

But by then both Elsie and Frances were tired of the whole fairy business. Many years later, Elsie looked at a photograph of herself and Frances taken with Hodson and said: 'Look at that – fed up with fairies!' Both Elsie and Frances have since agreed that they humoured Hodson to a sometimes ludicrous extent. This naïve admission played right into the hands of their critics. Quite apart

from 'playing Mr Hodson along' there were still the allegations of faking the whole fairy business in the first place and when more fairy photographs were not forthcoming, the 'Cottingley incident' seemed all set to be relegated to the dusty gallery of 'famous fakes'. Yet the episode is not closed. . . .

Above left: a map of the Cottingley area, showing the 'beck' where Elsie and Frances claimed to have photographed the fairies

Above: Geoffrey Hodson, a clairvoyant recommended by Sir Arthur Conan Doyle, pictured here with Elsie, aged 20, and Frances, 14, in 1921. He had personal experience of fairies and gnomes and was to publish his *Fairies at work and play* in 1922

Left: Bernard Partridge's famous caricature of the aging Conan Doyle. Though still chained by public opinion to his great fictional character Sherlock Holmes, he is seen with his head in the clouds of Spiritualism

The Cottingley fairies revisited

Ever since two young girls took 'fairy photographs' in the 1920s controversy has raged over them. Even into the 1970's, Elsie and Frances were reaffirming the authenticity of their pictures

THE FIRST PHOTOGRAPH of fairies taken by Elsie Wright of Cottingley, near Bradford, in 1917 has threatened to become overexposed in the occult-conscious late 20th century, for the photograph of the sprites pictured in front of a pleasant-faced Frances has been reproduced so often that it is in danger of becoming a sort of visual cliché. It is especially irritating to those who find the whole fairy business distasteful, even fraudulent; they object, shrilly at times, to the strangely artificial look of the fairy dancers – although they are less vocal on the other four photographs that were subsequently taken. The believers, as always, believe, and speak of 'more things in Heaven and Earth . . .'

The position of critics on the one hand and champions on the other may be summed up thus:

The 'prosecution' points out that Elsie painted and drew well, that she had always seemed immersed in drawing fairies, had been fascinated by the art of photography and had worked at a photographer's, and seemed suspiciously evasive in the 1971 BBC-TV *Nationwide* interview. Both Elsie and her cousin Frances admit to a strong sense of humour; both admit to having deceived the medium Geoffrey Hodson during the 1921 investigation (in terms of giving overgenerous endorsements to his descriptions of teeming fairy life in and around the beck). No third party was ever present when the five photographs were taken. The girls spent hours together playing down at the beck, which was well away from the house and concealed, by 40-foot (12-metre) banks, from public view. They shared a fair-sized attic bedroom in which they could have hatched their plots. In 1978 the 'Amazing Randi' (a professional American stage illusionist and self-appointed debunker of all paranormal phenomena) and a team from *New Scientist* subjected the photographs to 'enhancement' – a process used to bring out greater detail from Moon photographs – and thought they could see strings attached to some figures. Randi also pointed out that the figures in the first photograph bore a resemblance to those in an illustration in *Princess Mary's gift book*, published in 1914.

The 'defence' asserts that Elsie's job at the photographer's lasted only six months and amounted to running errands and cleaning up prints. She drew fairies because she saw

Above: the young Elsie Wright's watercolour *Fairies flying over a cottage*. She often painted fairies, because, she said, she often saw them

Left: an illustration from *Princess Mary's gift book*, which was very popular in 1914. These fairies bear some resemblance to those allegedly seen and photographed at Cottingley

Most people do not believe in fairies and therefore, to them, any alleged fairy photographs must be fakes. To sceptics there is no question about it: the Cottingley fairies were cut out of a children's book and superimposed, very cleverly (for no one has conclusively proved that they were faked), on photographs of the cousins, Elsie and Frances.

There was no shortage of material had they wanted to search for fairy 'models'. Fairies were common enough in children's books around the turn of the century. Most girls of their age, living at that time, could have described a fairy, for most illustrations reflected a similar, traditional fairy image.

In fact, Elsie and Frances's fairies were, if anything, slightly more fashion-conscious than, say, those pictured in the popular *Princess Mary's gift book* of 1914. The Cottingley fairies had up-to-the-minute bobbed hair and beaded Charleston dresses (although Elsie's gnome remained traditionally grotesque).

When psychical researcher E.L. Gardner visited Cottingley in the 1920s

Several critics pointed out that the Cottingley fairies looked suspiciously similar to those featured in the advertisement for Price's night lights (above right). One sceptic, William Marriott, produced this deliberate fake (above left) by superimposing the 'night light' fairies on a picture of Sir Arthur Conan Doyle

Some fairies of the era:
Above: a ring of fairies from Florence Harrison's *In the fairy ring* (1910)

Above right: a girl with fairies, from *Princess Mary's gift book* (1914)

Left: fairies dancing, by E. Gertrude Thomson from William Allingham's *The fairies* (1886)

he claimed mediumistic powers for both girls, but especially for Frances. He believed that the elemental spirits – fairies – used loosely-knit ectoplasm emanating from the girls with which to form visible bodies, visible, that is, only to the girls and the eye of the camera. The exact form they took was, he hazarded, 'chosen' by the subconscious minds of the girls, hence the strange mixture of traditional and contemporary. But, for whatever reason, both girls stopped seeing fairies after 1921.

them often and, anyway, her drawings were no better than might be expected from a fairly talented 16-year-old. As for the *Gift book* illustrations – fairies dancing around are bound to resemble each other and the ones in the Christmas 1914 publication lack wings. The string in the report in *New Scientist* of 3 August 1978 may be printing streaks, and even real figures would not stay absolutely motionless in the breeze that usually blew gently down the beck; and where might they be hung from? And what variety of invisible 'string' was used at the time? By the time Hodson came they were bored and nodded confirmation for the sake of peace and quiet. Elsie prevaricated because she wanted the matter to be forgotten. They did not have the motivation, materials, time, privacy, or expertise to fake the photographs. And, most significantly, they have always maintained they saw fairies and photographed them.

Newspapers, magazines and television companies have become increasingly interested in Elsie and Frances since Peter Chambers of the *Daily Express* discovered where Elsie lived in 1966. He quotes Elsie as saying that the fairies might have been 'figments of

Below: *Fairies by a stream*, a watercolour by Elsie Wright. She and her cousin were obsessed with fairies when they were young and this obsession is used by both the 'defence' and the 'prosecution' to explain the photographs. The sceptics use it to explain the motivation behind the 'fakes' and the believers claim that the obsession arose quite naturally because the girls saw fairies all the time

my imagination'. She may have made this rather bald statement simply to rid herself of unwelcome publicity. On the other hand she may have implied that she had successfully photographed these 'figments' of her 'imagination'. Significantly, in the years since the Cottingley fairies were photographed, research into 'thoughtography' (notably Dr Jule Eisenbud's work with Ted Serios in the United States) and experiments in Japan have indicated that thought-forms may indeed be photographed.

Elsie and Frances interrogated

For five years Elsie managed to avoid publicity; then, in 1971, BBC-TV's *Nationwide* programme took up the case. For 10 days she was interrogated, taken back to Cottingley and subjected to this sort of thing:

(The interviewer points out that, since the original fairy investigator, E. L. Gardner, died the year before, Elsie might wish to be more explicit.)

Elsie: I didn't want to upset Mr Gardner . . . I don't mind talking now . . .

(It is then suggested that Elsie's father had a hand in matters.)

Elsie: I would swear on the Bible father didn't know what was going on.

Interviewer: Could you equally swear on the Bible you didn't play any tricks?

Elsie (after a pause): I took the photographs . . . I took two of them . . . no, three . . . Frances took two . . .

Interviewer: Are they trick photographs? Could you swear on the Bible about that?

Elsie (after a pause): I'd rather leave that open if you don't mind . . . but my father had nothing to do with it I can promise you that . . .

Interviewer: Have you had your fun with the world for 50 years? Have you been kidding us for 10 days?

(Elsie laughs.)

Elsie (gently): I think we'll close on that if you don't mind.

More objective was Austin Mitchell's interview for Yorkshire Television in September 1976. On the spot where the photographs had allegedly been taken, the following dialogue took place:

Mitchell: A rational person doesn't see fairies. If people say they see fairies, then one's bound to be critical.

Frances: Yes.

Mitchell: Now, if you say you saw them, at the time the photograph was taken, that means that if there's a confidence trick, then you're both part of it.

Frances: Yes – that's fair enough – yes.

Mitchell: So are you?

Frances: No.

Elsie: No.

Frances: Of course not.

Mitchell: Did you, in any way, fabricate those photographs?

Frances: Of course not. You tell us how she could do it – remember she was 16 and I was

10. Now then, as a child of 10, can you go through life and keep a secret?

The Yorkshire Television team, however, believed the 'cardboard cutout' theory. Austin Mitchell duly appeared on the screen, personable as ever, with a row of fairy figures before him set against a background of greenery. He flicked them around a little (perhaps to reassure viewers that elementals had not invaded the prosaic surroundings of Kirkstall Road, Leeds).

'Simple cardboard cutouts,' he commented on the live magazine programme. 'Done by our photographic department and mounted on wire frames. They discovered that you really need wire to make them stand up – paper figures droop, of course. That's how it could have been done.'

But quite apart from the pronouncements of critics and champions, tapes, letters and newspaper cuttings are now available for anyone who would delve deeper into the fairy photographs. Understandably, Elsie and Frances would rather people kept away and respected their privacy after the passage of so many years.

The critics – Lewis of *Nationwide*, Austin Mitchell of Yorkshire TV, Randi, and Stewart Sanderson and Katherine Briggs of the Folklore Society – all these are fair-minded individuals interested in balancing probability on the available evidence. This extremely delicate balance did seem to have shifted in favour of the ladies' honesty during

Above: a rare 'cup and ring' stone, found in Cottingley Glen, close to the beck. Such strangely marked stones are traditionally associated with supernatural activities and have often been linked with fairy sightings

the 1970s but, obviously, many points could still be elucidated by further research.

Austin Mitchell said 'a rational person doesn't see fairies', and there are some sociologists who would say that rationality might be socially constructed. One's 'rationality' mostly depends on one's personal experiences and one's reading. There are, believe it or not, hundreds of instances of people claiming to have seen fairies. A perusal of Conan Doyle's book *The coming of the fairies*, or *Visions or beliefs* by Lady Gregory and the poet W. B. Yeats, should prove that more than a handful of such claims have been made.

The author has now met seven people who claim to have seen nature spirits. One of them, an ex-wrestler of powerful build – an unlikely figure to consort with sprites – is adamant in his assertions. It is interesting to note how many are prepared to listen to him with an unusual degree of tolerance.

It is usually possible to demolish individual accounts; taken collectively, however, some patterns begin to emerge. William Riley, the Yorkshire author, puts the five fairy pictures into perhaps the most relevant context: 'I have many times come across several people who have seen pixies at certain favoured spots in Upper Airedale and Wharfedale.'

Once upon a time...

The Cottingley photographs have, since their first publication, been regarded by many as proof that fairies exist. But they have recently been the subject of new analysis that seems to prove they cannot be genuine

ONE DAY IN JULY 1917, 16-year-old Elsie Wright borrowed her father's camera and took a picture of her 10-year-old cousin Frances Griffiths playing by the river close to their home in Cottingley, Yorkshire, England. They gave the film to Elsie's father to develop – and he was astonished to find that Frances's figure was surrounded by dancing fairies.

That, at least, is the beginning of the story of the remarkable Cottingley fairy photographs, five of them in all, that have caused so much excitement as proof of the existence of fairies, as we have seen. But the truth is not so romantic. For no fairies were really photographed in Cottingley – the village was merely the site of a childish prank that grew

Above: an illustration by Claude Shepperson for Alfred Noyes's poem *A spell for a fairy*, which appeared in *Princess Mary's gift book*, published in 1915. The fairies bear a remarkable similarity to those of the famous Cottingley photographs – and it is known that Frances Griffiths, one of the two girls who allegedly photographed the fairies, possessed a copy of the book

into an enormous deception.

The two young girls insisted that they had seen and photographed fairies, that much is certain. The pictures were striking enough – indeed remarkable, if they were genuine. Real fairies in a real wood, many people insisted.

It was Sir Arthur Conan Doyle, the famous creator of Sherlock Holmes, who introduced these fairy photographs to the world, describing them as 'the most astounding photographs ever published', and assuming that they were indeed pictures of *real* fairies. His article, published in the *Strand Magazine* of November 1920, was something of a bombshell, and one reader complained that for a few weeks 'no one talked of anything but fairies.' Conan Doyle's opinions were presented against the better judgement of many experienced psychical researchers, who realised that the evidence for the pictures' authenticity had not been sufficiently explored. Many researchers were, from the beginning, convinced that the pictures were far from genuine, and it was generally agreed among experts that the two girls who produced them had simply made copies of fairy drawings on stiff card or paper, had posed with these and photographed them. The only problem was that no drawing that could reasonably be supposed to be the original of the fairies that appeared in the girls' photographs had been found. At the same time, the girls themselves continued to insist that the fairies were genuine.

Not quite innocent?

The fairies do indeed give the marked impression of being cut-outs. And Elsie was actually a proficient artist for her age, and was quite capable of making such drawings. She had also worked for a few months as an assistant in a photographer's shop in Bradford, and so it is clear that she was not quite the innocent young thing Conan Doyle had in mind when he published his sensational article.

In particular, Elsie's father suspected trickery. Elsie's mother, however, was herself interested in the Theosophy of Russian mystic Madame Blavatsky, and was therefore probably aware of the Theosophical teaching that held that thought forms could be materialised so that clairvoyants were able to perceive them. Certain members of the Theosophical Society had, in the previous decade, actually published reproductions of painted and drawn thought forms invisible to ordinary people – and these, alongside the ever-popular psychic photography were sufficient to persuade many people that it was possible that the girls had indeed seen and photographed the fairies.

In the face of much cross-questioning, in the months after the publication of the photographs, and in later years during interviews given to newspaper and television reporters, Frances and Elsie insisted that the pictures were not hoaxes – although some of the statements they made were curiously ambiguous. An interview conducted as late as 1975 found them insisting on their original story. However, there is certainly a double meaning in Elsie's statement, recorded in a BBC interview: 'I've told you that they're photographs of figments of our imagination and that's what I'm sticking to.'

The girls never took a photograph in the presence of a third party. A further series of picture-making experiments was conducted during the middle of August 1920, but once again these were made by the two cousins, with no one else present. The whole validity of the series of fairy pictures, therefore, hangs upon the words of the girls themselves. Despite this fact, however, the story of the

Below: Frances Griffiths and a group of dancing fairies in the first of the Cottingley photographs. Comparison to a vignette illustration of *A spell for a fairy* (bottom) reveals similarities: the left-hand figures are almost identical, whereas the two right-hand figures have merely been transposed – and the large fairy wings clearly draw their inspiration from the colour illustration of the same poem that also appears in the book

The truth is that, at the time at which Doyle was introduced to these pictures, he was already in the process of writing a book about fairies. Clearly, then, Doyle already had a strong interest in fairies, and he went on to make use of all the Cottingley pictures in his next publication, *The coming of the fairies*, from which he made a large amount of money. It must be remembered, too, that – as Leon Berger has pointed out in a letter to the magazine *The Unexplained* – he had another, more compelling, reason for wishing to prove that the fairies were real. Doyle's father, who spent most of his life in mental asylums, saw fairies regularly – and Doyle may have felt that, by establishing the physical existence of fairies, he might at the same time be able to prove his father's sanity.

Whatever the reason, Doyle clearly had a vested interest in proclaiming the pictures genuine. It may well be that the girls had told little white lies to back up their initial fantasy – what children would not? – but it was Doyle who pushed these pictures into what became a public hoax. As a result of Doyle's publication, the two young girls found themselves entrenched in a position of dishonesty from which retreat was quite impossible.

The final proof

It was clear to many researchers that the pictures must be cut-outs. But the only real hope of *proving* this – in the face of what Elsie and Frances said – was to find the original pictures that the girls had copied. These were discovered in August 1977 by this author, who was then working on 19th-century fairy illustrations.

The drawings were illustrations for a poem by Alfred Noyes, *A spell for a fairy*, in which the poet instructs the reader how to make fairies visible. The charming illustrations were drawn by Claude Shepperson for *Princess Mary's gift book*, which was sold in vast numbers as part of a money-raising

Cottingley fairies was only partly created by Elsie and Frances. It was much more the creation of the media.

Perhaps the two girls *did* indulge in making 'figments of the imagination'. Indeed, as we shall shortly see, there may now be no doubt that the fairies were faked. But their prank or joke turned into a sort of monster for them, and the snapping of that camera shutter in 1917 was for them rather like the opening of Pandora's box. Shortly an enormous weight of publicity was brought to bear upon these photographs, supported by the fluent pen of Conan Doyle – who in fact knew nothing at all about psychic photography, and had his own reasons for wanting to believe that fairies were real.

scheme, the 'Work for women' fund, during the First World War.

The final vignette illustration to this poem is, without doubt, the original picture from which the fairies of the first Cottingley picture were constructed. The remarkable thing is that the girl who copied this (presumably Elsie, as she was the older and more artistically talented of the two) actually made no significant change to the individual figures of the fairies in the Shepperson drawing – they merely appear in the photograph in a different order. Elsie's drawing is clumsier, and she added butterfly wings to the figure.

An uncanny resemblance

Assuming the girls did indeed copy or trace the Shepperson vignette, they showed very little imagination. The one difference is that the Cottingley fairies have large wings, while those in the vignette have only diminutive wings. However, the wings in the colour plate that also accompanies the poem were evidently the model for the cut-out fairies. It is clear that the girls used the wings of the fairies of the colour plate in order to make their own creatures more fairylike. The wing structures in the colour plate and the vignette

Right: an illustration by Arthur Rackham for *A midsummer night's dream*, in an edition that appeared in 1908. Rackham was among those who, on the first appearance of the Cottingley photographs, suspected that the fairies might not be genuine. He believed, however, that they were derived from his own popular fairy drawings – whereas, in fact, they were direct copies of book illustrations by Claude Shepperson

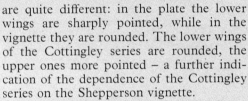

Below: an illustration by Charles Altramont Doyle – Sir Arthur Conan Doyle's father – from the diary he kept while incarcerated in various lunatic asylums. Charles Doyle believed he saw fairies – and it may have been the desire to prove his father's sanity that prompted Sir Arthur's interest in fairies, and his championship of the Cottingley pictures

THE BIRD IS MIMICING THE ELF.

are quite different: in the plate the lower wings are sharply pointed, while in the vignette they are rounded. The lower wings of the Cottingley series are rounded, the upper ones more pointed – a further indication of the dependence of the Cottingley series on the Shepperson vignette.

There may be no doubt that the photographs were made in a spirit of fun, and were probably well-intended 'genial' forgeries. It was a childish lark that got out of hand. The resemblance between vignette and photograph is far too obvious for anyone to suppose that the girls intended serious deception. It was inevitable that someone would at a future time observe the marked similarity between the two, and realise that the photographs were not genuine. This, of course, makes the later insistence of Elsie and Frances on the truth of their story all the more difficult to understand. They were, in a sense, victims of the media, and especially of the influence of Conan Doyle who – albeit unwittingly – through his own personal interests turned a clever hoax into a life-long fraud. It is no wonder that, in a television interview in 1975, Elsie and Frances admitted that the photographs had caused them no end of trouble.

Cottingley: at last the truth

Were there really fairies in the woods at Cottingley? And did two children succeed in photographing them? After over 60 years, Elsie and Frances revealed the truth about the famous Cottingley pictures

THE COTTINGLEY FAIRY photographs made a journalistic sensation when they first appeared, in an article in the *Strand Magazine*, towards the end of 1919. And ever since they have been regarded as perhaps the most convincing evidence ever presented for the existence of fairies and the spirit world. But, in late 1981 and mid 1982 respectively, Frances Way (née Griffiths) and Elsie Hill (née Wright), who took the photographs – now, of course, old ladies – admitted that the first four pictures were fakes. Speaking of the first photograph in particular, Frances has told the present author on more than one occasion: 'My heart always sinks when I look at it. When I think of how it's gone all round the world – I don't see how people could believe they're real fairies. I could see the backs of them and the hatpins when the photo was being taken.'

How was the hoax set up? It started, as both ladies agree, with the best of intentions. Frances, she says, was able to perceive many forms of fairy life at the beck at the bottom of the garden of the Wright household and was, understandably, continually drawn back to the stream. Occasionally she fell in and wet her clothes, and was severely told off.

Elsie was much moved by the tears of her cousin, and sympathised with her when she blurted out to the adults that the reason why

The Cottingley fairy photographs were, their originators now admit, copied from illustrations in *Princess Mary's gift book*. Their champion, Conan Doyle, should have realised this – his story 'Bimbashi Joyce' (below) appeared in the same book

BIMBASHI JOYCE

BY A. CONAN DOYLE

Painting and Drawings by R. TALBOT KELL[

It was in the days when the tide of M which had swept in such a flood i Great Lakes and Darfur to the co Egypt, had at last come to its full, i begun, as some hoped, to show si; turn. At its outset it had been teri had engulfed Hicks's army, swept ovei and Khartoum, rolled behind the Briti as they retired down the river, and finally c spray of raiding parties as far north as .

she went so often to the bottom of the garden was because there were fairies to be seen there. Although Elsie lacked Frances's keen perception of fairy life, she was sensitive to atmosphere and had a fine appreciation of the mysticism of nature.

Partly to take Frances's mind off her troubles, and partly to play a prank on grown-ups who sneered at the idea that fairies could be seen, but who cheerfully perpetuated the myth of Santa Claus, they conspired to produce fairy figures that they could photograph convincingly. Frances had a copy of *Princess Mary's gift book*, and the girls used a series of illustrations by Arthur Shepperson as a model from which Elsie –

who had received some art training from the college in nearby Bradford – constructed the lively fairy figures. They carefully cut the figures out using sharp tailor's scissors borrowed from Frances's mother, who worked as a tailoress in Bradford; they secured them to a bank of earth using hatpins. The girls took the famous photographs, dropped the cut-out figures into the swirling brook, and went home. How they gave the film to Mr Wright, and his surprise at seeing the fairy figures develop on the prints, is history.

The attitude of Elsie and Frances to the whole question of the fairy photographs is a typical Yorkshire one – to tell a tall story with a deadpan delivery and let those who will believe it do so. Indeed, Elsie has often said as much: 'I would rather we were thought of as solemn faced comediennes.'

About a month after the first photograph

was taken Elsie felt that she, too, would like to be photographed with a nature spirit of some kind. She made a gnome cut-out, which was duly hatpinned into the ground. Frances was a less expert photographer than Elsie and, according to her, the elongated hand in the picture is due to 'camera slant'; believers in the authenticity of the photographs have, however, attributed it to 'psychic elongation'.

If the second picture is examined, it is easy to see the point of a pin in the gnome's midriff. But Conan Doyle, after examining the print, concluded that the point was an umbilicus and that therefore birth in the fairy kingdom might be a similar process to human birth!

The two photographs were printed and circulated among the girls' friends in the autumn of 1918, and the matter gradually languished, with neither girl admitting to the truth of the affair, rather preferring to keep people guessing.

The following year Polly Wright, Elsie's mother, went to some Theosophical meetings, and so the prints came to be circulated at the Society's conference in Harrogate in the summer of 1919. By early 1920, they were in the hands of Edward Gardner, photographic and slide specialist of the Theosophical Society in London and president of the Blavatsky lodge and he tried repeatedly to persuade Polly to ask the girls to take more photographs. She, however, ignored his letters – and it was not until Doyle declared his own interest in the subject in June 1920 that matters began to develop in public.

In the summer of 1920, Gardner at last succeeded in persuading the girls to take a further series of photographs. These three last photographs were believed by both Gardner and Conan Doyle to constitute proof that it was possible to photograph fairies.

Frances, on the other hand, has always marvelled at the fact that anyone could believe them to be genuine. The flying fairy in the third photograph was pinned to the branch behind it; it was drawn freehand by Elsie, and seems to Frances to be out of proportion. The fairy offering flowers to Elsie in the fourth photograph was attached to a branch in a similar way, and sports a fashionable hairstyle that has attracted much comment.

The two cousins are divided about the authenticity of the fifth picture. To the casual eye, it looks very much like the result of a simple overlapping of photographs, but Frances insists that it is a genuine photograph of fairies. 'It was a wet Saturday afternoon and we were just mooching about with our cameras and Elsie had nothing

Below: the second Cottingley picture, which shows Elsie Wright playing with a gnome, was taken in August 1917. The point of the hatpin on which the paper cut-out figure was supported can plainly be seen as a protrusion on the gnome's stomach. Conan Doyle interpreted this as an umbilicus – a clear indication that birth in the fairy kingdom might be similar to human birth

Encouraged by Edward Gardner, the photographic and slide specialist of the Theosophical Society in London, Frances Griffiths and Elsie Wright took three more fairy photographs at Cottingley during the summer of 1920. The third picture (above left) shows Frances with a fairy in flight; this was drawn freehand by Elsie, and attached to the branch behind it with a hatpin. Both Frances and Elsie admit that the fourth picture (far left) was taken in a similar way – but Frances maintains that the final picture (left) is genuine: 'I saw these fairies building up in the grasses and just aimed the camera and took a photograph'

prepared,' she says. 'I saw these fairies building up in the grasses and just aimed the camera and took a photograph.' Elsie, on the other hand, insists that all five photographs are of cut-outs. It must be borne in mind that Frances has often said that it is as if some psychological blockage prevents her remembering events surrounding the photographs with any accuracy; yet this discrepancy in the cousins' accounts of taking the photographs remains curious.

The second set of photographs was hailed with joy by Gardner. And, trapped by their first trick, Elsie and Frances had no choice but to remain silent; the consequences that would have resulted from any disclosures must have seemed terrifying to them.

Looking for fairies

In 1921, Conan Doyle asked the clairvoyant Geoffrey Hodson to go to Cottingley to check the girls' observations – essentially, to see if he, too, could see the fairies. His lengthy descriptions of fairy life, endorsed by the overawed Elsie and Frances – who saw nothing while Hodson was present, as they disclosed in a television interview in 1975 – appeared as key pages in Doyle's *The coming of the fairies* in 1922. Hodson went on to become a distinguished writer on clairvoyance; it is impossible to rule out the possibility that his experience may actually have been genuine.

This author once asked Elsie point blank whether she could still endorse her statements to Hodson as reproduced in Conan

Doyle's book. 'You'll have to make your own mind up about that,' she said – again with just a suspicion of that deadpan Yorkshire humour.

What conclusions are there to be drawn? Four of the five pictures, for certain, are hoaxes. Both Elsie and Frances, however, insist that the fairies themselves were real. Frances saw them particularly often:

The first time I ever saw anything was when a willow leaf started shaking violently, even though there was no wind, I saw a small man standing on a branch, with the stem of the leaf in his hand, which he seemed to be shaking at something. He was dressed all in green.

Gradually, she began to see more and more of the elves. And in the summer of 1918, Frances saw fairies as well as elves:

They were real fairies. Some had wings and some not. . . . They were once sitting in a patch of sunlight on a low bank. . . . It all seemed so peaceful and friendly. . . . Sometimes they came up, only inches away, but I never wanted to join in their lives.

Finally, she says, 'I became so used to them that unless they did something unusual I just ignored them.'

Do fairies exist? Can they be photographed? What is certain is that the Cottingley photographs cannot be regarded as proof of the existence of fairies. It is up to each of us to decide whether those people who report seeing fairies actually see them, or whether they merely imagine them.

The banks of the beck at Cottingley – where, Frances still maintains, she saw fairies. So, even if the Cottingley photographs are fakes, whether or not fairies exist remains an open question

Connection and coincidence

We have all experienced coincidences that seem too perfect and bizarre to be the result of mere chance. It has been suggested that a rational explanation can be found for the pattern that apparently determines our lives, but many people still adhere to the belief that an all-powerful force is in control.

Sublime and ridiculous

The frequency of hilarious coincidences leads naturally to the idea that they are perpetrated by a cosmic prankster. But cosmic jokes may go beyond humour; as Zen Buddhism teaches, laughter and enlightenment can be very close indeed

FEW OF US have not felt at times that our lives are manipulated by forces beyond our control and comprehension, especially when the most trivial events can take on a mysterious significance of their own. Consider the case of Essex policeman Peter Moscardi. In 1967 the telephone number of his police station was changed to 40116. To a friend he inadvertently gave a wrong number, 40166. Several days later, patrolling an industrial area with a colleague, he investigated a factory. It was late at night, the door was open, and a light burned inside, but the building was empty. While Moscardi was in the office the telephone rang – it was his friend. Moscardi looked down at the telephone – and found that the number was the one he had mistakenly given his friend. Later they learned that the manager had forgotten

to lock up the factory, something that had never happened before.

When faced with incidents of such staggering improbability – and most of us can cite similar personal experiences – the word 'coincidence' seems feeble and dismissive. It explains nothing. We cling to such vague, but useful, notions as good or bad luck. But perhaps, it has been conjectured – and the idea is put forward only half in jest – these weird events are engineered by a mysterious cosmic joker, a sort of demented fairy godmother whose wand is a fool's slap-stick.

In the capricious and perverse world of the cosmic joker there are many varieties of prank. Perhaps the most spectacular of these are coincidences – especially those of name and number. The German psychologist Wilhelm Stekel spoke, in 1911, of 'the compulsion of the name'. We all know of examples – here is one from the *Daily Telegraph* of 3 June 1982: a duck farmer in Lincolnshire employs two people called Crow, four called Robbins, a Sparrow, a Gosling and a Dickie Bird. There are other varieties of 'the compulsion of the name' – such as the Canadian goose that crashed through the window of a house in Derby while the occupant was listening to a record by Frankie Laine, *Cry of the wild goose*.

The serious world of science, too, comes in for the prankster's ministrations. One thinks of noisy predictions by astronomers that have failed miserably – like the prediction that the comet Kohoutek, when it passed close to the Earth in 1973, would be a spectacle. In the event, it could hardly be seen with the naked eye. The pranks continue: in April 1982 a New Zealand government department cancelled an earthquake alert when it was found that the ominous seismograph readings they were receiving from remote stations were caused by excited wallabies hopping nearby; and a famous American university had to admit, to its great embarrassment, that for over a decade no one had noticed that one of its dinosaur skeletons was wearing the wrong head.

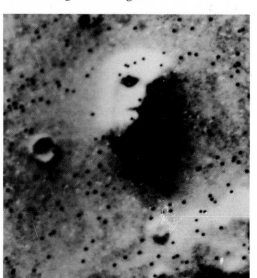

Left: among the strange and absurd natural phenomena chronicled in this 1958 issue of *Fate* magazine is a fall of frogs from the sky. It is events such as these that have prompted the suggestion that the world is governed by a cosmic joker. But what is the purpose behind his jokes?

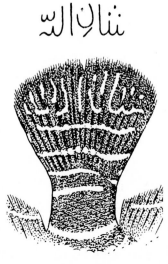

Left: the Camel Rock, near Santa Fe in New Mexico, USA; and the apparent image of a human face in a stalactite cave in Wiehl near Cologne in West Germany (below). Such visual coincidences – unlikely images that occur naturally – are known as *simulacra*. Rock simulacra are found all over the world and, wherever they occur, have generally been subjects of veneration for centuries

There is a dark side to the cosmic joker, too. In *The book of heroic failures*, Stephen Pile tells the story of a farcical but tragic event that took place during the British firemen's strike of 1978. The army took over responsibility for firefighting operations, and on 14 January they rescued a cat that had become trapped up a tree. The old lady who owned the cat was overjoyed and invited them all in for tea. But, says Stephen Pile, 'Driving off later, with fond farewells completed, they ran over the cat and killed it.'

The victim of an improbable series of accidents, for example, can perhaps be forgiven for thinking he is the victim of a curse – or that 'Someone up there doesn't like me.' Most of us have just enough paranoia to feel 'got at', usually when we are depressed, but the feeling passes and our sense of humour

Far left: does the surface of Mars bear huge effigies of human figures? This photograph, taken by the Viking I Orbiter on 25 July 1976 from a distance of 1162 miles (1873 kilometres), shows a rocky outcrop 1 mile (1.6 kilometres) across

Left: the marks on the tail of the butterfly fish from Zanzibar read, in old Arabic, 'there is no God but Allah'. Fishermen allegedly threw these fish back into the sea out of respect for the legend on their tails

puts it into perspective. In paranoid schizophrenia, however, these feelings get out of hand.

The yachtsman Donald Crowhurst, who ended his life tragically by drowning himself in 1969, had fallen into schizophrenia as his vessel drifted in mid Atlantic. Shortly before his suicide, he began to write a cynical parable in his ship's log. He felt our lives are manipulated by cosmic tricksters called 'chess-masters'. He believed that 'the explanation of our troubles is that cosmic beings are playing games with us':

God and his son were playing together in the cosmos. . . . The game they were playing was called turning apes into gods. It was a jolly just game, and . . . it was played according to one simple rule, the apes were not allowed to know anything about gods.

A similar cynicism, but born of disillusionment rather than madness, has led to the conspiracy theory of human history, which holds that almost every civilisation has been instigated and manipulated by powerful and insidious organisations, usually secret, of bankers, religions, cults and secret societies. A space-age variation of this is Erich von Däniken's now discredited theory that human evolution is the product of intervention by space-travelling aliens using genetic engineering. In Andrija Puharich's biography of Uri Geller, Geller claims that the source of his psychokinetic power is a group of super beings, deep in space, that have similarly manipulated human development. If this is true, however, one has to smile at the thought that the best these godlike machines can do is bend our cutlery!

The subjective connection

A significant number of keen minds have recognised what American psychologist Dr Jule Eisenbud has called 'subtle ordering tendencies or dispositions hidden in the very warp and woof of the universe'. The German philosopher Arthur Schopenhauer (1788–1860), whose ideas about the nature of the unconscious influenced Freud and Jung, believed that something more than mere physical causality influences men's lives; he called it 'the subjective connection'. The real significance of coincidences, he wrote in 1850, exists only in relation to the individuals who experience them. To others involved in the event, people for whom it has no significance, it passes unnoticed into the background of everyday life. 'The world is indeed comic,' wrote the master of Gothic horror, H.P. Lovecraft, 'but the joke is on mankind.'

The discussion of coincidences and their meaning has attracted the likes of Carl Gustav Jung, Paul Kammerer – a scientist engaged in pioneering work on the inheritance of acquired characteristics, who committed suicide when the results of his research with midwife toads were alleged to be rigged – Arthur Koestler and Sir Alister

Connection and coincidence

Hardy, all of whom have concluded that the phenomena of coincidences are somehow beyond the usual chains of cause and effect in space and time. Some contemporary researchers go as far as to suggest that these synchronistic events – as Jung termed them – might actually be arranged in some mysterious way by the collective unconscious.

In describing the subjective nature of synchronistic experiences, many writers have used the familiar simile of life being like a film or a play or a novel directed or written by some mysterious power. Science fiction writer Larry Niven has used the imagery of mankind as puppets in the hands of alien puppet-masters in several of his books, including *Ringworld*. The real argument among those who explain life in this way is over the identity of the puppeteer, author or director: God, angels, demons, cosmic imps, conspirators, aliens – or ourselves? It is the last possibility that provides the most interesting debate.

Writing in *Psychic* magazine in October 1975, Jule Eisenbud encapsulated the proposition:

> Theoretically . . . there is nothing that would be beyond accomplishment by the most innocent-looking observer. . . . At most he would be doing unconsciously, and with no manifest effort, what a movie director goes to great pains to do on a conscious level, that is, deploying props, natural surroundings and events, and the wide capabilities of 'central casting' . . . with special effects as needed. Since all . . . behaviour on the part of the players would be rationalized, no one would be any the wiser.

We certainly control the 'reality' of our dreams in this way. The stumbling block of applying this idea to real life, however, is the difficult problem of just how 'the fate of one individual invariably fits the fate of another so that each is the hero of his own drama, while simultaneously figuring in a drama foreign to him,' as Schopenhauer put it.

Top: the Death's Head hawk-moth carries the spine-chilling image of a human skull on its body. But what possible meaning can human remains have for the moth's predators?

Above: Donald Crowhurst, the yachtsman who died tragically in 1969 by drowning himself in mid Atlantic. He saw the cosmic joker as a cruel and sinister figure who amuses himself at the expense of human beings. As he wrote in his ship's log shortly before his suicide, he came to believe that 'the explanation of our troubles is that cosmic beings are playing games with us'

'This is something that surpasses our powers of comprehension.'

Whatever the identity of the cosmic joker, he is breathtakingly skilful at juggling with everything at once. And he still manages to be boundlessly creative and magnificently audacious. Here is another link with the subconscious mind: action that is unerringly swift, perfectly timed and appropriate is the characteristic of that unselfconscious state shared by the somnambulists and the hypnotised, martial artists and meditators, saints and sages – and incidentally some children, madmen and drunks. They appear to have access to a primal, childlike, unconditioned state of mind – to the personal and collective unconscious – that has reached its perfect expression in Zen Buddhism with its celebration of the playful or comic spirit.

Deliberate absurdity

Of all philosophies, Zen Buddhism may be of the most help to us in coming to terms with the cosmic joker, because it appears to have mastered the phenomenology of absurdity. In his analysis of Chinese philosophy, *The Chinese mind* (1967), E.R. Hughes described Zen teachings as 'consciously and deliberately paradoxical, even with the intention of causing laughter, to make evident the incongruities of the human situation'. What else can one say of a school of thought that numbers among its masters the eighth-century Teng Yinfeng, who died standing on his head with the deliberate intention of turning conventional values upside down in the hope some people would take life less

Right: Zen Buddhist monks on the steps of a temple in Kyoto, Japan. Many of the teachings of Zen are designed to be paradoxical or amusing in order to provoke laughter. Laughter, the followers of Zen believe – whether it comes about through the abrupt release of tension or through the 'getting' of a joke – can lead to the 'sudden awakening' of enlightenment. The Dada movement in the visual arts achieves a similar effect in its use of outrageous or nonsensical images, as in the photo-montage *Santa conversazione* (left) by Max Ernst (1891–1976). In cosmic jokes is the Universe laughing at itself?

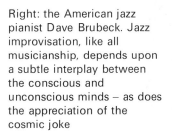

Right: the American jazz pianist Dave Brubeck. Jazz improvisation, like all musicianship, depends upon a subtle interplay between the conscious and unconscious minds – as does the appreciation of the cosmic joke

Left: the black side of the cosmic joker's humour is illustrated by a story related by Stephen Pile in his *The book of heroic failures*. During the 1978 firemen's strike in Britain the army, who had taken charge of firefighting services, were called out by an old lady whose cat had become trapped up a tree. After rescuing the cat, they were invited to tea by the overjoyed owner. But, as they left the house, they ran the cat over and killed it

seriously? The difference between a healthy appreciation of a cosmic joke and the paranoid reaction is that the former recognises its absurdity and delights in it, while the latter imbues it with a deadening seriousness.

As M. Conrad Hyers points out in *Zen and the comic spirit*, the child, the madman, the fool and the sage share a common ground in which they transcend the limits on behaviour and imagination accepted by the majority. The child has not yet learned to carve up the world into neat but arbitrary categories, nor is he governed by them; the madman cannot help himself as he confuses categories; the fool confuses categories deliberately, as do those great fools of art, the Dadaists and the surrealists; and the sage has gone beyond our need for categories and thus returns to the childlike state.

The Zen masters have always taught by exploiting the parallels between the instant in which we get the point of a joke, and the 'sudden awakening' of *satori* ('enlightenment'). Laughter is an explosive response to a situation that has suddenly been plunged into contradiction or reduced to absurdity, says Hyers, and it is this abrupt relief of tension that takes us by surprise, precipitating laughter in the 'getting' of a joke – and of illumination.

Whatever the ultimate origin of cosmic jokes, we certainly perceive them as an example of wit, and it seems reasonable to draw another parallel, this time between *koans* – the paradoxical riddles given to Zen students for meditation – and anomalous phenomena of any kind. The often meaningless pranks of the cosmic joker, unexplained or inexplicable, like *koans*, challenge our presumptions and expectations, making us reflect on the mysteries of our existence. Ufology's leading scientist, the astronomer Dr J. Allen Hynek, characterised the UFO problem with its parade of absurd entities and their even stranger behaviour, preposterous names and seemingly impossible craft, as 'both shocking and paradoxical'. This is, of course, an excellent description of a *koan*.

Cosmic jokes are phenomenological riddles, specially formulated, perhaps, by our collective unconscious, for the enlightenment – and enjoyment – of those with eyes and minds open wide enough to perceive them. It is an exquisite irony that something so universal should come from the trivial. As that great Zen master of the West, W.C. Fields, said, 'It's a funny old world. You're lucky to get out of it alive.'

Only make-believe?

Which comes first – the facts or the fiction? Does art, as most people believe, imitate life? Or can the 'impossible' happen and the reverse occur? Several disturbing cases seem to indicate that it can – and all-too-frequently does

THAT ART TAKES REALITY as its starting point is familiar enough an idea. Novelists generally describe situations that find an echo in their readers' experience, many artists are inspired by nature and others paint directly from it – some famous artists have, indeed, painted from photographs. But the idea that nature follows art – that real life somehow replicates the visual arts and literature – is altogether stranger. And yet there is some evidence to suggest that this does, indeed, happen – that, perhaps, the power of the creative mind is strong enough not only to inspire the imaginations of other people but to alter the very structure of reality.

Perhaps the most famous example of fact following fiction was the tragic sinking of the liner *Titanic* in 1912, which was alike in most details to a novel written 14 years earlier about the sinking of a ship called the *Titan*. Nor do the coincidences end there. One of the *Titanic* passengers who died was the journalist, W. T. Stead. His writings and lectures frequently used the image of a shipwreck as a simile for death, and the panic of a drowning person for the disorientation he believed was the state of the discarnate spirit in the period following death.

And the series of coincidences goes on with the near miss of a coal boat named *Titanian* in 1935. This vessel nearly went down after hitting an iceberg that was very close to the position of the *Titanic* accident. Finally, there is a more recent postscript, which happened to the Melkis family of Dunstable, Bedfordshire, in July 1975. They were watching a film about the *Titanic* tragedy on television when, just as the ship was about to strike the iceberg, their roof caved in. The cause was a chunk of ice of unknown origin from the sky.

How can we account for real-life events apparently replicating fictional ones? Are they mere accidents of chance – or are they inherently meaningful? Are they only pre-cognitive – or are they something more? The real mystery is how the immensely complicated chains of cause and effect of everyday life can result in a significant conjunction of people, places, names, values, and so on, in such a way as to make it meaningful to observers. Is it possible that the alleged sources of inspiration for fiction – such as

angels, spirits and other discarnate entities, as well as dreams – hold the answer? Perhaps. But before we can find it, we need to examine the phenomena themselves. Consider these examples.

In December 1975 France's most wanted man, Jean-Charles Willoquet, was arrested by members of the anti-gang squad – while he was watching a television drama based on the anti-gang squad. The Canadian postcode for a farmer named McDonald contained the sequence EIEIO. During a television showing of the film *Around the world in eighty days* in April 1975, the Dumfriesshire village of Ruthwell was blacked out just as the heroes were about to set off in their hot-air balloon – because a two-man balloon, similar to the fictional one, crashed into the power lines. In this light the Universe does not seem to be like Sir Isaac Newton's 'great machine', nor the 'great thought' of Sir Arthur Eddington, but more like a great dream of a universal sentient being. The synchronistic phenomena of our existence seem to have more in common with dream events than with anything else. And, like dreams, many of these events have a dark side, dealing in death, disaster and destruction, as the following examples of intrusive fate show.

In 1975 a book by David Boulton, *The making of Tania Hearst*, suggested that the kidnapping of the publishing heiress Patricia

Left: police surround the burning wreckage of a house in Los Angeles in 1974, in which five members of the Simbionese Liberation Army (SLA) were killed. The SLA had kidnapped – and won over – publishing heiress Patricia Hearst (right, posing against the SLA flag). For a time the FBI believed that James Rusk, the author of the pornographic novel *Black abductor* (1972), had not only inspired the Hearst kidnapping, but also probably organised it – so closely did the characters and events in his book resemble the case. The 'heroine' was even called Patricia. But Rusk proved to be innocent of such a conspiracy. Was this another example of Charles Fort's allusion when he said 'We are being played with'?

Hearst in 1974 was inspired by a pornographic novel, *Black abductor*, published in 1972. In the book, an heiress called Patricia is snatched from a campus as her boyfriend is beaten up; messages are sent to her parents via personal columns in newspapers; she is seduced by the young black, leader of the small revolutionary group she eventually joins. FBI investigators interrogated James Rusk, who wrote *Black abductor* under a pseudonym, because they were convinced that Patty Hearst's kidnappers, the Simbionese Liberation Army (SLA), had copied

the plot – or worse, that Rusk had planned it with them. Rusk was as astonished as they at the high degree of coincidence. And even if the SLA had been copying his plot, they had no guarantee the heiress would be won over, as she was in real life.

On 8 December 1971 opera star Marie Collier fell to her death from the balcony of her London home. She had been talking to her financial adviser about a new tour of the United States when she opened a window and fell out. Marie Collier had come to fame in the role of Tosca, who leaps to her death

Left: a scene from the film *Around the world in eighty days* (1956). During a television showing in 1975 the Dumfriesshire village of Ruthwell suffered a power cut when a two-man hot-air balloon crashed into the local power lines – just as, on screen, the heroes set off in their balloon. Would the accident have occurred if the film had not been shown at the time the real-life balloon sailed over the village?

Connection and coincidence

Left: in 1971 opera star Marie Collier was apparently happily discussing future plans with a manager when she opened her window and fell to her death. Her last role was that of Tosca, who leaps from a wall to her death

from a wall in the last act. It was Collier's last role before she fell from the window.

One of Julie Christie's most memorable films is *Don't look now* (1973), a dramatisation of a novel by Daphne Du Maurier, in which a couple are haunted by the spirit of their young child who had drowned in a pond outside their country home. The fictional plot came horribly true in March 1979 for Jonathan and Lesley Heale, who were living at Julie Christie's farmhouse in Wales. The film star was just leaving after a visit there when Lesley Heale found her 22-month-old son floating in the large duckpond near the house. She waded in and recovered him, just as the father in the film had done. And the boy had drowned in just 2 feet (60 centimetres) of water. This gruesome coincidence was said to have shattered all concerned.

Victim – or creator?

A somewhat similar story is told by Alan Vaughan in his book *Incredible coincidence* (1979), which makes it seem as if the authors of these fictions that become fact might be more responsible for the events than we can imagine at present. Certainly such people as authors, actors and film makers seem to be involved more than any other group. Vaughan writes:

> My introduction to synchronicity came from Professor Hans Bender, of the Freiberg University Institute for the Border Areas of Psychology, in Germany, in 1968, when I was studying there on a grant from the Parapsychology Foundation. Bender was researching the dreams of an actress and found that about 10 per cent of them had a synchronistic correspondence to her *later* acting roles. For instance, she dreamed of being on a ship with a baby.

The baby fell from her arms into the water, and she dived in after it. Two years later she played a role in a television film in which she enacted the improbable scene of her dream.

The 'fact follows fiction' effect also applies to fairytales and fables. Consider this as a version of Snow White: according to the *Sunday Express* (19 August 1979) a gang of seven dwarfs was arrested in Barcelona, Spain, for a series of shotgun raids on jewellery stores. It turned out that they were masterminded by a tall, good-looking blonde whose first name was Nieves, which means snow in Spanish. Another story, printed in the *Daily Express* (3 September 1975) recalls Cinderella, with a twist. At Palma in Majorca, 20-year-old Maria Bispal was arrested for 14 robberies. Her spree came to an end when she lost a shoe while fleeing from the scene of her latest crime. Enter the handsome detective. The shoe fits, and Maria confesses all to him – and off they all go to court (judicial, not royal).

A related question is how myths arise.

Above: the Heale family took over the Welsh home of actress Julie Christie – and found themselves enacting the roles of the parents in the 1973 film *Don't look now*, played by Julie Christie and Donald Sutherland (above right). Just as in the film, their toddler drowned in a pond near the house

Tomorrow's folklore is being created today, partly in the observation of unexplained phenomena. The recurrence of certain types of phenomenon seems to indicate that the collective unconscious contains archetypes that it projects onto the real world. Take this event: just four weeks after the Comoro Islands, situated between Madagascar and the African mainland, obtained independence from France in 1975, Ali Soilih seized power from the elected president with the help of a French mercenary, Colonel Bob Denard. Within a few months Soilih ruled the country with ruthless authority. He was then told by a witch that he could be killed only by a man with a dog. Immediately he ordered all dogs on the island killed. In the third year of his reign of terror, Soilih was overthrown and killed – by a man with a dog. As it happened the same Denard, who brought his pet Alsatian with him, led the successful fight against the dictator. The motif of a head of state trying to evade a fatal prophecy by eliminating the sources of the threat against him is familiar as a recurring theme in myth: Pelias and Jason, and Laius and Oedipus come to mind immediately.

If archetypes are able to project their organising influence onto the everyday world, then we might expect every thing, place, person, event or item of information such as a name, date or meaning, to form part of an unknown number of these organising patterns. These would be a kind of equivalent of the genetic code, activated by circumstance to give a developing situation its synchronistic character. Such an influence attaching itself to both the place of the *Titanic*'s doom, and to the variations of the ship's name and circumstances, might have drawn the various elements of the *Titanian*'s near miss together by acting upon billions of tiny probabilistic events.

When faced with such events, it is inadequate to try to explain them in terms of life copying art. The idea of art imitating

Right: Colonel Bob Denard, the French mercenary who, in 1975, aided the dictator Ali Soilih to take over the Comoro Islands, off the African mainland – and three years later led the rebellion that resulted in Soilih's death. The dictator had been warned by a witch that he would meet his end only at the hands of a man with a dog, and he had duly had all dogs on the islands put to death. But Denard had his Alsatian with him when he led the coup . . . Such synchronicities help create folklore, and are perhaps the agents of our inescapable doom

nature is familiar enough – but in fact the influences are bound to be in both directions. Perhaps we underestimate our own abilities to shape the world about us, abilities that are well-known to every village shaman, healer, magician and mystic. And, as we have seen, authors' creative powers are sometimes strong enough to give their work a life of its own.

Here is another example, told to author Arthur Koestler by the writer Pearl Binder. In the autumn of 1966 she was planning a satirical novel – eventually published as *Ladies only* (1972) – with a colleague, George Ordish, and his wife Olive:

On the spur of the moment I suggested, 'Why shouldn't it be in the future, when the population explosion will have made London almost uninhabitable? There would be camps set up in Hyde Park for the homeless. Let's

Above: the wreckage of *Morning Cloud*, yacht of the then British Prime Minister Edward Heath, is hauled ashore in 1974. This was the latest disaster to befall Heath's three yachts that bore that name; it was also the worst, for two crew members lost their lives. And five days before, Mr Heath had posed for publicity photographs at the launch of John Dyson's book *The Prime Minister's boat is missing*

have a refugee professor camping out there.' 'Viennese,' put in Mr Ordish, 'a broken-down old servant.' 'All goulash and sentiment,' added Mrs Ordish. 'With one of those unpronounceable Hungarian-sounding names . . . Nadoloy . . . Horvath-Nadoly.' And we went on to think of other characters.

A couple of days later we were astounded to read a news item in the morning press reporting that a homeless foreign old man had been found by police wandering alone at night in Hyde Park. He gave his name as Horvath-Nadoly.

All three authors shuddered with a strange thought: this wretched character had, apparently, stepped straight out of their imaginations. Pearl Binder wrote: 'We felt we had invented this tramp, and in the process brought him to life. . . .'

Above: the assassination of King Umberto I of Italy by the anarchist Bresci on 29 July 1900. His death and important events in his life were astonishingly closely paralleled by the life of another Umberto – a restaurant proprietor in a small town in northern Italy

Below: the German philosopher Arthur Schopenhauer (1788–1860), who believed that coincidences were a reflection of the 'wonderful pre-established harmony' of the Universe

Coincidences and connections

Every one of us has, at some time, experienced an unnerving coincidence. Mathematicians explain them away as mere chance events – but there are those who seek deeper reasons

ON THE EVENING OF 28 JULY 1900, King Umberto I of Italy dined with his aide in a restaurant in Monza, where he was due to attend an athletics meeting the next day. With astonishment, he noticed that the proprietor looked exactly like him and, speaking to him, he discovered that there were other similarities.

The restaurateur was also called Umberto; like the King, he had been born in Turin – and on the same day; and he had married a girl called Margherita on the day the King married his Queen Margherita. And he had opened his restaurant on the day that Umberto I was crowned King of Italy.

The King was intrigued, and invited his double to attend the athletics meeting with him. But next day at the stadium the King's aide informed him that the restaurateur had died that morning in a mysterious shooting accident. And even as the King expressed his regret, he himself was shot dead by an anarchist in the crowd.

Another strange coincidence connected with a death occurred much more recently. On Sunday 6 August 1978 the little alarm clock that Pope Paul VI had bought in 1923 – and that for 55 years had woken him at six every morning – rang suddenly and shrilly. But it was not six o'clock: the time was 9.40 p.m. and, for no explicable reason, the clock started ringing as the Pope lay dying. Later, Father Romeo Panciroli, a Vatican spokesman, commented, 'It was most strange. The

These foolish things...

The most striking coincidences often involve the most commonplace of objects or occasions, like the bizarre experience related by the Chicago newspaper columnist Irv Kupcinet (left):

'I had just checked into the Savoy Hotel in London. Opening a drawer in my room, I found, to my astonishment, that it contained some personal things belonging to a friend of mine, Harry Hannin, then with the Harlem Globetrotters basketball team.

'Two days later, I received a letter from Harry, posted in the Hotel Meurice, in Paris, which began "You'll never believe this." Apparently, Harry had opened a drawer in *his* room and found a tie with my name on it. It was a room I had stayed in a few months earlier.'

The Renaissance philosopher Pico della Mirandola, one of a long line of thinkers, starting with Hippocrates, the 'father of medicine', who believed that the world was governed by a principle of wholeness – and that coincidences could be explained as like events seeking each other out

Pope was very fond of the clock. He bought it in Poland and always took it with him on his trips.'

Every one of us has experienced a coincidence – however trivial – at some time or other. But some of the extreme examples seem to defy all logic, luck or reason.

Powers of the Universe

It is not surprising, therefore, that the 'theory of coincidence' has excited scientists, philosophers and mathematicians for more than 2000 years. Running like a thread through all their theories and speculations is one theme: what are coincidences about? Do they have a hidden message for us? What unknown force do they represent? Only in this century have any real answers been suggested, answers that strike at the very roots of established science and prompt the question: are there powers in the Universe of which we are still only dimly aware?

Early cosmologists believed that the world was held together by a kind of principle of wholeness. Hippocrates, known as the father of medicine, who lived at some time between 460 and 375 BC, believed the Universe was joined together by 'hidden affinities' and wrote: 'There is one common flow, one common breathing, all things are in sympathy.' According to this theory, coincidence could be explained by 'sympathetic' elements seeking each other out.

The Renaissance philosopher Pico della Mirandola wrote in 1557: 'Firstly, there is a unity in things whereby each thing is at one with itself. Secondly, there is the unity whereby one creature is united with the others and all parts of the world constitute one world.'

This belief has continued, in a barely altered form, in much more modern times. The philosopher Arthur Schopenhauer (1788–1860) defined coincidence as 'the simultaneous occurrence of causally unconnected events.' He went on to suggest that simultaneous events ran in parallel lines and the selfsame event, although a link in

The lying-in-state of Pope Paul VI. At 9.40 p.m. on 6 August 1978, as the Pope lay dying, his bedside alarm clock – set for six in the morning – inexplicably began to ring

Connection and coincidence

totally different chains, nevertheless falls into place in both, so that the fate of one individual invariably fits the fate of another, and each is the hero of his own drama while simultaneously figuring in a drama foreign to him. This is something that surpasses our powers of comprehension and can only be conceived as possible by the virtue of the most wonderful pre-established harmony. Everyone must participate in it. Thus everything is interrelated and mutually attuned.

Probing the future

The idea of a 'collective unconscious' – an underground storehouse of memories through which minds can communicate – has been debated by several thinkers. One of the more extreme theories to explain coincidence was put forward by the British mathematician Adrian Dobbs in the 1960s. He coined the word 'psitron' to describe an unknown force that probed, like radar, a second time dimension that was probabilistic rather than deterministic. The psitron absorbed future probabilities and relayed them back to the present, bypassing the normal human senses and somehow conveying the information directly to the brain.

The first person to study the laws of coincidence scientifically was Dr Paul Kammerer, Director of the Institute of Experimental Biology in Vienna. From the age of 20, he started to keep a 'logbook' of coincidences. Many were essentially trivial: people's names that kept cropping up in separate conversations, successive concert or cloakroom tickets with the same number, a phrase in a book that kept recurring in real life. For hours, Kammerer sat on park

Dr Paul Kammerer who, in 1919, published the first systematic study of coincidence

benches recording the people who wandered past, noting their sex, age, dress, whether they carried walking sticks or umbrellas. After making the necessary allowances for things like rush-hour, weather and time of year, he found the results broke down into 'clusters of numbers' of a kind familiar to statisticians, gamblers, insurance companies and opinion pollsters.

Kammerer called the phenomenon 'seriality', and in 1919 he published his conclusions in a book called *Das Gesetz der Serie* (The law of seriality). Coincidences, he claimed, came in series – or 'a recurrence or clustering in time or space whereby the individual numbers in the sequence are not connected by the same active cause.'

Coincidence, suggested Kammerer, was merely the tip of an iceberg in a larger cosmic principle that mankind, as yet, hardly recognises.

Like gravity, it is a mystery; but unlike gravity, it acts selectively to bring together in space and time things that possess some affinity. 'We thus arrive,' he concluded, 'at the image of a world mosaic or cosmic kaleidoscope, which, in spite of constant shufflings and rearrangements, also takes care of bringing like and like together.'

The great leap forward happened 50 years later, when two of Europe's most brilliant minds collaborated to produce the most searching book on the powers of coincidence – one that was to provoke both controversy and attack from rival theorists.

The two men were Wolfgang Pauli – whose daringly conceived exclusion principle earned him the Nobel Prize for Physics – and the Swiss psychologist-philosopher, Professor Carl Gustav Jung. Their treatise bore the unexciting title: *Synchronicity, an*

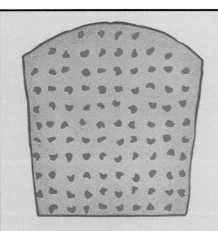

The cluster effect

In his book *Homo Faber* Max Frisch tells the extraordinary story of a man who, through a series of coincidences, meets the daughter he never knew he had, falls in love with her and sets in motion a train of events that results in her death. But Faber, a rational man, refuses to see anything more than the laws of chance in his story:

'I don't deny that it was more than a coincidence which made things turn out as they did, it was a whole series of coincidences. . . . The occasional occurrence of the improbable does not imply the intervention of a higher power. . . . The term probability includes improbability at the extreme limits of probability, and when the improbable does occur this is no cause for surprise, bewilderment or mystification.'

Few people could be so matter-of-fact in the face of the events Frisch describes – but Faber may be right. Every mathematician knows that a random distribution of events produces – surprisingly – a clustering effect, just as cherries randomly distributed in a cake will tend to be found in groups (left) rather than in the orderly arrangement one might expect (far left). The mathematician is not surprised by coincidences, or clusters of random events – but neither can he predict them!

Above: Wolfgang Pauli (1900–1958), the Nobel prize-winning physicist who, together with the eminent psychologist C.G. Jung, introduced the concept of *synchronicity* to help explain the occurrence of coincidences

Right: the decorated dome of the mosque of Madresh, Isfahan, Iran. The pattern represents the eternal pilgrimage of the soul – it unrolls in a continuous thread like the breath of the Universe, by which all things are connected. Modern physics suggests that this idea of 'interconnectedness' may be of use in providing non-causal explanations of events that are now dismissed as coincidence

acausal connecting principle. Described by one American reviewer as 'the paranormal equivalent of a nuclear explosion', it used the term 'synchronicity' to extend Kammerer's theory of seriality.

Order out of chaos

According to Pauli, coincidences were 'the visible traces of untraceable principles'. Coincidences, elaborated Jung, whether they come singly or in series, are manifestations of a barely understood universal principle that operates quite independently of the known laws of physics. Interpreters of the Pauli-Jung theory have concluded that telepathy, precognition and coincidences themselves are all manifestations of a single mysterious force at work in the Universe that is trying to impose its own kind of discipline on the utter confusion of human life.

Of all contemporary thinkers, none has written more extensively about the theory of coincidence than Arthur Koestler, who sums up the phenomenon in the vivid phrase 'puns of destiny'.

One particularly striking 'pun' was related

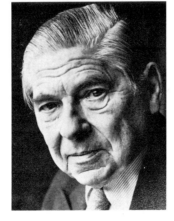

Above: Arthur Koestler, a science journalist who has written extensively about the search for a scientific explanation of coincidence – and its philosophical implications. It was he who coined the apt phrase 'puns of destiny' to describe the phenomenon

to Koestler by a 12-year-old English school-boy named Nigel Parker:

Many years ago, the American horror-story writer, Edgar Allan Poe, wrote a book called *The narrative of Arthur Gordon Pym*. In it, Mr Pym was travelling in a ship that wrecked. The four survivors were in an open boat for many days before they decided to kill and eat the cabin boy whose name was Richard Parker.

Some years *later*, in the summer of 1884, my great-grandfather's cousin was cabin boy in the yawl *Mignonette* when she foundered, and the four survivors were in an open boat for many days. Eventually, the three senior members of the crew killed and ate the cabin boy. His name was Richard Parker.

Such strange and seemingly meaningful incidents abound – can there really be no more to them than mere coincidence?

Against all the odds

It is a curious fact that the most striking coincidences often involve the most trivial of events. If, as many people believe, coincidences have some inner meaning, why are they apparently so pointless?

THE BRITISH ACTOR Anthony Hopkins was delighted to hear he had landed a leading role in a film based on the book *The girl from Petrovka* by George Feifer. A few days after signing the contract, Hopkins travelled to London to buy a copy of the book. He tried several bookshops, but there wasn't one to be had. Waiting at Leicester Square underground station for his train home, he noticed a book lying apparently discarded on a bench. Incredibly, it was *The girl from Petrovka*. That in itself would have been coincidence enough, but in fact it was merely the beginning of an extraordinary chain of events. Two years later, in the middle of filming in Vienna, Hopkins was visited by George Feifer, the author. Feifer mentioned that he did not have a copy of his own book. He had lent the last one – containing his own annotations – to a friend who had lost it somewhere in London. With mounting astonishment, Hopkins handed Feifer the book he had found. 'Is this the one?' he asked, 'with the notes scribbled in the margins?' It was the same book.

Dr Paul Kammerer, the former Director of the Institute of Experimental Biology in Vienna – and one of the first men to try to define the 'laws of coincidence' – would have relished that example. He was particularly fond of literary coincidences, and there are several in his book *Das Gesetz der Serie* ('The law of seriality'), published in 1919, which introduced the theory of 'seriality'.

Kammerer's work was also too early to include another literary coincidence, which was experienced by Dame Rebecca West, the novelist and historian. She found herself at a dead end when she went to the Royal Institute of International Affairs to research a specific episode in the Nuremberg trials:

I looked up the Trials in the library and was horrified to find they were published in a form almost useless to the researcher. After hours of search, I went along the line of shelves to an assistant librarian and said, 'I can't find it, there's no clue, it could be *any* of

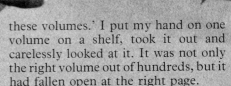

these volumes.' I put my hand on one volume on a shelf, took it out and carelessly looked at it. It was not only the right volume out of hundreds, but it had fallen open at the right page.

Kammerer – who committed suicide in 1926 – suggested that coincidences occurred in series or clusters and defined 'seriality' as 'a recurrence of the same or similar things or events in time or space.' Seriality, he concluded, 'is ubiquitous and continuous in life, nature and cosmos. It is the umbilical cord that connects thought, feeling, science and art with the womb of the universe which gave birth to them.'

Thirty years later, the Nobel prize-winning physicist Wolfgang Pauli and the philosopher-psychologist Professor Carl

Gustav Jung extended Kammerer's work with their theory of 'synchronicity'. Jung defined the word as 'the simultaneous occurrence of two meaningful but not causally connected events . . . a coincidence in time of two or more causally unrelated events which have the same or similar meaning.'

Although approaching the theory of coincidences from different directions, all three men hinted at a mysterious and barely understood force at work in the Universe, a force that was trying to impose its own kind of order on the chaos of human life.

If this seems fanciful, one of the most prolific of all contemporary thinkers on the subject, Arthur Koestler, points out that current biological – as well as physical – research strongly suggests a basic tendency of nature to create order out of disorder.

Not surprisingly, sceptics reject these theories. They explain coincidence in terms of the laws of probability: if something *can* happen then, however small the probability of the event, you should not be too surprised if it eventually *does* happen. A classic example is that a monkey at a typewriter, pressing the keys at random, will eventually – 'as time tends to infinity', as the mathematicians say – type out the entire works of Shakespeare. As science writer Martin Gardner puts it, 'Trillions of events, large and trivial, happen to billions of human beings every day. Therefore, it is inevitable that surprising things occur now and again.'

Another example is the unlikely chance of a bridge player being dealt all 13 cards of one suit. The odds are something like 635 billion to one. Yet, according to probability theory, if enough bridge hands are dealt, it will eventually happen. And indeed it did. Vera Nettick, of Princeton, New Jersey, found herself holding all 13 diamonds. She bid a grand slam and had the memorable experience of being able to lay her incredible hand down on the table.

The followers of seriality and synchronicity – and their later developments – think otherwise. Dealing cards and spinning coins are one thing, they claim. But bizarre coincidences that throw together people or events represent an entirely different force at work.

In his early researches, Kammerer classified coincidences – and he had collected hundreds of examples, often quite trivial, to support his theories – into various types. These mainly depended on the order in which they occurred, the number of parallel coincidences, whether they related to names, numbers or situations, and the elements they had in common.

Modern research now divides coincidences into two main categories, the trivial – like the incredible bridge hand – and the significant. Significant coincidences are subdivided into clearly recognisable types: the literary coincidence (like Dame Rebecca West's experience in the library), warning coincidences, useful coincidences (where the right thing happens at the right time), it's-a-small-world coincidences (bringing people together when least expected) and conjuring coincidences, incidents that are like examples of psychic sleight-of-hand.

Nazis in Fleet Street?

There are classic examples in each category, but the quintessential literary coincidence happened just before the Allied invasion of Europe in 1944.

Every aspect of the huge campaign – to drive out the Nazis and end the Second World War – was top secret and referred to only by codewords. The operation itself was known as OVERLORD. The naval spearhead was disguised by the name NEPTUNE. The two French beaches where the landing was to take place were coded UTAH and OMAHA. And the artificial harbours to be used to supply the troops at the beach-head were known as MULBERRY.

Incredibly, in the 33 days before D-Day, 6 June, each of these secret words appeared as the answer to a clue in the London *Daily*

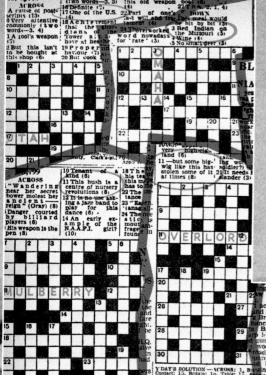

Left: by an amazing coincidence, many of the key code words used in the strategic planning of the Allied invasion of Europe in 1944 – OVERLORD, NEPTUNE, MULBERRY, UTAH, OMAHA – appeared as solutions to *Daily Telegraph* crossword clues in the weeks before D-Day. Security men quickly checked the *Telegraph* offices – but found no Nazi spy, only schoolmaster Leonard Dawe, who had been compiling the crossword for 20 years

Telegraph crossword. The key word OVER-LORD appeared only four days before the landing.

Security men immediately descended on the Fleet Street offices of the *Telegraph*, expecting to bag a Nazi spy. Instead, they found schoolmaster Leonard Dawe, who had been harmlessly compiling the paper's crossword for 20 years. Dawe was flabbergasted, and took a long time to convince them that he had been totally ignorant of the significance of the words.

The clairvoyant photograph
For an extraordinary conjuring coincidence, however, one can do no better than listen to the curious, and strangely inconsequential, experience of Mrs Eileen Bithell, of Portsmouth, Hampshire.

'For more than 20 years, a framed sign saying Closed on Wednesdays hung in the window of my parents' grocery shop. A few days before my brother's wedding, the sign was taken down to be altered. When we removed it from the frame, we discovered to our surprise that the sign had been painted on the back of a photograph. There was an even bigger surprise. The picture showed my brother's bride-to-be as a small girl, in the

Top: a game of bridge in progress. Card games provide the opportunity for the most spectacular, if trivial, of coincidences

Above: Sir James Jeans (1877–1946), the eminent physicist who remarked that science shows that the Universe looks more like 'a great thought than a great machine'

arms of his future father-in-law.

'Nobody knows how this particular photograph came to be used as the shop sign. For none of the people were known to my family at the time the sign was put up. Yet now, 20 years later, our two families were to be joined in marriage.'

Coincidences like these support the view of Sir James Jeans, the British scientist who died in 1946, who once commented, 'the stream of knowledge is heading towards a non-mechanical reality; the universe begins to look more like a great thought than a great machine' – or, as Eddington put it, 'The stuff of the world is mind-stuff.'

The rational and the occult
In his book *The challenge of chance*, Arthur Koestler suggested that coincidences 'can at least serve as pointers towards a single major mystery – the spontaneous emergence of order out of randomness, and the philosophical challenge implied in that concept. And if that sounds too rational or too occult, collecting coincidences still remains an amusing parlour game.'

Some coincidences start slowly and seem to gain momentum as one improbability follows another. One to cap any 'parlour game' was recounted by a former Fleet Street editor, now a distinguished author. For reasons that will become obvious, all the names have been changed; here is the story:

'Around 12 years ago, when I was editor of a weekly magazine in London, I met and fell in love with a Fleet Street woman journalist named Jackie. Some time afterwards, I parted company with the magazine after a difference of opinion and immediately went, with Jackie, on a Press trip to Capri. What I *didn't* know was that, in the meantime, the girl had met someone else. She had joined a Press party aboard a Swedish ship and had fallen in love with Egon, the shipping line's PRO [public relations officer].

'Six years elapsed in which everyone changed places. Jackie and I split up. She married Egon. He eventually broke with the shipping line. They got a new PRO, a girl named Jan. And Harry was appointed editor of the magazine.

'Then, like some supernatural "action replay", it all started happening again. Harry had an almost identical difference of opinion with the management and left. He immediately went on a previously-arranged Press facility trip . . . to Capri. Who should be on the same trip – again – but Jackie. The man in charge of the visit was her husband, Egon. Meanwhile, I was on the same Swedish ship on which Jackie and Egon had first met and had been introduced to his successor, Jan, who was completely unaware of the earlier relationships. We are now married. And all five of us live in the same area.'

Strange tricks of fate

Some people seem to be able to sense in advance the clusterings of random events that we call coincidences, and use them to their advantage. Can we all learn from these cases?

IT WAS ONLY WHEN his train steamed into Louisville station that George D. Bryson decided to break his trip to New York and visit the historic Kentucky town. He had never been there before and he had to ask where to find the best hotel. Nobody knew he was in Louisville, and, as a joke, he asked the desk clerk at the Brown Hotel, 'Any mail for me?' He was astonished when the clerk handed over a letter addressed to him and bearing his room number. The previous occupant of Room 307 had been another, and entirely different, George D. Bryson.

A remarkable coincidence, by any standards, but made particularly piquant by the fact that the man who tells it most frequently is Dr Warren Weaver, the American mathematician and expert on probabilities, who believes in the theory that coincidences are governed by the laws of chance, and rejects any suggestion of the uncanny or paranormal in coincidences.

On the opposite side of the fence are those who follow the 'seriality' or 'synchronicity'

In 1891 an unknown Englishman named Charles Wells became an overnight sensation as *The man that broke the bank at Monte Carlo*, as a music-hall song later called him. Using no apparent system, he three times 'broke' the 100,000-franc 'bank' allocated to his roulette table at the famous Monte Carlo casino (seen as it is today, above left; in a contemporary drawing from the *Illustrated London News*, above right). Can coincidence explain how Wells was somehow able to sense the winning numbers? We shall never know; after winning for the third time, Wells disappeared, taking his secret with him. He was never seen again

theories of Dr Paul Kammerer, Wolfgang Pauli, and Carl Gustav Jung.

Although the three men approached the theory of coincidences from different directions, their conclusions all hinted at a mysterious and barely understood force at work in the Universe, a force that was trying to impose its own kind of order on the chaos of our world. Modern scientific research, particularly in the fields of biology and physics, also seems to suggest a basic tendency of nature to create order out of chaos.

The sceptics, however, stand firm. When events are happening at random, they argue, you are bound to encounter the clusterings we call 'coincidence'. It is even possible to predict such clusterings or, at least, to predict the frequency with which they are likely to happen.

If you toss a coin many times, the laws of probability dictate that you will end up with an almost equal number of heads and tails. However, the heads and tails will not alternate. There will be runs of one and runs of

Connection and coincidence

the other. Dr Weaver calculates that, if you toss a coin 1024 times, for instance, it is likely that there will be one run of eight tails in a row, two of seven in a row, four of six in a row and eight runs of five in a row.

The same is true of roulette. 'Evens' once came up 28 times in succession at Monte Carlo casino. The odds against this happening are around 268 million to one. Yet the randomness experts claim that, as it *could* happen, it did happen – and will happen again somewhere in the world if enough roulette wheels keep spinning long enough.

Mathematicians use this law, for example, to explain the fantastic series of winning numbers that earned Charles Wells the title – in song – of *The man that broke the bank at Monte Carlo*.

Wells – a fat and slightly sinister Englishman – became the subject of the popular music-hall ditty in 1891, when he broke the bank at the Monte Carlo casino three times. He used no apparent system, but put even money bets on red and black, winning nearly every time until he finally exceeded the 100,000 francs 'bank' allocated to each table. On each occasion, attendants lugubriously covered the table with a black 'mourning' cloth and closed it for the rest of the day. The third and last time Wells appeared at the casino, he placed his opening bet on number five, at odds of 35 to 1. He won. He left his original bet and added his winnings to it. Five came up again. This happened five times in succession. Out came the black

Above: Dr Warren Weaver, the American mathematician and probability expert whose study of coincidence has led him to oppose any suggestion that a paranormal force is involved

When a commuter train plunged from an open drawbridge into Newark Bay in New York (below), over 30 people lost their lives. By an ironic coincidence, this tragic incident won many New Yorkers large sums of money. A newspaper picture of the accident (left) showed the number 932 on the rear coach of the train, and many people, sensing some meaning in the number, put their money on it in the Manhattan numbers game – and won

cloth. And out went Wells with his winnings, never to be seen there again.

The seriality and synchronicity theorists – and those who have extended the work of Kammerer, Pauli and Jung – accept the idea of 'clusters' of numbers. But they see 'luck' and 'coincidence' as two sides of the same coin. The classic paranormal concepts of ESP, telepathy and precognition – recurring elements in coincidences – might offer an alternative explanation of why some people are 'luckier' than others.

Modern research breaks coincidences down into two distinct types: trivial (like spinning coins, runs of numbers and amazing hands of cards) and significant. Significant coincidences are those that shuffle together people, events, space and time – past, present and future – in a manner that seems to cross the delicate borderline into the doubtful region of the paranormal.

Macabre significance

Sometimes a coincidence occurs that seems to link, almost capriciously, the rival theories. After a New York commuter train plunged into Newark Bay – killing many passengers – work started on recovering the coaches from the water. One front-page newspaper picture showed the rear coach being winched up, with the number 932 clearly visible on its side. That day, the number 932 came up in the Manhattan numbers game, winning hundreds of thousands of dollars for the hordes of people who – sensing an occult significance in the number – had put their money on it.

Modern researchers now divide significant coincidences into several categories. One is the warning coincidence, with its presentiment of danger or disaster.

Warning coincidences often have an extraordinarily long reach, which is why many

are ignored or go unrecognised. That was certainly the case with three ships, the *Titan*, the *Titanic* and the *Titanian*. In 1898, the American writer Morgan Robertson published a novel about a giant liner, the *Titan*, which sank one freezing April night in the Atlantic after hitting an iceberg on her maiden voyage.

Fourteen years later – in one of the world's worst sea disasters – the *Titanic* sank on a freezing April night in the Atlantic after hitting an iceberg on *her* maiden voyage.

The coincidences did not end there. The ships, both fact and fiction, were around the same tonnage and both disasters occurred in the same stretch of the ocean. Both liners were regarded as 'unsinkable', and neither carried sufficient lifeboats.

Coincidence and premonition

With the extraordinary story of the *Titanian*, the *Titan-Titanic* coincidences begin to defy human belief. On watch one night in April 1935 – during the *Titanian*'s coal-run from the Tyne to Canada – crewman William Reeves began to feel a strong sense of foreboding. By the time the *Titanian* reached the spot where the two other ships had gone down, the feeling was overpowering. Could Reeves stop the ship merely because of a premonition? One thing – a *further* coincidence – made the decision for him. He had been born on the day of the *Titanic* disaster. 'Danger ahead!' he bellowed to the bridge. The words were barely out of his mouth when an iceberg loomed out of the darkness. The ship avoided it just in time.

Another category is the 'it's-a-small-world coincidence', which brings together people and places when least expected – a phenomenon vouched for by Arthur Butterworth, of Skipton, Yorkshire.

During the Second World War, while serving in the army, he ordered a secondhand book on music from a London bookseller. The book eventually reached him at his camp

Coincidence links the fates of the *Titanian* (above) and the famous *Titanic*. Both hit icebergs in the same waters; but the *Titanian* survived

Below: Charles Coghlan, whose dead body made an immense sea journey before being cast up on the shore of his home town

– disguised by the usual military postcode – in the grounds of Taverham Hall, near Norwich. Standing at the window of his army hut, he opened the parcel and, as he did so, a picture postcard – presumably used as a bookmark – fell out. The writing on one side showed the postcard had been written on 4 August 1913. To his astonishment, when he turned it over, the picture showed 'the exact view I had from my hut window at that very moment . . . Taverham Hall.'

If coincidence can reach so easily across time and space in its quest for 'order out of chaos', it is not surprising that it can stretch beyond the grave, too.

While on a tour of Texas in 1899, the Canadian actor Charles Francis Coghlan was taken ill in Galveston and died. It was too far to return his remains to his home on Prince Edward Island, in the Gulf of St Lawrence – more than 3500 miles (5600 kilometres) away by the sea-route – and he was buried in a lead coffin inside a granite vault. His bones had rested less than a year when the great hurricane of September 1900 hit Galveston Island, flooding the cemetery. The vault was shattered and Coghlan's coffin floated out into the Gulf of Mexico. Slowly, it drifted along the Florida coastline and into the Atlantic, where the Gulf Stream picked it up and carried it northwards.

Eight years passed. Then, one day in October 1908, some fishermen on Prince Edward Island spotted a long, weather-scarred box floating near the shore. Coghlan's body had come home. With respect mingled with awe, his fellow islanders buried the actor in the nearby church where he had been christened as a baby.

Chance? Destiny? A mere trick of 'randomness'? Or that strange and powerful force, striving to make sense of the Universe, that some call coincidence?

The meaning of coincidence

Are coincidences merely random events, as mathematicians would have us believe – or is there much more to them? The psychologist C. G. Jung developed an extraordinary theory about the phenomena

'COINCIDENCE' IS A WORD that is often levelled by rationalists at anyone who presumes to suggest that evidence exists for paranormal phenomena. But in recent years defenders of the paranormal have found their own weapon in the concept of 'sychronicity' developed by the great psychologist and philosopher Carl Gustav Jung.

For Jung, a tireless champion of open-mindedness, calling an event 'coincidence' did not automatically shut the door on any further examination of the facts. Coincidences happen – fact. Further and more important, coincidences often seem to have *meaning* to the percipients – also an established fact. Jung pointed out that there can be few people who have not had some experience in their lives that they recognise as 'meaningful coincidence'. Many of us may be reluctant to try to explain or evaluate these events for fear of being accused of credulity or superstition. But at the same time we often feel that there is more to them than mere chance.

In his essay on synchronicity, subtitled *An acausal connecting principle*, Jung bravely ventures into this unexplored area (which he describes as 'dark, dubious and hedged about with prejudice'). He reminds us that the natural laws by which we live are based on the principle of *causality*: if this happens, that follows. Empirical observation and experiment prove that this is so, every time. But, Jung insists, there are *facts* that the old principle of causality cannot explain.

Below: Professor J. B. Rhine, the American pioneer ESP researcher whose work was cited by Jung as objective evidence for the existence of an active force behind coincidence

Jung's study of coincidence was stimulated by his own experiences. One extraordinary case involved a golden scarab (below), Egyptian symbol of rebirth, and its European relative, the rose scarab (right)

He cites evidence from the many well-authenticated phenomena gathered by psychical researchers – material on ESP collected by Dr J.B. Rhine, verified cases of precognitive or clairvoyant dreams, and the 'meaningful coincidences' chronicled by researchers such as Dr Paul Kammerer.

Jung was drawn to this mass of material by an intriguing sense that it might contribute in a major way to a greater understanding of the human psyche. In his pioneering essay on synchronicity he is concerned to 'open the field', in the hope that a more thorough and comprehensive tilling will come later. And he is doubtless right to think that his work will inspire later researchers – his preliminary thoughts are breathtaking, for anyone who can overcome prejudice.

Jung is at pains to emphasise what he sees as the true significance of many synchronistic events (his term for meaningful coincidences or 'symbolic parallels'), in which he sees a stirring or 'constellating' of *archetypes* – those immensely powerful motifs that seem to underlie human consciousness. He offers several examples of constellation from his own experience, including the case of a patient whose rationalist preconceptions had set up rigid barriers against the progress of her analysis. She was relating a dream to Jung that involved a golden scarab – a particularly potent symbol of regeneration,

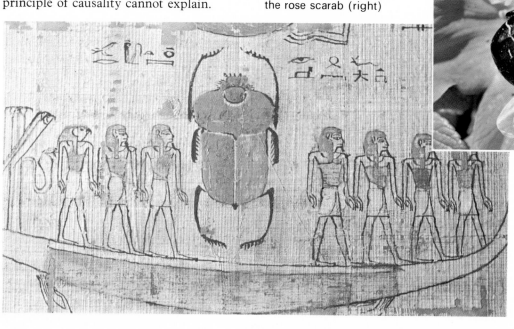

especially in ancient Egypt. As she spoke, an insect flew in at the window – and, with astonishment Jung identified it as one of a species that is the closest thing to a scarab beetle that can be found in Europe. Since 'rebirth' is one way of expressing the transformation that is the goal of Jungian psychotherapy – and since this oddly resonant reinforcing of the rebirth archetype led to a breakthrough for Jung's patient – it is clear how important meaningful coincidence can be.

But isolated phenomena, however remarkable, do not help to build up a workable hypothesis, and Jung went looking for empirical material. He was well aware that he was looking in areas where the scientific establishment said such material did not exist – but then, he points out wryly, so was Galileo. In fact, he chose to examine a body of traditional processes where the idea of synchronicity is taken for granted – that is, the forms of divination that are essentially techniques designed to interpret the meanings of coincidence.

Chinese horoscopes
First he examined the *I Ching*, that ancient Chinese means of summoning our 'intuitive' faculties to aid, or even supplant, our reason in making judgements. From there he turned to traditional astrology, where he put aside the dubious and subjective 'analysis' of character traits and focused instead on a 'harder' connection: the planetary aspects,

The promising Hollywood actor James Dean (right) was killed in a tragic motoring accident in September 1955. Afterwards, when the wreck (above) was towed to a garage, the engine sipped and fell onto a mechanic, breaking both his legs. The engine was bought by a doctorwho put it into a racing car and was killed shortly afterwards. In the same race, another driver was killed in a car with the drive shaft from Dean's car. Dean's car was later repaired – and a fire broke out at the garage. It was displayed in Sacramento, and fell off its mount, breaking a teenager's hip. Then, in Oregon, the truck on which the car was mounted slipped and smashed into a shop front. Finally, in 1959, it broke into 11 pieces while sitting on stationary steel supports

Below: a diagram invented by Jung and Pauli to explain their idea that acausality may be a ruling principle of the Universe

especially conjunction of Sun and Moon, long associated by astrologers with marriage. And his empirical search turned up an interestingly high percentage of married couples whose horoscopes *did* show the aspects in question.

Jung would have been very interested in the recent work of the young French statistician Michel Gauquelin, who has sought – and found – correlations between people's professions and the presence in their horoscopes of certain astrological elements.

Perhaps inevitably, however, this aspect of Jung's research has been the one that has attracted the most censure from those who wish to discredit him. People – mostly journalists – who have never read a word of Jung's own voluminous writings are now firmly convinced that he was a credulous crank, or a charlatan, because he 'believed' in astrology, alchemy and other weird subjects. But in fact Jung's own conclusions were that, while he accepted that the results of his experiment were not statistically valid – and that, even if they were, they would not prove the validity of astrology – they did provide him with a set of data concerning the phenomenon of synchronicity.

From his observations Jung draws some conclusions about synchronicity

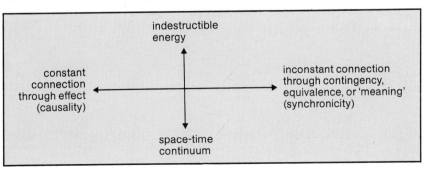

indestructible energy

constant connection through effect (causality)

inconstant connection through contingency, equivalence, or 'meaning' (synchronicity)

space-time continuum

Connection and coincidence

A 19th-century Chinese porcelain dish showing the eight trigrams, or symbols of the primary subdivisions of creation; the symbol in the middle represents the positive and negative forces in life, *yang* and *yin*. These concepts were central to the *I Ching*, a Chinese method of divination studied by Jung in his research into coincidences

and the crucial role that the human psyche plays in it. Coincidences may be purely random events but, as Jung points out, as soon as they seem to carry some symbolic meaning they cease to be random as far as the person involved is concerned. He even considers the idea that the psyche may somehow be operating on external reality to 'cause' coincidences – or that, as in precognitive dreams, the external phenomena are somehow 'transmitted' to the psyche. But he quickly concludes that, because such ideas involve a suspension of our known 'laws' of space and time, we are not capable of ascertaining whether these hypotheses are relevant. And so he comes back to his own theory of an 'acausal' connecting principle governing certain chains of events.

In the face of a meaningful coincidence, Jung says, we can respond in any one of three ways. We can call it 'mere random chance', and turn away with our minds clamped shut; we can call it magic – or telepathy or telekinesis – which is not a great deal more helpful or informative. Or we can postulate the existence of a principle of acausality, and use this idea to investigate the phenomenon more thoroughly.

In the course of doing this Jung puts forward the unsettling thought that space and time may have no real objective existence. They may be only concepts created by the psyche in the course of empirical science's attempts to make rational, measurable sense of the Universe. It is certainly true that these concepts have little true meaning in the systems of thought of many primitive tribes. And, as many leading Jungians have pointed out, a great deal of damage has been done to conventional ideas of space and time by post-Einsteinian advances in particle physics, where so often causality vanishes and probability rules. So, if space and time are merely mental concepts, it is quite reasonable to suppose that they will be capable of being 'conditioned' by the psyche.

Using this hypothesis, Jung goes on to pose a fascinating question. He assumes that, when a meaningful coincidence happens, an image – perhaps from the unconscious – comes into consciousness, and an 'outer' objective phenomenon coincides with it. The psyche perceives meaning in this juxtaposition of events. But what if the meaning could also exist *outside* the psyche? What if meaning exists within the phenomenon itself – just as causality exists, demonstrably, within objective cause-and-effect phenomena?

Rationalising the absurd

To put it another way, for clarity: we perceive causality with our minds – so, in a way, it can be regarded as a psychic event. Experiment proves that causality always obtains in 'outer', objective events so we know that it, too, has an objective existence. But equally, we perceive acausal connections (meaningful coincidences) with our minds, so we know that acausality is a mental – or psychic – phenomenon. Could it also be that it actually happens in the outer world, and so has an objective existence of its own?

In short, might it not be that acausality is a cardinal structural principle of connection that lies at the very foundation of outer reality, a fourth to join the great triad of space, time and causality?

The implications of the idea are almost too difficult to imagine – in part, as Jung was the first to appreciate, because to pursue the possibilities further involves the extraordinary task of setting the psyche to investigate the deeper reaches of itself. But this is, of course, the central purpose of depth psychology. And the rewards for attempting such a piece of research could be immense – Jung's idea of synchronicity does, at the very least, indicate vast frontiers, philosophical as well as psychological, that await exploration.

Jung made his pioneering steps untroubled by his awareness that he would have to travel along some paths in the 'dark and dubious' areas that orthodox science is inclined to dismiss as superstition – mankind's ancient and still thriving traditions of divination, magic and the paranormal. We may still hope that a time will come when fear, prejudice and mental laziness will no longer prevent other people from setting out to determine whether Jung's idea of synchronicity may indeed lead to new ways of perceiving the nature of mind, the nature of matter – and the nature of Nature itself.

A tale of two murders

Two murders committed in the same place on the same day, but exactly 157 years apart, with the suspected murderer named Thornton in each case – this is the bizarre Erdington affair. But was there anything more than coincidence involved?

IF THE PRINCIPLES underlying astrology are correct, people born in the same – or similar – astrological conditions should have broadly similar lives. There is certainly no lack of anecdotes about people born at the same time on the same day many years apart, with the same astrological conditions prevailing at the two dates, whose lives have, indeed, revealed marked similarities.

One of the better-known examples is that of Queen Elizabeth I and the late Dame Edith Sitwell. Although they were born 350 years apart, they had much in common – even down to facial similarities. Their birth charts display many intriguing resemblances: both were born on 7 September, between 3.00 and 4.00 p.m., and both had the ascending sign of Capricorn in their horoscopes. Neither woman was welcomed into the world: Lady Sitwell, Dame Edith's mother, wanted her first-born to be a boy, while Elizabeth's mother, Anne Boleyn, suffered execution through giving birth to a daughter, as Henry VIII desperately wanted a son. Neither Elizabeth nor Dame Edith married, each wrote verse and was subject to melancholic fits.

There appears, however, to be a certain amount of evidence suggesting that not only do people who are born on dates on which the

prevailing astrological conditions – the alignments of the planets – are similar suffer similar fates, but that events that occur on those dates can bear uncanny resemblances to one another. The strange case of the 'identical' Erdington murders apparently comes into this category. Two girls of the same age (and, according to some sources, the same birth dates) were the victims of murders committed on the same day of the year – but with a time difference of 157 years. The identical factors in the two cases are so striking and so numerous that it could be argued that some kind of astrological influence must have governed the actions of those who committed the crimes.

On 27 May 1817, 20-year-old Mary Ashford was found dead, apparently murdered, at Erdington, then only a village, 5 miles (8 kilometres) outside Birmingham. On 27 May 1974, Barbara Forrest, aged 20, was strangled and left in long grass near the

Connection and coincidence

children's home in Erdington at which she was a nurse.

That in itself is perhaps a remarkable coincidence, but no more. It is when one examines each case in detail that the identical factors begin to proliferate. Both in 1817 and 1974 Whit Monday was on 26 May. Barbara Forrest and Mary Ashford had both been raped before being murdered and their bodies were found within 400 yards (360 metres) of one another, death taking place at approximately the same time of day. It would appear (though there must be some doubt about this in the case of Mary Ashford) that there were attempts by the killers to hide the respective bodies. And the coincidences do not end there. Both girls had visited a friend early in the evening of the Whit Monday to change into a new dress and then go on to a dance. After each murder a man was arrested

Previous page: Queen Elizabeth I (1533–1603) and the English poet Dame Edith Sitwell (1887–1964). Both ladies were born on 7 September, between 3.00 and 4.00 p.m.; both were unwanted babies, neither married, both wrote verse and each suffered from periodic fits of melancholy. There is even a marked resemblance between their faces. People born at times of similar astrological conditions are known as astrological time twins – and astrology predicts that their lives should follow broadly similar courses

Left: a contemporary engraving of Mary Ashford, whose body was found on 27 May 1817 in a flooded sandpit close to Erdington – then a rural village, as this photograph of Mary's house (previous page), taken decades later, shows. The scene of the events of the night of 26 May 1817 (below) includes the spot on which an uncannily similar crime was committed exactly 157 years later – the Pype Hayes Children's Home, then Pipe Hall. In both cases the man accused of the murder was called Thornton – and in both cases he was acquitted

– and in each instance his name was Thornton. To round off this narrative of astonishing parallels, both men were charged with murder but were acquitted.

It was when the police were checking through archives after Barbara Forrest's death that they came across full reports of the murder of 1817 – and noted these similarities with amazement. At 6.30 a.m. on 27 May of that year a labourer making his way to work in Erdington found a pile of bloodstained female garments not far from Penn's Mill. He reported his find to the police and a search of the whole area was carried out. Eventually two sets of footprints, those of a man and a woman, were discovered leading in the direction of a flooded sandpit.

Bloodstained clothing

The footsteps ended at the edge of the water in the pit. This was searched, and the body of Mary Ashford retrieved from it. Her clothing was bloodstained and there were bruises on her arms. She was a well-known local girl, and it was not long before all her movements of the previous day were traced. On the Whit Monday, 26 May, she had travelled from Erdington to Birmingham to sell dairy produce at the market, having arranged to go to a Whitsuntide dance at the Tyburn House Inn that evening. She returned to Erdington about 6 p.m., went to a friend's house and changed into a new print dress for the dance, to which she went accompanied by a girl named Hannah Cox.

The two girls thoroughly enjoyed themselves at the dance, which ended about midnight. For most of the evening, Mary Ashford danced with a young bricklayer named Abraham Thornton. He, Mary, Hannah Cox and her partner, Benjamin

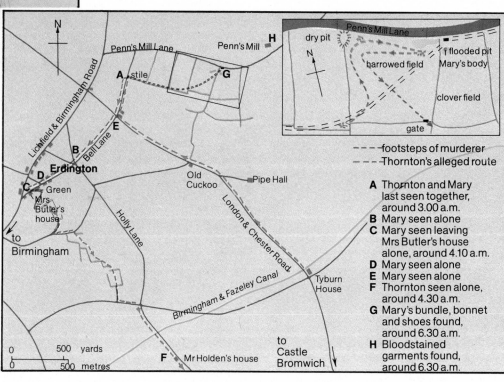

A Thornton and Mary last seen together, around 3.00 a.m.
B Mary seen alone
C Mary seen leaving Mrs Butler's house alone, around 4.10 a.m.
D Mary seen alone
E Mary seen alone
F Thornton seen alone, around 4.30 a.m.
G Mary's bundle, bonnet and shoes found, around 6.30 a.m.
H Bloodstained garments found, around 6.30 a.m.

Carter, walked together towards their respective homes as far as a place known as the Old Cuckoo, a little short of Erdington village. Hannah and Benjamin then went off in another direction.

At about 3.30 a.m. on 27 May, Mary Ashford was seen walking towards the home of Mrs Butler, Hannah Cox's mother. Evidence was given that she was 'walking very slowly and alone'. Arriving at Mrs Butler's house, Mary changed her party dress for her working attire and at 4 a.m. she said goodbye to Hannah Cox and said she was going home.

Mary was seen twice more after leaving Mrs Butler's house. Joseph Dawson testified to seeing her alone at 4.15 in Bell Lane, and 10 minutes later Thomas Broadhurst swore that he, too, saw her unaccompanied in the same lane. After the discovery of her body Abraham Thornton was interviewed and questioned about the murder.

Indignant suspect

'I can't believe she is murdered,' said Thornton. 'Why I was with her until four o'clock this morning.' Although astounded to hear that Mary had been murdered, it did not dawn on him for one moment that he was suspected of having killed her.

Later that day, however, Thornton was taken into custody and searched. He admitted having had sexual intercourse with the girl, but denied rape or murder. Although medical evidence in that era could hardly be called scientific, or be compared to the forensic evidence of today, the suggestion was that Mary had been sexually assaulted.

In his deposition Abraham Thornton confirmed that he and Mary had walked home part of the way with Hannah Cox and Carter. 'When Carter and Hannah left us Mary and I walked on over the fields until we came to a stile,' he stated. 'We sat talking for about a quarter of an hour. Soon afterwards we went to the Green at Erdington where I waited outside while Mary changed her dress. But Mary did not come out of the

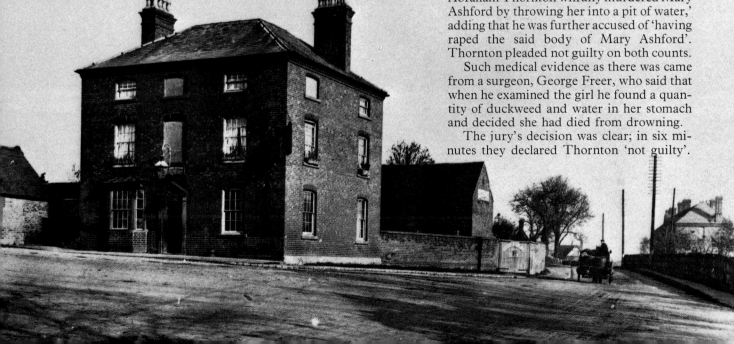

Above: Mary Ashford as she looked on the night of her murder. She attended a Whit Monday dance at the Tyburn House Inn (below), and spent the evening dancing with a young bricklayer, Abraham Thornton (overleaf top). She left the dance in Thornton's company, and was seen several times with him before her body was found next morning

house so, being tired of waiting, I went home alone.'

Fortunately for Thornton, there was confirmation that he was alone about this time. A Mr Holden, together with another man and woman, testified to seeing him – as, too, did John Haydon, a game-keeper, who talked to him for a quarter of an hour. Further to this testimony William Jennings, a milkman, stated that 'I saw Abraham Thornton about 4.30 in the morning, walking alone. . . .'

No one had seen Mary and Thornton together after they were sighted at 3.00 a.m. at a stile at the top of Bell Lane. The two had been seen by various people in this period, but always each was alone – they were never together. There was also the fact that the distance in a straight line from the flooded sandpit to the point where Thornton was last seen was nearly 1½ miles (2.4 kilometres) – or, by the route Thornton himself claimed to have used, 2 miles (3.2 kilometres). This fact alone, combined with the time factor, meant that at least some of the testified evidence was false. If Thornton walked to Erdington with Mary, as he claimed, then those witnesses who asserted that they saw Mary alone in Bell Lane must have been mistaken. Equally, it was clear that if Thornton's story was to be believed, the footsteps of a man that were found leading across those fields in the direction of the flooded sandpit could not have been his. Yet the female footprints were positively identified as belonging to Mary Ashford by two workmen at the nearby mill, who removed the dead girl's shoes and measured them against the footprints.

Abraham Thornton was brought to trial in August 1817 at the Warwick Assize Court before Mr Justice Holroyd. The case attracted considerable attention and a contemporary account of the trial stated that 'by six o'clock in the morning great numbers of people had assembled before the gates of the County Hall.' The charge was that 'not having the fear of God before his eyes, but being moved by the instigation of the devil, Abraham Thornton wilfully murdered Mary Ashford by throwing her into a pit of water,' adding that he was further accused of 'having raped the said body of Mary Ashford'. Thornton pleaded not guilty on both counts.

Such medical evidence as there was came from a surgeon, George Freer, who said that when he examined the girl he found a quantity of duckweed and water in her stomach and decided she had died from drowning.

The jury's decision was clear; in six minutes they declared Thornton 'not guilty'.

Connection and coincidence

Today that verdict would settle all arguments, but in the early part of the century, under an ancient law, it was possible for William Ashford, Mary's brother, to appeal against the verdict and so demand a second trial. This was fixed for 17 November 1817, and Thornton then appeared before Lord Ellenborough at the Court of the King's Bench. At this trial Thornton made legal history by being the last man in Britain to take advantage of an old law called 'Trial by Battel'. This involved Thornton renewing his plea of 'not guilty' and throwing down a gauntlet from the dock for the right to challenge William Ashford to trial by battle.

The law of England

'Not guilty,' Thornton declared, 'and I am ready to defend this plea with my body.' Thereupon Ashford's counsel disputed Thornton's right to trial by battle, claiming that it was 'an obsolete practice, which has long since been out of use'. But Lord Ellenborough ruled that it was 'the law of England'. If Ashford had picked up the gauntlet, the two men would have fought with weapons until one was beaten, or gave in. If Thornton had lost, he would have been executed immediately. If he had won, he would have been freed. Having had no response to his challenge by 21 April 1818, Thornton was formally discharged. He later emigrated to the United States.

The mystery of Mary Ashford's death lies not so much in the fact that her killer was never discovered as in the – admittedly remote – possibility that this might not have been a case of murder. On the other hand Barbara Forrest's death seems quite definitely to have been caused by strangulation. Her body, also partly clothed, was found hidden by long grass in a ditch some eight days after she disappeared. She had worked at the Pype Hayes Children's Home; Michael Thornton, a Birmingham child care

Below: Abraham Thornton's 'gage of battel'. At Thornton's trial for the murder of Mary Ashford, the jury pronounced him 'not guilty'. Mary's brother William appealed against the verdict and forced a second trial. Thornton then invoked the ancient law of 'Trial by battel', throwing down the gage of battel and declaring that he was ready to defend his innocence with his body. Ashford refused the challenge, and Thornton went free

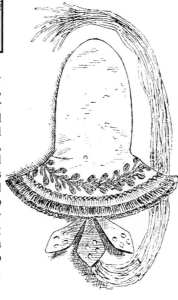

Right: Barbara Forrest, who was murdered 157 years to the day after the murder of Mary Ashford in 1817. The man charged with her murder was also called Thornton. Was this mere coincidence – or were the two murders somehow caused by the prevailing astrological conditions?

officer, who also worked as a supervisor at the home, was charged with her murder.

At the trial in March 1975, Mr Justice Croom-Johnson ruled that there was insufficient evidence to continue the trial and directed the jury to find Thornton not guilty. Despite the fact that the prosecution had had the entire seven months during which Thornton had been kept in Winson Green Prison to prepare its case, it was unable to offer any positive evidence against him.

There is one dissimilarity between these two so similar murders that is, curiously, extraordinarily striking. Mary Ashford's body was found within a few hours, although Erdington was then a village and her body was hidden in a flooded sandpit. Yet, while Erdington today is a built-up area of Birmingham, it took more than a week before Barbara Forrest's body was found in the ditch. And there are two other strange features of these cases. Although there is, of course, no photograph of Mary Ashford, sketches of her drawn after the celebrated trials suggest a marked resemblance to Barbara Forrest. A fellow worker with Barbara Forrest also declared that about 10 days before Barbara was murdered, she was heard to say: 'This is going to be my unlucky month. I just know it. Don't ask me why.'

Is this case simply a question of an extraordinary series of coincidences, or could it be that the astrological conditions on 27 May 1817 and 27 May 1974 somehow caused the murders of the two girls? To follow this hypothesis too far leads quickly to absurdities. But the 'twin' Erdington murders remain enigmatic – and not, quite, dismissible as mere coincidence.

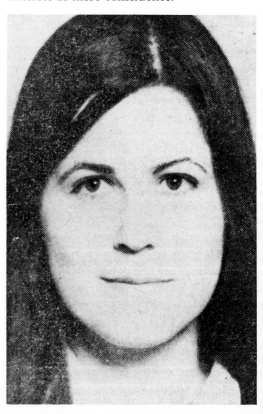

Once in a lifetime

The subject of coincidences is endlessly fascinating – above all to those to whom they happen. There are many extraordinary examples which lead to the belief that meaningful coincidence is not at odds with a rational view of life

A LIVELY CORRESPONDENCE on coincidences appeared in the *Daily Graphic* in 1905. Among the gems was a letter from the playwright Arthur Law. It told how, 20 years earlier, he had written a play featuring the sole survivor of a shipwrecked vessel, the *Caroline*. This fictional character was called Robert Golding. A few days after the play was first staged, Law was astonished to read a newspaper account of the sinking of a vessel called the *Caroline*. All hands had been lost, with one exception – a sailor whose surname was Golding!

The Nobel prize-winning physicist Wolfgang Pauli, for one, has concluded that coincidences can be regarded as the visible traces of untraceable principles. The American science writer Martin Gardner, however, remains sceptical: 'It is easy to understand how any one personally involved in a remarkable coincidence will believe that occult forces are at work.' Yet, even if there is no agreement on a definite answer to the question of what lies behind coincidences, it is undeniable that sceptics and believers alike find coincidences inescapably fascinating. For all coincidences make one wonder, and the more idiosyncratic examples never fail to fire the imagination.

Oddly enough, writers and musicians seem to have more than their fair share of remarkable coincidences – judging by their colourful after-dinner talk. Not every such tale is verifiable, but one event that is fully authenticated involved the world-famous oboist Leon Goossens.

In 1952, Leon Goossens lost his pocket diary on a bus. He quickly replaced it with a new one bought at the village shop near his home in Lewes, Sussex. Some weeks later, he lost the replacement diary – this time while crossing a field. The field was searched, but the diary remained hidden in the grass.

Over a year later Leon Goossens was walking across the same field, when he stopped to light a cigar – and spotted the lost diary close to his feet. By now, it was no more than a battered relic, but something prompted him to pick it up and flick through it. The months of sunshine, rain and snow had warped and split the bindings open, revealing that the covers had been stiffened with squares of newspaper. There was nothing

Left: the playwright Arthur Law, whose play *Caroline* featured one Robert Golding, the sole survivor of a shipwrecked vessel, the *Caroline*. Law's story was entirely fictional – but a few days after the play opened, he read an account of the sinking of a vessel called the *Caroline*. Its sole survivor was named Golding

surprising in that – millions of bindings are prepared in the same way. But in this case he found himself staring at a piece of newsprint that startled him. For there, pasted into the front cover, was a 19-year-old gossip column item referring to his own marriage in 1933. If the event had occurred in 1933 itself it would have been amazing enough. But considering the vast amount of newsprint that appeared during that 19-year-period, the odds against this coincidence are astronomically high – if they can be calculated at all!

It is little wonder that, when faced with events like these, people are led to think that there must be some form of guiding power behind 'meaningful coincidences'. They would certainly sense some such power in the next case – one of the most intriguing and moving in the annals of coincidence.

Leonhard Frank, the German playwright and novelist, gained international fame in 1926 with his novel *Carl and Anna*; it was converted into a play and later filmed. Encouraged by this success, he looked back at his very first novel, written in 1914 – *The robber band* – and decided to write a sequel called *The singers*.

In *The singers* Frank presented all the characters from *The robber band* in their middle age, with the spirit of adventure knocked out of them. Most of these characters were based on people Frank had known,

Connection and coincidence

but there was one new character in the novel who had no basis in reality. This was Hanna, a graceful springy child, slender without being thin. A hot-blooded stranger, olive and rose-coloured, who made play, despite the innocence of her sixteen years, with all the qualities of seductive femininity

Frank was certain that he had created Hanna out of his own imagination; she was no more than his ideal of girlhood – a dream image modelled on no one he had ever met or known. *The singers* was published in 1927, and the author considered it his finest work.

Two years later, in Berlin, Leonhard Frank finished yet another novel and found himself spent and exhausted from the effort. He began to spend time idly sitting at the Romanisches Café in an attempt to relax his overworked brain. And there one day, close by, he saw the Hanna he had 'invented'. She wore a white beret perched on her shoulder-length, raven-black hair. And, just as he had pictured it, her delicate face was olive and rose-coloured. When she smiled

she exposed a regular arc of teeth in her fresh, young, rather large mouth, involuntarily giving to her smile the

Below: the German author Leonhard Frank and his wife Charlotte. Frank first saw Charlotte in the Romanisches Café (right) in Berlin in 1929, where he was struck by her uncanny resemblance to a character

he had created. Haunted by her memory, he did not see her again for 19 years, when they met by chance at a farm to which they had both fled to escape the New York heat wave of 1948 (below right)

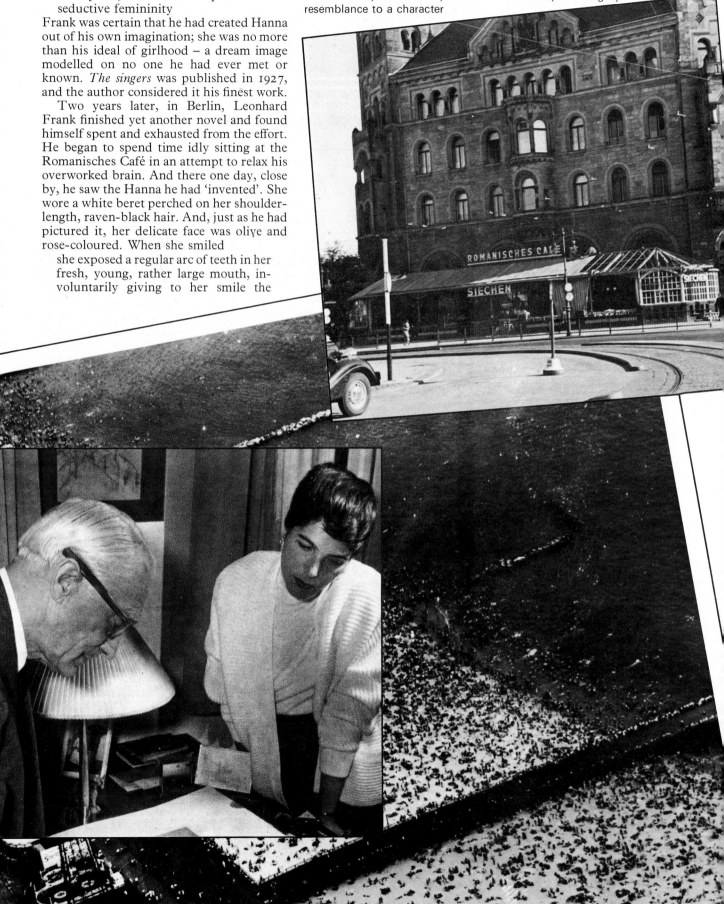

began to suffer from attacks of giddiness, and left the city for the countryside. He went to a farm whose owner took in paying guests; he had stayed there the previous year.

Once at the farm, he sat on low garden wall calmly drinking in the cool air – and then his heart began to race. There on a bench in front of the farmhouse sat 'Hanna', the ideal who had stepped straight from the pages of his book. She looked just as she had looked 18 years earlier – only the clothes were different. He sat dumbfounded. He had found her – in a strange continent, out of 150 million inhabitants, on a remote farm to which only a few dozen visitors ever came!

He was content to wait until the next afternoon before speaking to her. Then he

enchantment of a still-hidden gleam of womanhood – a hot-blooded girl standing on the brink of life.

What moved Frank more than anything else was her expression: 'emotional strength, suffused with humour and high-spirits, and in her eyes and mouth . . . an irresistible curiosity about life'.

As he watched her, Frank became aware that other customers and even the waiters were taken with the girl – her special qualities were obvious to everyone. It should have been an occasion for elation, but a melancholy feeling overwhelmed the writer – he was painfully conscious that he was 48 and this girl was hardly more than 20. Still, he had to follow his impulses and talk to this incredible creature. But before his chance came, a tall, thin youth hurried in, addressed the girl as Charlotte, apologised for being late and swept out holding 'Hanna's' arm.

For weeks afterwards Leonhard Frank haunted the café, hoping to see the girl once more – but she never returned and no one knew who she was or where she lived. Then, three years later, his last chance of meeting 'Hanna' disappeared. For Frank had to leave Germany to escape persecution, and perhaps death, at the hands of the Nazis. His exile eventually led him to the USA, where he worked as a Hollywood scriptwriter.

In July 1948, he found himself caught up in a record heatwave that hit New York. He

Above: the celebrated oboist Leon Goossens. In 1952, he lost a pocket diary while crossing a field. Over a year later, he was walking across the field when he came across the diary. He picked it up – and found that the cover had been stiffened using a square of newspaper carrying a gossip column item about his own marriage, 19 years before (top)

told her about the sighting at the Berlin café and about his search, and assured her that she was truly one of his characters. Without prompting, she immediately offered the name 'Hanna'. He was overjoyed that she too recognised the affinity, but his joy faded when she revealed that the young man at the café was now her husband. But Frank's passion was too great to smother and impulsively he tried to kiss her; but she pushed him away and for the next three weeks she avoided him. Then they met, danced and talked the whole night through and the next morning she rang her husband and told him that she must have a divorce. The husband dutifully bowed out and Leonhard and

Return of the rings

Stories of rings lost and found in the most unlikely of circumstances are among the most persistent in the annals of coincidence. In 1980 one Joseph Cross, of Newport News, Virginia, USA, lost his ring when it fell into floodwater during a storm. In February 1982 a restaurateur in Charlottesville, Virginia, found the ring – inside a fish. In Britain, on 28 March 1982, the *Sunday Express* and *News of the World* reported that, two years after farmer Ferdi Parker lost an antique wedding ring, a vet found it in a cow's stomach while performing an autopsy. On 13 September 1982 many

British newspapers reported the remarkable tale of Joy Manley, who lost a ring 11 years earlier while working as a pillow stuffer in a bedding factory in Somerset. It was returned to her after Marshall Hazzan, of Wilmslow, Cheshire, investigated a lump in his pillow, found the ring and passed it on to the bedding firm. And the *Sunday Mirror* on 18 July 1982 reported the affecting story of pensioner Albert Thornton, who was weeding a flower bed at his home in Tolworth, Surrey, when he found his wife's wedding ring, which she had lost 15 years before. It was their silver wedding.

Charlotte were married. Small wonder that Frank found that these amazing coincidences 'confirmed once again my belief that accident in human life may be synonymous with destiny'.

Yet despite the allure and magic of such stories, there are other factors that must be considered dispassionately. We have to realise that in judging coincidences we are hardly able to evaluate the events realistically; the data needed are never fully to hand. A real-life example will serve to illustrate this.

Chance encounter

A BBC producer on his way down London's Oxford Street to Broadcasting House suddenly remembered a book sale that he had seen advertised. He reversed direction, darted down a side-street that led to the place in which the sale was being held – and bumped straight into an old friend from his schooldays in Wales. The friend still lived in Wales, was in London for the day and was in that street at that moment only

because he had a last-minute change of plans. They were both amazed at the strange chain of circumstances that had brought them together.

But the producer began to make a few calculations. He reflected that for over 20 years he had walked along Oxford Street at least 20 times a week, but in all that time he had met only one person from his home town. And yet Oxford Street was a veritable magnet for visitors. So how many old friends had he *missed* meeting in all those years? Of course, there could be no answer to that question. But the question itself highlights the missing factor in most coincidences – for we never know how many pathways *fail* to converge. So we see coincidences in isolation and exaggerate their significance.

But for all that, who wants total knowledge? Most people are happy enough to cherish coincidences as happenings that add an extra sparkle to living – an attitude that is harmless enough and hardly at odds with a rational view of life.

Right: Oxford Street, London, on a typically busy weekday morning. A BBC producer, making his way along Oxford Street towards Broadcasting House one day, met an old school friend, who lived in Wales, in a side street. Both were astonished at the coincidence that had brought them together in such an unlikely place – but the producer later fell to wondering whether their meeting really was so very unlikely. He reflected that for over 20 years he had walked along Oxford Street at least 20 times a week; and Oxford Street is a magnet for visitors to London. What was perhaps more extraordinary was that he had not met *more* old friends

Profiles of the paranormal

It is claimed that the fragility of our orthodox boundaries of reality is vividly illustrated in detailed case studies of people with paranormal abilities, or those who make a study of the paranormal. However, deeper investigation shows that some of these cases are more indicative of human ingenuity than the existence of 'another world'.

A miracle in Tibet

It seemed as if Sadhu Sundar Singh's fate was sealed when he was sentenced to die in a deep, dry well without food, light and air – and yet he escaped almost unhurt. Was it a miracle?

ALL FAITHS HAVE THEIR SAINTS, mystics and visionaries, who have experiences expressed to them in the vocabulary of their own culture. A Roman Catholic may see a vision of the Virgin Mary, a Quaker may receive a revelation from the 'inner light', a Muslim may experience a communication from Mohammed, a secular poet find himself for an instant at one with the Universe and spend the rest of his life trying to express the glory of that moment's insight.

Such experiences can be used as propaganda for this or that form of belief. But they are shared by individuals of too many faiths and non-faiths to be accepted as evidence for one particular form of truth.

The story of Peter's miraculous escape from prison, when chained between two guards (Acts 12), is one that even many Christians find difficult to accept. Yet a 20th-century Christian, Sadhu Sundar Singh, not only claimed to have had a similar experience but also spoke of witnessing an extraordinary vision, one that was to change his life.

Sundar Singh's story begins in India, in the early 1890s, when he was still a young boy growing up in a wealthy Sikh family. His mother, a deeply religious woman, had taken Sundar to visit a *sadhu*, a holy man who has chosen the life of a homeless wanderer in search of truth. The meeting between the young boy and the old mystic had a profound effect on Sundar. He at once made it his resolve to search for God. When he was 14 his quest was intensified by the deaths of his mother and elder brother. A year later, possibly as a result of the missionary influences that were prevalent in India at the time, he struck out against Western religion. Christianity was anathema to him, and to show his hatred he stoned local Christian preachers and publicly burned the Bible in his village.

Three days after this denouncement Sundar is said to have received the sign he had been so fervently looking for. After praying all night he had a vision. In the vision Jesus Christ appeared to him and said in Hindustani: 'How long will you persecute

Right: an Indian holy man. It was a meeting with just such a man that was to start the young Sundar Singh on his search for God

Sadhu Sundar Singh (left) was undaunted by the hostile terrain of the Himalayas (below) and by the reception committee he knew would be waiting for him when he crossed to Tibet

me? I have come to save you. You pray to know the right way. Take it.'

Sundar's search had ended and, perhaps, no one was more surprised than he that it should end with a revelation from a Christian God.

This was only the beginning of Sundar's story; with his personal quest now over a new journey of evangelism had begun. He was baptised into the Christian Church in 1905 but, after taking an Anglican ordination course, he decided that the conventional priesthood was not for him. His new-found faith was not a fragile thing but then neither was his sense of Indian culture and tradition. Sundar believed he could spread his own vision of Christ only if he remained unfettered by denominational bonds. Not for him the dog-collars and suits that he had seen other converted Indian priests wearing. Nor was he willing to block out his awareness of the ever-present spirit world, a world that was close to the hearts of some of the primitive villagers among whom he lived and later preached.

To resolve his dilemma he took the unique

Good Lord deliver us

Acts 12: 1–17 relates a miracle that has no apparent rational explanation. Peter was imprisoned during one of Herod's anti-Christian purges. Chained between two soldiers, he was awoken in the night by a light in his cell. An angel appeared before him, struck off his chains and led him to freedom, bolts, bars and locks proving no obstacle. Peter 'came to himself' in the city street. Until then he thought he was dreaming but, finding his experience to be real, he went to the home of his friend where a girl, hearing his voice, reported that it was his spirit outside the house. When Peter's friends saw him they were amazed by his account of his escape.

In the 20th century, Sundar Singh's miraculous escape was to cause similar surprise and disbelief.

step of becoming a Christian sadhu, preaching the Gospel without material resources and relying on charity. As a sadhu he was allowed access to areas that would have otherwise been closed to him; as an Indian holy man, albeit a Christian one, he was less likely to alienate the very people he was trying to convert.

Sadhu Sundar Singh made it his special business to evangelise in Tibet. And it was in that strange and mysterious country that the miracle is said to have taken place. He crossed the Himalayas several times on foot and, though it was not easy to make converts in a Buddhist country, his zeal remained undiminished. It was during one of these trips that he was arrested and condemned to death for preaching Christianity.

Buddhist law forbids a true disciple to kill, so criminals are executed in ways that, by means of legal fictions, exonerate Buddhists from direct responsibility. Sundar's death sentence could have taken a variety of forms – one method was to sew the victim into a water-saturated bullock's skin. The skin would then be put out to dry. As it slowly contracted, so the person within was gradually smothered to death. Sundar's fate was to be as unpleasant. He was beaten, stripped of his clothes and then violently thrown down a dry well, topped by a heavy iron lid. By his own account, the floor of the well was carpeted with the human bones and putrid flesh of previous victims.

Time starts to run out

It was only a question of time before he either was suffocated by the stench of death or died from starvation. One thing, however, sustained him. When he had first seen his vision of Christ he reported experiencing a strong sense of peace and joy. This feeling, he claimed, remained with him always, even at times of distress and persecution. The effect of the vision – which, he maintained, was objective and entirely different from many other mystical experiences he was to have later on – was permanent. That feeling of peace and joy stayed with him throughout the duration of his incarceration.

Sundar passed the time in prayer until, on the third night, he heard the key grating in the lock above and the rattle of the withdrawn cover. He claimed that a voice called to him to seize the rope that was lowered. His arm had been injured during the beating he had received, but fortunately there was a loop in the rope into which he placed his foot and he was then hauled up the well and was

for three days in the conditions he had to endure would, undoubtedly, feel confused and disorientated when eventually released. Perhaps this explains why he was unaware of any human presence when he finally gained his freedom. Another discrepancy is how, given the conditions of Sundar's entombment, he could have known he had been there for three days – although, of course, someone may have told him of this later.

A sceptic would have strong grounds, too, for pointing out that the tale rested on the unsupported witness of a single man. That man, besides a constant stream of mystical visions, had experienced other wonders. He claimed to have made contact with a secret Indian Christian brotherhood whom he urged to declare themselves publicly; and to have met a *rishi* (hermit) of great age, the Maharishi of Kailash in the Himalayas, who dwelt in a cave 13,000 feet (4000 metres) above sea-level and imparted to him a series of apocalyptic visions. The apocalyptic visions were never recorded; the secret Christian brotherhood never declared themselves. The sceptic could argue that for all his concern with Christian truth, the Sadhu was a bit of a romancer given to flights of fantasy.

A taste for the bizarre

In truth, however, the sceptic should be left to believe what he wants to believe. Miracle or no miracle, it cannot overshadow the fact that Sundar was a genuinely good man who, in his own lifetime, was revered by many as a saint.

Sundar himself always tried to play down his psychic and mystical experiences and his possession of a gift of healing. He found that a reputation for miracle-mongering pandered to the public's taste for the bizarre and diverted attention to himself and away from the Christ it was his concern to preach. His own view of the affair in Tibet was that it had been heavenly forces at work. However, he would probably have been the last person to have wanted to make a production out of the so-called miracle. Romancing to glorify himself or even the God he served was foreign to him.

In the 1920s Sadhu Sundar Singh had become something of a household name. He made many trips, financed by friends, to Ceylon, Burma, Malaysia, China, Japan, America, Australia and Europe. He preached wherever he went and met with prominent churchmen, among whom he had a high reputation. Through these trips he made a deep impression on thousands of ordinary people of many races. There were few who regarded him as a holy confidence trickster who told lies to support a cause in which he had come to believe. He continued to make trips to Tibet, and the country that had been the source of his deepest revelation also turned out to be the place where he met his end. Sundar Singh disappeared without trace, somewhere in the Himalayas, in 1929.

free. He claimed he heard the lid being replaced and relocked. When he was out in the fresh air, the pain in his injured arm simply disappeared and he is said to have rested until morning then returned to the local caravanserai, an inn where groups of travellers rested. He remained there for a short while before he resumed preaching.

The reappearance of a man thought to be dead and safely entombed caused a furore. Sundar was arrested, brought before the head Lama and ordered to describe his escape. His own explanation of what had happened only enraged the Lama, who declared that someone must have stolen the key. But, when he found it was still on his girdle, which never left him, he was said to have been terrified. The Lama, apparently cowed by the possibility that the escape was a product of divine intervention, ordered Sundar to leave immediately and to go as far from the city as possible.

This then was the miracle in Tibet, when Sundar Singh was supposedly plucked from certain slow death by an act of God. But was the hand that saved him divine or human? Certainly Sundar's account has its weaknesses. For example, how was it that, after his release, he was able to make it all the way back to the caravanserai without anyone commenting on his nakedness? In fact, such a sight was not as unusual in Tibet as it would have been in Britain, say. There is, however, no getting away from the fact that someone could have stolen the key that could secure Sundar's release, or there may have been a duplicate. Anyone who had been locked up

Three lamas in front of a pilgrimage shrine. The men carry traditional ritual objects – prayer wheels and rosaries. Buddhism as practised in Tibet is an amalgam of the Buddhism of India and indigenous religious beliefs

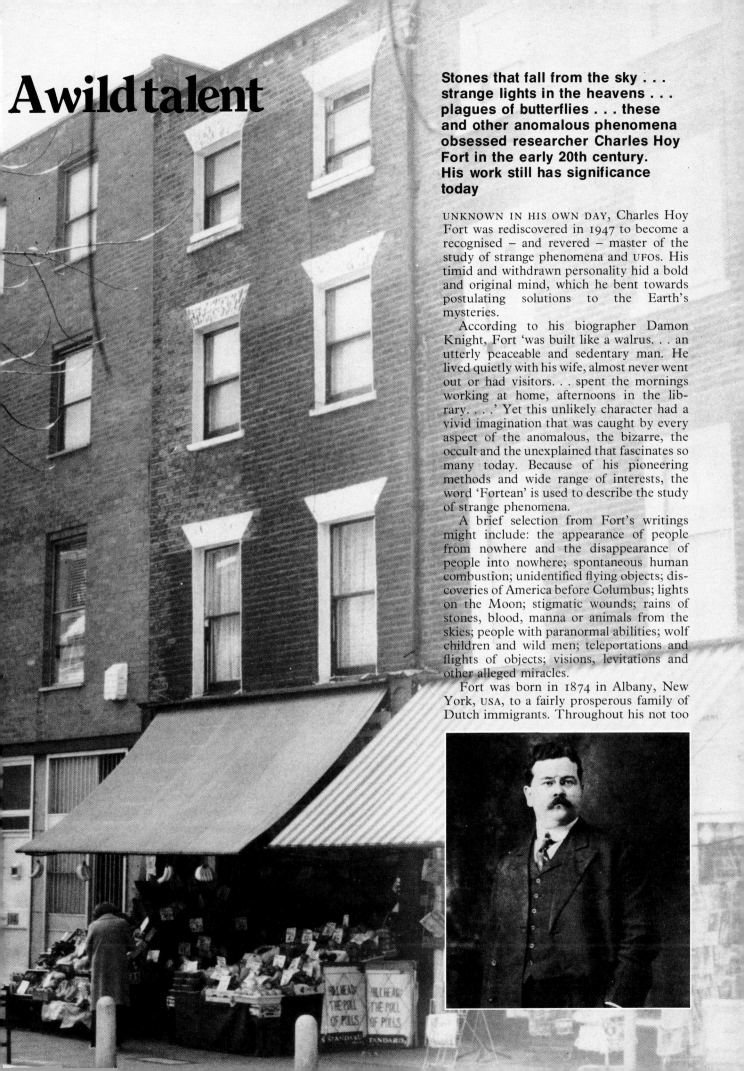

A wild talent

Stones that fall from the sky . . . strange lights in the heavens . . . plagues of butterflies . . . these and other anomalous phenomena obsessed researcher Charles Hoy Fort in the early 20th century. His work still has significance today

UNKNOWN IN HIS OWN DAY, Charles Hoy Fort was rediscovered in 1947 to become a recognised – and revered – master of the study of strange phenomena and UFOs. His timid and withdrawn personality hid a bold and original mind, which he bent towards postulating solutions to the Earth's mysteries.

According to his biographer Damon Knight, Fort 'was built like a walrus. . . an utterly peaceable and sedentary man. He lived quietly with his wife, almost never went out or had visitors. . . spent the mornings working at home, afternoons in the library. . . .' Yet this unlikely character had a vivid imagination that was caught by every aspect of the anomalous, the bizarre, the occult and the unexplained that fascinates so many today. Because of his pioneering methods and wide range of interests, the word 'Fortean' is used to describe the study of strange phenomena.

A brief selection from Fort's writings might include: the appearance of people from nowhere and the disappearance of people into nowhere; spontaneous human combustion; unidentified flying objects; discoveries of America before Columbus; lights on the Moon; stigmatic wounds; rains of stones, blood, manna or animals from the skies; people with paranormal abilities; wolf children and wild men; teleportations and flights of objects; visions, levitations and other alleged miracles.

Fort was born in 1874 in Albany, New York, USA, to a fairly prosperous family of Dutch immigrants. Throughout his not too

In his quest for stories of anomalous phenomena, Charles Fort (previous page) spent several years in the 1920s among the archives of the British Library (right) at the British Museum in London. During his 'London period' he lived in Marchmont Street (previous page), then a run-down area, close to the British Museum. He unearthed thousands of reports of extraordinary happenings, including cases of spontaneous human combustion, inexplicable flash floods and falls of red rain. Fort offered a characteristic non-explanation for such phenomena saying, 'we are being played with'

happy childhood, Fort suffered much physical punishment at his father's hands, which made him hate authority. His rebellions prepared him for a life questioning authority and dogma. When he was 18 he left home to hitch-hike around the world in order, as he saw it, to put some 'capital into the bank of experience'. One day Fort boasted to a bedridden neighbour of his travels, but the man was not impressed. He too had travelled when he was younger, but it was only when he was confined to his room, he said, that he began to extract lasting values from his experiences. This impressed Fort very much and he later wrote: 'I [realised] that one should not scatter one's self upon all life, but center upon some one kind of life and know it thoroughly.' And that is what he did for the remaining 35 years of his life.

Fort's 'grand tour'

In 1897, at the age of 23, Fort read every scientific book and journal he could find and, within a few years, had amassed 25,000 notes on the infallible public face of authoritarian science. He burned them because 'they were not what I wanted.' He resumed what he called his 'grand tour', reading through the world's major newspapers and scientific journals and taking notes on small squares of paper in a cramped shorthand of his own invention. By 1915 he had several tens of thousands of notes, and he began writing two books. One was called X and explored the idea that life on Earth has been controlled by events or beings on Mars. The other was called Y. In this Fort presented evidence indicating that a sinister civilisation existed at the South Pole. In writing to his friend Theodore Dreiser, the influential American

novelist, he commented: 'You have at least one thing to be thankful for – I might have begun with A.'

Then Fort's luck turned – an uncle died leaving him just enough income to relieve him from the worry of earning his daily bread. Dissatisfied with the lack of publishing interest in his unusual books, Fort burned the manuscripts of X and Y and promptly began a third gleaned from his fabulous collection of notes. Dreiser was taken with the new work, *The book of the damned*, and persuaded his publisher to issue it.

When it appeared in 1919, most critics did not know what to make of it. It obviously presented a radical critique of contemporary science but it was fragmented, choppy and hard to follow. Eminently quotable, by turns compassionate, violent, poetic, ironic and deceptively wise, it was written in a difficult stream-of-consciousness style.

Fort was a cynic about scientific explanations. He observed how scientists argued for and against various theories, facts and kinds of phenomena according to their own beliefs rather than the rules of evidence. He was particularly appalled at the way in which any datum that did not fit one scientist's view, or the collective view, was ignored, suppressed, discredited or explained away. Fort called such rejected data 'the damned' because they were 'excommunicated' by science, which acted like a religion.

Fort did not like to be told what to think and expected his readers to think for themselves as well. His favourite technique was to state the bald facts flatly and then criticise them according to their validity and usefulness. Then he would present some 'expert's'

According to Fort almost anything can, and sometimes does, fall from the sky, to heap knee-deep around the bewildered onlooker. Among the many eyewitness accounts are descriptions of the classic 'fire from heaven' (below) and rains of various artefacts, such as the steel ingots that fell on the citizens of Basel, Switzerland, in the late 15th century (right)

case or explanation, and put in opposition to it a few, often fantastic, theories of his own based on precisely the same evidence. Whether the results gripped the readers' belief or sense of humour, he left up to them. For example, throughout his writings he expressed doubts about the Darwinian theory of evolution. Again, in *The book of the damned* he anticipated the von Däniken premise of 'ancient astronauts' by over 40 years. In thinking aloud about the strange vitrified forts of Scotland, he imagined that they had been destroyed in some ancient space war. 'I think we're property,' he wrote, and elaborated his meaning: 'That once upon a time, this Earth was No-Man's-Land, that other worlds explored and colonised here, and fought among themselves for possession, but now it's owned by something, all others warned off.' In *Wild talents* he elaborated:

I now have a theory that, of themselves, men never did evolve from lower animals: but that, in early and plastic times, a human being from somewhere else appeared upon this Earth, and that many kinds of animals took him for a model, and rudely and grotesquely imitated his appearance, so that today, though gorillas of the Congo, and of Chicago, are only caricatures, some of the rest of us are somewhat passable imitations of human beings.

Travels of a prophet
The year after the publication of *The book of the damned*, Fort fell into a depression. He again burned his notes – which numbered 40,000 – and set sail for London. He could hardly contain his joy at the masses of material in the British Museum. In the next eight years he undertook his 'grand tour' several more times, at each pass widening his horizons to new subjects and new correlations. During this period, his belief in the eventuality of space travel developed, and he was sometimes to be heard giving forth on the subject to an uncomprehending crowd at Speaker's Corner in Hyde Park.

At this time Fort wrote *New lands*, the least successful and most cranky of his books. It was largely a satirical attack upon the pomposity of astronomers, who, he said, were 'led by a cloud of rubbish by day and a pillar of bosh by night . . . .' In 1929, Fort and his wife returned to New York and he began to work on *Lo!* He completed his last book, *Wild talents*, which dealt with the occult or psychic abilities of humans, in 1932, during progressive blindness and weakness. A few weeks later, on 3 May 1932, he was admitted to hospital; he died within a few hours. He took notes almost to the end; the last one said simply: 'Difficulty shaving. Gaunt places in face.'

In 1931, the year before Fort's death, Dreiser and another novelist, Tiffany Thayer, organised a meeting to launch the Fortean Society. Fort was not altogether

A monstrous regiment

Long before the term 'psychic warfare' was coined, Charles Hoy Fort came up with the startling idea of harnessing psychic powers to conquer the enemy. He envisioned a fighting unit of 'poltergeist girls' on the battlefield.

This passage on such poltergeist activity from his last book (*Wild talents*, 1932) illustrates his typical style of throwing out his thoughts.

'. . . A squad of poltergeist girls – and they pick a fleet out of the sea, or out of the sky – if, as far back as the year 1923, something picked French airplanes out of the sky – arguing that some nations that renounced fleets as obsolete would go on building them just the same.

'Girls at the front – and they are discussing their usual not very profound subjects. Command to the poltergeist girls to concentrate – and under their chairs they stick their wads of chewing gum.

'A regiment bursts into flames, and the soldiers are torches. Horses snort smoke from the combustion of their entrails. Re-inforcements are smashed under cliffs that are teleported from the Rocky mountains. The snatch of Niagara falls – it pours upon the battlefield. The little poltergeist girls reach for their wads of chewing gum.'

Such a regiment would surely be the ultimate in deterrent weaponry.

surprised, but declined the presidency. He had actually put his objection to such an organisation several years before. In 1926 in a reply to the science fiction writer Edmund Hamilton's discussion of the growing number of people who had read Fort and wished to pursue his ideas, Fort wrote:

> That we shall ever organise does not seem likely to me . . . . The great trouble is that the majority of persons who are attracted are the ones we do not want; Spiritualists, Fundamentalists, persons who are revolting against science, not in the least because they are affronted by the myth-stuff of the sciences, but because scientists either oppose or do not encourage them.

Nevertheless, Thayer founded the Fortean Society and it enjoyed much success in its early years. But because Thayer championed ever more cranky ideas – a flat Earth, for example – the society, and its journal *Doubt*, petered out with his death in 1959.

Method in his madness?

Today we can appreciate the method in Fort's madness as we see some of his wildest data in a wider context. For example, we acknowledge him as one of the main influences upon the developing study of UFOs, not least because such writers as Eric Frank Russell and Vincent H. Gaddis were originally members of the Fortean Society. Gaddis was already contributing articles on mysterious crafts and lights in the skies before the famous sighting by Kenneth Arnold at Mount Rainier, Washington, USA, in 1947, when the term 'flying saucers' was coined. Thirty years previously Fort had begun to collect notes on lights and dark objects seen dancing, speeding and hovering in the skies over many countries. He wondered then if they were the aerial transports of alien visitors – 'super-constructions' as he called

Top: a sea monster, one of the many 'impossible' creatures listed by Fort as having been reported by sober, reliable witnesses – and dismissed totally by equally 'reliable' scientists

Above: Theodore Dreiser (1871–1945), the American writer who was passionately concerned with projecting Fort as an immensely readable and worthwhile researcher. As he wrote in his review of Fort's *Lo!* (right): 'Charles Fort is the most fascinating literary figure since Poe.' But unlike Poe's works, Fort's were non-fiction – or were they?

them. He also conjectured that some of them might be little-known forms of natural phenomena.

Fort must also be credited with the discovery that UFO sightings come in 'flaps', as exemplified by the series of sightings of mystery airships across America (1896–1897), and Britain (1904–1905 and 1908–1909). At those times, no known airship could match the mystery crafts' speeds, design or powerful lights. It was this groundwork that prepared the early ufologists for the study of the wave of 'missile-like meteors', later called 'ghost rockets', that were sighted throughout northern and western Europe in 1946. If there were aliens with technologies in advance of ours, Fort mused in *New lands*, they might be able to project images of themselves onto Earth. Or, they might have appeared on Earth in person in earlier times and been taken for apparitions or demons. So that if we consider the history of apparitional phenomena, could not, as Fort asked, many of the 'appearances [be] beings and objects that visited this Earth, not from a spiritual existence, but from outer space'? Although Fort was being deliberately provocative, this passage does anticipate the psychological, psychical and paraphysical dimensions of close encounter experiences of the 'contactees' of today.

Another fundamental contribution by Fort to contemporary theorising is his notion of teleportation as a primary force for distribution of matter, objects and life forms throughout the Universe. From his acquaintance with the literature of Spiritualism, he was aware of the phenomenon of

LO! by CHARLES FORT

Acclaimed by

THEODORE DREISER
"Charles Fort is the most fascinating literary figure since Poe. His books thrill and astound me."

BOOTH TARKINGTON
"He is colossal, magnificent . . . Anyone interested in unorthodoxies, who enjoys having his imagination staggered and his mind dazzled, should read this vigorous and astonishing book."

JOHN COWPER POWYS
"I am struck sharply and starkly by the curious genius of Charles Fort. He creates that curious awe in the mind, in the presence of this inexplicable universe, which Goethe in *Faust* declares to be one of man's noblest attributes."

Left: the 'airship' that was seen over Peterborough, Cambridgeshire, on 23 March 1909, and which featured in *Lo!* Two constables, going about their duties at 5.10 a.m., saw and described the object as being 'somewhat oblong and narrow in shape, carrying a powerful light'. It also sounded like a powerful motor ticking over. Fort reported that several accounts of other strange aerial phenomena were received by sensationalist newspapers – but were not used by them. Fort suggested that the reason for this was that 'unaccountable lights and objects in the sky are not supposed to have sex'

Below: part of the vitrified fort near Strathpeffer, Ross and Cromarty, in the Highland region of Scotland. Fort was ahead of his time in ascribing the vitrification to intense heat from the fires of battle

It was the operation of this force of teleportation within the sphere of living creatures that most fascinated Fort. He could explain falling fishes or frogs in terms of the animals being whisked away from wherever they were abundant to some point in a distant sky, from which they then proceeded to fall. This could account for the sudden appearance of animals far from their usual habitats, or the appearance of fish in a freshly dug pond. What he called the teleportive force might even come under human control from time to time: poltergeist phenomena, levitation, bilocation or psychokinesis could occur consciously. Many of these ideas were eagerly seized upon by such American science fiction and fantasy writers as Robert Heinlein, Theodore Sturgeon, James Blish, Charles Harness, August Derleth and Philip Jose Farmer, some of whom were also members of the Fortean Society.

Over a two-year period when he was in his early fifties, Fort wrote a series of four letters to the *New York Times* in which he maintained that aliens were patrolling the skies. They were regarded as crank letters. When he died, the same dignified newspaper called him a 'foe of science' in its obituary on him. Fort would probably have expected such an epithet from people who had never tried to understand him. But his reputation has leaped over the *Times*'s opinion. Today some people regard Charles Hoy Fort as a prophet and visionary – and few who have studied him are prepared to dismiss him entirely.

'apports' – objects that materialise in the seance room. He felt that apports had an affinity to the appearances and disappearances of people, things and animals, the mysterious transportations and flight of objects usually, but not necessarily, during 'hauntings', and the phenomena of things and animals that fall in the open air in improbable circumstances. Fort coined the word 'teleportation' to describe such phenomena when he was writing *The book of the damned*. He saw teleportation as one of the basic forces of nature. It not only distributed life forms among the planets, but actually shifted materials of which they were built and shaped their environment. In the early days, wrote Fort, this force would have been extremely active. But as life and matter became more equally distributed among the inhabitable worlds, and became better established in their new homes, the need for the force would lessen. Eventually, he said, it would become vestigial, functioning erratically: 'The crash of falling islands – the humps of piling continents – and then the cosmic humour of it all – that the force that once heaped the peaks of the Rocky Mountains now slings pebbles at a couple of farmers near Trenton, New Jersey.'

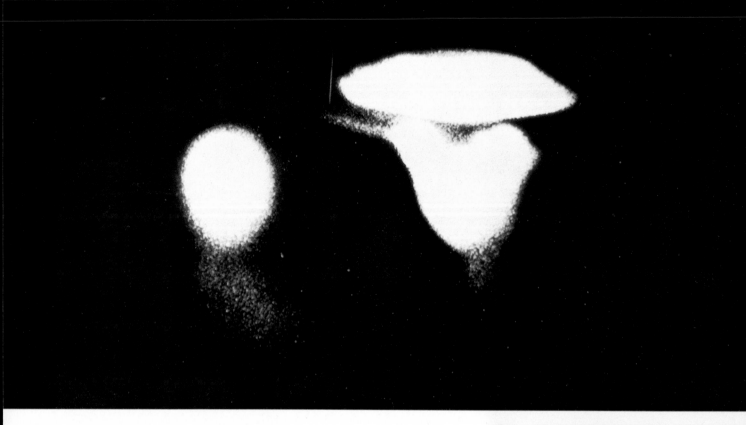

A wise fool

Did Charles Fort stumble onto some cosmic understanding as a result of collecting anomalous phenomena ignored by scientists? It may be that science today would gain by following up some of Fort's leads

THE PUBLICATION OF *The book of the damned* by Charles Hoy Fort in 1919 changed the standard of reporting of anomalous phenomena in American newspapers for the better. Nonetheless, there was a sting in the tail. For whenever journalists reported a sighting of a sea serpent, or a home disrupted by a poltergeist, or a shower of frogs, they would comment to the effect that 'here is another datum for the archenemy of science, Charles Fort.'

This unfortunate reputation of Fort as an enemy of science lingers. Anyone who has read his books, however, must disagree. Fort was extremely well-versed and up to date in nearly all branches of science in his day and understood the scientific method, the rules of evidence and proper scholarship. Fort had looked closely at the great and impressive edifice of science and found it full of cracks. He found scientists who made pontifical pronouncements without bothering with the facts of the case, who substituted dogma for true scientific enquiry, who suppressed, ignored or explained away embarrassing data. He felt that anomalies held significance for science and should be studied. To understand that significance, it is necessary to look briefly at how science develops and changes.

Above: a UFO photograph of 1965, listed in the Condon Report as a possible fake. Fort's interest in and notes on UFOs helped set the stage for the development of present-day ufology

Right: Galileo demonstrates his telescope to Florentine nobles. The first person to use a telescope for the study of the skies, Galileo made a series of important findings in the early 17th century – but his work was rejected by hide-bound scholars and the then all-powerful Church because it went against accepted ideas

The history of science is not one of orderly progression; it resembles more a battle, full of seemingly chaotic advances, retreats and skirmishes. This view of disorder and accident in scientific progress has been endorsed in one of the essential works on the history of science, *The structure of scientific revolutions* (1962) by Thomas Kuhn. At any time in its history, says Kuhn, a science is the prisoner of the 'basic preconceptions' of the day. These preconceptions are limiting factors, which he calls 'paradigms'. But paradigms are essential to the formal expression of a science because they serve as models or structures with which to organise whole areas of knowledge and to provide the context for explanations.

Kuhn shows that the rise of a new paradigm in science, and the demise of the outdated one, is not the 'graceful surrender' by fair-minded individuals that science propagandists would have us believe. It is often as painful and protracted as any religious or political revolution, and for much the same reason. Scientists are human beings with all the weaknesses and worries of human beings. They have a great deal invested in their job, their status and their credibility – factors of more value to their security than the ideal of an open mind. Above all, they tend to be loyal to the familiar paradigm.

The classic example of reluctance to accept something new is that of the group of Italian scientists who refused to look through Galileo's telescope lest they, like the Jesuit Clavius, be tempted to abandon their comfortable view of a geocentric Universe on seeing Jupiter's satellites through the instrument. Indeed, the revolutions of moons about Jupiter, the model for the new idea of the solar system, remained in contention for

many years after Galileo proposed the idea.

A new paradigm, or the data that leads to it, can seem threatening, even sinister. So the body of orthodox science behaves like an invaded organism and closes ranks against the 'infectious' data. Eventually the anomalies mount up and there comes a time when they can no longer be ignored. There ensues a crisis period during which whole fields of science are broken apart and the pieces reassembled incorporating the new data. What was once anomalous is now accepted or explained as a self-evident fact. Recurrent crisis is not only typical of scientific progress,

Above: this illustration from Marco Polo's account of his Asian travels in the 13th century shows the fantastic creatures that, he had heard, lived in India. Such travellers' tales are still part of the data base of anomalous phenomena

Below: Antoine Lavoisier, the 'father of modern chemistry'. Despite his distinction as a scientist, he dismissed out of hand the existence of meteors – and helped prevent their being studied by science for decades

Kuhn says, it is essential to it. In *Lo!*, Fort called science 'the conventionalization of alleged knowledge', explaining: 'it acts to maintain itself against further enlightenment, but when giving in, there is not surrender but partnership, and something that had been bitterly fought then becomes another factor in its prestige.'

The main aim of orthodox science is to consolidate the field of knowledge, not to seek out oddities of fact or theory. Repeatability and regularity are preferred to anomalousness.

Age-old oddities

The study of strange phenomena is clearly not in the same stage of development as mainstream science. In the field of 'anomalistics', as some American scholars call it, collections of oddities have long abounded, however. Many of the works of the Greek philosophers such as Pliny, Pausanias and Athenaeus are rich in Forteana. So are the writings of travellers such as Ibn Batutah and Marco Polo and of the compilers of early bestiaries and natural histories such as Olaus Magnus and Edward Topsell. Their work forms a vast data base on the subjects currently lumped under the heading of 'the unexplained'.

If this data base corresponds roughly to what Kuhn calls the 'morass' of data at the early point of a science, then we are only awaiting the coming of that organising paradigm to begin our transformation into scientists. Once again Fort points the direction, giving us a particularly useful expression. He says that orthodox science is, by its own definition, 'exclusionist'. A scientific experiment, for example, is an attempt to isolate something from the rest of the Universe. The flaw of orthodoxy lies in its attempts to put things into units or categories. Yet anyone who has seriously investigated strange data knows that they defy categorisation. Exclusionist science functions well enough but bases its criteria on arbitrary decisions. As science progresses, such distinctions become obsolete and collapse. Thus in the early 19th century many biologists still regarded living things as essentially different from non-living things: for these 'vitalists' there was an unbridgeable gap between the animate and inanimate worlds. But from 1828 onwards, as chemists learned to synthesise organic

compounds (compounds such as urea or acetic acid, which are produced by living organisms), the distinction between the animate and the inanimate lost its fundamental importance for chemists, and to present-day scientists seems little short of superstition. They tend to forget that many of the dividing lines drawn by today's science – such as that between mind and matter, for example – may be redrawn or abandoned; and they slavishly accept or reject data by criteria that are, at best, transient. It is clear that this arbitrary structure predetermines how we interrogate the Universe – and how we interpret its answers. The German physicist Werner K. Heisenberg wrote: 'What we observe is not nature itself, but nature exposed to our method of questioning.' So light will behave like a wave or a particle according to the context in which it is investigated. Or, as the duck said with peculiar logic in *Alice in Wonderland*: 'When *I* find a thing, it's usually a frog or a worm.'

Left: Werner Heisenberg, a Nobel prize-winner for his work in nuclear physics. The quantum theory, to which he made a great contribution, was not taught at one of Britain's ancient universities for 30 years after its formulation – a striking example of how scientists will sometimes resist new ideas from even their most distinguished colleagues

Below: spectra – bands of coloured light formed when white light is broken up. The theory that light is made up of waves was accepted by scientists because of its success in explaining spectra and other phenomena. But today light is considered to behave as a wave form *or* as a stream of particles (photons), depending on the experimental circumstances. This progression in the way that scientists explain light shows how a paradigm can change

The barriers between the acceptable and unacceptable in science are changing all the time. What is magic or superstition to one era may become the science of the next. The great French chemist Antoine Lavoisier told the Academy of Sciences in 1769 that only peasants could believe stones could fall from the sky, because 'there *are* no stones in the sky.' His influence prevented scientific study of meteorites – the 'stones from the sky' – until 1803.

But some barriers are breaking down. Today's life sciences contain much rehabilitated folklore: old herbals have been used for new pharmaceuticals and the practices of shamans have been adapted for new treatments. Apparitional phenomena, once the preserve of theologians and demonologists, are now the subject of psychical research and psychology. A number of Fort's special correlations – strange lights on the Moon, curious aerial lights and sounds that accompany or precede earthquakes, lunar periodicities in biological processes and behaviour, lake monsters and UFOS – are all matters of serious academic study today.

In answer to how strange phenomena could relate to the main body of science, Fort suggested that it was science that would make the move to assimilate anomalous phenomena by adopting a more radical, inclusive approach. Inclusionists would 'substitute acceptance for belief', he said, but only temporarily until better data or theories arose. This is exactly what true scientists do, of course, because for them enquiring after the truth is more important than being right or first. Inclusionism would recognise a state of existence in which all things, creatures, ideas and phenomena were interrelated and so 'of an underlying oneness'. From his thousands of notes, Fort came to the realisation that the Universe functioned more like an organism than a machine and that, while

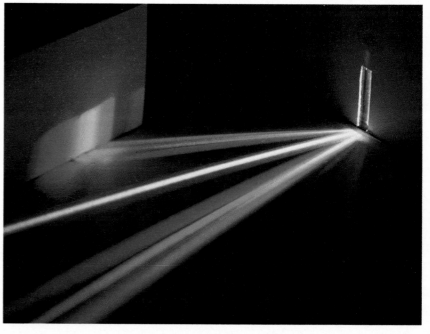

general principles applied universally, eccentricities, deviations and anomalies were the inevitable result of local expression of those principles. This almost mystical view anticipates C.G. Jung's notion of the collective unconscious and similar beliefs that appear in the cosmologies of primitive and animistic religions. Yet another theory in which the world is seen as functioning more like an organism than a machine emerged in 1981 – Dr Rupert Sheldrake's revolutionary principle of formative causation. This appears to offer philosophical tools for exploring continuity and synchronicity by postulating a resonance between forms of similar structure, whether living or not, that operates outside time and space.

Portents of change

In earlier times, most cultures had an appreciation of anomalies that we have lost. They also had some framework in which to study them, usually as omens or portents of social change, as Jung has suggested UFOs might be. Priests in rural Scandinavia in the late medieval period were obliged to report to their bishops anything contrary to the 'natural order'. Their chronicles that survive are treasure troves of sea serpent sightings, falls of mice and fish, animal battles and other strange phenomena.

Today such stories are absent from the scientific journals, where Fort found them, and are used as small filler paragraphs in the newspapers, written inaccurately and for laughs. Apart from a few excellent specialist magazines, the only regular journals devoted to the reporting and discussion of Fortean phenomena are two American publications, the *Journal* of the International Fortean Organisation and *Pursuit*, published by the Society for the Investigation of the Unexplained (SITU), and Britain's independent

Left: Charles Hoy Fort at his super checkerboard. He invented a game called super checkers (draughts), which was so complicated that it usually took all night to play it to the end

Below: a medieval fool. The jester poked holes in the customs and beliefs of his society – a role Fort played in ridiculing the scientific establishment of his day

Bottom: the simply marked grave of Fort at Albany, New York, where he was born

Fortean Times. The only scientific body concerned with anomalous phenomena is the Center for the Study of Short-Lived Phenomena, formerly part of the Smithsonian Institution in Washington DC, USA. It is now a successful self-funding venture. The establishment in London in 1981 of the Association for the Scientific Study of Anomalous Phenomena (ASSAP) may be a sign of hope for interdisciplinary studies of all sorts in the future.

One day, when orthodox science widens its circle of attention, the task of assimilating Fortean phenomena will have been made easier by the dedicated collectors of obscure and weird data. Their true function, in relation to mainstream science, is elegantly stated in a line from Enid Elsford's book on the medieval fool: 'The Fool does not lead a revolt against the Law; he lures us into a region of the spirit, where . . . the writ does not run.'

For the present author at least, Charles Hoy Fort was science's fool.

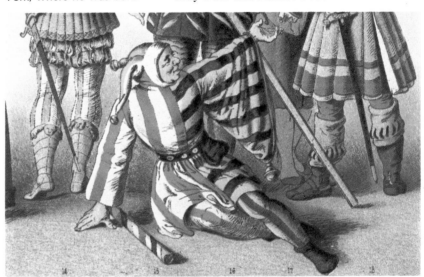

The unknown prophet

In 1914 an unidentified Frenchman was captured by German forces in Alsace. During an all-night session of questioning, the man made some extraordinary revelations to his captors – about the future of the war, and of the world

IN AUGUST 1914 ANDREAS RILL, a carpenter from Untermühlhausen on active service in Alsace, wrote two letters to his family in Bavaria, Germany. In these letters he told how he and another soldier had captured a Frenchman who proved to be a somewhat unusual prisoner. After capture, he was questioned all through the night – and during the questioning he began to speak about the future of the war. In his first letter, Rill wrote that the Frenchman was a 'strange holy man who said incredible things. If we knew what would happen during the years to come, we would throw away our weapons today.' And then the carpenter reported what their unusual prisoner told them: the war was to last for five years and Germany was going to lose it; a revolution would then follow, although it would not really end. Everyone would become a millionaire; there

Above left: Andreas Rill, the Bavarian carpenter whose letters home while on active service in Alsace in 1914 were more than a little out of the ordinary. For in one of them (left) he told of a Frenchman he had taken prisoner – a man who had been able to tell him the course the war was to take

'when there is a 4 and 5 in the year [1945], Germany will be pressed from all sides and totally plundered and destroyed'; foreign powers would occupy Germany. But, by virtue of its resourcefulness, Germany would recover. In the first letter Andreas Rill noted further that 'Italy will be against us in this war within a year and will be on our side in the second war'; many German soldiers would die in Italy. The letters tell of a third war beginning with an invasion by Russia of south-east Germany; this was to happen during 1947 or 1948, and during the war that followed the 'mountains will spit fire'; 'between the Danube and the Inn everything will be totally erased'; 'the streams are so shallow that no bridges will be needed to pass'; in Russia the rulers would be killed; there would be so many dead people that there would be no one to bury them.

Suspicion of authenticity

At first sight the letters are astonishing – the details are so extraordinarily accurate, even down to dates. When they were presented for examination to the Freiburg Institute for Border Areas of Psychology and Mental Hygiene, the first reaction was suspicion as to the authenticity of the letters. But experts in criminology testified that there are no signs that the letters are forged, or that parts of them were altered after they were written. The son of the author of the letters, Siegmund Rill (born 1906), told Professor Hans Bender and this author during a visit to his home in Weil, Bavaria, that everyone in the neighbourhood remembered Andreas Rill and his letters very well. After the first predictions had proved to be accurate, Andreas Rill told the story of the strange Frenchman to several of his friends in local pubs. Reportedly Rill became almost blasé, and somewhat fatalistic, after he saw one prediction after another fulfilled: the German defeat in the First World War, inflation and, finally, the upsurge of Nazism under Hitler. At that time the prophecies of the unidentified French prisoner became widely known in Bavaria, and one day a police crime squad showed up at the Rills' home to question him about his conviction that the future would bring tyranny. The son told us that it was only by chance that his father escaped imprisonment in a concentration camp.

During the 1950s the letters came into the possession of one Father Frumentius Renner, who published them in a mission journal, where they passed almost unnoticed. Until Professor Bender learned about the existence of the letters, no efforts were made to examine their authenticity or to establish the true identity of the mysterious prophet. It was a comparatively easy matter, at the Freiburg Institute, to have the letters checked by criminologists, but it was the work of some years to uncover the visionary.

Through careful tracing of members of

Above: Dr Hans Bender (left) of the Freiburg Institute for Border Areas of Psychology and Mental Hygiene examines one of the Rill letters with Father Frumentius Renner. Father Renner came across the letters in the 1950s, and published them in a mission journal – but, unaccountably, they passed almost unnoticed

Right: Adolf Hitler. According to Rill, the unknown Frenchman not only predicted the course of the First World War, but also forecast the establishment of the Weimar Republic, Hitler's rise to power, and the Second World War and its outcome

would be so much money that it would be thrown out of windows and no one would bother to pick it up. (At this point the author of the letter remarked: 'Ridiculous!') At this time the Antichrist would be born; he would be a tyrant, passing new laws every day; the people would become poorer without realising it. This time would begin around 1932 and would last for nine years. In 1938 preparations for war would begin; this war would last three years and it would end badly for the dictator and his followers; the people would rise against him in anger; things would become known 'that are simply inhuman'; everyone would be very poor; Germany would be torn apart.

Andreas Rill's second letter contains some details of the predictions of the end of this war: 'The man and his sign will disappear,' and hatred and envy would be rife; and

the Rill family and a minute analysis of the war journal of the company with which Andreas Rill had served, we tried to find the exact spot at which the Frenchman was captured. Andreas Rill's sons told us that the visionary was apparently a rich man who gave away all his earthly wealth to join a monastery in Alsace. Before that he was said to have belonged to a Freemason's Lodge in Colmar. Our researches revealed that Rill's company must have been around Colmar in Alsace when the prophet was interviewed. Siegmund Rill was sure that his father met the visionary in a monastery near Colmar; and we confirmed that part of Rill's company was housed in a Capuchin monastery at Sigolsheim, 6 miles (10 kilometres) from Colmar, at the time. Some years later, in 1918, Rill and his company were stationed at Turckheim, near Colmar. His son told us that Rill took the opportunity to go, on foot, to the monastery to look again for the visionary, but was told that he had died in the meantime.

We checked the lists of inhabitants of all

Above: the monastery at Sigolsheim, Alsace, where the Freiburg Institute's search for the identity of the mysterious French prophet eventually led them. Their researches revealed that a Frater Laicus Tertiarius – a person who lives in a monastery as a guest of the religious community – had died at Sigolsheim in 1917. Rill had captured the French prophet in 1914; in 1918, when his company was stationed at Turckheim (see map, left), he apparently walked to a monastery to look for the visionary, but was told he had died. Turckheim is within walking distance of Sigolsheim; could the French prophet have been the unknown Frater Laicus Tertiarius?

the Capuchin monasteries in the area and found one slight clue that might point towards the person we were looking for: in the Sigolsheim monastery there had lived a certain Frater Laicus Tertiarius who had died at some time after 1917 but before Rill's second visit to the place. A Frater Laicus Tertiarius is a person who is not a member of a monastery, but who lives there as a guest. It could well have been that the prophet would not have been immediately accepted as a member of the monastery, particularly if he had been a rich man and a Freemason in his earlier life. Furthermore, it is easy to reach Sigolsheim by foot from Turckheim, so this may well have been the place that Andreas Rill visited when stationed in Turckheim in 1918.

We found several passages in the war journal that might have a bearing on the prophecies. One prediction the Frenchman made – noted in one of the Rill letters – was that a certain Corporal G., who ridiculed the visionary, would not come home from the war and that his body would not be buried, but would be eaten by ravens. True enough, on 23 September 1914, Corporal G. went missing while on a patrol. The war journal notes that his remains were found and identified in February 1915. The war journal also contains a note, concerning Corporal G. and dated the day of his disappearance, from the private journal of Colonel Schleicher putting it on record that the corporal was 'seeing spirits again.'

It remains puzzling that such a detailed

and important prophecy did not become better known. Why should the Frenchman tell his visions only to his German captors? Was this the only prophecy he ever uttered? This is hard to believe; but we are left with no more substantial evidence than the two letters written by Andreas Rill to his family.

An important aspect to consider is, of course, how good the precognitions turned out to be. Andreas Rill's first letter is an

account of what the Frenchman said, while the second represents Rill's reflections on his experience with the visionary. The second letter, written some days after the first, also gives details about a third world war. It seems that Rill selected from the prophet's words only those aspects of the third war prophecy that related to his home, Bavaria. In considering the predictions of the three wars, we should bear in mind that the prophet was French, and although the author of the letters reports that he spoke several languages (it is most probable that he spoke German with the soldiers), some misunderstandings may have arisen through the prisoner's imperfect command of the German language. Considering the Frenchman was interviewed for many hours at night, it is hard to believe that Rill could have remembered all he said.

Psychological studies of reports of witnesses show how poorly people are, in general, able to recollect events they have experienced. One should not forget, too, that the prisoner's prophecies were of the highest interest among the soldiers and that discussion may have prompted embroidery of the truth.

But the prophecy does, with fair accuracy, forecast political developments in Europe for many years to come. The successful predictions include the duration of the First World War from 1 August 1914 to the armistice of 11 November 1918; revolution and the establishment of the Weimar Republic on 9 November 1918; the leftist revolution and

Above: Warsaw pact manoeuvres in Poland in 1981, and (right) an anti-nuclear-weapon demonstration that took place in Bonn, West Germany, also in 1981. The French prophet forecast a third world war that was to take place between 1946 and 1948: 'mountains will spit fire'; 'everything will be totally erased'. This did not, of course, happen – but could the French prophet have been 'tuning in', not to actual events in the future, but to the general climate of anxiety about the nuclear arms race that has existed ever since the atomic explosions that ended the Second World War?

its failure to retain power; inflation until 1923; the election of the Nazi party in January 1933; the occupation of Czechoslovakia in March 1939; the attack on Poland in August 1939; the occupation of Norway and Holland in May 1940; the attack on Russia in June 1941; the landing of Allied forces in Sicily in July 1943; Hitler's suicide and the surrender of Germany in May 1945, and its occupation by American, English, French and Soviet troops; the loss of German territory and the division into two states; and the rapid recovery of the Federal Republic of Germany under chancellor Adenauer.

What of the predictions concerning a third world war? A psychic who gives an accurate prediction in one case may, of course, be totally wrong in another. At Freiburg we have experienced this time and again in experiments with the famous psychic Gerard Croiset. Thus the prediction of a war yet to come may well be completely wrong. The time when it was supposed to take place, 1946 to 1948, has passed. This may mean that the prediction is erroneous. But the dates may also have been noted wrongly, or the prophet, speaking a foreign language, may have given them wrongly.

There is no question that in Europe now a possible third world war, with its horrifying potential for destruction, is felt as a constant

imminent danger. The psychic may have 'picked up' this general anxiety and mistaken it for the events actually happening.

Whether it is a precognition of potential danger or mere fantasy – or something in between – the case of the French prophet, with such detailed predictions fulfilled with such accuracy, remains a puzzling and enigmatic footnote in the files of parapsychology.

In the 17th century, Kenneth Odhar – the prophet of the Seaforth family – was hailed as one of the greatest Highland seers ever. And it seems that his predictions continue to be fulfilled today

IF WE ARE to give folklore and historical legend any credence at all, the power of 'second sight' has been commonplace in the Highlands of Scotland – and in Ireland whence the Celtic people of the north came – for centuries. Until the 18th century, every glen and braeside from Lochaber to the far tip of Caithness had, it would seem, its resident 'wise' man or woman, traditionally the seventh child of a seventh child, who through the power of God or fairies inherited the gift of *taibh-searachd* – prophecy.

After the last Jacobite uprising ended with the disastrous battle of Culloden in 1746, the clans were considerably reduced in number and their remnants exiled and scattered to the West Indies, North America, and later Australia and New Zealand. But the tradition of the 'Highland seer' lived on; even today his descendants are looked upon tolerantly and with respect.

In the 19th century there was a quickening of interest in the 'romantic' Highlands. George IV encouraged the trend by appearing at Edinburgh with his portly frame wrapped in the newly invented 'Royal Stewart' tartan, a fashion followed by the Prince Consort, who went as far as to design a tartan wallpaper and carpet for Balmoral, and Sir Walter Scott had already fanned the flame with his popular historical novels.

In the wake of this 'romanticism' came the folklorists, indefatigably tramping over the heather in search of quaint tales and superstitions. One of the more respected of these

Baile-na-Cille in Uig on the Isle of Lewis, reputedly the place where Kenneth Odhar, the Brahan seer, received his precognitive powers. According to legend, he either found or was given a magic stone, and it was in this that he was able to see the future. It seems that Kenneth paid dearly for his gift, for one tale has him half-blinded, and several accounts describe him as 'cam' – one-eyed or squinting

was Andrew Lang, himself a Scotsman, an active member of the Society for Psychical Research, and the author of, among other books, *The making of religion* (1898), which dealt with examples of second sight among primitive societies. Turning to his homeland, Lang examined the evidence for and against the powers of the native seers. In a paper published in 1899, he was able to 'unblushingly confess the belief that there probably are occasional instances of second sight, that is of "premonitions"'.

However, Lang urged that all the evidence in each individual case be considered, pointing out that the strongest cases must rest on prophecies that had been recorded before their 'fulfilment', thus ruling out the possibility of romantic hindsight. Obviously, the more explicit the prediction, the more convincing its detailed fulfilment would be.

Under these terms, the posthumous claims made for Coinneach Odhar of Mackenzie, the Brahan seer, stand up to considerable scrutiny. Famous in his lifetime as the resident prophet of the mighty Seaforth family, he came to be regarded as one of the most impressive Highland seers ever when, 150 years after his death, his predictions regarding the unusual circumstances of the family's extinction came precisely true.

Coinneach – Gaelic Kenneth – was born in the parish of Uig on the Isle of Lewis around the year 1600. According to Alexander Cameron of Lochmaddy, who chronicled many of the seer's prophecies some years after his death, it was at some time during his early teens that Kenneth's powers developed. Several versions of their origins exist, all involved with the supernatural. According to one, his mother, tending her cattle in the graveyard of Baile-na-Cille near Uig, met

Prophet by appointment

the ghost of a daughter of the King of Norway, who gave her a blue stone in which Kenneth would see the future. Other accounts tell how Kenneth himself was given a white stone with a hole in it by the fairies, and it was through this that he was able to see coming events.

Whatever the source of his powers, news of them spread to Kenneth's feudal overlord, Kenneth Cabarfeidh – Staghead – Mackenzie, who in 1609 had been created first Lord Mackenzie of Kintail. The chief's stronghold was Brahan Castle, a few miles from Dingwall on the Cromarty Firth, and at his summons Kenneth Odhar went to live on the Brahan lands. Soon after Odhar's arrival the old chief died and was succeeded by his son, who was created first Earl of Seaforth in

Above: the writer and psychical researcher Andrew Lang (1844–1912), who examined the evidence for second sight in his native Scotland. He confessed to a belief in the existence of 'premonitions', saying: 'I know too many examples among persons of my acquaintance . . . to have any doubt about the matter'

Left: a *taibhsear* – seer – of the Highlands. Such figures commanded respect in the community as it was widely believed that the power of second sight was a gift from God, or inherited from the fairies

Below: the battle of Culloden, 1746, which – in one of his more memorable prophecies – the Brahan seer accurately predicted over 100 years before

1623; it was the first Earl's grandson who was to build Odhar's fame.

Kenneth, third Earl of Seaforth, was roughly the same age as Kenneth the poor prophet and seems to have been fascinated by him. He released the seer from his job as farm labourer on the Brahan estate and, although still lodged in a sod-roofed cottage, Odhar the Lewisman – who spoke only Gaelic – was introduced into local learned society.

He cannot have been a cheerful companion, for his predictions invariably involved bloodshed or disaster, pronounced with a dour relish. On one occasion, for instance, an elderly man, Duncan Macrae of Glenshiel, asked the seer to tell him 'by what means he would end his days'. Odhar immediately replied that he would die by the sword. Such an event seemed so unlikely that Odhar stood in danger of being discredited:

for one thing, Macrae had been distinguished in the Mackenzie army in clan wars without coming to harm, and for another there had been no tribal feuding for years. Nevertheless, recorded his kinsman and contemporary the Reverend John Macrae of Dingwall, Duncan Macrae died as predicted, the victim of a misunderstanding. In 1654 General Monck led a troop of Parliamentary soldiers up to Kintail and a company of them met Macrae walking in the hills behind his house. Addressed in a language he did not understand and startled by the strange uniforms, Macrae put his hand to his broadsword and was immediately cut down: 'This was all the blood that General Monck or his soldiers, amounting to 1500 men, had drawn.'

The weeping widow

Most of the time the seer's advice was unsolicited, and his predictions were interesting only because they proved accurate. One day he announced that 'A Lochalsh woman shall weep over the grave of a Frenchman in the burying place of Lochalsh.' Frenchmen were virtually unknown north of Edinburgh, and yet within a few months the Earl of Seaforth discovered that a Lochalsh woman had married a French footman who died young; the widow had taken to weeping by his graveside every day.

Doubtless these insights into the immediate future enthralled Odhar's contemporaries, but it was his long range predictions that fascinated the likes of Andrew Lang. Odhar gained nothing from them personally, not even prestige, for their fulfilment lay far in the future, and this as much as their accuracy gives them the hallmark of genuine precognition.

One pronouncement that was marvelled at when it proved true was that in the village of Baile Mhuilinn, in the west of Sutherland, there would live a woman named Baraball n'ic Coinnich (Annabella Mackenzie) who would die of measles. In about 1860 there was a woman of that name living in the

land but, said Kenneth, one day it would 'be under lock and key, and the Fairies secured within'. In the mid 19th century it became a cemetery, and today is surrounded by a fence with a locked gate.

For the Mackenzies of Fairburn, cousins of Seaforth, Odhar could see nothing but doom. Over the years he predicted gruesome fates for them, combined with financial ruin and final obliteration; eventually, Odhar said, a rowan tree would grow from a crack in Fairburn Tower, and a cow would calve in its upmost chamber. In Odhar's time the tower was new and strong, but in the 18th century, when its owners lost their lands following the Jacobite rebellion, it fell into ruin. In 1851 a cow did make its way up the narrow and precipitous stairway and calved in the top room, while a rowan tree sprang from a fissure half way up the tower wall and grew to a considerable size before dying in the summer drought of 1957.

village, but she was 95 years old and it seemed unlikely that her death would be caused by that disease; then, a few years later, Annabella died – as predicted – of measles.

In 1630 Seaforth 'lent' Odhar to a 'gentleman from Inverness', who wrote down a string of the seer's utterances. One well-authenticated pronouncement was made on the way to the gentleman's house. Crossing a bleak patch of moorland, Odhar said: 'Oh! Drummossie, thy bleak moor shall, ere many generations have passed away, be stained with the best blood of the Highlands. Glad I am that I will not see that day . . . heads will be lopped off by the score, and no mercy will be shown.' One hundred and sixteen years later the battle of Culloden was fought on that very spot.

Mystery of the moving stone

Another startling prediction concerned an 8-tonne stone that marked the boundaries of the estates of Culloden and Moray. The day would come, said Odhar, when the 'Stone of Petty' would be moved mysteriously from its position on dry land and re-erected in the sea of Petty Bay. It is a matter of record that during the stormy night of 20 February 1799 the huge stone was uprooted and ended in the sea some 250 yards (230 metres) from the shore line. No satisfactory explanation of its moving has ever been put forward.

In another of his predictions Odhar spoke of 'strings of black carriages, horseless and bridleless', which would pass through the Highlands, led by 'a fiery chariot' – a fair description of the railways of mid Victorian times. He also stated that ships with sails would pass behind the 'fairy hill' of Tomnahurich near Inverness; they began to do so when the Caledonian Canal was opened in the 1820s. Tomnahurich itself was common

Some of the seer's accurate predictions: of the common land at Tomnahurich that became a cemetery (above) in the 19th century, he said it would be 'under lock and key and the Fairies secured within'; of the advent of the railways (right) he said 'horseless' carriages would be led by a 'chariot of fire'; and the downfall of the Fairburn Mackenzies, he rightly said, would be signalled by the birth of a calf and the sprouting of a rowan tree in the ruin of Fairburn Tower (below)

Famous last words

When the mighty Seaforth family sentenced their resident seer to death, they also condemned themselves. For in his final utterance the prophet foretold only doom and destruction for the Seaforth line

POPULAR FAITH in the prophecies of Kenneth Odhar, the most distinguished of Highland seers, was strong and widespread in the mid 17th century. Many of his predictions were well-known and were passed on from generation to generation: some came true in his lifetime, others long after his death; many are still unfulfilled.

Some of Odhar's prophecies may have been helped by his natural shrewdness. The strange, sulphurous waters of Strathpeffer, a few miles north of Brahan, had been shunned by locals as poisonous for years, but Odhar claimed that

> Uninviting and disagreeable as it now is, with its thick crusted surface and unpleasant smell, the day will come when it shall be under lock and key, and crowds of pleasure and health seekers shall be seen thronging its portals, in their eagerness to get a draught of its waters.

In 1818, Strathpeffer became a fashionable spa, and the pump room, normally kept locked, is still a centre for health cures.

On the other hand, his prediction of a disastrous flood 'from a loch above Beauly', which would destroy a village in its vicinity, was unlikely in the extreme. There was no loch anywhere near Beauly, which stands at the innermost point of Beauly Firth. However, in the 20th century a dam was built across the river Conon at Torrachilty, a few

Right: the pump room at Strathpeffer mineral wells. The Brahan seer's prophecy that one day the waters would draw crowds of 'health seekers' astonished the local people, for it was popularly believed that the Devil himself washed there. However, in the late 18th century it was discovered that the waters had healing properties, and in 1818 Strathpeffer was established as a fashionable spa

Below: in 1966 heavy rain caused the hydro-electric dam at Torrachilty to overflow and this, in turn, caused the river Conon to burst its banks. The flooding created havoc in the village of Conon Bridge, destroying buildings, crops and cattle. The precise nature of this disaster had been foreseen, centuries before, by the Brahan seer

miles away from Beauly, and in 1966 it unexpectedly overflowed. The flood water killed hundreds of sheep and cattle, destroying grain, fences and buildings in the village of Conon Bridge, some 5 miles (8 kilometres) 'above Beauly'.

Odhar's end was surprisingly unforeseen, considering his gifts, but it did cause him to forecast with uncanny accuracy the end of his patron's line. Kenneth, third Earl of Seaforth, was a staunch Royalist who led a troop of his Mackenzie clansmen during the Civil Wars against Cromwell's army along the Scottish borders. After the death of Charles I he was imprisoned but, after the Restoration, was held in high esteem by Charles II, being granted extra lands and winning the hand of Isabella Mackenzie, sister of the Earl of Cromarty.

In the mid 1660s the Earl was sent to Paris by King Charles, and several months passed without Isabella receiving a letter from him. One night, Isabella asked the seer to tell her what her husband was doing. Odhar said that he saw him in a splendid room, well and happy, and 'indisposed' to return home yet. Isabella pressed him to tell her more, and the incautious prophet told her that the Earl was 'on his knees before a fair lady'.

The Countess immediately ordered the seer to be burned to death in a tar barrel as a

witch. Odhar was astonished and filled with dismay at her reaction: he had expected reward for his prophecies, not condemnation. But the Countess's decision was upheld and, attended by representatives of the Kirk, Odhar was taken to Chanonry Point on the Moray Firth for execution. There, he begged the ministers to write down what he was going to say.

Speaking in his native Gaelic, he said that he saw a Seaforth chief, the last of his house, who would be deaf and dumb. He would have four fair sons, all of whom he would follow to the tomb. One of them would die on the water. His daughter, whom the prophet described as 'white hooded', would come from lands to the east to live at Brahan, and she would kill her sister. Thus all the Seaforths would die. The seer continued:

And as a sign by which it may be known that these things are coming to pass, there shall be four great lairds in the days of the last deaf and dumb Seaforth – Gairloch, Chisholm, Grant, and Raasay – of whom one shall be buck-toothed, another hare-lipped, another

When Kenneth, third Earl of Seaforth (left), patron of the Brahan seer, was abroad on business, his wife Isabella (below), having had no word from him, summoned the seer to Brahan castle (below left: the castle in ruins) to give an account of her husband. The seer told her that he could see the Earl with another woman, and Isabella was furious. Unfortunately for the seer, she directed all her anger against him and condemned him to be burned as a witch

half-witted, and the fourth a stammerer.

There would also be a laird of Tulloch, 'stag like', who would kill four wives in succession, but the fifth would outlive him.

Odhar was executed near the modern Chanonry Point lighthouse, by the road from Fortrose to Fort George ferry; the place is marked with a stone slab. But the memory – and the implied threat – of his predictions lived on, not least in the minds of the Seaforth family. For the next hundred years their fortunes fluctuated, and several of them must have wondered if extinction were close at hand. For their activities in the risings of 1715 the family were stripped of their titles, but these were restored in 1726, and the Seaforths subsequently became staunch

Hanoverians, growing richer and more powerful by the year. The title of Earl of Seaforth died out with its holder in 1781, but the chieftainship passed to a second cousin who seemed destined to bring even greater honours to Brahan.

Francis Humberstone Mackenzie was born in 1754 and early in his life became member of parliament for Ross and Lord Lieutenant of the county. During the revolutionary wars with France he raised a regiment that subsequently became the Seaforth Highlanders, and in 1797 he was created Baron Seaforth of Kintail. In 1800 he became Governor of Barbados, and in 1808 he was promoted to Lieutenant-General of the army. As well as his military interest, Seaforth was an amateur painter of great

having another 30 illegitimate offspring in Tulloch gained him the nickname 'the stag'.

Odhar's final prophecy came true within a few years of Seaforth's death. His eldest surviving daughter Mary had married Admiral Sir Samuel Hood in 1804; and when Hood died at about the same time as Seaforth while commanding the East Indian station, Mary returned home in widow's weeds to take over her father's lands: this formal dress included a white hood – so that she was both 'hooded' in fact, as Odhar had said she would be, and 'Hood' by name. One day she was driving her younger sister, the Hon. Caroline Mackenzie, through the woods by Brahan Castle when the ponies bolted and the carriage overturned; Lady Hood was merely bruised, but her sister died of her injuries.

The prophecies of the Brahan seer form a perennial guessing game for those Highlanders who know of them, for from time to time they still appear to come true – as in the case of the Conon Bridge disaster. One of the

talent, and he sponsored not only Sir Walter Scott, but also the painter Sir Thomas Lawrence and the scientist Sir Humphry Davy in their early years. He was happily married to the niece of Lord Carysfort, who bore him four sons and six daughters; altogether he presented a picture of enduring, well-established worth.

But the truth of the matter was that the prophet's predictions had begun to come true for Seaforth when he was 12 years old. In that year an outbreak of scarlet fever at his boarding school killed several of his fellow pupils and rendered Seaforth totally deaf; over the years his speech became affected, and towards the end of his life he could communicate only by making signs or writing notes.

His eldest son William Frederick died as a baby in 1786 and eight years later his second son George died at the age of six. His third son, Francis, a midshipman in the Royal Navy, was killed in his eighteenth year in a skirmish at sea – 'dying on the water', as Kenneth had foretold, in November 1813. Finally his last son, another William Frederick, the 24-year-old MP for Ross, died suddenly in August 1814. Seaforth himself died in January of the following year and was buried with his ancestors at Fortrose Cathedral. His contemporaries and neighbours, as the *Edinburgh Daily Review* pointed out in Seaforth's obituary, were the buck-toothed Sir Hector Mackenzie of Gairloch, the harelipped Chisholm of Chisholm, the retarded Laird Grant, and the stammering Macleod of Raasay. They also included Duncan Davidson, Laird of Tulloch, but it was to be many years before his part in the prophecy was fulfilled. When he died, Tulloch – then Lord Lieutenant of the county of Ross – had had five wives, four of whom had died in childbirth. Between them they had borne him 18 children, while his reputation for

Above: the stone at Chanonry Point, Fortrose, commemorating the 'legend of Coinneach Odhar, better known as the Brahan seer'. It was here that, in his final hour, the seer made his last prediction. 'I see far into the future,' he said, 'and I read the doom of the race of my oppressor. The long-descended line of Seaforth will, ere many generations have passed, end in extinction and sorrow. . . . More than a century later, the Seaforth line came to an end just as the seer had foretold

Right: one of the seer's well-known proclamations concerned the depopulation of the Highlands, which began in the 18th century when many tenant farmers were evicted to make way for sheep on the land. This cartoon dates from the mid 19th century, when the problem was compounded by landowners charging high rents, forcing crofters to move south or, in many cases, emigrate

most remarkable of the seer's predictions related to the emptying of the Highlands of crofters in order to breed sheep. This came to pass with the Highland clearances of the mid 18th century. But the seer went on to say that those Highlanders driven away to far off lands as yet 'undiscovered or explored' would return to work in the Highlands in the days when the 'horrid black rains' should fall. Today, many Canadians, Texans and New Zealanders of Highland descent work in Scotland, notably in connection with offshore oil rigs and nuclear plants and submarine sites.

Naturally, the natives are curious: do the Brahan seer's 'black rains' – *siantan dubha* – refer to North Sea oil? Or do they refer to a fall-out of a much more sinister nature?

The great escape

When his parachute went up in flames 18,000 feet above Berlin, Flight Sergeant Nicholas Alkemade decided to jump rather than burn to death. The miracle was that he survived to tell the tale

FLIGHT SERGEANT Nicholas Alkemade was a little nervous at the thought that this was to be his thirteenth bombing mission over Germany. Just 21 years old, he had the loneliest, most dangerous job in RAF Bomber Command: tail-gunner in a Lancaster. Still, he and the crew of *S for Sugar* had survived so far.

Besides the danger, being tail-gunner in a Lancaster was uncomfortable. There was room enough in that tiny perspex bubble for the gunner, his ammunition and four Browning machine guns. And that was all. Even the parachute had to be stowed outside the turret. At 20,000 feet (6000 metres) it could get very cold indeed – and 24 March 1944 was a chilly spring night.

Little bothered the flight from 115 Squadron as they droned over the German mainland. A little flak above Frankfurt, then Berlin – already lit up by Pathfinder flares and the sharp beams of searchlights trying to ensnare the 300 Allied bombers that had come to pound the beleaguered enemy capital that night. At last, Alkemade heard the magic words: 'Bombs away!' Two tonnes of high explosive and nearly three of incendiaries dropped away. At once the pilot, Jack Newman, turned the big plane toward home and safety.

There was one massive explosion. Then cannon shells tearing down the fuselage towards Alkemade. Two ripped through his turret, shattering the perspex. Splinters dug into him. Then he saw the attacker: a lone Junkers 88, closing in now to finish off the

Top left: an Avro Lancaster bomber. Capable in some versions of carrying 10 tonnes of bombs, it was used against German industry as well as in incendiary raids on enemy cities – like the one Sgt Alkemade flew in March 1944

Top right: the versatile Junkers 88 was adapted to many combat roles. A night fighter version crippled Alkemade's *S for Sugar* – and brought about a miracle

Above: Nicholas Alkemade, alive and well despite several close encounters with death

wounded bomber. Alkemade aimed and fired, his tracer arcing toward the enemy, now only 50 yards (45 metres) distant. The Junker's port engine exploded and it dipped away, doomed. Alkemade was elated.

Not for long. Flames were already leaping past the remains of his turret. In a moment Jack Newman's voice came over the intercom: 'You'll have to jump for it. Bail out. Bail out.' Unfortunately, that, for Alkemade, meant retrieving his parachute from its rack behind him – somewhere amid those tongues of fire. He shoved open the doors into the fuselage momentarily and gaped at the blaze within. But this was his only hope. He tried again, spotted the parachute – then watched in horror as it disintegrated in flames.

'My stomach seemed to drop out of my body,' he said. 'I now knew that I was going to die. I said to myself, "You've had your lot."'

But not, he decided, by being burnt to death. 'Better a quick, clean death than frying.' Nicholas Alkemade was going to jump. Tearing off his already melting oxygen mask, he managed to manoeuvre the turret so that the hole faced toward the rear again. Then he somersaulted backwards into space.

Sheer relief at once replaced the terror. Alkemade felt perfectly calm. As he later put it: 'It was perfectly quiet and cool, like resting on a cloud . . . as though I was lowered onto a super-soft mattress. There was no sensation of falling. . . . I thought, well, if this is dying, it's not so bad.'

Indeed he felt so peaceful that he was able to calculate that from 18,000 feet (5500 metres) it would take him 90 seconds to hit the ground. And he had been looking forward to his next leave in a week's time. Now he wouldn't be seeing his girlfriend Pearl. Lying on his back in the air, he gazed at the

stars and thought how foolish Man's struggles seemed. Then he passed out.

Alkemade couldn't understand why he felt so cold. He was supposed to be dead. He opened an eye. A star shone through the fir trees above him. He dug out his cigarette case and lighter, suddenly desperate for a smoke, then checked the time. It was 3.10 a.m. and he had been unconscious for three hours. 'Jesus Christ,' he said out loud. 'I'm alive.'

Somehow, the trees had broken his fall. Eighteen inches (45 centimetres) of snow made a final cushion. He had dropped over 3 miles (5 kilometres) out of the sky and lived to tell the tale. Not only that – he was hardly damaged at all. Some burns, a badly twisted right knee, but everything else seemed to work. He couldn't walk, and then began to worry about exposure. 'The prospect of being a POW didn't seem so bad. I wanted to be found.'

Members of the local *Volkssturm* heard the blasts from his regulation whistle, and found him still smoking his cigarette. When they picked him up he fainted. And then the problems began.

He was taken to hospital, and tried to explain what had happened to a doctor. 'Nix parachute,' he announced. The doctor smiled mirthlessly and tapped his head gently. Obviously Alkemade was mad. At Dalag Luft POW camp near Frankfurt it was no better. Alkemade suffered three interrogations and solitary confinement for sticking to his unbelievable story. He was clearly lying, and just as clearly he was really a spy.

But Alkemade heard that a Lancaster had been reported crashing on the night of 24 March near where he was found. Perhaps it was *S for Sugar*. And perhaps the remains of his parachute could be found in the wreck. Lieutenant Hans Feidal of the Luftwaffe was eventually persuaded to look into the story. Sure enough, the harness of the tail-gunner's

parachute was there, and was brought back. Alkemade tried it on. The snaphooks and lift webbing were still tied down with thread – and would have broken had the parachute been opened. Then the Germans found the scorched handle of the ripcord in the wreckage. The camp commandant could only pronounce Alkemade's escape a miracle.

His fellow prisoners later presented him with the flyleaf of a Bible. On it was written:

DALAG LUFT

It has been investigated and corroborated by the German authorities that the claim made by Sergeant Alkemade 1431537 RAF, is true in all respects, namely that he made a descent from 18,000 feet without parachute and made a safe landing without injury, his parachute having been on fire in the aircraft. He landed in deep snow among fir trees.

Corroboration witnessed by:

Flt Lt H. J. Moore, Senior British Officer.

Flt Sgt R. R. Lamb 1339582.

Flt Sgt T. A. Jones 411 Senior British NCO. Date 25.4.44.

Nicholas Alkemade survived his thirteenth bombing mission, against all the odds. And he continued to live a charmed life. He worked in a chemical factory in his home town of Loughborough after the war. Once a 224-pound (100-kilogram) steel girder fell on him. He was hauled out for dead, but walked away with a bruised scalp. On another occasion he was drenched with sulphuric acid. He had an electric shock that threw him into a hole where he lay breathing chlorine gas for a quarter of an hour, and lived to tell that tale as well. Someone, somewhere, is looking after Nicholas Alkemade.

Below: the cramped quarters of a Lancaster's tail gun bubble. A rear gunner was known in the RAF as 'arse-end Charlie' – an attempt at humour that failed to disguise the high mortality rate that went with the job

Below right: the airman's view of an incendiary raid on a sleeping German city. These attacks were intended to demoralise the civilian population. Though very destructive, they failed in their psychological objective

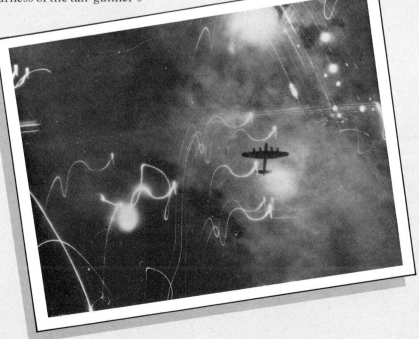

Bizarre dreams of a gallows that would not work haunted both the convicted man and his executioner in the Victorian Babbacombe murder case. This chapter relates the strange story of the man who could not be hanged

James Berry, the hangman who failed to execute John Lee. In the 19th century most hangmen worked as freelances, receiving their commissions from local county sheriffs, who were the officers charged with carrying out the death sentence. Berry worked as an executioner from 1884 to 1892 and during that time executed 134 men and women

called them 'dreams of things that never will be, and which is (*sic*) impossible.'

What distressed him most about these dreams was that they concerned the failure of his equipment. In the worst one, he stood on the gallows desperately working the lever that released the trapdoor for the fatal drop – but the trap stayed shut.

By the strangest of coincidences, the dream that so shook Berry gave sublime confidence to a man named John Lee, who was to dream it too.

In the late autumn of 1884, Berry came across the name John Lee in the columns of his local newspaper. Lee had been accused of killing Miss Emma Ann Whitehead Keyse, a former maid of honour as well as a friend to Queen Victoria. She was found battered to death, her oil-soaked clothing on fire, in her dining room on the night of 15 November 1884. Among her servants at The Glen, the house where she lived in Babbacombe in Devon, were 19-year-old John Lee, her footman, and his half-sister, Elizabeth Harris, the cook. It was Elizabeth Harris who gave the alarm and was the principal witness at the Exeter Assizes the next month.

Lee, the court was told, was a convicted petty thief who had been hired by the kindly rich woman at a wage of four shillings a week. Lee had come under suspicion of theft again and, though Emma Keyse had given him another chance, she had docked his wages by half. On the night of the murder, Elizabeth

Third time lucky

ON THE NIGHT BEFORE he became a public hangman, James Berry began to suffer from bad dreams. This upset him the more because, as he repeatedly asserted, his waking conscience was clear. The stocky, 32-year-old Yorkshireman was the son of a woollen worker who had a profound belief in Methodism and law and order. Berry inherited these beliefs, and so chose the police force as his first career.

During his 10 years as a constable in the West Riding, Berry had become friendly with William Marwood, executioner to the City of London and County of Middlesex, and had learned most of the tricks of the trade from him. When the old man died in September 1883, Berry, having left the police force, applied for the post. He did not get it. Indeed, he did not receive his first hanging commission until March 1884: he was to hang two men at Calton Prison, Edinburgh, for a fee of 20 guineas (£21), a second-class return rail ticket from his home in Bradford, Yorkshire, and his board and lodging. As he lay waiting for the dawn of that first assignment, the dreams began.

Berry later refused to use the word 'nightmare' to describe his unsettling visions. He

The scene of the murder at Babbacombe, Devon, shown in a contemporary engraving (right) and in a modern photograph (far right). Miss Keyse, the murdered mistress of the villa known as The Glen, was an austere, wealthy and God-fearing woman who regarded her servants as children for whom she was responsible

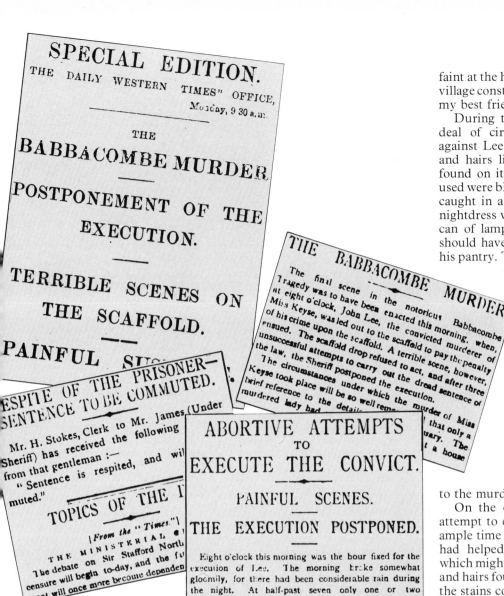

SPECIAL EDITION.
THE DAILY WESTERN TIMES" OFFICE,
Monday, 9 30 a.m.

THE
BABBACOMBE MURDER.
POSTPONEMENT OF THE EXECUTION.
TERRIBLE SCENES ON THE SCAFFOLD.
PAINFUL SUS...

THE BABBACOMBE MURDER.

The final scene in the notorious Babbacombe Tragedy was to have been enacted this morning, when, at eight o'clock, John Lee, the convicted murderer of Miss Keyse, was led out to the scaffold to pay the penalty of his crime upon the scaffold. A terrible scene, however, ensued. The scaffold drop refused to act, and after three unsuccessful attempts to carry out the dread sentence of the law, the Sheriff postponed the execution.

The circumstances under which the murder of Miss Keyse took place will be so well reme... brief reference to the detail... murdered lady had ...

...ESPITE OF THE PRISONER— SENTENCE TO BE COMMUTED.

Mr. H. Stokes, Clerk to Mr. James (Under Sheriff) has received the following from that gentleman :—
" Sentence is respited, and wil... muted."

TOPICS OF THE I...
|From the " Times."|
THE MINISTERIAL ...
The debate on Sir Stafford North... censure will begin to-day, and the fu... ment will once more become dependen...

ABORTIVE ATTEMPTS TO EXECUTE THE CONVICT.
PAINFUL SCENES.
THE EXECUTION POSTPONED.

Eight o'clock this morning was the hour fixed for the execution of Lee. The morning broke somewhat gloomily, for there had been considerable rain during the night. At half-past seven only one or two loiterers were to be observed in the neighbourhood of the

faint at the horrible sight. When he faced the village constable he said tearfully: 'I have lost my best friend.'

During the police investigation, a great deal of circumstantial evidence built up against Lee. His clothing was bloodstained and hairs like those of his employer were found on it; the knife and chopper he had used were bloodstained too. The maid he had caught in a faint found bloodstains on her nightdress where he had touched her. And a can of lamp oil, which his half-sister said should have been full, was found empty in his pantry. The very proximity of the pantry

Left: headlines from the local press carrying news of the abortive execution – and granting of respite – on 23 February 1885. Later the same week the *Devon Evening Express* published a letter written by Lee to his family before his 'execution' in which he said, 'They have not told six words truth, that is, the servants and that lovely step-sister who carries her character with her'

to the murder scene told against him.

On the other hand, Lee had made no attempt to escape, though he probably had ample time before the alarm was raised. He had helped to carry his mistress's body, which might well account for the bloodstains and hairs found on his own clothing. Some of the stains could easily have been Lee's own, since he had gashed his hand while smashing the window to let out smoke; those on the maid's nightdress and on the knife and chopper were almost certainly his. And, although the chopper may have been used in the murder, equally it may not have been.

Lee repeatedly swore his innocence, but the prosecution claimed he had a motive: he had killed his employer because she had cut

Harris said, she had awoken in her smoke-filled room, made her way to the dining room and found the body.

Her mistress's head had been battered in and her body doused in lamp oil and ignited in an apparent attempt to hide the crime. According to the cook's testimony, Lee had emerged from his pantry adjoining the dining room, smashed a window to let out the smoke and cut away burning wood and fabrics with a knife and chopper. He had steadied one of the maids, who had become

his paltry wages in half. In vain the defence pointed out that two shillings were better than none, and that Lee and the whole household were thrown out of work by Emma Keyse's death. Nevertheless the jury found Lee guilty. Asked if he had anything to say before sentence was passed, Lee drew himself upright in the dock and said calmly: 'I am innocent. The Lord will never permit me to be executed.'

Later there were murmurings that Lee's half-sister, whose evidence against him was so important, had been seeing a lover. In the prim Emma Keyse's household, this would have been a far worse offence than petty theft, and instant dismissal would probably have been Elizabeth Harris's lot. Perhaps, the rumours went, she had been discovered with her lover by her employer, and he had struck out in panic – leaving Elizabeth Harris to eradicate the crime by lighting the fire. Whatever the truth, such conjecture came too late to help Lee.

James Berry was nearing the end of his first full year as an executioner and, with about a dozen successful hangings to his credit, he felt that he might be called upon in the Lee case. And in the first week of February he received an official commission from Henry M. James, under sheriff of Devonshire, to hang John Lee at Exeter jail for the murder of Emma Ann Whitehead Keyse. The sentence was to be carried out at 8 a.m. on Monday 23 February 1885. Berry arrived at Exeter two days before.

Machinery of death

On the night before the execution, Berry pointed out what he considered to be short-comings in the scaffold's machinery of death. He told the prison governor that the leaves of the oak trapdoor were too light; that spring clips should be set in the walls of the pit beneath to catch the doors as they fell open; that the iron strips edging the doors were too thin and that the bolts holding the trap shut were badly adjusted. The governor explained that the scaffold had been moved and re-erected by a gang of convicts, but had been used without any problems a few months before. Using a sandbag weighing the same as Lee, Berry tested the lever several times, and each time the trapdoor dropped perfectly.

Later that night, Lee had a final interview with the prison governor and the chaplain. The governor told him that there was no possibility of a reprieve. Lee merely shrugged, reasserted his innocence and added mysteriously: 'Elizabeth Harris could say the word which could clear me, if she would.' Both men noted Lee's coolness.

On the morning of the execution, Berry was disturbed to learn about Lee's dream of the night before: his own uneasy vision from another angle. For Lee had dreamed that he was standing on the gallows with the noose around his neck – and the trapdoor did not

fall when the hangman pulled the lever. Lee had laughed when he told his dream, saying: 'You see, I shan't be hanged today. You will never hang me. You wait and see.'

When Berry entered the condemned cell at 7.56 a.m., Lee rose from his bunk to meet him, rather pale but calm – as Berry put it later, 'the coolest customer I ever handled'. Berry, Lee, the governor and four warders set out across the prison yard, preceded by the chaplain reading the service. At the door of the shed housing the scaffold, they were met by the under sheriff and the prison surgeon. Ten newspaper reporters watched from positions by the shed windows. According to some of their reports, as Lee entered the shed a white dove alighted on the roof and then flew over the prison walls.

The grim party ascended the steps of the gallows. Berry led Lee to the centre of the trap, strapped his legs together below the knee, fixed the noose around his neck and placed the white hood over his head. The chaplain faced him. The hangman then stepped back, kicked out the restraining pin and pulled the lever. The rattle of the bolts being drawn was heard – but the trap failed to fall.

It was the moment that both Berry and Lee had lived before in their dreams. For a few seconds Berry gaped at the fully drawn lever under his hand, and then he moved forward and stamped on the trapdoors. They remained firmly closed. Two warders joined him, thumping on the traps with their heavy boots.

Six minutes elapsed before Berry –

Below: a modern artist's impression of the scaffold in Exeter jail (left), where John Lee's execution was to take place. The gallows was contained in an old coach shed in the prison yard. A heavy beam had been let into the brickwork at either end of the shed and an iron eye bolt set into the centre of the beam to take the rope. Directly under this a platform had been built with a double-leaved trapdoor in its centre. The trap was held shut by two iron bolts running underneath it; these were withdrawn when a lever on the platform (normally held in the safe position by a metal pin) was drawn back. The key words used by the hangman were 'straps, noose, hood, pin, lever, drop' and if all went smoothly the whole thing could be over in 12 seconds from the moment the condemned man stepped onto the trap

'clearly shaken', as the reports said – took off the hood and noose from Lee, who was 'ashen, but not whiter than some of the witnesses'. He was led off while Berry tested the trap with the sandbag again: it worked perfectly.

Lee was brought back, and this time Berry yanked the lever back with such force that it bent under his weight. But the doors remained firm under Lee's feet. For the next 20 minutes, Berry, the carpenter and the prison engineer worked on the scaffold and tested it repeatedly. They greased the bolts, planed the doors, and were finally satisfied.

Back came Lee and the chaplain. As the latter recalled: 'The lever was pulled again and again. A great noise was heard, which sounded like the falling of the drop. But to my horror, when I turned my eyes to the scaffold, I saw the poor convict standing upon the drop as I had seen him twice before. I refused to stay any longer.' In fact the

Above: a contemporary engraving of a public execution, a macabre relic of medieval England that persisted until 1868. After that time executions were carried out within the prison, with only official witnesses present

chaplain buckled at the knees and was caught by a warder, then led off the gallows with Lee. Everyone was in a tremulous state and some of the warders were in tears. But John Lee kept his composure.

A messenger was sent to London to report to the Home Secretary. Meanwhile, Lee was asked if there was anything he would like and he said that he could eat another 'last' breakfast. He ate the huge repast ordered for Berry, who had lost his appetite completely.

That evening a telegram arrived from the Home Secretary granting Lee a respite, and his sentence was subsequently commuted to life imprisonment. Berry too began a life sentence of a kind: not only did his dream of the jammed trapdoor recur more frequently, but he had to face constant questions about the Lee affair from everyone.

A lucky escape?

The most plausible explanation for the jammed trapdoor was not put forward until 40 years later, when most of the principals were dead. This theory was that a fault in the construction of the platform had caused the problem: a plank of wood, set edge on to the trapdoors, had been warped and therefore arched upwards in the middle. When the chaplain stood on it opposite Lee to read the prayers, the plank straightened out and jammed under the hinged side of the trap. When the sandbag was used for testing, the chaplain was absent and the trap worked.

But how could the plank withstand the violent stamping of three men? And if it were the true explanation, Lee's escape would be even more remarkable: for if he had not been moved at exactly the same time as the chaplain, the chances are that the trap mechanism would have worked.

Lee served 20 years in prison. Shortly after he came out in 1905 he married a woman who had apparently waited for him, and the couple went to the United States. There he died in 1933. He declared his innocence to the end of his life, and insisted that divine intervention had saved him.

As for Berry, the fiasco at Exeter had one personal satisfaction: he was invited to collaborate with Lieutenant-Colonel Alten Beamish, Royal Engineers, who was attached to the surveyor's department of the Home Office, in designing a 'standard' gallows. Their design was fitted in British prisons until the abolition of the death penalty for murder in the late 1960s.

Long before his own death in 1913, however, Berry had turned strongly against capital punishment. But though he had turned to religion with renewed fervour, he spurned the theory of divine intervention for Lee's miraculous escape from the gallows. For, he would ask, why should God intervene for Lee and not for the many other almost certainly innocent victims among the 134 men and women he had hanged in eight years as a public executioner?

With a nod or a wink

The old belief that a corpse will react to the presence of its murderer seems to have found horrific expression in the strange case of Joan Norkot; an 'impossible' story of the rotting corpse that winked at the guilty parties

ONCE DEAD AND BURIED few people have shown signs of life, but those that have, or are rumoured to have been reanimated, have naturally enough inspired the witnesses with awe and fear. In the case of Joan Norkot, who died in 1629, her brief moment of posthumous glory did more; it was enough to point the finger of accusation – almost literally – at her murderers, and subsequently to secure their conviction.

Such was the course of justice in 17th-century England. In those days of widespread superstition it was firmly believed that the body of a murder victim would bleed at the touch of the assassin, and considered binding legal evidence if it did so.

The strange case of Joan Norkot was rediscovered in 1851, when it was one of the legal and historical occurrences selected from the day books of Dr Henry Sampson for inclusion in the July edition of *The Gentleman's Magazine and Historical Review*. In 1851 pragmatism, fact and scientific evidence were the order of the day, as this Victorian journal's prefatory remarks on the case show:

The next extract contains a narrative of a very singular legal case, which comes down to us upon the most unquestionable authority – that of the old Serjeant who, after having been an original member of the Long Parliament of Charles I, lived as father of the bar to congratulate King William on his accession in 1688. . . . It would be difficult to parallel the following relation of superstition and miserable insufficiency of legal proof. . . .

Top: the Long Parliament of 1640, in which John Mainard (above) had sat, living long enough to see William III come to the throne in 1688. Yet his intellect remained as sharp as ever and he was considered an impeccable witness to the bizarre case of Joan Norkot

Left: the resuscitation of Margaret Dickson, a murderer who was hanged in 1728. But Joan Norkot had actually decomposed – how could she have revived?

The 'old Serjeant' in question was one Sir John Mainard, 'a person of great note and judgment in the law', whose version of the Norkot incident was recorded in a manuscript 'fair written with his own hands' and discovered among his papers after his death at the age of 88 in 1690; a copy of it was taken by a Mr Hunt of the Temple, who gave it to Dr Sampson for his records.

Joan Norkot lived in Hertfordshire – it is not known exactly where – with her husband Arthur, her infant son, her sister Agnes and brother-in-law John Okeman, and her mother-in-law Mary Norkot. By all accounts a cheerful, good-looking woman, happily married and a good mother, Joan was well-known to the locals, who expressed surprise and horror when it was revealed that one morning she had been found with her throat cut, apparently the victim of a violent attack, still clutching her child in her arms. Her family claimed that it was suicide.

So had Joan committed suicide? On the night of her death, said Mary Norkot and the Okemans, Joan's husband had been away, visiting friends. They further claimed that there had been 'a deal of trouble' between Arthur and Joan of late, and that on her last evening alive she had been 'in a sour temper, and some despondency'. So maybe, in a fit of despair, she had plunged the knife into her throat. But this was not good enough for Joan's friends and neighbours. In the weeks following the inquest rumour grew to such an extent in the village that it directly challenged the legal verdict. With new evidence coming to light from investigations at the Norkot cottage, it was widely believed that Joan could not have killed herself. Acting on popular opinion,

the jury, whose verdict was not drawn into form by the coroner, desired the coroner that the body, which was buried, might be taken up out of the grave, which the coroner assented to, and thirty days after her death she was taken up, in presence of the jury and a great number of the people.

The touch test

It was at the exhumation, according to the testimony later given in court by the local clergyman, that the test of touch decreed by superstitious custom was made. Mainard takes up the story:

. . . the four defendants present, they were required, each of them, to touch the dead body. Okeman's wife fell on her knees and prayed God to show token of their innocency, or to some such purpose. . . . The appellers did touch the dead body, whereupon the brow of the dead, which was of a livid or carrion colour (that was the verbal expression in the terms of the witness) began to have a dew or gentle sweat [which] ran down in drops on the face, and the brow turned and changed to a lively and fresh colour, and the dead

Left: a portrait said to be of Sir Nicholas Hyde, the Lord Chief Justice at Hertford Assizes (below) in 1629 when Joan Norkot's family were tried for her murder. At first it was thought that Joan had committed suicide, but the local people suspected foul play and her body was exhumed. Each member of Joan's family was compelled to touch the grisly remains, which then winked and raised a finger – damning evidence against them in those days. Once the case was brought to court other, more conventional, evidence came to light, and the accused were convicted of Joan's murder and duly hanged – except for her sister-in-law Agnes, who was reprieved because she was pregnant. The motive for the murder remains obscure

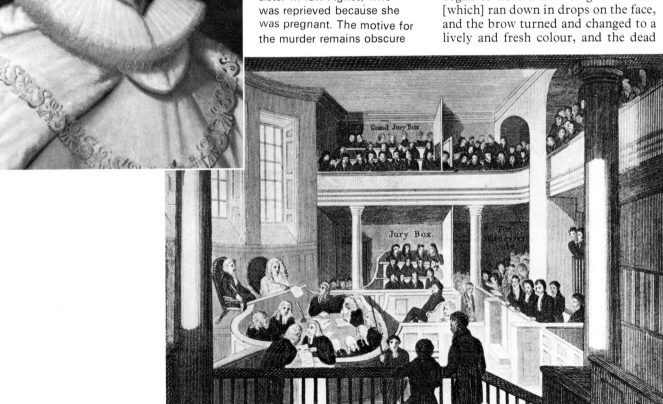

opened one of her eyes and shut it again, and this opening the eye was done three several times. She likewise thrust out the ring or marriage finger three times and pulled it in again, and the finger dropt blood from it on the grass.

This, in 1629, was irrefutable proof of homicide, and once the furore that necessarily accompanied Joan Norkot's sudden return to the land of the living (and equally abrupt return to eternal sleep) had died down, the jury altered its verdict.

Although it was now declared that Joan Norkot had been 'murdered, by person or persons unknown', the eye of suspicion had come to rest firmly on Arthur, Mary, Agnes and John, and they were subsequently tried at Hertford Assizes – and at first acquitted.

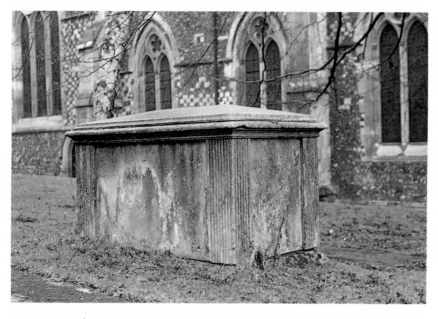

Below: an altar tomb. There are many legends of 'mysterious' rappings coming from such tombs, and of skeletons found bent and twisted inside them. Premature burial was common – comatose or cataleptic people were often thought to be dead and were duly buried, only to die of asphyxiation, thirst or horror. Yet it seems that Joan Norkot was well and truly dead when her body was exhumed, so premature burial can be ruled out as an explanation for her brief reanimation

'The evidence' weighed so heavily against them, however, that presiding Judge Harvy suggested 'that it were better an appeal were brought than so foul a murder should escape unpunished.' Joan Norkot's orphaned son became the plaintiff in the appeal, which was duly lodged against his father, grandmother, aunt and uncle. Said Mainard himself, '. . . because the evidence was so strange I took exact and particular notice of it.' In the trial the events at the graveside were soberly recounted by the local parish minister, described by the chronicler as a 'grave person' but one whose name has not survived.

Not surprisingly, the officiating judge, Chief Justice Nicholas Hyde, doubted the old cleric's evidence. 'Who saw this beside yourself?' he asked the witness. 'I cannot swear that others saw it,' replied the minister, 'but my Lord, I believe the whole company saw it, and if it had been thought a doubt, proof would have been made of it, and many would have attested with me . . . .'

Further, less fantastic evidence was then brought against Mrs Norkot senior and the Okemans, adding to the argument that if no

one had gone into the cottage between the time when Joan retired for the night and when she was found dead, then they must be her murderers. Joan had been found lying in her bed with the bedclothes undisturbed, and her child with her – indicating that suicide had not taken place in the bed, in fact not at all. Her throat was cut from ear to ear and her neck broken, and if she first cut her throat, she could not break her neck while lying in the bed, or vice versa.

Murder most foul

Clearly the dead body had been moved and there had been a half-hearted attempt to conceal the evidence. Moreover, the bloody knife had been firmly embedded in the floor some distance from the bed, point towards the bed, haft towards the door. However violent her death throes, there is no way that Joan Norkot – had she actually taken her own life – could have thrown the blade into that position. Lastly, there was the bloody print of a left hand on top of Joan's own left hand, an item of evidence that Chief Justice Hyde questioned but eventually accepted.

The four prisoners were then brought forward but had no defence to offer. Arthur Norkot's alibi collapsed when it was revealed that he had not visited the friends he had claimed to be staying with for several years. The jury retired and when it returned found Norkot, his mother and Agnes guilty of murder. Okeman was acquitted. The three guilty persons each cried out, 'I did not do it! I did not do it!' but, nevertheless, judgement was passed. Norkot and his mother were sentenced to death and duly hanged, but Agnes Norkot was reprieved when it was discovered she was pregnant.

In his reconstruction and discussion of the case in *Unsolved mysteries* (1952), Valentine Dyall suggests a possible – though speculative – reason for the murder:

The motive for the crime remained obscure, though it was generally supposed that Arthur Norkot had believed his wife unfaithful. The other two women of the family, known to be jealous of Joan's good looks and position as mistress of the house, probably made willing accomplices – while John Okeman, a simple fellow, was bullied into silence.

But there is no logical explanation for the incredible scene that took place when Joan was disinterred. We can toy with the notion of premature burial, but there can be no doubt that Joan Norkot was well and truly deceased when she was laid to rest. Perhaps exposure to the elements had an immediate chemical effect on her decaying flesh, explaining the 'lively and fresh colour' of her brow, but how did Joan's eye wink, and her finger move and yield fresh blood?

Maybe it was just that Joan Norkot, in the course of divine retribution, awoke fleetingly from death to ensure that justice was done.

Worldwide wonders

Any explanations offered for the many reports of seemingly fantastic occurrences will have to be on a global scale. The coffins in Barbados that move by themselves and the Chinese children who can read with their armpits are just two examples of paradoxes demonstrating that no area on Earth is without its incredible phenomena.

Turning in the grave

The mysterious movement of lead-cased coffins in a sealed tomb in Barbados in the 19th century was believed by many to be the work of some supernatural force. What really happened?

THEY SAY the dead tell no tales. And since the corpses interred in a Barbadian graveyard vault early last century were, apparently, the only human agencies present when the actual coffins they were laid in moved, there naturally exists no immediate first-hand account of this eeriest of mysteries.

The so-called 'creeping coffins of Barbados' crept, with some alacrity, into West Indian folklore between 1812 and 1820. Indeed, this was no isolated incident, but a phenomenon that repeated itself with chilling regularity until the nerve of the vault's owners and the local dignitaries finally ran out. At the time the tomb in question, situated near the entrance of the graveyard of Christ Church, overlooking the bay at Oistins on the south coast of the island, belonged to the Chase family. It was a solid affair, built of large, cemented blocks of coral, 12 feet long by 6 feet wide (4 metres by 2 metres), sunk halfway into the ground and sealed off by a great marble slab. Anyone trying secretly to get in (or out) of the vault would have found it an arduous task.

Two burials took place before anything happened. On 31 July 1807 Mrs Thomasina Goddard's funeral was held, and on 22 February 1808 that of the infant Mary Anna Maria Chase. Then, on 6 July 1812, pallbearers and mourners arrived to lay to rest Dorcas Chase, the elder sister of Mary Anna Maria. Several of the men heaved the door open – struggling with its great weight – and the coffin was lifted down to the portals of the tomb. Peering into the darkness from the few first steps, the leading pallbearers were greeted by a truly sepulchral sight. Mary Anna Maria's coffin had moved to the corner opposite the one in which it had been placed; Mrs Goddard's had been flung aside against

a wall. Something more than a draught had moved them – both coffins were cased in lead. Without pausing to ask questions the labourers lifted them back into position, placed Dorcas's among them and sealed the vault up again. But who or what had tampered with the dead – and why? Amazed and frightened, the mourners chose to put the blame on the Negro slaves who had assisted at the funeral of the first Chase sister.

So were the Negroes to blame? There was reputedly little love lost between the patriarch Thomas Chase and the black slaves he employed. Chase was by all accounts a cruel man whose tyrannical behaviour had driven his daughter Dorcas to kill herself. It seems improbable though that anyone bearing a grudge against him would have gone to such lengths to inflict such trivial damage.

The work of malign spirits?

As it was, Chase himself died within the month; and on 9 August 1812 his coffin was placed among the other three, which this time had remained undisturbed. A few years slipped by with no reason for anyone to believe that anything untoward was taking place in the Oistins churchyard. On 25 September 1816 the vault was reopened for the burial of a little boy, Samuel Brewster Ames. Once again the coffins lay in disarray – and the accusing eye was again turned on the Negro labourers, who promptly denied all charges and shrank in fear from what they considered the work of malign spirits: Negroes regarded the dead with superstition and were in fact the most unlikely of suspects. There was little the mourners could do, however, but return the coffins to their rightful places, leave Master Ames among them and block up the doorway with the great slab – which they did, hastily. It was opened again on 17 November for the interment of Samuel Brewster, whose coffin was being transferred to the Chase vault from its original home in a St Philip graveyard. The mystery surrounding the vault was now so

well-known that a crowd gathered in anticipation of fresh disturbances.

It was not to be disappointed. All of the coffins had shifted ground. That of Mrs Goddard, who had been lying in 'rest' now for nearly a decade, had finally given up under the strain and fallen apart. An exhaustive search of the vault proved futile – the walls, floor and roof were as solid and unyielding as ever. And yet for the third time there were unmistakable signs of violent activity within. Would it happen again? One wonders with what sense of dreadful, resigned foreboding the mourners repositioned the coffins (tying and bundling the remnants of Mrs Goddard's against the wall) and cemented the great door back into place.

Nearly three years passed before the vault was opened again – during which time it received thousands of curious visitors. On 17 July 1819 the funeral of Thomasina Clarke took place. It seems that the mystery was now a major national issue, for Viscount Combermere, the Governor of Barbados, and two of his officials attended the funeral. In front of hundreds of hushed spectators the marble slab was cut free by masons and dragged aside by a team of slaves. Inside, all was chaos; every coffin had moved save only the shattered fragments of Mrs Goddard's, which had remained in their little pile. The vault was searched again. Nothing. Not one clue. Undeterred, the labourers lugged the coffins back. Sand was then sent for and sprinkled over the floor of the tomb so that it formed a smooth, thick carpet that would surely show the traces of the mysterious coffin mover. Once the door was replaced

The bay at Oistins on the south coast of Barbados received thousands of visitors in the years between 1812 and 1820. The tourists flocked to Christ Church graveyard to see at first hand the vault of the Chase family where, it was rumoured, someone – or something – was tampering with the dead

Combermere left the impression of his seal in the cement and others did the same.

No recently deceased Barbadian was brought to the vault when it was opened again on 18 April 1820. Public speculation and excitement about the strange goings-on had mounted to such a degree that no one had the patience to wait for someone to pass on before the mystery could be finally solved or abandoned. After prolonged debate that could lead to only one conclusion, Viscount Combermere, the Honourable Nathan Lucas, Major J. Finch (secretary to the Governor), Mr R. Bowcher Clarke and Mr Rowland Cotton journeyed to Christ Church, collected the Reverend Thomas Orderson and repaired to the graveyard with a band of quaking Negro labourers.

The seals on the cement were intact – no one had therefore since removed the door and entered that way. And from the outside the vault was as solid as ever. Combermere ordered the cement to be chipped away and the huge slab was dragged aside, causing a strange, grating noise. This was the result of one of the larger lead coffins having been thrown up against the door, against which it now lay. Mary Anna Maria's tinier coffin, meanwhile, had been sent flying to the far end of the vault with such violence that it had damaged the coral wall. The other coffins

were scattered about, but there were no tell-tale marks in the sand to suggest what might have moved them. The Honourable Nathan Lucas, reporting the incident, had this to say:

> I examined the walls, the arch, and every part of the vault, and found every part old and similar; and a mason in my presence struck every part of the bottom with his hammer, and all was solid. I confess myself at a loss to account for the movements of these leaden coffins. Thieves certainly had no hand in it; and as for any practical wit or hoax, too many were requisite to be trusted with the secret for it to remain unknown; and as for negroes having anything to do with it, their superstitious fear of the dead and everything belonging to them precludes any idea of the kind. All I know is that it happened and that I was an eye-witness of the fact!!!

Whatever, or whoever, it was that caused the coffins in the Chase vault to wander between those four walls was given no further opportunity to do so. All of the coffins were lugged out and given more peaceful resting places elsewhere in the churchyard. The vault remains open and unused to this day.

'Werewolves and vampires'

There have been other cases of coffins refusing to stay put. Discussing the Barbados mystery in his book *West Indian tales of old*, Sir Algernon E. Aspinall makes reference to the *European Magazine* of September 1815, which cites a vault at Stanton in Suffolk, England, where on at least three separate occasions, and, as at Oistins, behind a sealed door, coffins had moved off their raised biers; during one of these 'manoeuvres' the heaviest coffin – another eight-pallbearer affair – had climbed onto the fourth step of the vault. 'Whence arose this operation, in which it was certain that no-one had a hand?' asked the *European Magazine* writer. Needless to say, the people of Stanton were as shocked as the Barbadians. In 1867 Mr F. C. Paley, son of the rector of Gretford, near Stamford in Lincolnshire, England, wrote to *Notes and Queries* concerning the repeated movement of heavy lead coffins (also cased in wood) in a local vault; his letter was corroborated by a witness who commented that some of the coffins had moved to a leaning position against the wall.

The superstitious people of Arensburg on the Baltic island of Oesel immediately blamed vampires and werewolves when similar trouble occurred in the town cemetery in 1844. The crisis started in June with the 'spooking' of horses belonging to visitors to the graveyard. Some of these horses bolted, others fainted or dropped dead; many, so the story goes, went mad. The fault was laid at the door of the Buxhoewden family vault. When a funeral service in the family chapel was interrupted by eerie sounds from the

The entrance to the Chase vault in Christ Church graveyard, Oistins. The vault has stood open and empty since 1820, when all the coffins it contained were removed and buried in another, more peaceful, place

Viscount Combermere, the Governor of Barbados, supervised the sealing of the Chase vault after the funeral of Thomasina Clarke on 17 July 1819. When he returned nine months later to check on the state of the tomb he found the coffins in total disarray – and yet the seals on the door had remained intact

adjacent burial chamber, the bravest of the Buxhoewdens entered the tomb to find that the coffins of their late relatives had been thrown around. Rumours of 'devilry' spread and there was great fear and consternation in Arensburg. The president of the local ecclesiastical court, the Baron de Guldenstabbé, headed an official enquiry and personally visited the vault, which had been put back in order and locked. The coffins had moved again.

Determined to get to the bottom of the mystery, the Baron set up a committee to investigate it. They went further than their Barbadian cousins and had the floor of the vault ripped up, hoping, in vain, to find a secret passage. They suspected ghouls, though none of the coffins had in fact been robbed. Forced to give up their fruitless search, the committee laid not sand but ash throughout the vault and chapel and, as at Oistins, left secret seals that would break if the door were opened by any means. For three days and nights the place was guarded by soldiers. Then the committee returned: the seals were unbroken, the ashes were untouched and the coffins were everywhere they shouldn't have been – some standing on their heads, one so badly cracked that a bony arm protruded from it. Lacking the patience of the Barbadians who had put up with this sort of thing for eight years, the Arensburg committee and the Buxhoewdens immediately had the coffins moved elsewhere and put an end to the vault's activities.

What causes coffins to move about, whether they are in vaults in Barbados, in England or on an island in the Baltic Sea? There is no ready explanation. The 'traps' set up by the various investigators – the secret seals and the sand or ash covered floors – strongly indicate that no human villains are involved. That in Barbados it was malevolent Negro slaves – or the malevolent spirits suspected by the Negroes themselves – seems implausible. Among those who have considered the supernatural and paranormal possibilities are Sir Arthur Conan Doyle, who believed that the Oistins coffins moved because of the strange physical powers that are supposed to reside in the bodies of the prematurely dead – like the young Chase girls and Samuel Brewster Ames. There is more credence in the theory proffered by George Hunte, author of *Barbados*, who suggests that 'gas from decomposing bodies and not malevolent spirits was responsible for the violent separations and disarray of the sober arrangements which were made by undertakers'.

What about water in the vaults? Could the coffins have floated? The Chase vault was not only watertight but high and dry too; underground currents can be ruled out. The man who confirmed Mr Paley's letter about the Gretford coffins believed they floated into their strange positions when the vault was

Below: drawings made by eyewitness Nathan Lucas to show how the coffins were originally placed in the vault (left) and how they were found in April 1820 (right). However, there are discrepancies between the account given by Lucas and those of other witnesses, and a second set of drawings (bottom) – also said to have been made on the spot and at the time the tomb was opened – is generally accepted to be a more accurate portrayal of the arrangement of the coffins

Frank Russell compared the drawings in his chapter on the coffin phenomenon in *Great world mysteries* (published in 1957):

As first placed, three large coffins were put in a neat row with the middle one set slightly further away from the vault's door. Three smaller coffins sat tidily on top of the big ones. All had their feet towards the door, their heads towards the back of the vault, their longitudinal axes parallel to the side walls.

When found out of place all coffins were in varying but fairly regular stages of reversal, their heads now being more or less towards the door, their feet more or less towards the back wall. They look exactly as if caught when rotating at snail's pace around their own centres of gravity, some having twisted farther than others, their axes now cutting through an arc of about 120 degrees. The picture they present is that of a swirl, or a spiral effect, like so many metal shapes, heavier at one end than the other, spun around by some force gravitational, gyroscopic, electromagnetic or goodness knows what.

However inconclusive, Russell's suggestion seems the most plausible. Superstition and fear though – slamming the door shut on the case of the creeping coffins of Barbados and abandoning the vault (as at Arensburg) – precluded further scientific research into the whole weird business, which remains wreathed in mystery. All that is known for sure is that for eight macabre years in the Chase vault at Oistins there were, to adapt the words of Emily Brontë, 'unquiet slumbers for the sleepers in that quiet earth'.

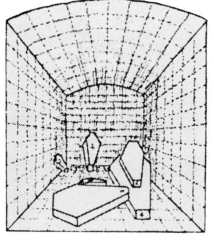

flooded – but there is no evidence that it ever was. Since the events at Arensburg all took place within a few weeks, any sign of flooding would have been noticed; none was. Lead coffins *can* float – they need something to float on, however.

The movements of the Oistins coffins could be ascribed to earth tremors. Barbados lies on a seismic belt and is framed by fracture zones; moreover there is a volcano on the nearby island of St Vincent. The slightest underground tremor could have displaced the coffins – but why only those in the Chase vault? The theory is dubious. Stanton, Gretford and Arensburg are not known for seismic activity.

Most of the coffins in the vault at Barbados were made of lead, so ordinary magnetic forces did not cause the mischief. And yet some such force may provide the answer to the mystery. One vital clue has emerged from the investigations of the Barbadians. At the time of the last burial there in 1819 someone saw fit to make a drawing of the vault in a state of orderliness; and another of its supposedly chaotic appearance when it was opened for the final time in April 1820. Eric

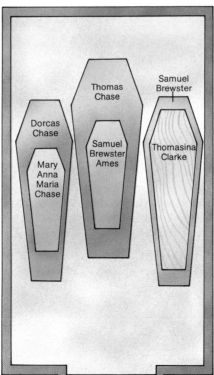

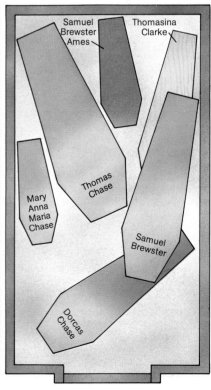

Secrets of the stone towers

The picturesque *trulli*, with their unique conical roofs and mysterious painted symbols, intrigue the traveller to Puglia in southern Italy. Are these symbols magical or mundane?

THERE IS ONLY ONE PLACE where the curious structures known as *trulli* can be found: the region of Puglia in southern Italy. And the biggest cluster of these distinctively turreted buildings is located in Alberobello, a small town 20 miles (35 kilometres) north of Taranto in the very heel of the boot of Italy.

From a small one-room cowshed to a whole complex of dwellings, sometimes of two or three levels, the most notable element of this architecture is the conical roof, which gives the trulli their name. In the singular form of trullo, this Italian word was probably derived from the Latin *turris*, meaning 'tower'. But some scholars support the notion that the name comes from the Greek word for a measuring cup that, when inverted, is shaped like a trullo.

The origin of these unique trulli is hotly disputed. Suggestions that the roofs were derived from Mycenean or Etruscan tomb designs have never gained much credence, but it is generally agreed that the distinctive form must have been brought by an early wave of migration from a Levantine or African country.

There is another special thing about the trulli, which is that the people who live in them often paint a white symbol on the conical towers. These symbols in themselves represent one of the most intriguing aspects of the folklore of Puglia, and the strange fact is that nobody has been able to offer a satisfactory explanation as to when and why

Below: the little town of Alberobello in Italy has the largest concentration of the structures known as *trulli,* whose origin is shrouded in mystery

Below right: this monogram on one of the trulli roofs of a large Alberobello hotel is made up of a capital A over a cross. There are two double meanings in this symbol: the cross represents the 'tree' upon which Christ died and the *albero* ('tree') in the town's name. The whole symbol then stands both for the town and for the beauty of the Christian cross

the local inhabitants began to so decorate their homes.

As we might expect from a country steeped in the traditions of the Western Church, the majority of the symbols that appear on the trulli are Christian. By far the most frequently used is that of the simple Latin cross, but there are many variations of cross forms.

Were the symbols merely Christian, it is unlikely that they would have attracted much attention. However, some of the symbols are distinctly un-Christian, and are derived from a wide variety of sources including astrology, the *qabalah* and alchemy. Such symbols have excited the interest of scholars, but have also given rise to some rather far-fetched theories as to the intentions of the peasant farmers

produced by Rudolf Koch in 1930, for some of the symbols appear to be taken directly from this source.

However, this group of 'forgeries' should not deflect us from the genuine trulli symbols, though information about them is hard to come by. When questioned about the signs, for example, local residents are not particularly helpful – simply because their own information is so sketchy. One or two admit readily that they merely follow the outline of the existing symbols because it has always been done that way in the family. When they do try to explain the origin of the symbols they paint on their roofs, they show little knowledge of the actual meanings of the signs. One trulli dweller said that the symbol:

is 'the cross of Christ'. This tells little of the story. For it is almost certainly a variant of

who probably originated the custom of decorating the trulli towers with symbols.

The earliest mention of the symbols seems to be in the 17th century, and records show that they were generally restricted, then as now, to the agricultural areas of Puglia. A few scholars have argued that the practice of trulli painting started only in the 20th century; but there are photographs of the 1890s in existence that show trulli painted with symbols. The age of the symbols themselves has been much debated, without conclusion. Some say they date from the beginning of the Christian era; others believe they originated in the 15th and 16th centuries, even though some borrowing from earlier periods would naturally have taken place.

The influence of the tourist industry has undoubtedly caused the proliferation of the symbols. For example, in preparation for a visit to the town of Alberobello by Mussolini in 1934, the official tourist board actively encouraged the painting of the symbols on the trulli. Photographs of the town at that time show a profusion of symbols. Not surprisingly, one of the prominent and frequent ones was the most common of the Fascist symbols:

Above: one of the simpler trulli symbols is this letter R, which is probably the initial of the family living there

Right: the most common symbol on the trulli is the Latin cross. There are also many variations of cross forms, which speak for the Christian heritage of those who paint the symbols

Below: samples of the symbols painted on the trulli roofs especially for the visit of Mussolini to Alberobello in 1934

Bottom: a random selection of some of the more unusual symbols found on the Alberobello trulli

This same section of Alberobello, seen in the late 1960s from much the same place as a photograph of the 1934 event, revealed a single forlorn painting of an ordinary cross.

It is all too apparent that this sudden flourishing of symbols in 1934 had little to do with the tradition of trulli painting. Many of the symbols were copied, often rather inexpertly, from books on astrology and alchemy. In fact, it is tempting to think that some official in the tourist board had access to the influential if unreliable book of symbols

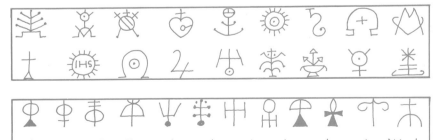

The trulli symbols are most often painted in a chalk pigment paint, which calls for frequent renewing. This constant overpainting tends to thicken lines and has the effect of changing the forms. For example, some of the 'swallows' or birds:

have with the passage of time turned into angels:

The strong capital letter P on one trullo in Alberobello is without doubt a result of the overpainting of the Greek letter rho:

which was one of the many monograms of Christ. As such, it was a powerful protective symbol among the early Christians. The rho and its variants – especially that of the chi rho:

the early Christian symbol that in turn is derived from the Greek letter phi:

The graphic form of a circle with a vertical line through it suggests the idea of a spiritual descent into the 'globe' of the world, and is therefore easily linked with the central Christian tenet of Christ's descent to Earth. But there is also a logical basis for the adoption of phi as a Christian symbol. This is because Christ was linked with the idea of light, and the Greek word for light is *phos*, which begins with the letter phi. This letter appears on early Christian tombs, in which use it implies that the soul of the departed would not find itself in the realm of darkness – the Hades of the Greeks – but would ascend into the world of light: even into the bosom of Christ, known as the 'light of the world'.

Some of the modern trulli symbols are little more than the initials of the owners' names. Slightly more esoteric is the monogram found on one of the trulli roofs of a large hotel in Alberobello, made up of the capital letter A over a cross. This cross is obviously intended to have a double meaning – it is the 'tree' upon which Christ died, and it is also the tree, *albero*, in the name Alberobello, which means 'beautiful tree'. The whole symbol on the trullo therefore has a double meaning: it refers to the town, and also to the idea of the cross being made beautiful by the redemptive act of Christ. The A also stands for the *alpha*, which is one of the standard early Greek symbols adopted by the Christians to symbolise the idea of 'beginning', a reference to the new Christian era.

A strong letter P, which may have come about by the thickening of the lines when the Greek letter rho, which resembles the Roman letter P, was painted over many times

the first two letters of the Greek word for Christ – are still found on some of the trulli in their original form. Now, in the case of this particular P, it is clear that the original form of the rho was lost as it was overpainted, till it was transformed into a symbol that the person who repainted it could recognise and understand. Some of the inhabitants think that such a trulli P stands for the Latin word *pax*, meaning 'peace'. But one local woman gave a simpler explanation when she said that it was used because the trullo itself was in the street named Portabella.

Certainly the modern generation do not show the same pride in painting their trulli symbols as did the older generation. From photographs taken in Alberobello and its environs in the early 1970s, it is evident that fewer and fewer of the towers are being decorated. There are far more television aerials than there are mystical symbols over the roofs!

The Christian ethos still remains, of course, and so the cross and its many variants still predominate. By and large there appears to have been little change in the local view of the power of the cross since medieval times. More than likely the trulli dwellers would echo the sentiments of that infamous book used during the Inquisition, the *Malleus maleficarum* ('The witches' hammer'), which proclaimed that demonic power and the evil eye might be curtailed merely by making the sign of the cross in the air. They do just that with their trulli symbols.

THE UNUSUAL TRULLI of Puglia in southern Italy are the more fascinating because of the white symbols on their distinctive conical roofs – the 'towers' that give the structures their name. And these symbols have been painted on by the trulli dwellers over generations. But there is some doubt as to whether the symbols are as old as is often suggested.

For example, certain of the symbols used for the signs of the zodiac and planets are far from ancient, those representing Pisces, Jupiter and Saturn being:

These forms were adopted widely only some time after the invention of printing in Europe in the mid 15th century. The older symbols for these three examples are:

The fact is that none of these early symbols are found on the trulli; there are only modern ones.

Similarly, if the trulli symbols really were derived from very early sources, the Sun symbols would be different. The most common ones on the trulli roofs are:

The first of these is the image of the Sun within the Greek letter omega and the second is the 'double Sun'. But none of the trulli roofs bear the much earlier symbol:

which dates from at least the 8th century.

Generation after generation of Italians living in the old structures known as *trulli* have decorated their roofs with symbols painted in white. Their age and significance, however, remain a mystery

Above: the symbol for the planet Venus is one of the genuinely old markings on the trulli roofs. It can be traced back to pre-Christian Greek horoscopes

Below: a vista of the little town of Alberobello in southern Italy presents a charming picture. The intriguing symbols on the trulli roofs have attracted scholarly interest as well as tourists

White symbols-black arts?

This curious form was derived from two of the Greek letters in the word 'sun'.

The symbol for the planet Venus:

is very old, being traceable to pre-Christian Greek horoscopes. This symbol, which does appear on one or two trulli, is still much used by modern astrologers and has been adopted by biologists to represent 'female'. But the occasional use of a genuinely ancient symbol does not make a case for the antiquity of all of them.

There has been much speculation on the origin and purpose of many of the trulli signs. Some writers have even gone to the length of claiming that a number of the symbols are derived from satanic sources and are linked to black magic and diabolic rites. Those who make such claims indicate that they are unfamiliar with the history of symbolism. An example of this is the writer who traced a direct connection between the swastikas on the trulli and the dark god Moloch, to whom small children were sacrificed in the pre-Christian era. The swastika is one of the most widespread symbols in the world, connected essentially with a solar or cosmic mysticism. It could have no relationship with Moloch – just as it originally had none with the Nazis, who gave it a diabolic connotation.

It can be said with certainty that not one of the surviving trulli symbols is directly linked with the thousands of sigils derived from magical scripts, secret alphabets, black magic symbolism and the profusion of symbols contained in diabolic and occult treatises. One serious scholar of symbolism pointed out in 1940 that the greater number of the trulli signs are Christian, others being 'pagan, astrological, as well as floral and

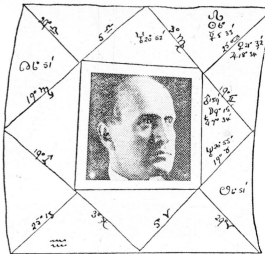

The ignominious end of the Italian dictator Mussolini (above) and the horoscope that predicted it (right). The trulli of Alberobello were specially painted for Il Duce's visit in 1934 – and some of the astrological symbols could be read as a sly snub to the leader

Below: one of the Christian interpretations of the pierced heart symbol is that it represents the wounded heart of the Virgin Mary

geometric'. Keeping in mind that the floral and geometric symbols are themselves possessed of special meanings, though sometimes still unexplained, then this would appear to be a fair summary of the scope of the trulli symbolism.

Pagan symbols are doubtlessly found on the trulli. The clearest example is of relatively recent usage, however: it is the double v the standard symbol, as we have seen, for the Italian Fascist movement. This naturally figured large in the series of symbols painted in welcome to Mussolini on his visit to the Puglian town of Alberobello in 1934.

Curiously, this pagan symbol had a special significance, though it became evident to non-occultists only in retrospect. This significance hinges on the fact that the Fascist symbol is virtually an inverted M, the first letter of Mussolini's name. After Mussolini had been shot by Italian partisans in April 1945, his body was hung upside down in the streets of Milan, an object of ridicule – the

The custom of painting symbols on the trulli roofs seems to be dying out, as shown by this photograph of Alberobello taken in the early 1980s

man inverted like his initial M. Only an occultist would have seen the full implication of this, for it was well-known in occult circles that a violent end had been predicted for the dictator. The English astrologer who worked under the pseudonym of 'Raphael' had published his commentary on Mussolini's horoscope as early as 1932: he had predicted the European conflict, as well as Mussolini's ignominious death by violence. Another symbol in the Mussolini horoscope is cited as a further presage of violence representing the 'revolutionary' planet Uranus.

Whoever painted the symbol for Saturn:

on the trulli roofs could hardly have intended a welcome to the leader, for Saturn is the darkest of the astrological planets and foretells of great evil. In some respects, this seemingly innocent symbol points directly to the interfering hand of the tourist board, for two such symbols appear on the trulli specially painted for Mussolini's visit, and both are painted in exactly the same way. There are at least a dozen different ways of drawing the modern symbol for this planet, and so we can surmise that these identical two were copied from a single source. Probably the trulli dwellers who so copied them did not know that they were cocking an occult snook at the Fascist ruler.

The predominance of the cross on the trulli roofs tells us that the majority of the symbols are of Christian origin. This has tended to influence the interpretation of their meanings. M.L.T. Verardi, an Italian sociologist who made a careful study of the trulli, put much emphasis on this Christian element, and consequently he often missed the occult element where it did exist. For example, he read the significance of the symbol for Uranus:

in Christian terms, insisting that the top part was derived from the first two letters of the standard form IHS, a contraction of Jesus, and that the bottom part represented Christ resting triumphant on the globe of the world. In fact, this is a standard symbol of Uranus, the H being derived from the initial of its discoverer, Sir William Herschel. However, had Verardi examined one of the trulli 'Uranus' symbols more closely, he would have seen that the painter had put a dot in the centre of the circle. This changes the meaning considerably, and carries it into the realm of occultism. This symbol and its variant:

which also appears on a trullo, are actually the common symbolic forms for the planetary spirit of the Sun, named Och in the medieval occult manuscripts. Each of the seven planetary spirits, and the related planetary angels, have symbols attached to them, and are also derived from the medieval lore of symbolism, yet this Och symbol is the only one that has found its way onto the roof of a trullo.

Verardi also allowed his preoccupation with Christian symbolism to colour his interpretation of the symbol:

This has been on the same trullo since the late 1960s and has been repainted at least once. Earlier photographs, made during the period of Verardi's study (he died in the 1950s), show a slight distortion of the sign, but on the whole the form has been preserved by the trullo owner with a fair exactness. Now, for some reason, Verardi traced the form of this symbol to an intertwined heart, a specifically Christian symbol. This is a most unlikely interpretation – but the precise significance of the symbol does remain unknown. It is possible that it is a truncated phi symbol, or it could possibly be based on a 16th-century alchemical symbol used to denote gold, the object of the alchemical search.

Curiously, the pierced-heart symbols:

said by some to be the wounded heart of the Mother of God and by others to be the heart of Jesus transfixed by the lance of the Roman Longinus, seem to be disappearing from the trulli roofs. Pictures taken at the end of the 1960s clearly show such symbols, but these same trulli roofs were bare in the early 1980s.

Will the tradition of painting symbols on the trulli of Puglia die out before the enigma of their exact origin and history is solved? It would be a pity if this were to happen.

The great Siberian fireball

In 1908 a vast area of Siberia was devastated by the explosion of a huge fireball. Trees were scorched and felled, and the skins of many animals broke out in scabs. Could this have been a nuclear explosion? What could have caused it?

ON THE MORNING OF 30 JUNE 1908, farmer S. B. Semenov was sitting on his porch in the isolated Siberian trading station of Vanavara, 500 miles (750 kilometres) north-west of Lake Baykal. It was still only 7.15 a.m., but the day was already well under way; the Sun rises early in midsummer this far north. Nearby, Semenov's neighbour P. P. Kosalopov was pulling nails out of a window frame with pincers. Neither man could have had an inkling of the drama they were about to witness.

Suddenly, Semenov was startled to see, towards the north-west, a brilliant fireball that 'covered an enormous part of the sky'. Semenov twisted in pain, for the fireball's heat felt as though it were burning his shirt. Next door, Kosalopov dropped his pincers and clasped his hands to his ears, which felt as though they were burning. He first glanced at his roof, suspecting it to be on fire, then turned to Semenov. 'Did you see anything?' Kosalopov asked. 'How could one help but see it?' replied the frightened Semenov, still stinging from his burns.

A few seconds later, the blinding, bright blue fireball, trailing a column of dust, exploded 40 miles (65 kilometres) from Vanavara with a force that knocked Semenov off his porch, where he lay unconscious for a few seconds. On coming to, he felt ground tremors that shook the entire house, broke the barn door, and shattered windows. In the house of Kosalopov, earth fell from the ceiling and a door flew off the stove. Sounds like thunder rumbled in the air.

The great Siberian fireball of 1908 was an event so exceptional that it excited a controversy that continues to this day. Explanations for it range into the realm of the bizarre, including the remarkable hypothesis that it was caused by nothing less than the emergency landing of a nuclear spacecraft,

The aftermath of the explosion on 30 June 1908 of a huge fireball that 'covered an enormous part of the sky' over Tunguska, Siberia (map inset, right), must have looked much like a forest fire (top); for up to 20 miles (30 kilometres) around the site of the explosion, trees were blown down, and the intense heat of the blast set the forest alight

Thirteen years after the Tunguska explosion, Soviet mineralogist Leonid Kulik (above) led an expedition to the site, travelling by horse-drawn sled and boat (right). His route is shown in the map (above right). Kulik found dramatic evidence of the blast – whole forests of scorched and uprooted trees (left)

perhaps even of extra-terrestrial origin.

The area on which the object fell, in the valley of the Stony Tunguska river, was sparsely inhabited by the Tungus, a nomadic, Mongol-like people who herded reindeer. Near the centre of the fall, north of Vanavara, several Tungus were thrown into the air by the explosion, and their tents were carried away in a violent wind. Around them, the forest began to blaze.

As the dazed Tungus cautiously inspected the site of the blast, they found scenes of terrifying devastation. Trees were felled like matchsticks for up to 20 miles (30 kilometres) around. The intense heat from the explosion had melted metal objects, destroyed storehouses, and burned reindeer to death. No living animals were left in the area but, miraculously, no humans were killed by the blast. There were also reports that a mysterious 'black rain' had fallen in the area.

The effects of the Tunguska blast were seen and felt for 600 miles (1000 kilometres) around. Reports from the district of Kansk, 400 miles (600 kilometres) from the blast, described boatmen being thrown into the river and horses being knocked over by shock waves, while houses shook and crockery crashed off shelves. The driver of the Trans-Siberian express stopped his train for fear of a derailment when the carriages and rails began to shake.

Other effects were noted around the world, but their cause remained a puzzle for a long time, as news of the fireball and explosion did not become widely known for many years. Seismic waves like those from an earthquake were recorded throughout Europe, as well as disturbances of the Earth's magnetic field. Meteorologists later found from microbarograph records that atmospheric shock waves from the blast had circled the Earth twice.

Echoes of distant Siberia

A woman in Huntingdon, England, wrote to *The Times* to report that the night skies were so bright that shortly after midnight on 1 July 'it was possible to read large print indoors. . . . At about 1.30 a.m. the room was quite light, as if it had been day. It would be interesting if anyone would explain the cause of so unusual a sight.' But, at that time, no one *could* explain.

Similar eerie night-time effects were noted over much of Europe and western Asia after the fall. Reports from this area record nights up to 100 times brighter than normal and crimson hues in the sky, like the glare from fires towards the north. The strange lights did not flicker or form arches like the *aurora borealis*; they were like effects that followed the outburst of Krakatoa, which injected vast clouds of dust into the atmosphere.

At the time of the Tunguska fall, Russia was entering a period of major political upheaval and the national press did not give any coverage to what it saw as a minor event in a remote part of the empire. Despite the exceptional nature of the Tunguska event, news about it remained buried in local Siberian newspapers until 13 years later, when word of it reached a Soviet mineralogist, Leonid Kulik.

Kulik had a particular interest in fallen meteorites, not least because of the rich source of iron they could provide for industry. He became convinced that the object that had fallen on 30 June 1908 in the valley of the Stony Tunguska river was an iron meteorite even larger than that which formed the vast Barringer crater in Arizona 25,000 years or so ago.

After years of planning, Kulik set out in 1927 on an expedition to reach the site of the

Tunguska fall. From the railway town of Taishet, Kulik and his team crossed 400 miles (600 kilometres) of frozen *taiga* by horse-drawn sled until they reached Vanavara. There, they heard the remarkable stories of the inhabitants, convincing Kulik more than ever that he was on the track of a truly enormous meteorite.

A sudden snowfall held up progress for over a week. On 8 April, Kulik, a colleague, and a local guide set out on horseback on the final leg of the journey. They marched northwards through scenes of increasing devastation: birch and pine trees lay on the ground where they had been uprooted by the force of the shock wave 19 years before. Many of the trees had been scorched or even set alight by the same intense heat that farmer Semenov had felt in Vanavara.

Surveying the blast area from a ridge, Kulik wrote:

> From our observation point no sign of forest can be seen, for everything has been devastated and burned, and around the edge of this dead area the young twenty-year-old forest growth has moved forward furiously, seeking sunshine and life. One has an uncanny feeling when one sees 20- to 30-inch [50- to 75-centimetre] thick giant trees snapped across like twigs, and their tops hurled many metres away to the south.

Visit of the god of fire

Kulik wanted to press on the remaining few miles to the centre of the blast, but the Tungus guides were superstitious, for their legends said the area had been visited by the god of fire, and they would go no further. Kulik had to return to Vanavara to recruit new guides, and another month passed before he arrived again at the devastated area and finally reached the centre of the fall – to

Above: members of the Tungus tribe, who were the most directly affected by the Tunguska explosion. They reported that, after the blast, many of their reindeer broke out in scabs – a fact that has led some scientists, assuming that the scabs were evidence of radiation sickness, to suggest that a nuclear explosion had occurred

Right: The area of devastation in Tunguska, showing the centre of the explosion and the direction of the fallen trees, together with three different suggestions of the path taken by the fireball. The path indicated by the solid red arrow was proposed by scientists K. P. Florensky and V. G. Konenkin, and is now generally considered to be the correct one

discover the great riddle of Tunguska.

Of the giant crater he had expected there was not a sign. Instead, he found a frozen swamp and a curious stand of trees which, despite being at the centre of the explosion, had escaped the effects of the blast that had levelled everything around them. Whatever object caused the explosion, it had never reached the ground. Although he returned to the area with bigger expeditions in subsequent years, Kulik never found any fragments of meteoric iron.

So if the Tunguska blast was not caused by the impact of an iron meteorite, what *was* the cause? In 1930, the English meteorologist Francis J. W. Whipple, assistant director of the Meteorological Office, proposed that the event had been caused by the collision of the Earth with a small comet, a suggestion supported by the Soviet astronomer A. S. Astapovich.

The popular view of a comet is a giant glowing ball of dust and gas trailing streamers for millions of miles, as with the spectacular Halley's Comet in 1910. But such brilliant comets are the exception rather than the rule. A dozen or more comets may be tracked by astronomers each year, but few or none of them ever become visible to the naked eye. Most comets are smaller and fainter than those illustrated in astronomy books; some comets, particularly old ones, may show no tail at all.

According to the most popular theory, a comet resembles a dirty snowball of frozen gas and dust. Old comets run out of gas to become nothing more than loose 'bags' of low-density rocks. Such an object would indeed cause a blazing fireball as it burned up by friction after plunging at high speed into the Earth's atmosphere, eventually shattering explosively as the forces of deceleration overcame its own strength. The mid-air blast of such an object would explain why there was no crater or meteorite fragments at

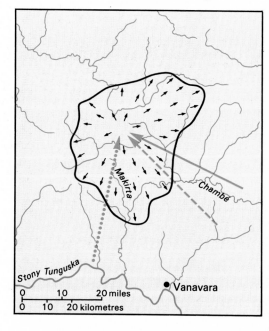

Tunguska. But critics of the comet theory argued that no comet had been seen in the sky before the Tunguska blast.

There has been a host of alternative explanations, including a bizarre suggestion that a mini black hole blasted into Siberia. According to astronomical theory, mini black holes, with the mass of an asteroid packed into the size of an atomic particle, could have been formed in the maelstrom following the Big Bang explosion that is believed to have marked the origin of the Universe. The passage of a mini black hole through the Earth would, according to University of Texas physicists A. A. Jackson and Michael Ryan, have all the observed effects of the Tunguska fireball – except that the mini black hole should have carried right on through the Earth and emerged in the north Atlantic, producing similar spectacular effects as it departed. Unfortunately for the theory, no such effects occurred.

Spacecraft from Mars?

Of all the theories for the Tunguska blast, the most controversial was put forward in 1946 by the Soviet science-fiction writer Alexander Kazantsev. Disguising his theory as a fictional story, Kazantsev proposed that the explosion over Siberia had been caused by the burn-up of a nuclear-powered spacecraft, perhaps from Mars. Kazantsev speculated that the aliens had come to collect water from Lake Baykal, the largest volume of fresh water on Earth. As the craft plummeted into the atmosphere it heated up by friction until the engines erupted in a mid-air blast like the Hiroshima bomb.

Soviet ufologists Felix Zigel and Alexei Zolotov have supported the exploding nuclear spacecraft idea. Zigel even proposed that the craft performed a crazy zig-zag as it desperately attempted to land, although none of the eyewitnesses actually reported seeing the fireball change course.

Right: the flight path of the Tunguska fireball in the area immediately surrounding the impact point, as reconstructed by Soviet ufologist Felix Zigel from the study of the damage created by the atmospheric shock wave, and the evidence given in a number of eyewitness accounts. The arrows through towns indicate the direction in which the object appeared to be travelling

Below: some of the evidence of large-scale destruction found by Kulik and his team 13 years after the blast: scorched trees, knocked flat by the force of the explosion or, where they were still standing, of stunted and scrubby growth

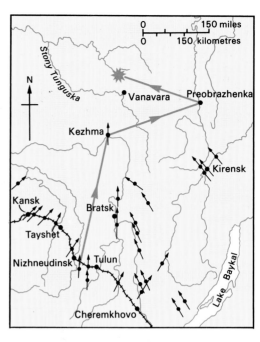

Another science-fiction writer, John Baxter, in his book *The fire came by*, published in 1976, followed Kazantsev in comparing the effects of the Tunguska explosion with those of the Hiroshima bomb – the strong thermal flash, the updraught of heated air that caused a 'fiery pillar', and the characteristic clump of trees that remained standing at the centre of the Tunguska devastation, as they had under the explosion point of the Hiroshima bomb.

There was even talk of deadly radiation at the site. One of the characters in Alexander Kazantsev's story speaks of a man who, shortly after examining the Tunguska blast area, died in terrible pain as if from an invisible fire. 'It could be nothing other than radioactivity,' explains the fictional character. In fact, there is no record that anyone died from the Tunguska blast – but the Tungus people reported that reindeer in the area broke out in scabs, which modern writers such as Baxter have attributed to radiation burns.

Expeditions to the area noted an accelerated growth of vegetation around the blast site, again attributed by some to genetic damage from radiation. There were reports in popular writings that radioactivity had been detected in the wood from the area, and an analysis of radiocarbon from tree rings in the United States by Nobel prize-winner Willard Libby showed an increase in radiocarbon following 1908. All of which seemed to indicate that the Tunguska explosion could have been nuclear.

This theory raises some alarming questions – for the Tunguska explosion occurred a good 30 years before the first nuclear tests. Who, or what, could have caused a blast of such proportions?

The Tunguska explosion was the disastrous end of a visitor from space. But was that visitor a spacecraft or a fragment of a comet? The latest scientific research would seem to provide an answer

SIBERIA, 30 JUNE 1908: a brilliant fireball blazed through the Earth's atmosphere, exploding at a height of 5 miles (8 kilometres) above the valley of the Stony Tunguska river with the force of a 12½-megatonne nuclear bomb. According to one popular theory, the Tunguska explosion really was a nuclear blast, caused by the burn-up of a nuclear-powered alien spacecraft. But another leading theory says the Tunguska object was the head of a small comet. What evidence is there to back up these rival theories?

Important clues to the nature of the Tunguska explosion were obtained on three expeditions to the site, in 1958, 1961 and 1962, led by Soviet geochemist Kirill Florensky. His 1962 expedition used a helicopter to chart the disaster area. Instead of looking for large meteoritic fragments, as Leonid Kulik had done in the late 1920s, Florensky's team sifted the soil for microscopic particles that would have been scattered by the burn-up and disintegration of the Tunguska object. Their search proved fruitful. The scientists traced a narrow tongue of cosmic dust stretching for 150 miles (250 kilometres) north-west of the site, composed of magnetite (magnetic iron oxide) and glassy droplets of fused rock. The expedition found thousands of examples of metal and silicate particles fused together, indicating that the

Below: Willard F. Libby, one of a team who thought they had found an increase in atmospheric radioactive carbon-14 following the Tunguska explosion

Bottom: within a year of the explosion, Tunguska looked like this: fresh green growth pushing through the dead timber

Tunguska object had not been of uniform composition. A low-density stony composition containing flecks of iron is believed to be typical of interplanetary debris, particularly meteors ('shooting stars'), which are themselves composed of dust from comets. The particles spread north-west of the Tunguska blast were apparently the vaporised remains of a comet's head.

These actual samples of the Tunguska object should have been enough to settle the controversy once and for all. Florensky wrote about his expeditions in a 1963 article in the magazine *Sky & Telescope*. The article was entitled, 'Did a comet collide with the Earth in 1908?' Among astronomers, the comet theory has always been the front runner. In his article, Florensky said that this viewpoint 'was now confirmed'.

Radiation check
Florensky's expedition carefully checked for the existence of radiation at the site. He reported that the only radioactivity in the trees from the Tunguska area was fallout from atomic tests, which had been absorbed into the wood. Florensky's party also looked in detail at the acceleration of forest growth in the devastated area, which some had put down to genetic damage from radiation. Biologists concluded that only the normal acceleration of growth after a fire, a well-known phenomenon, had taken place.

But what of the 'scabs' reported to have broken out on reindeer after the blast? In the absence of any veterinary report one can only speculate, but most likely these were not

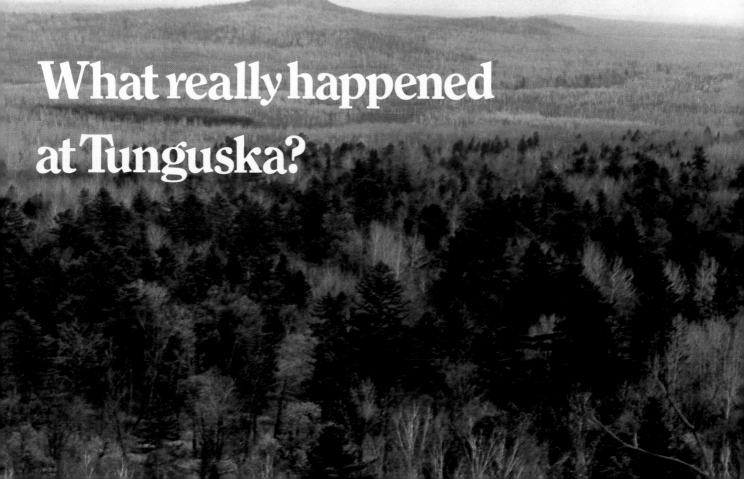

What really happened at Tunguska?

caused by atomic radiation but simply by the great flash of heat given out by the blast, which also set fire to the trees. Humans near enough to have felt the heat of the fireball showed no signs of radiation sickness, and remained alive and healthy when Leonid Kulik visited the site over a dozen years later.

Believers in the nuclear explosion theory quote investigations in 1965 by three American physicists, Clyde Cowan, C.R. Atluri, and Willard Libby, who reported a 1 per cent increase in radiocarbon in tree rings following the Tunguska blast. A nuclear explosion releases a burst of neutrons, which turn atmospheric nitrogen into radioactive carbon-14 that is taken up by plants along with ordinary carbon during their normal photosynthesis. If the Tunguska blast were nuclear, excess radiocarbon would be expected in the plants growing at the time.

To test this prediction, the American scientists examined tree rings from a 300-year-old Douglas fir from the Catalina Mountains near Tucson, Arizona, and also from an ancient oak tree near Los Angeles. They found that the level of radiocarbon in the rings of both trees had jumped by 1 per cent from 1908 to 1909. The picture is confused by erratic fluctuations of up to 2 per cent that exist in the levels of radiocarbon measured in the tree rings from year to year. Therefore a 1 per cent radiocarbon increase is not outside the range of normal fluctuations caused by natural effects. An important double-check was made by three Dutch scientists on a tree from Trondheim, Norway – much nearer the blast, where the radiocarbon effects would be expected to be more noticeable. Instead of a radiocarbon rise in 1909, they found a steady decrease around that time. Therefore the increase in American trees found by Cowan, Atluri and Libby must be due to local effects – and not to the Tunguska blast.

Pattern of destruction

Lastly, what about the clump of trees left standing at the centre of the Tunguska blast area, as were trees under the explosion point of the Hiroshima bomb, and the 'fiery pillar' seen after the explosion? In fact, these effects are not unique to a nuclear blast. Any explosion is followed by an updraught of heated air and a puff of smoke. Brilliant exploding fireballs happen frequently as chunks of solar system debris plunge into the atmosphere; fortunately for us, most of them are far smaller than the Tunguska object.

The clump of standing trees would be left behind by an aerial explosion of any kind, as shown by the scale-model experiments of Igor Zotkin and Mikhail Tsikulin of the Soviet Academy of Sciences' meteorite committee. They set off small explosions over a field of model trees, and found they were able to reproduce the pattern of felled trees including the central standing clump.

Therefore it seems that all the 'evidence'

The healing processes of the Siberian forest have not yet obliterated the scars of the 1908 explosion. Within a few years saplings had grown between the trunks strewn on the ground (top). But even today the fallen trees are still evident beneath a covering of moss and foliage (above)

adduced for a nuclear explosion at Tunguska is either misinterpretation or mischievous distortion.

Remarkably, the Tunguska event was repeated on a smaller scale over North America on the night of 31 March 1965. An area of nearly 390,000 square miles (1 million square kilometres) of the United States and Canada was lit up by the descent of a body that detonated over the towns of Revelstoke and Golden, 250 miles (400 kilometres) south-west of Edmonton, Alberta, Canada. Residents of those towns spoke of a 'thunderous roar' that rattled and broke windows. The energy released was equal to several kilotonnes of TNT.

Scientists predicted the meteorite's point of impact and set out to look for a crater, much as Leonid Kulik had done in Siberia half a century before. Like him, they were unsuccessful. Scanning the snow-covered ground from the air, the scientists were unable to find traces of the meteorite, or of a crater. Only when investigators went into the area on foot did they find that a strange black dust coated the snow for miles around. Samples of this dirt were scraped up, and proved to have the composition of a particularly fragile type of stony meteorite known to scientists as a carbonaceous chondrite. The Revelstoke object fragmented in mid-air, raining thousands of tonnes of crumbly black dust upon the snow. Significantly, witnesses to the Tunguska blast described just such a 'black rain'.

Clinching evidence for the cometary nature of the Tunguska object comes from the results of the latest Soviet expeditions to the site, reported in 1977. Microscopic rocky particles found in the 1908 peat layers have the same composition as cosmic particles collected from the upper atmosphere by rockets. Thousands of tonnes of this material are estimated to be scattered around the fall area. Along with these particles of rock from space were jagged particles of meteoric iron. The Soviet researchers concluded that the Tunguska object was a comet of carbonaceous chondrite composition. This comes as no surprise, for astronomers are finding that a carbonaceous chondrite composition is typical of interplanetary debris.

But if it was a comet, why was it not seen in

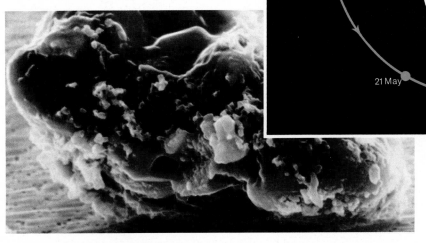

Top: how the Tunguska explosion may have happened. The comet Encke could have shed a rock fragment that was captured by the Earth

Above: this dust grain, magnified 10,000 times, was collected in the stratosphere. It is thought to have come from a comet

Left: the rings of recent Tunguska trees (top) are thicker than those of trees killed in the disaster (bottom). Some scientists claim that radioactivity from the explosion caused a spurt in plant growth

the sky prior to impact? Firstly, it always stayed close to the Sun so that it was lost in glare; and secondly, it was too small to have ever become bright enough to see even in a dark sky. Astronomers now believe that the Tunguska object was actually a fragment broken several thousand years ago from Comet Encke, an old and faint comet with the shortest known orbit of any comet around the Sun. A Czech astronomer, Lubor Kresak, pointed out in 1976 that the orbit of the Tunguska object, deduced from the direction and angle at which it struck the Earth, is remarkably similar to that of Encke's comet. Dr Kresak estimates that the body had a diameter of only about 100 yards (100 metres) when in space, and a mass of up to a million tonnes. Dust from its disintegration in the atmosphere caused the bright nights observed in the northern hemisphere in the period following the Tunguska event.

'The identification of the Tunguska object as an extinct cometary fragment appears to be the only plausible explanation of the event; and a common origin with Comet Encke appears very probable,' concludes Dr Kresak.

What is more, an event like Tunguska can happen again. Astronomers have found a number of small asteroids whose orbits cross the path of the Earth. For instance, in 1976 a direct repetition of the Tunguska event was avoided by hours as a previously unknown asteroid with a diameter of a few hundred yards swept past the Earth at a distance of 750,000 miles (1.2 million kilometres). Astronomers estimate that an object the size of the Tunguska comet hits the Earth once in about 2000 years on average. So it is only a matter of time before we are hit again – and next time it could do a lot of damage.

A catalogue of curiosities

China, encompassing one fifth of mankind, has its fair share of mysterious happenings. Many of these cases came to light when, for three brief years, the veil of official censorship was lifted

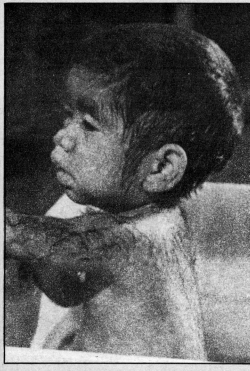

Left: Zhu Xiulian, born in 1977 in Guangdong Province, has been covered in black hair since her birth. In all other respects she is a normal child, active and intelligent

Below: one of the most famous of Chinese hairy children, Yu Zhenhuan, born in 1977. His parents were horrified when he was born and were tempted to let him die. Now the state is helping them with his upbringing

FROM THE EARLY PART OF 1979, the Chinese press printed a steady stream of reports covering the whole range of strange phenomena. Like reports of any sort from that vast and largely inaccessible country, these could rarely be followed up by Western observers and are therefore open to a number of interpretations. The best we can do in assessing them is to compare them with the patterns emerging in the rest of the world.

In December 1981 the Chinese newspapers were ordered to curb their coverage of strange phenomena, particularly human freaks and prodigies. 'There is a problem with the social effects of such stories,' said an official report. There does indeed seem to have been a decrease in the volume of strange reports in 1982, so let us consider what was gleaned from the three-year period up to the official clampdown.

With a population approaching 1000 million, it is hardly surprising that all conceivable oddities of the human form occur in China. Many human freaks were reported.

The average Chinese is perhaps the least hairy individual on the planet, so the phenomenon of the hairy child is all the more unusual in China. The Hong Kong newspaper *Ta Kung Pao* of 10 January 1980 reported that 32 such individuals had been found in China, spread over 10 provinces. Although isolated cases had been reported over the years, it was little Yu Zhenhuan (whose name means 'shock the Universe') that made the condition famous. Western journalists have handled his story in their usual degrading fashion, calling him 'monkey-boy', 'wolf-boy', freak, mutant . . . but to the Chinese he is simply *mao hai*, a hairy child.

Yu Zhenhuan was born on 30 September 1977 in Shaotzugo People's Commune in Liaoning Province, north-east China. His parents, Yu Wenguang, 27, and Song Baoqin, 25, were horrified to find their baby covered in jet-black hair at birth: his eyebrows merged with the hair on his forehead, and his entire body except for his lips, palms, soles and the tip of his nose was hirsute. He even had hairy ears.

There was, it seems, some dispute as to whether Zhenhuan should be allowed to live, but he survived long enough to come to the attention of the Chinese Academy of Sciences, and after that his future was assured. His family was given a new house and a state subsidy to look after him, and at the age of

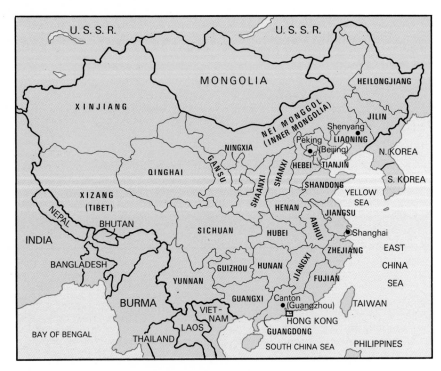

U.S.S.R. U.S.S.R.
MONGOLIA
XINJIANG HEILONGJIANG
NEI MONGGOL (INNER MONGOLIA) JILIN
NINGXIA Shenyang LIAONING
Peking (Beijing) N.KOREA
QINGHAI GANSU SHANXI HEBEI TIANJIN S. KOREA
SHAANXI SHANDONG YELLOW SEA
XIZANG (TIBET) HENAN JIANGSU
NEPAL BHUTAN
INDIA SICHUAN HUBEI ANHUI Shanghai
BANGLADESH ZHEJIANG EAST
GUIZHOU HUNAN JIANGXI CHINA
YUNNAN FUJIAN SEA
BURMA GUANGXI Canton (Guangzhou) TAIWAN
VIET-NAM HONG KONG
LAOS GUANGDONG
BAY OF BENGAL THAILAND SOUTH CHINA SEA PHILIPPINES

eight months he starred in his first film, a documentary shot at Shenyang, the provincial capital.

By the end of 1979 his hair had turned from black to brown. It varied in length in different parts of his body: 3 inches (7 centimetres) around the shoulders, 2 inches (4.5 centimetres) on his back, 1 inch (2.5 centimetres) on his abdomen. Apart from that, he was very much a normal child. All his senses were in good working order, x-rays and intelligence tests showed nothing abnormal. He had a slightly enlarged heart, and at four to five months was taller than an average child. His head and ears were large, and he cut his teeth late, at about one year. He laughed a lot and, apart from a little trouble with a boil and eczema, was perfectly healthy. The hair parted at the side of his body and thickened towards the mid-lines of the back and abdomen, forming whirls at various places.

Zhenhuan had a sister two years older than himself, who was perfectly normal. Apart from his maternal grandfather and uncle, who had slightly hairy calves and thick beards, none of his immediate relatives showed similar traits.

All human foetuses are covered with fine down after five to six months' development, but this hair is usually shed before birth. The cause of the *mao hai* atavism apparently remains mysterious, but it has been determined that the trait is inheritable. And the hirsute individual keeps his pelt throughout his lifetime.

To balance these stories, reports of completely hairless folk began to emerge. In February 1981 the New China News Agency said that seven such people had been discovered in east China. Zhang Juling, a 10-year-old girl, was one of these. Her father

Above: the provinces and autonomous regions of China. The stories of paranormal happenings that have come out of China originate in all parts of this vast country

Right: these two Siamese twins, Liu Sen-Ti and Liu Sen-Kai, were 64 years old when this picture was taken in the 1940s. In their prime they had made a great deal of money touring Europe and America. Now, having fallen on hard times, they were about to return to vaudeville in Nanking. Their act was a simple one: it consisted of answering questions from the audience about the details of their everyday life

said that with a magnifying glass minute hairs could be detected on her skin, 'but these hairs fall off as soon as the weather turns cold.' (One would expect that, if this were to happen, it would be when the weather turned *warm*.)

Then there were two brothers in Yunnan Province – Yang Tianzhao, 26, and Yang Tianshun, 21. Their hairlessness was accepted by their fellow villagers, simply because clean-shaven heads are a way of life in the region. Their peculiarity came to light only when a medical team carried out an investigation in the village. Though the brothers had no hair at all, not even in their nostrils, hair follicles could be seen under the skin in the pubic region and armpits, and on the scalp. The brothers seldom fell ill and they sweated normally, unlike some of the other hairless people. Their youngest brother, who died at the age of 18 months, was also hairless. But their two surviving sisters had thick black hair on their heads.

Chen Li, 15, whose address was not reported, was congenitally unable to perspire, since he lacked sweat glands and hair. In summer he bathed in rivers a dozen times a day to keep cool, and had to cover himself from head to toe with wet towels before he could fall asleep.

An unidentified boy of 15 in Shiling Commune, Jiangsu Province, was known as 'fire body'. After falling ill in 1971 he refused

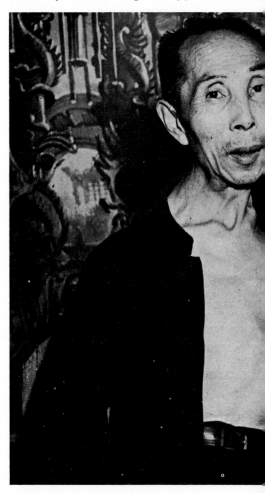

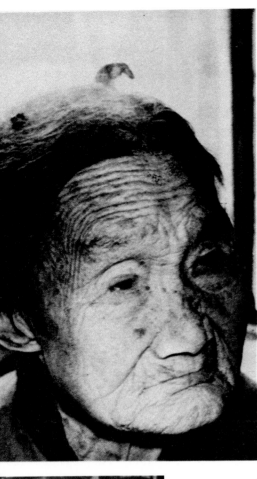

Left: an 88-year-old woman, Zhao Lishi ('Madam Chow'), found herself growing small horns. It took about six months to reach the stage of development seen here. A similar condition, in which bony protrusions develop *inside* the skull, is not uncommon in elderly women

not – were reported around this time in the *South China Morning Post*. A baby born at the Tsan Yuk hospital, Hong Kong, had four legs and four arms. It died 13 hours after birth. And in Manila, Philippines, a boy with two heads, three feet and three hands died five hours after birth.

A surgical operation on an 88-day-old girl, carried out at Anshan in Liaoning Province on 4 December 1979 disclosed four parasitic foetuses growing in her abdomen. In total, they weighed 11½ ounces (325 grams). The largest was 6 inches (15 centimetres) long and had well-developed hands, feet and hair.

In 1980 Lin Eryi, a 17-year-old male of Gutian County, Fujian Province, complained of difficulty in breathing and vomited blood and human hair. Diagnosing a tumour, surgeons operated and discovered a foetus, carried since birth in the thoracic cavity. Weighing more than 2¼ pounds (1 kilogram), it had underdeveloped hair, teeth and eyes.

At the age of 68 Wang Yinge of Angua County, Hebei Province, had a calcified foetus removed. It had been embedded in her abdominal cavity for 31 years. All those years ago it had burst out of the womb and entered the abdominal cavity, where it died at the age of about seven months and became calcified. It weighed 4 ounces (121 grams) and was 4½ inches (11.5 centimetres) long.

Death of a monkey-man

According to the *Shanghai Wenhuibao* (early 1980), local scientists had exhumed and were examining the remains of Xu Yunbao, who died in a fire in 1962, aged 23. Born in Sichuan Province, Xu was entirely covered in hair and bent at the waist. His skull was only 3 inches (8 centimetres) in diameter at birth; he grew to be only 3 feet 5 inches (105 centimetres) tall. Referred to as a 'monkey-man', Xu used all four limbs for walking, refused clothing even during the winter, and preferred raw corn to cooked food. The paper denied he was either monkey or ape, but it admitted he had 'a strong wild nature and liked to catch people'. His mother, 72, his two brothers and his two sisters were still alive and apparently normal. There is a strange twist to this story, reported in the official *Guangming Daily*. The mother had apparently disappeared for 27 days in 1939, in a forest area frequented by the 'wild men', or Chinese yeti, of Hubei Province. 'She admitted she had been seized by the ape-men but denied having any relations with them,' said the paper. The clear implication was that the hairy boy was a yeti-human half-breed.

According to reports in May 1980, an old woman of 88 in Hebei Province grew two horns on the top of her head some six months previously. The larger of the horns was said to be ¼ inch (6 millimetres) long, yellowish brown and without feeling. An American

to wear any clothing, even playing naked in the snow during winter. In the previous 10 years he had not caught cold or any other illness, and was growing up normally otherwise.

Wu Xiaoli, a baby girl from Miangyang in Sichuan Province, always felt hot and went naked because she was apparently allergic to clothes; she was nicknamed 'fire baby'.

The oddest freak story from China emerged at the beginning of 1980. Zhang Ziping, 35, a deaf-mute farmer from a remote mountain village in Huize County, Yunnan Province, had his second head surgically removed. The 'parasitic' head, in some sources reported as normal-sized, but actually about 8 inches (20 centimetres) round, was growing on the right side of Zhang's face. It had hair and 12 teeth, but the eyes, eyelids, nose and mouth were not fully developed. The cranium was normally shaped and covered an egg-sized brain, which is said not to have functioned. Plastic surgery restored Zhang's face, and he was said to be looking for a wife.

A two-headed baby was born on 16 August 1980 in an army hospital in Tianjin, to unidentified parents. Weighing 7 pounds (3.3 kilograms) at birth, the baby also had two oesophaguses, two respiratory systems and two stomachs, but one heart, liver and anus. When the left hip was injected, the left head cried; when the left head was fed, the right head cried.

Two other freak births – one in China, one

doctor, Martin Bruber, told the New York *Midnight Globe* that this was a case of hyperosteosis frontalis. This is a bony, tumourlike growth that normally occurs on the *inside* of the skull and is nearly always confined to elderly women, frequently suffering from diabetes or obesity. But he had never heard of a case where the horns grew on the *outside* of the skull.

The less restrained *New Thrill* of Malaysia identified the woman as 'Madam Chow' of the Chiao Ho district in Hebei Province, and said she was in normal health, not obese or diabetic. It also said that the horns grew to be 2 inches (5 centimetres) long. When both horns were that length, they started to turn downward, and allegedly came to resemble deer horns. The same newspaper mentioned an unidentified Japanese with 3-inch (7.5-centimetre) horns. And it referred to another report from China of a man with 10-inch (25-centimetre) horns, which later dropped off to leave stumps. These then started to form into an 's' shape.

In February 1981 there were some more tantalising reports in *New Thrill*. There was a report of a five-year-old boy with a tail: he was said to be more advanced than other children of his age in many respects. Also, a Peking newspaper had gone to great lengths to debunk a reported mermaid and 'fish with legs', of which a picture (said to be a photomontage) had been circulating in Peking.

An elixir from ants

In the same month the *Shanghai Wenhuibao* carried the story of 87-year-old Yan Zhongshan, who had discovered a wondrous tonic made from ants. It seems that since 1964 he had been collecting ants, washing them in pure water, drying and grilling them and then grinding them up into powder and cooking them up in an omelette, from which he made pills. A regime of one pill a day throughout the winter had given Yan exceptionally sharp eyes and ears; and, having lost his teeth when he was 72, he had now grown a new set, strong enough to crack nuts with – or so he claimed.

Luo Shijun of Jiangxi Province, in southern China, celebrated his hundredth birthday on 12 December 1981. According to the *Shanghai Wenhuibao* (6 April 1982), he discovered one morning that 27 new teeth had grown from his previously toothless gums. An official in his village, who could not believe his eyes, gave Luo a piece of dried meat which the peasant chewed readily. There is no mention of ant pills here.

New teeth or not, some Chinese live on to a very ripe old age. A candidate for oldest Chinese emerged from the census of 1982. Lan Buping, of Guangxi Autonomous Region, was born on 13 April 1846, according to a Canton newspaper in July. He still went occasionally into the mountains to cut firewood, said the paper, and could drink 2 pints (1 litre) of rice wine at one sitting.

However, in September 1980 the journal *New Physical Culture* reported that an ex-Buddhist monk, Wu Yunqing of Shaanxi Province, claimed he was born in 1838, making him 142 years old. He told interviewers he had prepared wood for his coffin three times. The first two lots rotted away, and the third now served as floorboards in his room. The old man gained national celebrity, but two journalists checked local records and established he was born on 13 December 1898, making him an 82-year-old fraud.

In April 1981 the Xinhua News Agency reported two giant children. Three-year-old Jin Rui already weighed 89 pounds (40.5 kilograms) and was polishing off 2 pounds (0.9 kilograms) of food a day. He weighed almost 15 pounds (6.8 kilograms) when he was born on 23 May 1978 in Hubei Province. One month later he weighed 26 pounds (11.8 kilograms), and was eating four meals of porridge a day. The report also mentioned Liu Debiao, 6, from Jiangsu Province, who was 4 feet 9 inches (1.45 metres) tall, weighed 91 pounds (41 kilograms) and could carry a man almost twice his weight on his back.

Rounding off this sombre cabinet of curiosities is the gruesome project of Dr (or Professor) Qi Yongxiang. In December 1980 the *Shanghai Wenhuibao* stated that in 1967 a female chimpanzee had been inseminated with a man's sperm, and was three months pregnant when Red Guards smashed the laboratory and the chimpanzee died. Dr Qi, who was identified as a 'researcher in medicine' in the north-eastern city of Shenyang, was involved in the original project, and wanted to resume the experiments to create what he called a 'near-human ape'.

Having an enlarged brain and tongue, it should be able to grasp simple concepts and talk some kind of language. Organs from the monster could possibly be used as substitutes for human or artificial organs in transplants. The creature could drive a car, herd animals, guard forests and other natural resources, and be used for exploration of the seabed,

Above: two hairless brothers from Yunnan Province. Yang Tianzhao (right) was 26 when this picture was taken in 1980: his brother Yang Tianshun was five years younger. They lack hair completely – it does not even grow in their nostrils

Below: Wu Yunqing became a national celebrity in 1980 when he claimed to have been born in 1838. But journalists showed that he was born 60 years later

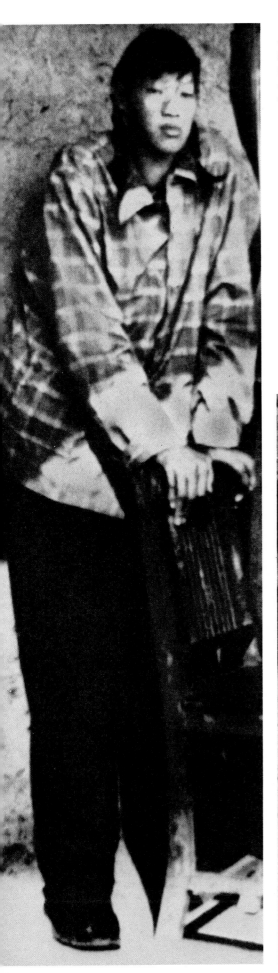

Left: the tallest woman in the world, Zeng Jin-Lian, stood 8 feet 1 inch (2.46 metres) high. She was only 17 years old when she died of diabetes in 1982

Below: three-year-old Jin Rui of Hubei Province. Seen here at the age of 35 months, he already weighed a prodigious 89 pounds (40.5 kilograms) and was eating 2 pounds (1 kilogram) of food each day

outer space and the centre of the Earth.

Chimpanzees and humans are remarkably similar genetically. A chimp has 48 chromosomes while a human has 46. It is assumed that the only major rearrangement has been the fusion, during human evolution, of two pairs of chromosomes to produce one pair. The differences between horses and donkeys, which can mate to produce the infertile mule, are considerably greater.

Professor Neil Moore, an associate professor in the department of animal husbandry at Sydney University, commented: 'You cannot say blandly the whole thing is stupid. All one can say is that it is possible to obtain fertilisation between many species, but the chance of survival of [a man-ape] embryo is remote.'

If such a hybrid could survive, though, it would have notable advantages as a worker, according to Dr Qi: since it would be classed as an animal, there need be no qualms about killing it if necessary.

Pieces of the Chinese puzzle

The Chinese seem more receptive than Westerners to the paranormal; top scientists take part in 'wild man' hunts, and ordinary people take fright at the disaster prophecies of astrologers

SIX PARTY WORKERS from the Shennongjia forestry region in Hubei Province, central China, were driving along a road near Chunshuya village at 1 a.m. on 14 May 1976. Suddenly they came upon a strange tail-less creature, with reddish fur, lying in the road. The driver kept his headlights directed onto the creature while the others went forward to investigate. They approached to within 6 feet (2 metres) of it, and one of them tossed a stone at the animal's hindquarters. It rose on its hind legs and lumbered off into the darkness. It was neither a bear nor any other animal they had ever seen before. A telegram reporting the incident was sent to the Institute of Palaeoanthropology and Vertebrate Palaeontology of the Chinese Academy of Sciences. There were other reports of a similar beast from the region during 1976.

The mountainous area covered by Shennongjia and its neighbouring regions Qinling and Bashan has a temperate climate. It is thinly populated and is the home of many rare plants and animals, such as the giant panda. There are undoubtedly new animal species to be discovered, perhaps including some large ones: zoologists have discovered a new variety of bear, the Shennongjia white bear, in this area. The vast forests are supposed to be the home of the *yeren* or wild man (also called a *xuěrén*), described in folk tales and writings of the last 2000 years.

Other provinces of China also produce stories of wild men. Wang Zelin, once a student of biology, claimed to have seen a creature of an unknown type while he was travelling in south-western Shaanxi in 1940. 'It looked like those plaster reconstructions of the Peking Man,' he said, 'only much more hairy, and it had an ugly protruding snout.' Peasants living in the locality tell of encounters with the yeren, which 'walk like humans, but have faces like monkeys'.

In 1962 reports of the yeren came from

Two members of a Chinese Academy of Sciences expedition scale a peak in the Shennongjia region in their hunt for a *yeren*, or wild man. The effort that the scientific establishment has put into finding the yeren has been massive, and has yielded apparent traces of the beast – hairs, excreta and so on. The yeren itself may have been sighted by the hunters on one occasion

Left: living proof that large creatures can exist undiscovered in the remote regions of China: the Shennongjia white bear, which was a relatively late discovery by zoologists. The bear may account for some yeren reports – but certainly not all

Below: Dr Zhou Guoxing, an anthropologist, pictured during the large yeren hunt mounted in March 1977. No yeren was captured, but a great deal of evidence of its existence was found

Bottom: some members of the Chinese Academy of Sciences expedition climb a hillside in Shennongjia in search of the yeren. The area, forested and mountainous, has yielded reports of the wild man for 2000 years

bog. There it was beaten to death with sticks by the women of the village. The peasants decided they had found the legendary 'man-bear'. They lopped off its hands and feet and sent them to the local government authorities, hoping for a reward. The remains were preserved by a biology teacher. In 1980 they came to light again, and for a while the press ran reports linking this creature with the Shennongjia sightings. However, it emerged in April 1982 that the Zhuatang creature had had a long tail, was about 5 feet (1.5 metres) tall, and was covered with long black silky hair. An examination of the hands and feet confirmed that they belonged to some kind of climbing monkey – not a yeren.

Hunt for the wild man

The Academy of Sciences has long taken a serious interests in reports of wild men. In 1959 it participated in the Tibetan Mount Everest expedition to study the 'abominable snowman', or yeti. The effort was interrupted, however, by fighting between the Tibetans and their Chinese rulers. In 1976, following the reports of yeren in the Shennongjia region mentioned above, the academy organised another search, under Yuan Zhenxin and Huang Wangpo. In March 1977 a 110-member expedition set out, composed of biologists, zoologists, photographers and teams of soldiers. It was equipped with rifles, tranquilliser guns, tape recorders, cameras and dogs. The search lasted eight months, but no creature was captured. Zhou Guoxing, an anthropologist with the Peking Museum of Natural History, said that at one point the search party came close to one of the creatures, but before it could be captured a nervous soldier accidentally shot himself in the leg. The shot brought expedition members rushing in from all directions and presumably frightened the creature away. However, a wealth of indirect evidence, in the form of footprints, hair and excreta, was discovered and studied. The

Xishuangbanna in a remote part of Yunnan Province. It prompted memories of previous sightings: one peasant told of having been with Nationalist Chinese soldiers who tracked eight of the creatures through thick forests for 10 days in 1947. One creature was killed and dismembered by the soldiers, who ate its flesh.

On 23 May 1957 a 13-year-old girl called Wang Longmei (though another report has it that she was called Xu Fudi) was grazing a few cows near a creek in Zhuatang village, in the coastal province of Zhejiang. It was drizzling, and the afternoon was dark, when a creature resembling a human being appeared and came towards her. She cried for help, and the beast panicked and stumbled into a

team also interviewed hundreds of people – teachers, hunters, herb collectors and others – who gave vivid accounts of encounters with the yeren.

A summary report of the expedition's findings appeared in the July 1979 issue of *China Reconstructs*:

> On June 19th, 1976, Gong Yulan, a 32-year-old member of the Qunli brigade of the Qiaoshang commune in Fang-xian county and her four-year-old child were in the mountains cutting grass when they saw some such creature scratching its back against a tree trunk.
>
> When our team questioned people in the area, the wife of the brigade leader recalled how Gong Yulan had come running to her door, all out of breath with great beads of sweat on her fore-head, saying: 'A yeren! A yeren!'
>
> Gong Yulan led us to the spot where she had seen the creature. On the tree trunk, 1.3 metres [4 feet 3 inches] from the ground, we found several dozen fine hairs of varying length. In August of the same year another group of investigators discovered two long hairs 1.8 metres [5 feet 11 inches] from the ground on the same tree trunk.

The hair was found to belong to a higher primate of some kind and definitely not to a brown or black bear. Four types of monkey live in the Shennongjia forests: the golden langur, the white-headed langur, the red-faced macaque and the great green monkey. But these are much smaller than the creature described by Gong Yulan and quite different in appearance.

After thousands of footprints, some up to 18 inches (45 centimetres) in length, had been studied, the investigators concluded that a fully grown yeren is anything up to 8 feet (2.4 metres) tall, weighs about 550

Above: Gong Yulan, the woman standing by the tree, recounts the story of the yeren she believes she saw on 19 June 1976. The beast was scratching its back against the tree; fine hairs were later found adhering to the trunk. They did not belong to any identifiable species of animal

Right: a plaster cast of what appears to be a footprint, found in Shennongjia in August 1977. Utterly unlike the prints left by any known creature, it prompts the speculation that it was made by a yeren

pounds (250 kilograms) and has a stride of more than 6 feet (1.8 metres). The footprints are like those of a human being, except that the oval big toe turns outwards.

Others used more subtle methods than the academy's to locate the yeren. It was reported that an enterprising scientist was walking through the wilds of Hubei Province, dressed in an ape suit and carrying a bundle of dates, with which he hoped to make a good first impression on the yeren when they met.

The academy scientists speculate that the yeren might be a descendant of *Gigantopithecus*, the hominid ape whose fossilised bones, 200,000 years old, have been discovered in Hubei. The scientists are clearly searching for a fairly conventional solution, and would have no time for hypotheses about apparitions or other paranormal phenomena.

Dragged into the depths

Like most regions of the world, China has its stories of lake monsters. In June 1980 there were reports of a monster in Menbu Lake, 310 square miles (800 square kilometres) in area, on the Tibetan Plateau. It had been seen by both farmers and party officials. Three witnesses reported seeing a strange animal with a body as big as a house, a very long neck, and a comparatively big head. One story tells of a farmer who was rowing on the lake when he was dragged down into it by the monster and disappeared for ever. Another story said that a cow left tied up near the lake disappeared, leaving traces of having been dragged into the water.

Three months later there was news of monsters in Lake Tian Chi ('the lake in heaven') at the other end of China, in Jilin

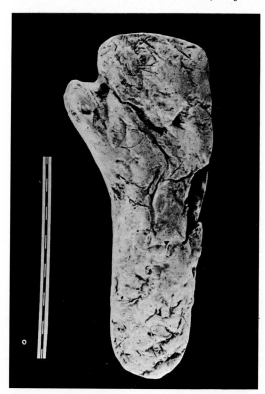

Province. The lake is in the crater of the volcano Baitoushan, which last exploded in 1702 – which makes nonsense of theories that the lake monsters are surviving dinosaurs!

The monster was described as having a flat beak like a duck, a head shaped like a cow's, and a body bigger than a cow's. Piao Longzhi, a meteorological worker on the mountain, fired shots at the beast in August 1980. Some of them seemed to graze its head. It was stated that a group of five monsters had been reported on one occasion.

Magical practices and all the occult arts have a long history in China, and belief in them still flourishes today. In January 1981 the news came out of Tibet that a work entitled *The book of heavenly prophecy* was circulating there. It had apparently first appeared 20 years previously, but was now gaining such attention that Lhasa Radio felt constrained to denounce it. The book encouraged people to eat as much as they could and buy as much clothing as possible, because doomsday was at hand: famine, drought and flood were said to be coming, and the Earth would then be destroyed.

The government-controlled radio denounced all this as nonsense. But in March China was appealing for international aid (to the tune of $700 million) because of famine; Hebei Province was suffering from drought (23 million people affected); and Hubei Province was suffering from flooding (with 20 million affected).

Then, at the end of March, about 4000 people sailed in 100 junks to Hong Kong, begging to be allowed to stay until 10 April. Astrologers and Taoist priests had predicted that an earthquake would hit the southern province of Guangdong during that period. British and Chinese experts agreed that their fears were groundless, landing permission was refused, and the junks were escorted back to sea. On 9 April, an earth tremor shook Guangdong for 10 seconds. Although it was only rated at 3 to 4 points on the Mercalli scale of felt intensity ('vibration like passing of heavy trucks . . . windows, dishes, doors rattle') it doubtless raised the prestige of those astrologers and priests.

Even the rocks seemed to be yelling for

Above: scores of fishing boats from Red China arrived in Hong Kong on 3 December 1980, fleeing from an earthquake that astrologers and priests had predicted. The boats were compelled by the authorities to return to their home ports – where an earth tremor struck on 9 April

Below: Lake Tian Chi, in Jilin Province, northern China. The lake is young, for it occupies the crater of a volcano that last exploded in 1702 – yet it is reported that monsters live in it

help around that time. According to the *Shansi Daily* in February 1981, cries for help were said to have been heard emanating from a rock that juts out of the Dongting Lake in Hunan Province. It was speculated that the rock in some way recorded the cries of drowning sailors and 'played them back' when the conditions of temperature and light were just right.

In October 1981 the *Canton Daily* reported a wonder of Yunnan Province. A 'dancing tree' had been discovered: 'When music is played near the tree, the trunk sways in time to the rhythm and its leaves turn from side to side. As soon as the music stops, the tree also immediately ceases to move.' This worked only with soft melodious music: the tree ignored loud martial music: 'When people standing near the tree talk softly, the tree will also begin to dance, but if the talking is loud and raucous, it does not move.'

Of the hundreds of millions of Chinese alive today it would be odd if some did not display unusual talents. But is it true that some strangely gifted children can read using their ears – and other parts of their bodies?

A 12-YEAR-OLD CHINESE BOY called Tang Yu was playing one day when he stumbled against a bystander. The boy said that, although only his ear touched the man's pocket, he was able to 'read' the brand name on a packet of Flying Wild Goose cigarettes in his breast pocket. To test the boy's claim, another man wrote a word on a sheet of paper and crumpled it into a ball. The boy placed the wad of paper next to his ear and after a while told the man what he had written on it.

The local paper, the *Sichuan Daily*, published an article about Tang Yu's talent in March 1979. It was severely criticised in Peking for publishing 'unscientific nonsense', and the mass media were advised to refrain from following up similar stories. One paper even accused little Tang Yu of sneaking a look when he performed these feats. It was recalled that a similar stir had been caused in the 1940s when the Chinese press carried a story about a girl, also in Sichuan, who was capable of surviving without food for several months. The story proved to be a fake: the girl was eating in secret.

This time, however, once the first report had gained currency, many others began to surface in different parts of the country. The political climate was right for speculation about the world of the paranormal: there was widespread talk of seeking truth empirically

The seeing ear

and not blindly following the party line.

Most of the reports involved children who were supposed to be able to 'read' not only with their ears but with the tops of their heads, their armpits, pigtails, buttocks, feet and so on. Many of the children were said to have more than one such paranormal faculty. A 25-year-old woman was found who, it was claimed, could read simultaneously and without confusion with five parts of her body; and a girl of nine was said to be able to read with 10 parts of her body.

Chinese historians found similar reports in classic works written over 2000 years ago. The Shanghai scientific journal *Nature* argued the validity of such phenomena in a series of 10 articles. For the rest of the year ESP became a major topic of conversation, not only in tea house gossip but also within the country's leading scientific and medical

Above: the front cover of the Chinese journal *Nature* of April 1980 showing just some of the children said to be able to 'see' with their ears, fingers and even armpits. This trend in psychic abilities began in 1979, when 12-year-old Tang Yu (bottom right of picture) stumbled against a bystander and found he could read the name on a cigarette packet in the man's jacket pocket – with his ear. It seems that Chinese scientists are taking such claims seriously and are strenuously investigating them under strict laboratory conditions

research establishments.

In an effort to determine the validity of these claims, scientists and doctors performed hundreds of tests on these gifted children. The most elaborate were organised in Shanghai by *Nature* from 4 to 10 February 1980. There were 14 subjects, aged between 9 and 25. They were tested before 10 audiences, totalling more than 2000 scientists, doctors, teachers and journalists, and the proceedings were filmed by the Shanghai Science and Education Studio. There was a holiday atmosphere at the tests, coinciding as they did with the Chinese spring festival.

The test subjects were seated in the centre of the hall. Behind each of them stood a monitor to minimise the possibility of trickery. Members of the audience left the hall, wrote words or pictures on sheets of paper, folded the papers, placed them in heavy paper bags or plastic boxes and then returned to the hall where they presented them to the children, who examined them using their own particular methods. The expressions of the children differed widely: some closed their eyes, some bowed their heads, others smiled or looked shy.

Little Jiang Yan was the star of the test on 6 February. Her performance almost brought the house down, according to the report in the Hong Kong newspaper *Ta Kung Pao* (31 July 1980). Her clear Peking accent rang from the loudspeakers: 'Mine is a cluster of yellow bananas painted on a green background!' She had 'read' this picture with the tip of her finger, with which she was allowed to feel about in a cloth sleeve. The six children tested on that day were given three papers each to 'read'; the results were 17 correct out of 18.

Telepathic armpits?

Much attention was focused on two young Peking sisters, Wang Qiang and Wang Bin. Not only could they read with their ears and armpits, but if one sister placed a message under her armpit, the other could read it telepathically.

In addition to being tested before large audiences, the 14 youngsters were also examined by a team of 30 experts and scholars in various fields. Some had been sceptics before the tests, but changed their minds afterwards. Among the converted was Wu Xueyu, director of the eye, ear, nose and throat hospital of the Shanghai No 1 Medical College. 'I surrender,' said the 70-year-old doctor. 'There is no arguing with facts.'

The Chinese-American physicist Dr Chih Kung Jen was among a team of specialists who conducted tests on 12 psychic children in the autumn of 1980. The children achieved a 98 per cent accuracy in 'reading' concealed messages with parts of their bodies. When holding the wrapped paper, he said, 'the children told us they experienced both a warmth and a tingling sensation in

Above: Lai Shi-Lung, professor of medicine at Canton Medical College and (right) Cyrus Lee, a Chinese American. Lai Shi-Lung is engaged on research into 'EHBF' – extraordinary human body functions – and is concentrating mainly on eyeless sight. Cyrus Lee is a professor of psychology who has done much to make the Chinese research on EHBF known in the West

their hands – like pin-pricks – and that the sensation travelled along the nerve lines of their bodies to their heads.'

Some scientists had some singularly un-enlightening ideas to offer by way of explanation, according to Meng Dòngming, a reporter with the official *Worker's Daily*: 'Most researchers tend to the idea that the skin of people with these sorts of abilities gives off a certain kind of radiation which can pass through objects and relay information back to the body for interpretation by the brain.' He quoted a professor as saying that the basis of the strange powers was that 'thoughts have substance.'

Chen Shouliang, dean of natural sciences at Peking University, studied a group of 40 children around the age of 10, picked at random. He was able to develop extra-sensory powers in 16 of them. He concluded that extra-sensory perception is a latent human ability.

Professor Wang Chu, deputy director of the department of radio engineering at the same university, reported on the descriptions given by the children he had studied with Chen Shouliang. At first, the children say, the image appears in their minds as a disordered jumble of dots and lines, which gradually rearrange themselves until the picture becomes clear. According to Chen and Wang's study, the faster this process takes place the more likely the child is to get the correct answer. The process speeds up as the child becomes more experienced in the use of the special sense, and is also influenced by the state of the child's health.

When the sisters Wang Qiang and Wang Bin returned to Peking after the Shanghai tests, the Traditional Chinese Medicine Institute arranged for an expert in *qigong* to train them. *Qigong* is literally '*ch'i* work', *ch'i*

Right: Tu Ping and Tu An, a sister and brother who attend a primary school near Wuhan University, mainland China, take part in an eyeless sight experiment. With their sight effectively blocked out they were asked to 'read' objects at a distance and have shown marked telepathic abilities. Here Tu Ping gleefully describes the target object – only five seconds after the beginning of the experiment

being 'breath', 'inner power', or non-muscular energy – the life force. It is the energy that flows along the acupuncture meridians, and is developed by practitioners of the 'internal schools' of martial arts, the most well-known of which is *t'ai chi chuan*. *Ch'i* masters are said to have extraordinary powers – 'rooting' to the ground and resisting massive efforts to push them over; repulsing attacks by means of an invisible force; transmitting a surge of energy, resembling electricity, or a strong magnetic attraction; and so on. One master, out walking in the street with a friend, is said to have been hit in the back by a pedicab, which rebounded 10 feet (3 metres) and tipped over. The master, without a break in the conversation, walked on as if nothing had happened. There are also accounts of masters projecting *ch'i* beyond the body to ring bells and snuff out candles at a distance. Was it this power that was used by two girls in Yunnan Province, discovered at the beginning of 1981, who could make tree branches break and flowers bloom, allegedly?

As a result of their *qigong* training, the armpit-reading sisters Wang increased their already remarkable powers. During tests, they were able to indicate the location of scars on the body of a fully clothed person and successfully described the shape of a pendant hidden under the clothing of another.

Related observations have been reported involving an 11-year-old boy, Xie Zhaohui. Doctors said he had the ability to describe, without touching a patient, the position of a foetus in the later stages of gestation, whether the liver is grossly inflamed as compared with a picture of a normal liver, and whether a fracture is simple or compound.

Another 11-year-old, Wei Ruoyang, appears to have even more highly developed 'x-ray' vision. 'Researchers took him to a reservoir near Peking and asked him to indicate the location of underground water pipes,' according to Meng Dongming of the *Worker's Daily*.

The places he pointed to corresponded

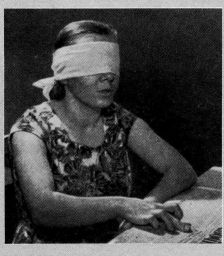

The ability to 'see' with parts of the body conventionally reserved for other functions is accepted as real by many scientists in the Soviet Union. Like the Chinese researchers, they have put a great deal of effort into studying the faculty, and there have been public demonstrations by gifted people. One of the most famous is Rosa Kuleshova, who is allegedly able to recognise colours through her fingertips (right). She told this to her doctor in her home city of Takil, in the Urals, in 1962. Her demonstration so impressed him that he reported her abilities to colleagues, including Professor Abram Novomeysky, who began to study her intensively. At first only two fingers of Rosa Kuleshova's right hand were sensitive; with training, both hands and other parts of her body, including the elbow, became able to 'see'. She became so adept she could 'read' print (above).

Even more excitingly, Novomeysky found that many people can develop similar abilities. Some could begin to distinguish colours within half an hour of making their first attempts. Other Russian workers began to train blind people in the skill of 'skin vision' and reported great success.

Experiment ruled out the possibility that the skin vision is due to telepathy or clairvoyance. Nor could it be due simply to the different 'feel', in the normal sense, of differently coloured surfaces; colours could be recognised through a sheet of glass and some subjects could recognise them when they held their fingers some way above the material being 'viewed'.

According to Professor Novomeysky, his experimental subjects reported that each colour had its own specific 'feel': yellow, it seems, is slippery, orange is hard and rough, and so on.

The fingertip test

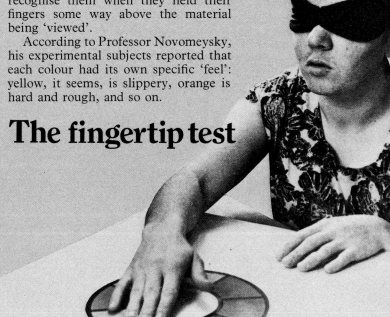

Left: Zhen Xiao-hui and her mother at their Canton home. The little girl has shown remarkable powers of EHBF, especially reading with her fingertips

Below: a group of psychically gifted children from Shanghai who demonstrated their bizarre talents to a group of visiting Americans, including parapsychologist Dr H. E. Puthoff, who cautiously reported this experience to the SPR conference at Cambridge in 1982

lock which had been sealed inside a box along with its key. Chen Yi placed her hand upon the sealed box for about 20 minutes, then declared: 'The key is now floating inside the box! Now the key is going into the keyhole and is turning the lock over.' When the box was opened, the key was indeed in the lock and the lock had been opened. . . .

In the autumn of 1981 the *Shanghai Wenhuibao* quoted Yu Guangyuan, vice-chairman of the National Science Commission, as saying that the ear-reading (and related) stories were 'ridiculous propaganda' and that such things had long been a popular 'magic trick' in China. It is true that cautious commentators have pointed out that parapsychological researchers must be conversant with the tricks of the illusionist's trade: if a professional magician can duplicate a feat, then paranormal ability in achieving it cannot be regarded as proved.

On the other hand, is it likely that such a large number of young children from all over

exactly with the locations as shown in official maps. Then they took him to the tombs of the Ming Dynasty emperors, to the north of Peking, and he correctly pointed to the location of two of the hidden entrances to one of the tombs. He also described the internal arrangements of another of the tombs, Chang Ling, but, as the tomb has not been opened by archaeologists, it is not possible to check at present whether or not he is right.

Strange powers everywhere

The *Taiyuan City Daily* reported in March 1981 that over 100 children with unusual powers had been found in the city. The paper claimed:

> Some children with supernatural powers develop from being able to read with their ears to having x-ray vision, telepathic powers, telescopic vision, and the ability to open locks, peel oranges, open and close flowers with the power of their thoughts alone.

Zheng Rongliang, visiting professor of biophysics at Johns Hopkins University in the United States, witnessed many psychic feats by Chinese children.

> In February of this year [1981] I attended a scientific conference in Shanghai in which 14 of the children demonstrated their really extraordinary abilities. In one demonstration, a young boy and girl sat holding stems with unopened flower buds in their hands. After about 20 minutes of concentration by these two subjects, these buds opened to reveal yellow blossoms. . . .
> A 12-year-old boy showed us he could use his mind power to make a watch or clock run faster or slower at will. A 12-year-old girl named Chen Yi opened a

China would be skilled in the techniques of the stage magician?

To assess the truth of the bizarre stories that emerged from China until 1981, when the authorities clamped down on them, is even harder than it is in the case of similar reports in the West. We must be grateful that we have been allowed even to glimpse this much of paranormal happenings in that country. It may be that the authorities will again relax their control on the reporting and investigation of strange events – more and more of what was once anathema is coming to be permitted or even encouraged. If they do, it will certainly show that in China there is an abundance of weird, wonderful and unexplained events that do not sit comfortably with orthodox scientific views.

A hint of hidden treasure

Since rumours of buried treasure on Oak Island began in 1795, speculators have spent a small fortune trying to find it, but despite the most determined efforts, the treasure remains as elusive as ever

ON A SUMMER'S DAY in 1795 a 16-year-old lad named Daniel McGinnis beached his canoe on the south-eastern shore of a small island in Mahone Bay, which makes a deep indentation in the southern coast of Nova Scotia. Why McGinnis chose this particular island for his excursion is unknown. Perhaps he was attracted by the feature that distinguishes the island from its neighbours – a thick covering of red oak, which had given rise to its unofficial name, Oak Island.

McGinnis set off for the interior of the island, following an old path through the trees. Presently he found himself in a clearing, where the oak trees had been cut down and a second growth was springing up to take their place. Curiously, however, there stood in the centre of the clearing a single, ancient oak. McGinnis noticed that one of its branches had been lopped off and that the stump overhung a depression in the earth from a height of about 15 feet (5 metres). The depression, and the fact that he could plainly see lacerations on the stump, which he took to be scoring from a rope, suggested to McGinnis that he had stumbled upon the site of buried treasure. He hurried back to his home town of Chester, 4 miles (6 kilometres) distant on the eastern shore of Mahone Bay, to enlist the aid of friends.

The following day McGinnis returned to Oak Island, accompanied by 20-year-old John Smith and 13-year-old Anthony Vaughn. With picks and shovels the boys set to work beneath the tree.

No sooner had they begun shovelling out the loose earth than they discovered that they were indeed following in someone's footsteps. For they found themselves in a clearly defined circular shaft, 13 feet in diameter, with walls of hard clay that bore the marks of

As the units of measurement used in early records of excavations at the Money Pit were Imperial, in this chapter the original measurements have not been converted into metric equivalents. The following conversion chart may be helpful.

1 inch=2.5 centimetres
10 inches=25 centimetres
1 foot=30 centimetres
10 feet=3 metres
100 feet=30 metres
1 mile=1.6 kilometres

Right: this diagram shows the various levels of the Oak Island Money Pit found by successive treasure-seeking expeditions from 1795 to 1850. The ingenious system of tunnels that ensured the flooding of the pit each time it was excavated beyond a certain depth can clearly be seen

Left: Oak Island lies off the coast of Nova Scotia, sheltered by the wide sweep of Mahone Bay. The aerial view (far right) shows how successive excavations have eaten away at the coastline close to the Money Pit, which is situated in the foreground of the photograph, to the right

Prince Edward Island

NOVA SCOTIA

Oak Island

ATLANTIC OCEAN

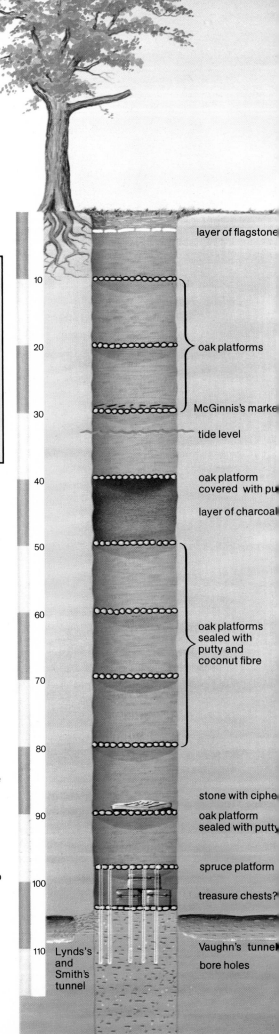

layer of flagstone

oak platforms

McGinnis's marke

tide level

oak platform covered with pu

layer of charcoal

oak platforms sealed with putty and coconut fibre

stone with ciphe

oak platform sealed with putty

spruce platform

treasure chests?

Lynds's and Smith's tunnel

Vaughn's tunnel

bore holes

picks. Four feet down they encountered a layer of flagstones, which could not have come from Oak Island. They hauled them out and kept digging. At 10 feet they ran into a platform of solid oak logs extending right across the shaft and firmly embedded in its clay walls. They managed to remove the logs and dug on. At 20 feet there was a similar platform, and at 30 feet yet another. With such limited equipment the lads could go no further – indeed, it was a prodigious feat for them to have got as far as they did. They returned to Chester to drum up more support, having first driven in stakes to indicate the depth they had reached.

Surprisingly, in view of the obvious allure of buried wealth and the intriguing nature of their discovery, the boys found no takers. Apparently Oak Island had a shady reputation. It was haunted – dangerously so. A Chester woman, whose mother had been one of the first settlers in the area, recalled that fires and strange lights had once been observed on the island. A boatload of men had set off to investigate these goings-on and had disappeared without trace. Clearly, the place should be given a wide berth.

It was nine years later, when the boys had grown into men, that help finally came forth in the shape of one Simeon Lynds, a well-heeled 30-year-old who became interested in the story as told him by Vaughn and who formed a syndicate to assist the original three in their quest. John Smith at least had not been idle all this time. He had managed to buy the land surrounding the excavation, and indeed over the next three decades would add to his holding, lot by lot, until he was in possession of the whole eastern end of the island. So it was that in 1804 a group of determined men, well-equipped for the task in hand and confident of success, descended on the mysterious Oak Island.

First they had to clear out the mud that had settled in the pit, but once they came to the sticks left nine years before, they were satisfied that their site had been unmolested during the intervening years. They now set to work in earnest. Reports of what they encountered between 30 feet and 90 feet down vary both in detail and in sequence, but the following account is accurate in its essence and does not sensationalise the discoveries made by the syndicate of 1804. At the 40-foot level they found another oak platform, this time covered in putty; at 50 feet, having dug through charcoal, they came upon yet another oak platform, this one sealed with coconut fibre. Then at regular 10-foot intervals there were more platforms, all of oak, either unadorned or covered with putty or coconut fibre.

Indecipherable inscription

At a depth of 90 feet they hit a flat stone, 3 feet long and 1 foot wide. It was not native stone and, of more significance, it bore an indecipherable inscription on the underside. This stone, with its strange markings, was surely a most valuable clue, but it was apparently treated in an off-hand manner. John Smith installed it at the back of the fireplace in the house he had built on the island, a move that was hardly calculated to preserve any message the stone was intended to convey. Half a century later the stone was exhibited in Halifax, as a lure for the recruitment of further funds for exploring the pit. At that time a professor of languages claimed to have cracked the code: 'Ten feet below two million pounds.' Someone who saw the stone in the early years of this century recalled in 1935 that whatever inscription there was had faded completely by the time he saw it, and his must be the final word – literally; no one has been·able to trace the stone since then.

The treasure hunters pressed on, now with a crowbar. The earth was so sodden that they had to haul up one cask of water to every two casks of earth. At 98 feet they struck

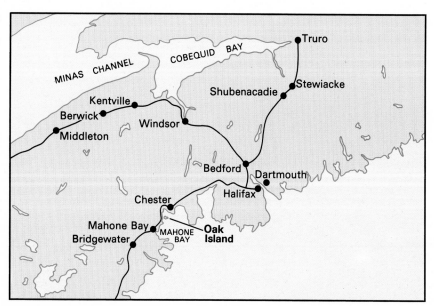

A map of Mahone Bay and Oak Island. It was here that the search for buried treasure began when, one summer's day in 1795, 16-year-old Daniel McGinnis paddled his canoe across Mahone Bay to explore Oak Island – and stumbled on the Money Pit

something solid, stretching across the entire width of the shaft. They reckoned that it was wood – and it required only a small leap of faith to conclude that it must be a chest. It was nearly nightfall on Saturday, and the men returned to their homes, confident that Monday morning would bring them riches beyond the dreams of avarice.

In fact, Monday morning brought nothing but disappointment. To their chagrin, they found the pit filled with water to within 33 feet of the surface. They tried to bale it out with buckets, but the level remained stubbornly unchanged. They rigged up a pump and lowered it to the 90-foot level. The pump burst, and the syndicate abandoned work for the year.

In the spring of 1805 they returned to the site and tried to drain the pit by digging another, deeper one alongside. At 110 feet, still dry, they tunnelled sideways towards the original shaft – to be greeted by a veritable Niagara. They were lucky to escape with their lives (as some of their dogged successors did not). By the following morning the débâcle was complete. Having once been only inches from their goal, so they had believed, they now stared glumly at two muddy pits, both filled with water to within 33 feet of the surface. They had exhausted their capital and now admitted defeat, blaming their misfortune on a caprice of nature. They would not be the last to mistake the identity of their unseen adversary.

For 44 years the Money Pit, as it was to become known, lay undisturbed, but then in 1849 a new syndicate was formed, with an ageing Anthony Vaughn acting in an advisory capacity. The Truro syndicate (named after the town in which it was formed) found both shafts caved in, but 12 days' hard labouring took them 86 feet down the original shaft. As had happened half a century before, the diggers left for home on a Saturday evening, light of heart. An inspection on Sunday morning showed nothing

amiss, and the men set off for church in Chester, doubtless to render heartfelt thanks. If so, their gratitude was premature. When they returned at 2 p.m., 'to their great surprise [they] found water standing in the Pit, to a depth of 60 feet, being on a level with that in the Bay.' Their attempts to bail it out were described in an account a few years later as being 'as unsatisfactory as taking soup with a fork'.

Undismayed, the Truro men decided to employ a pod auger (a horse-driven drill that could bring to the surface samples of what it penetrated) in order to determine precisely what it was that the pit contained below the 98-foot level. They erected a platform above the water and bored five holes, the first of them to the west of centre of the pit, the others progressively eastward across the pit. The first two revealed only mud and stones.

The third, however, was a different matter. In a written report, the man in charge of the drilling operations commented as follows:

The platform was struck at 98 feet just as the old diggers found it, when sounding with the iron bar [in 1804]. After going through the platform, which was 5 inches thick, and proved to be spruce, the auger dropped 12 inches and then went through 4 inches of oak; then it went through 22 inches of metal in pieces; but the auger failed to bring up anything in the nature of treasure, except three links resembling the links of an ancient watch chain. It then went through 8 inches of oak, which was thought to be the bottom of the first box and the top of the next; then 22 inches of metal, the same as before; then 4 inches of oak and 6 inches of spruce, then into clay 7 feet without striking anything.

This was certainly exciting, and the fourth bore was no anticlimax. Eighteen inches below the platform the drill appeared to scrape the side of a chest (so they surmised), and in fact splinters of oak were brought to the surface, along with what they took to be coconut fibre.

Double dealing

The fifth and final bore took a bizarre turn. The foreman, James Pitblado, was under instructions to remove every speck of material clinging to the drill when it was brought to the surface, so that it could be examined under a microscope. This he did, but not quite in the spirit intended. He was seen by one of the syndicate members to take something out of the auger, wash it, study it closely and slip it into his pocket. When challenged, he blithely retorted that he would display his findings at the next meeting of the syndicate directors. Incredibly enough, he was taken at his word. Instead of attending the board meeting, Pitblado found himself a backer, who promptly made an unsuccessful attempt to buy the eastern end of Oak Island. It was commonly believed that what Pitblado found was a jewel.

The Truro syndicate was now convinced to a man – and not without good reason – that two oak chests filled with loot lay, stacked one on top of the other, immediately below the 98-foot level. It remained merely to conquer nature's obstinacy over the matter of the water. In the spring of 1850 a new shaft was sunk some 10 feet to the west of the Money Pit: hard clay to a depth of 109 feet, and no flooding. Then another shaft was bored sideways into the Money Pit, just as in 1805, and with the same result: water burst in, half-filling it within minutes.

It is hard to credit, but it seems that it was only at this stage in the saga that anyone got round to questioning the source of all the water that was so bedevilling things. The story goes that someone tumbled into one of the pits, swallowed a mouthful and pronounced the water *salt*! In any case, it is a fact that only at this juncture was a connection made between the water in the shaft and the sea surrounding Oak Island. The association between the two was easily confirmed by noting that the water in the shafts rose and fell with the tides.

The composition of the soil ruled out any possibility of natural seepage (which would have made it impossible to dig the Money Pit in the first place anyway), so there was only one conceivable explanation. The Money Pit was in some way or other connected with the sea by a subterranean passage. How?

The answer was not difficult to find. A quick search on the nearest beach, 500 feet from the Money Pit at Smith's Cove, revealed all. When the tide ebbed, the sand 'gulched water like a sponge being squeezed'. A bit of spadework showed why. At a depth of 3 feet the workmen turned up a 2-inch layer of the now familiar coconut fibre. Beneath this was a 5-inch layer of kelp, or seaweed, then carefully arranged flat stones, criss-crossing one another. This 'sponge' extended for 145 feet along the beach, between low and high water marks. Next the searchers uncovered five box drains, skilfully constructed of flat stones, 8 inches apart, at a depth of 5 feet. These drains converged, fan-like, on a funnel-shaped sump hole, just above high-water mark. (When one of the drains was uncovered it was completely free of silt – a comment on the high quality of the original workmanship.) From the sump a tunnel ran inland and steadily downwards to the Money Pit, finishing its 500-foot course somewhere below the 98-foot mark.

The present-day observer, like the men from Truro, is driven to accept a remarkable conclusion – a conclusion that, were it not for incontrovertible evidence, he would be inclined to laugh out of court. Someone, at some time prior to 1795, had badly wanted to conceal something. Either by chance or by design, he set about his business on an obscure island in a Nova Scotia bay. He started by digging a shaft to a depth of over 100 feet. Then he constructed a 500-foot tunnel between the shaft and the beach at Smith's Cove, where he constructed a fiendishly clever bit of 'plumbing' that booby-trapped the approach to his hiding place. He then filled in the shaft, having rendered it inaccessible in its lower reaches, not haphazardly but in a most deliberate manner. Finally, having switched on the burglar alarm, as it were, he sailed off into the sunset, leaving behind the tell-tale oak tree.

The men from Truro were awed, as well they might be, but not overawed. What 17th- or 18th-century Man could ravel, 19-century Man could unravel. Or so he thought.

Smith's Cove on Oak Island. Here treasure hunters discovered the secret of why the Pit flooded each time they reached a certain level in their excavations

Over the years scores of prospectors made their way to Oak Island, each one convinced that he would recover the fabulous treasure from the ingenious Money Pit. But the pit remained impregnable

IF THE TREASURE SEEKERS of the Truro group had ever wavered in their belief in the existence of a fabulous hoard at the bottom of the Money Pit, the discovery of the ingenious flood tunnel enabled them to cast off any doubts. Quite apart from the sheer brilliance of the tunnel arrangement, the task of building the pit had been nothing short of Herculean. It was inconceivable that someone would go to such lengths to protect run-of-the-mill booty. The Money Pit must harbour a fortune, and it was well worth any amount of effort to reach it.

Accordingly, the workmen built a coffer dam 150 feet long across Smith's Cove, between the low-water mark and the catchment, hoping thereby to cut off the water supply. It would then remain only to pump the Money Pit dry once and for all. Unfortunately, a particularly high tide swept the dam away before it was completed. The Truro men then compounded their misfortune by misjudgement.

It should have been plain to them that it was possible to build a dam successfully, for how, without making one himself, could their mysterious predecessor have dug his tunnel in the first place? Yet instead of persevering with their original plan, they opted for a quicker, cheaper solution. They decided to intercept the tunnel between the shore and the Money Pit and to block it off. The reports are confused about how many fresh shafts they sank, and where, in an attempt to locate the tunnel. At one point they thought they had it, when they dislodged a boulder at a depth of 35 feet and were greeted by a surge of water. In fact, they

As the units of measurement used in early records of excavations at the Money Pit were Imperial, in this chapter the original measurements have not been converted into metric equivalents. The following conversion chart may be helpful.

1 inch=2.5 centimetres
10 inches=25 centimetres
1 foot=30 centimetres
10 feet=3 metres
100 feet=30 metres
1 mile=1.6 kilometres

Oak Island, which takes its name from the thick growth of red oaks that covers both its ends, seen here from the coast of Nova Scotia. A tiny, uninhabited island, it became a hive of activity after the discovery of the Money Pit in 1795. Through the years men and equipment were taken to the island by boat, but in 1963 Robert Dunfield, an American petroleum geologist, built a causeway from the mainland (this can be seen at the right of the photograph) to facilitate the transportation of heavy machinery

were far too close to the Money Pit for the flood tunnel to be so near the surface, and when they attempted to seal off the supposed tunnel by driving stakes and timbers into it, the water level in the Money Pit remained undisturbed. Thwarted, they resorted to an expedient that had been tried before. Fifty feet from the Money Pit, they dug down to a depth of 118 feet and then tunnelled sideways towards their goal. They were even more unlucky than their predecessors had been: the pit collapsed into the tunnel.

This was worse than anything that had happened before, and the Truro men believed that in the subterranean turmoil their treasure 'chests' had tumbled deeper into the shaft, perhaps to a depth of 150 feet. Whether or not that bleak conclusion was justified, this latest development was more than a minor setback. Where before there had been 'chests' lodged securely around the 100-foot mark, there was now chaos, a dreary sea of mud in which their dreams of wealth lay trapped. Their funds were exhausted, and they called a halt.

In 1859 the group re-formed, and the following year there emerged a new Truro syndicate, which nevertheless numbered some of the original members. More shafts were sunk, all with the purpose of blocking off or diverting the flow of water from the flood tunnel, and all with the same conspicuous lack of success. As many as 33 horses and 63 men were employed at the pumps at one time, and then in 1861 steam power was harnessed to the seemingly insuperable task of draining the Money Pit. The boiler burst, scalding one of the workmen to death. By 1865 the men from Truro had had enough and quit for good, making way for a new syndicate from Halifax, which was formed the following year.

Like the original Truro syndicate, the Halifax group set about things the sensible

Sinking into the quagmire

way. They tried to cut off the water at source by building a dam. As before, the tide demolished their handiwork before it was completed, and, as before, this single failure deflected the treasure seekers from their sound strategy. Instead of buckling down to the arduous business of building a *better* dam, they returned to the Money Pit. They pumped and they dug; they bored holes and dug some more, running branch tunnels laterally in an attempt to intercept the flood tunnel. This they finally accomplished, although it did them no good. They discovered that the flood tunnel, some 4 feet high and $2\frac{1}{2}$ feet wide, entered the Money Pit at a depth of 110 feet (that is, 10 feet below the supposed original location of the treasure). But finding the flood tunnel and cutting off the flow of water from the sea were two different matters, and in 1867 the syndicate gave up the unequal struggle. Before his death in 1938, one of the syndicate members, Isaac Blair, told his nephew Frederick Blair (who would himself be closely involved with many attempts to solve the Oak Island mystery during his long life): 'I saw enough to convince me that there was treasure buried there and enough to convince me that they will never get it.' Prophetic words.

A sound analysis

By now the pattern of failure was pretty clearly defined, and a quarter of a century was to elapse before the next brave attempt. Then in 1894 the Oak Island Treasure Company was established, with $60,000 capital. The young Blair drew up the prospectus, which was certainly sound enough in its historical analysis. Eager investors were told: 'It is perfectly obvious that the great mistake thus far has been in attempting to "bail out" the ocean.' The answer, it suggested, was 'to use the best modern appliances for cutting off the flow of water

Above: the head of the Money Pit at the time of the excavations by Frederick Blair's Oak Island Treasure Company. Over a period of about five years Blair and his associates made repeated attempts to drain the pit – but without success

Below: a group of eager prospectors at work at the Money Pit in about 1915. Blair's own funds had long since run out, but he continued to act as an adviser to other syndicates that arrived on the island. Right up to his death in 1954, Blair remained convinced that the elusive treasure would be found

through the tunnel at some point near the shore, before attempting to pump out the water'.

As so often before, an attempt to intercept the flood tunnel was made close to the Money Pit rather than near the shore (where it must lie nearer the surface), and with the usual inconclusive results. Then, again as before, the Money Pit itself was attacked – with added difficulty now because the century-long depredations had obscured its precise location. Blair and his associates found it, however, by working their way upwards from one of the side tunnels leading off an earlier shaft. (By this time a cross-section of the area would have resembled a rabbit warren.) They discovered the flood tunnel too, where it entered the Money Pit at the 110-foot mark. But the tidal water pressure was far too great to stem at that point.

It was 1897 by the time Blair and his colleagues belatedly turned their attention to the beach at Smith's Cove. They had no intention of building a dam, but they launched a determined assault on the flood tunnel, near its source. They bored five holes in a line running across the supposed path of the flood tunnel, and one of them yielded salt water, which rose and fell with the tides. They lowered 160 pounds (73 kilograms) of dynamite to a depth of 80 feet, and when they set it off, they observed considerable turbulence in the Money Pit. Assuming that they had finally destroyed the flood tunnel, they returned to the Money Pit and the pumps, but still the water poured in.

According to the traditional sequence of events, it was now time to start drilling. First they sank a 3-inch pipe, which came to rest against iron at 126 feet. Inside the pipe they lowered a drill, which went past the obstruction and struck what was identified as cement at 151 feet. Twenty inches further on the drill struck oak 5 inches thick. Then it hit what 'felt like' large metal objects, which persistent twisting and turning of the auger

dislodged, so that the drill could, apparently, slip between them. Then it struck loose metal, which was even more difficult for the drill to force its way through, then more of the large metal objects.

This was the first evidence of a buried hoard since the original Truro syndicate had bored through wood and metal in 1849. The drillers concluded that a layer of loose coin lay wedged between two stacks of metal bars – and they did not think the bars were iron.

They followed up this discovery with the application of sound technique, and only the most maddening bad luck prevented them from bringing samples to the surface. They tried to secure the drill hole by piping below 126 feet, and to that end they sent down a pipe of the same diameter as the drill ($1\frac{1}{2}$ inches) inside the 3-inch pipe. But at 126 feet the pipe was deflected by metal and struck what appeared to be the wall of the pit. They removed the pipe and sent the drill down again – but it followed the new, sterile path made by the pipe. The original hole down to the cement and the metal beyond was lost! Nor could other drills, sent down immediately afterwards, find that elusive hole. In one of these later drillings it was thought that the auger glanced off the outer edge of a chest. Finally, this particular avenue of attack had to be abandoned when at 126 feet the drill struck a channel of water, which spouted up the pipe at the rate of 400 gallons (1800 litres) per minute. This, of course, suggested that there were *two* flood tunnels, the second, deeper one providing back-up cover for the first.

A simple test proved that this was in fact the case. Blair poured red dye into the Money Pit when the water level was at its highest (that is, at high tide) and scanned the shore as the tide receded. The red dye surfaced in three separate places, 600 feet

Left: in 1971 the Triton Alliance Company lowered a submarine television camera into the Money Pit, which they had drilled to a depth of over 200 feet, and claimed that it revealed the presence of three chests – and a severed hand

Right: details of some of the major excavations of the Money Pit between 1850 and 1970. Despite the use of increasingly sophisticated machinery, which enabled successive expeditions to dig deeper and deeper into the ground, the pit still refused to give up its secret

Below: one of the shafts leading to the seemingly bottomless Money Pit. Since its discovery in 1795, hundreds of thousands of dollars have been poured into the pit and the lives of five men have been lost

from the Money Pit, only this time on the south shore.

In a futile attempt to intercept this second tunnel, Blair sank six shafts, and by the time he was finished – when the syndicate ran out of money – the only result was that the quagmire around the Money Pit was so bad that its precise location had become uncertain again. In the course of this series of persistent failures, however, Blair did uncover a mysterious object that served to convince his syndicate – and many later searchers – that beyond a shadow of a doubt, there was a cache of something buried in the Money Pit. In one of the drillings the auger brought to the surface a small ball of parchment that, when smoothed flat, revealed the letters 'v.i.'. What they stood for remains a mystery, but a scrap of parchment retrieved from such a depth is hard to dismiss. It was clearly evidence of some kind – but evidence of what?

Next came Captain Harry L. Bowdoin, a New York mining and marine engineer. He started well, clearing the Money Pit to a depth of 113 feet. From there he put down a core drill, which struck what was presumed to be cement at 149 feet. This caused great excitement. Were they finally on the threshold of a watertight treasure chamber? Alas, no. Nothing but yellow clay and stones for the next 18 feet. Then bedrock. A further 25 borings yielded no more, while experts at Columbia University pronounced the 'cement' to be 'natural limestone pitted by the action of water'. Bowdoin departed, declaring that the treasure was a myth.

Others came and went without adding anything to the considerable but infuriatingly inconclusive body of knowledge about the Money Pit. Then in 1931 William Chappell, who had operated the drill that had

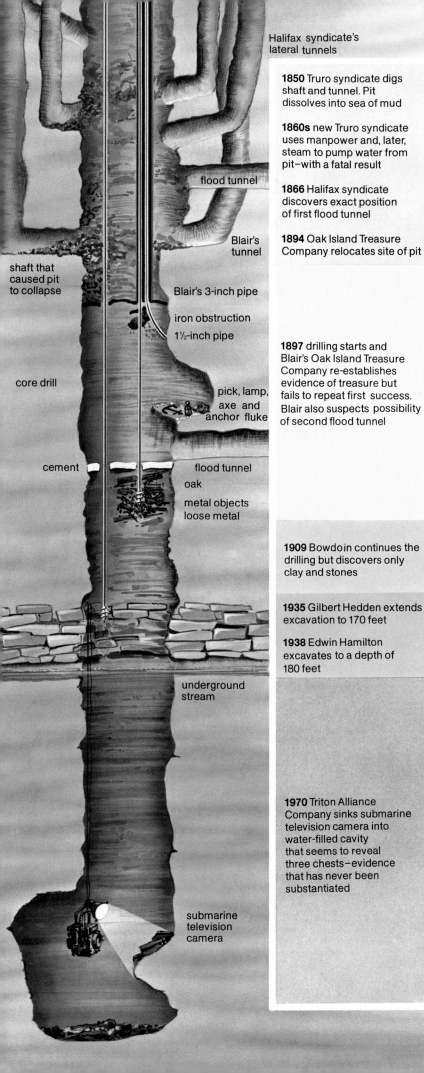

shaft that
caused pit
to collapse

Blair's 3-inch pipe

iron obstruction

1½-inch pipe

core drill

pick, lamp,
axe and
anchor fluke

cement

flood tunnel

oak

metal objects
loose metal

underground
stream

submarine
television
camera

Halifax syndicate's
lateral tunnels

flood tunnel

Blair's
tunnel

1850 Truro syndicate digs
shaft and tunnel. Pit
dissolves into sea of mud

1860s new Truro syndicate
uses manpower and, later,
steam to pump water from
pit—with a fatal result

1866 Halifax syndicate
discovers exact position
of first flood tunnel

1894 Oak Island Treasure
Company relocates site of pit

1897 drilling starts and
Blair's Oak Island Treasure
Company re-establishes
evidence of treasure but
fails to repeat first success.
Blair also suspects possibility
of second flood tunnel

1909 Bowdoin continues the
drilling but discovers only
clay and stones

1935 Gilbert Hedden extends
excavation to 170 feet

1938 Edwin Hamilton
excavates to a depth of
180 feet

1970 Triton Alliance
Company sinks submarine
television camera into
water-filled cavity
that seems to reveal
three chests—evidence
that has never been
substantiated

Oak Island Money Pit

brought up the piece of parchment more than
30 years before, returned for another attempt. Digging either in or near the Money
Pit (he and his old colleague Blair could not
agree on the location), Chappell uncovered,
at depths of between 116 and 150 feet, plenty
of evidence of earlier work – a pick, an oil
lamp, an anchor fluke, an axe head estimated
to be 250 years old. The only way such
objects could have been trapped at that
depth, Blair reasoned, was by a natural cavity
somewhere below the 100-foot mark (the
original location of the 'chests'), into which
all had fallen at some point in the siege.

Whether or not Blair had drawn the right
conclusion, he had certainly touched upon
the central irony of the quest. Each failure
had rendered subsequent attempts less likely
to succeed, despite the fact that as the years
rolled by, increasingly sophisticated techniques and equipment were available to the
searchers. During the middle 1930s Gilbert
Hedden, a New Jersey businessman, cleared
Chappell's shaft and lowered it to a depth of
170 feet. After two seasons' labour, he too
gave up and sold his equipment to Edwin
Hamilton, a machinery engineer. Hamilton
reached 180 feet, and while he found no
treasure, he at least found the place where the
second flood tunnel entered the Money Pit,
at a depth of 150 feet. He also proved that this
second tunnel, like the first, led from Smith's
Cove. The reason Blair's red dye had surfaced on the south shore was that at 180 feet
there was a natural stream flowing across the
pit in that direction.

An unsolved riddle

The catalogue of failures continued after the
Second World War, and in 1963 defeat was
accompanied by tragedy. A retired circus
stunt rider, Robert Restall, was overcome by
exhaust fumes from the pump that he was
using as he worked in the shaft. His son and
two other men died with him when they went
to his rescue. Then, two years later, a mighty
attempt was made by Robert Dunfield, an
American petroleum geologist. He even built
a causeway from the mainland to enable him
to get a 70-foot-high clam digger onto the
site. With this he dug a massive hole 80 feet
wide and 130 feet deep on the site of the
Money Pit. No luck.

In 1970 a group calling itself the Triton
Alliance Company took over Dunfield's con-
cession. A year later, Triton announced that
it had discovered a water-filled cavity at a
depth of 212 feet, and that a submarine
television camera had revealed what looked
like three chests and, gruesomely, a severed
hand, flesh intact. Divers were subsequently
lowered into the cavern at a depth of 235 feet.
They found neither chests nor hand. At this
stage it seemed unlikely that anyone would
ever solve the riddle of the Money Pit.

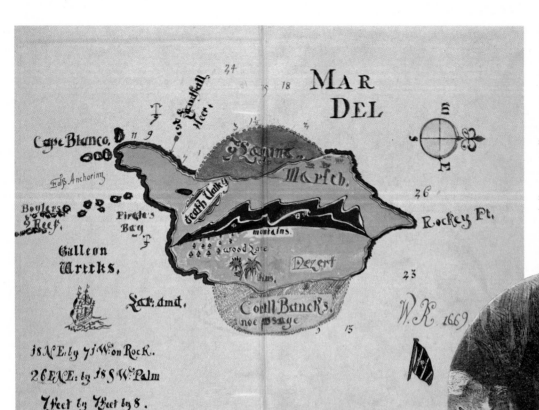

So near, yet so far

Who was the engineering genius behind the Money Pit? What did he bury there – and why? After years of investigation all hope of solving the mystery was abandoned. But there was one vital clue that everyone had overlooked

FROM THE MOMENT that Daniel McGinnis chanced upon the Money Pit in 1795 to the present day, attempts to salvage the supposed treasure have naturally gone hand in hand with speculation about the identity of those who buried it. There has been no shortage of candidates, from a tribe of Incas to a party of Norsemen. Dottiest of all, surely, is the theory that the Money Pit conceals manuscripts of Francis Bacon's that reveal his authorship of Shakespeare's plays. All along, however, the popular favourites for the role have been pirates – either pirates unknown or one particularly well-known pirate, Captain William Kidd.

This is hardly surprising, given the romantic association between pirates and buried treasure. And while, generally speaking, the pirate connection has been regarded as self-evident, there is at least one small piece of circumstantial evidence that appears to confirm such a suspicion. The oft-mentioned coconut fibre (if it was correctly identified) presumably came from the West or East

Indies, notorious haunts of pirates and buccaneers. Nova Scotia is far from the beaten track of piracy, but there is certainly no reason why some of the English maurauders who preyed so successfully on Spanish ships and towns in the Caribbean during the middle part of the 17th century, the notorious 'brethren of the coast', should not have made their way up the Atlantic coast.

It is an attractive theory that conjures up visions of pieces of eight, a frenzy of moonlit activity by desperate men with the sea at their backs, blood on their hands and avarice in their hearts. But it founders on the question of dates. It will be recalled that McGinnis found a clearing with young oaks springing up to replace those that had been felled. The red oaks of the North American and Canadian coast grow quickly, and McGinnis would have found mature trees towering above him, not saplings, had the Money Pit been dug a century and more before.

The identification of the pirate in question as Captain Kidd presents difficulties too. He

As the units of measurement used in early records of excavations at the Money Pit were Imperial, in this chapter the original measurements have not been converted into metric equivalents. The following conversion chart may be helpful.

1 inch=2.5 centimetres
10 inches=25 centimetres
1 foot=30 centimetres
10 feet=3 metres
100 feet=30 metres
1 mile=1.6 kilometres

was hanged for piracy at Wapping in 1701 and has subsequently been popularly associated with practically every tale of buried treasure that has ever been told. Nevertheless, Kidd and the mysterious Oak Island brush against each other in a strange way.

In 1935 a book entitled *Captain Kidd and his Skeleton Island* appeared in England. It included a map of an island and a set of directions. The map was based, according to the author of the book, Harold T. Wilkins, on the famous Kidd charts, which had recently come into the hands of a collector of pirate relics, Hubert Palmer. The charts, four of them, had been found hidden in three sea chests and an oak bureau – apparently genuine Kidd relics. All depict an unidentified island in greater or lesser detail, and they contain various markings and inscriptions (not all of them identical, although the island is always the same), including the initials w.k., the location 'China Sea' and the date 1669. These Kidd-Palmer charts, as they are known, were accepted by experts as being genuine 17th-century documents.

There are striking similarities between the island depicted in these charts and Oak Island, despite the 'China Sea' location. It has been suggested, incidentally, that the latter is both a red herring and, rather whimsically, a pun on *la chêne*, French for 'oak'. These similarities almost leaped off the page at Gilbert Hedden, who came across Wilkins's book as he was mounting his campaign on Oak Island in 1937. And Wilkins's drawing, apparently based on the original charts, contained these clear directions:

18 w and by 7 e on Rock
30 sw 14 n Tree
7 by 8 by 4

Hedden set out on a determined exploration of the area around the Money Pit with Wilkins's book open in his hands. Fifty feet

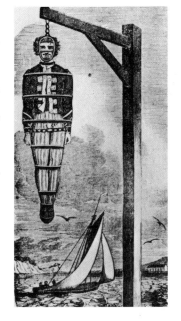

Below: this map, from Harold Wilkins's book *Captain Kidd and his Skeleton Island*, convinced prospector Gilbert Hedden that Skeleton Island was in fact Oak Island, and that there was indeed an immense treasure buried there. But the map came from Wilkins's imagination, and it bears little resemblance to any of the genuine Kidd-Palmer charts

north he came upon a large granite boulder with a hole drilled in it. When he told Isaac Blair of this, the old campaigner was reminded of a similar stone that he and his associates had come across 40 years earlier, down at Smith's Cove. The two men found the stone, similarly drilled, and paced out the distance between the two, which was approximately 140 yards. In an attempt to relate this distance to the information contained in Wilkins's book ('18 w and by 7 e'), they estimated that they had paced 25 rods (1 rod is 16½ feet).

Then two land surveyors were called in, who calculated a position 18 rods from the rock by the Money Pit and 7 rods from the one at Smith's Cove. From that point they measured 30 rods south-west, following the directions in the chart. And there, beneath tangled undergrowth, they found a triangle of beach stones, each side of which was 10 feet long; its base was enclosed in an arc, giving the appearance of a rough sextant. An arrow of stones ran 14 feet from the curved base of the triangle to its apex. The arrow pointed north, straight at the Money Pit. Hedden and Blair could make no sense of the third line of instructions, but they had seen enough to convince them that Captain Kidd's island and Oak Island were undoubtedly one and the same.

A mythical island

So persuaded was Hedden by this discovery that he journeyed to England to discuss it with Wilkins. Wilkins was flabbergasted. He explained that he had drawn the map from memory, that it was a composite of the four Kidd-Palmer charts that Palmer had only allowed him to glimpse, that he had had no chance to make a note of the directions that two of the charts contained. So where had Wilkins got those directions he published with his drawing – directions that had led Hedden to his discovery on Oak Island? The author was adamant: he had simply made them up. When pressed further by Hedden, Wilkins confessed that the *map itself* had come straight from his imagination too – that Palmer had refused his request for a sight of the original charts. As for Oak Island, he had never heard of it, had never seen its outline, had never in fact crossed the Atlantic. Yet he had to concede that his mythical island did indeed look like Oak Island, and that Hedden had proved that those fanciful directions did indeed correspond to something very real. By the time Hedden left England to return to Oak Island, Wilkins appeared to have convinced himself that he was no less than the reincarnation of Captain Kidd.

Hedden went away shaking his head in bewilderment, which is all anyone could do about this aspect of the Oak Island mystery until the answer to the Wilkins enigma was provided by Rupert Furneaux, in his book *Money Pit, the mystery of Oak Island* (1972). Furneaux discovered that Wilkins had lied to

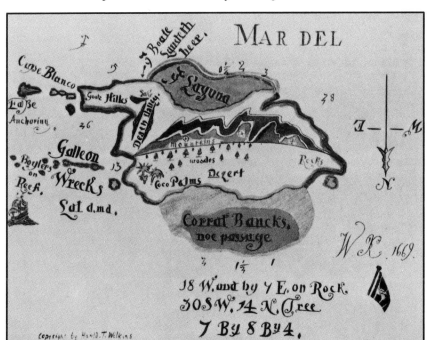

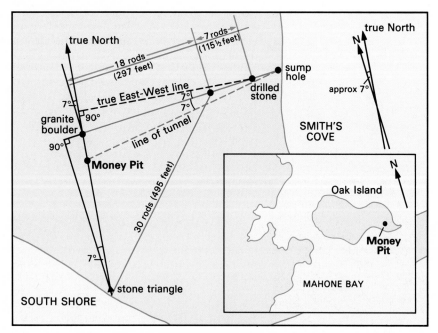

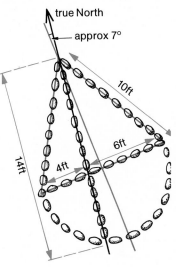

Top: the course plotted by Gilbert Hedden and Frederick Blair (who was still acting as unofficial adviser to operations on Oak Island), following the directions on Harold Wilkins's map. This led to the discovery of a triangle of stones (above) embedded in the soil beneath a dense tangle of undergrowth, and within the triangle was an arrow – pointing directly at the Money Pit

Hedden. Wilkins had in fact been corresponding with a Nova Scotian, who in 1912 had chanced upon a box containing charts among a pile of stones on an island 15 miles (24 kilometres) north of Mahone Bay. Those charts are now lost or hidden, but someone who had seen them was able to draw for Furneaux, from memory, the mystery island depicted in the charts, complete with directions. Moreover, in the charts the island was named Gloucester Isle, which, Furneaux had already discovered, was the name given to Oak Island when Mahone Bay was charted by the British Admiralty hydrographer, Joseph Frederick Wallet Des Barres, in 1773. The Des Barres charts of various parts of the Atlantic coast were not printed until later that decade, by which time the war raging between Britain and the American colonies would certainly have ensured that they were closely guarded documents. Hence, according to Furneaux, the inescapable conclusion is that whoever buried the charts that were discovered in 1912 had access to the Des Barres chart of Mahone Bay and merely added his own directions to mark the location of the Money Pit (*his* Money Pit, it follows). Wilkins had blithely reproduced these directions and the island shaped like Oak Island in his book on Captain Kidd, thereby adding confusion to genuine mystery – the mystery of who buried what on Oak Island. (There is a further mystery: the island in the Kidd-Palmer charts bears an unnerving resemblance to Oak Island; this is inexplicable.)

In his book Furneaux claimed to have worked out a plausible solution to the mystery, and he reasons his case carefully, sifting the known from the speculative, weighing the likely against the improbable. As he sees it, everything points in one direction.

Furneaux ridiculed the commonly held notion that the Money Pit and its elaborate defences were the work of pirates – the redoubtable Kidd or any of his ilk. First, the idea that pirates went around burying treasure chests is largely a fiction; it runs counter to the 'live for today' mentality of thieves in general and pirates in particular. Crews of pirate ships were paid on a share basis and on the nail, since, like all seamen, they demanded the right to squander their hard-earned money in time-honoured pursuits at the end of the voyage. Why would they help their captain to hide the spoils on some remote island to which they would, in all likelihood, never return?

This argument is mere conjecture, but it makes a great deal of sense. Even more telling is Furneaux's contention that to ascribe to pirate riff-raff a scheme so brilliant in conception and so masterful in execution is simply ludicrous. According to one authority whom Furneaux consulted, the tunnelling operation would have taken 100 disciplined men, working in three shifts, six months to accomplish. Whoever it was who directed them in this back-breaking enterprise, he was a trained engineer of outstanding quality.

Finally, there is the date of construction, which has already been mentioned in connection with the sapling oaks. If Furneaux was right that whoever did the job must have access to the Des Barres chart (which means that the work was undertaken some time after the mid 1770s), then pirates are ruled out virtually on that score alone, since their halcyon days in the Caribbean and along the Atlantic coast were long gone by that time.

A most important clue

So, if pirates were not responsible for the Money Pit, then who did built it? And how? And why? According to Furneaux, the date of construction provides the most important clue; he worked out an ingenious method for pinpointing that date. He reasoned that one of the many problems facing the mysterious mastermind was how to ensure that his tunnellers, working inland from Smith's Cove, kept on a straight line so as to run smack into the Money Pit. That line is 14° south of the true east-west line. Surely, according to Furneaux, he would have given his men, who were presumably working in dim light deep underground, one of the clearly marked cardinal points of the compass (west). If so, the magnetic variation west of north at the time must have been 14°. The magnetic values for Nova Scotia go back to 1750 and can be estimated for much earlier periods. It is thought that Oak Island would have recorded that particular variation in about 1611. It seems pretty certain that it did so in 1780.

Who would have wanted to conceal something of great value on Oak Island in 1780? The answer lies in the world around Oak Island in that year. General Sir Henry Clinton, commander-in-chief of the British forces in America, had been installed in his headquarters at New York for two years. The year of his appointment, 1778, witnessed France's entry into the war on the side of the colonists, and the combined threat to New York from the French fleet and Washington's army was very real. Clinton's fall-back position, should he have had to evacuate New York, was Halifax, about 40 miles (64 kilometres) north of Oak Island. Is it not reasonable to suppose, asked Furneaux, that at some point during these perilous years Clinton may have seized on the idea of removing to a safe place some of the huge quantities of specie (money for the conduct of the war) in his keeping? If so, an island in Mahone Bay, which was en route should he have had to fall back on Halifax, would make sense. Moreover, a friend and colleague of Clinton's, John Montrésor, had surveyed Mahone Bay some years earlier. Perhaps Montrésor suggested the site.

So, according to this theory, some time around 1780 a contingent of British sappers,

led by an unknown engineer of rare genius, descended on Oak Island and performed their great work. The shattering implication of this for generations of treasure seekers is that the money, if it was actually deposited there (the hiding place could have formed part of a contingency plan that was not put into operation), must have been recovered by those who had hidden it, since there is no record of Clinton's having to explain away a few missing millions when he returned to England.

How could such a recovery have been effected, given the Money Pit's fool-proof system of flooding? For years searchers had tried in vain to locate flood gates, which they reckoned the designer must have installed to enable him to shut off the water when he returned. A blind alley, according to Furneaux – and so, in effect, was the Money Pit itself. Furneaux suggests that after the Money Pit and the tunnels had been dug (but not connected), one or more branch tunnels were run outwards and upwards from the Money Pit; at the end of those upward-reaching tunnels, probably not far beneath the surface of the ground, the treasure was concealed. Then the Money pit was filled in, the flood tunnels were connected to it, and the treasure was thereby completely safeguarded. Only he who knew its precise location could find it (and perhaps he could do so without bothering to excavate the Money Pit). All others would flounder in the watery swamp of the Money Pit forever.

It must be admitted that this solution to the puzzle has a weightiness about it that is alien to the old skull-and-crossbones tradition. But before assenting to it too quickly, it is appropriate to ask whether it accounts for all the evidence. How, for example, does it make sense of the metal objects encountered by the drilling operations of 1849 and 1897? And what about that piece of parchment with the tantalising inscription 'v.i.'?

Top: Sir Henry Clinton, commander-in-chief of the British forces in America from 1778 to 1782, who may have been responsible for the Money Pit. According to one theory, Clinton ordered his miners and engineers (above) to build the pit as a hiding place for some of the war funds in his keeping

Right: tourists listen to the story of the Money Pit, of the generations of hopeful prospectors who searched for what they believed to be a fortune at the bottom of the pit – and of the mystery that still surrounds it

Riddle of Racetrack Playa

The stones move – and no one sees them do it. Yet thousands have seen their tracks in the dry lake beds that dot the Sierra Nevada mountains in the western United States. When – and how – do the moving stones make their mysterious journeys?

HIGH IN THE Sierra Nevada mountains, in the remote region of California's border with Nevada, there are places where stones move at night. Once, a band of pioneers was trapped in these rough, deeply channelled hills and unexpected dried-up lake beds, on their way to prospect or to settle in more hospitable places. Now it is part of the vast Death Valley National Park, of which the moving stones are a great attraction.

Perhaps the most famous of these dry lake beds, or playas, is Racetrack Playa, about $1\frac{1}{4}$ miles (2 kilometres) wide by 3 miles (5 kilometres) long and nearly 4000 feet (1200 metres) above sea level. The visitor's eye is immediately drawn to the scattered boulders and stones that litter this plain of hard, cracked mud. The quality of light at this altitude adds to the surreal effect, so that the rocks, with their snaking furrows behind them, give the impression of being both stationary and stirring. No one has ever seen the stones move – but move they do.

Over the years it was noticed that the rocks that moved had not rolled along but were pushed, leaving a groove the same size as their width behind them. Then in 1955 a geologist called George M. Stanley wrote in the *Bulletin* of the Geological Society of America (GSA) that he believed wind and ice were involved. Stanley was intrigued by the fact that groups of rocks often moved together. He suggested that sheets of ice formed around a group of rocks and that the wind raised the whole sheet slightly and propelled it along. This sounds plausible and was accepted for many years, especially after ice sheets embedded with rocks had been seen moving on other Californian playas. However, the ice layers on the Death Valley playas are extremely thin, and while they may be capable of moving smaller stones, even Stanley did not suggest they could shift the 300- to 600-pound (135- to 270-kilogram) boulders that had made tracks.

The mystery of Racetrack Playa became world-famous in the 1960s, and in 1969 it attracted the attention of Dr Robert P. Sharp, of the California Institute of Technology's geology department, who began a study of the moving stones that lasted seven years. He selected 25 stones of a variety of shapes and weights, up to about 1000 pounds (455 kilograms), named them, and used a metal stake to mark their position. Later he included five more rocks. When he was able to make the arduous journey to the playa over more than 30 miles (50 kilometres)

Opposite: the trail of a moving stone is marked by clear tracks behind it in the arid landscape of Racetrack Playa – one of the dried-up lakes of the Sierra Nevada mountains. The moving stones are a tourist attraction of the Death Valley National Park

These two sets of tracks show how far some of the moving stones travel (right) and how they can change direction (below)

the rock by its movement. This indicated that the rocks must have moved when the playa surface was soft, not during its hard-baked or frozen state. Sharp found that most of the recorded movements occurred in three periods: the particularly wet or stormy winters of 1968 to 1969, 1972 to 1973 and 1973 to 1974. Although only some of the stones moved during all three periods, Sharp could infer that rain was as important a factor as wind. The playas get very little rain – about 0 to 3 inches (0 to 8 centimetres) annually – but they are surrounded by about 70 square miles (180 square kilometres) of hills, which make a fine catchment area. Even a light rain in the area could result in a thin layer of water over most of the playa.

Because the surface of the playa is made of fine clay, the action of the rain creates a sheet of water with clay particles in suspension. If the water soaks the surface deeply enough or for long enough, the rocks get bogged down in soft, sticky clay. But when about a quarter of an inch (0.6 centimetres) of water collects, the surface is firm enough to support the rocks. 'The secret,' Sharp wrote in the GSA *Bulletin* in 1976, 'is to catch the play of wind and water at precisely the right moment.' He thinks that movement probably occurs within one to three days of wet or stormy weather when the surface is 'as slick as a whistle'. A powerful gust of wind is all that is needed to make the rock slide, and a slighter wind afterwards will keep it going. Sharp maintains that the surrounding hills scoop

of rough dirt road, he looked for any tagged rocks that had moved, staked their new position and measured the distance travelled.

During the seven-year study period, 28 of the 30 rocks moved. The longest track measured 860 feet (262 metres) but, as in all cases, this distance was reached by a number of smaller moves rather than all at once. The longest single movement was 659 feet (201 metres) by a 9-ounce (250-gram) cobble called Nancy. The direction of these movements was north-north-easterly, with a few deviations to the east and south-east, which matched the direction of the prevailing winds in the playa.

Sharp soon noticed that there was a ridge on the edges of the furrow and that a small heap of debris was pushed up at the front of

and channel the winds into the playa at sufficient speeds to start the rocks moving – and the smoother the bottom of a stone, the farther it will skid. He has also calculated the maximum velocity of a moving stone as about 3 feet (1 metre) per second.

The phenomenon of moving rocks is not unique to Racetrack Playa. Tracks have been observed on at least 10 other playas in California and Nevada, and from time to time, in the literature of geology, similar anomalies have been reported. In an article written in 1879 for the periodical *Nineteenth Century*, Lord Dunraven told of a strange sight on the shore of a lake in Nova Scotia the previous year:

> One day my Indian told me that in a lake close by all the rocks were moving out of the water, a circumstance I thought not a little strange. However, I went to look at the unheard of spectacle and, sure enough, there were the rocks apparently all moving out of the water on to dry land. The lake is of considerable extent, but shallow and full of great masses of rock. Many of these masses appear to have travelled right out of the lake and are now high and dry some 15 yards [14 metres] above the margin of the water. You may see them of all sizes, from blocks of, say, 6 or 8 feet [1.8 or 2.4 metres] in diameter, down to stones which a man could lift. Moreover, you find them in various stages of progress, some 100 yards [90 metres) or more from the shore and apparently just beginning to move; others halfway to their destination; and others again . . . high and dry above the water. In all cases there is a distinct groove or furrow, which the rock has clearly plowed for itself.

One of the 'walled lakes' in the state of Iowa, USA. According to Professor Charles A. White in a *Scientific American* article (1884), these walls were formed by deposits of compacted gravel, earth and boulders through the action of ice expansion in the shallow lakes. An early theory about the moving stones of the playas maintained that ice formation had caused their movement

Lord Dunraven noticed one enormous specimen some distance from the water's edge; earth and stones were heaped up in front of it to over 3 feet (1 metre) in height. A furrow the exact width of the rock extended down the shore and into the water until it was lost from sight in the depths.

This weird scene, remarkably similar to that on the playas, was explained in a letter to the *Scientific American* later in 1879. The writer, who signed the letter 'J.W.A.', claimed to have seen identical effects in other Canadian lakes. The effect is most prominent in shallow lakes that are partly bounded by steep banks or cliffs, according to the explanation. As ice forms it expands and pushes outwards in all directions. The cliffs form an immovable obstacle on one shore, however, doubling the thrust on the opposite, open shore. In shallow water the ice extends to the lake bottom and embeds the rocks there. As the ice expands, it takes the rocks and any other debris with it, depositing them farther along when expansion stops and a thaw sets in. As the lake ice expands and melts each winter, cumulative movements would be enough to drive the rocks onto the land. A similar explanation was proposed by Professor Charles A. White (*Scientific American* 1884) to account for the mystery of the so-called 'walled lakes' of Iowa, which were originally thought to be 'the work of an extinct race'. He said that successive expansions of ice in shallow prairie lakes gradually deposited substantial ridges of compacted earth, gravel and boulders around the perimeter of the lakes.

So we may know how the rocks move. But the surrealistic scene of playas, rocks and their snaking track marks can still awaken a keen appreciation of the wonder and mystery of the natural world.

What Happened at Hanging Rock?

The brooding Australian landscape, potent with ancient presences, was the backdrop for the mysterious disappearance of a school party in 1900; an event which has become a haunting modern legend

ST VALENTINE'S DAY 1900 dawned sunny and sparkling in the village of Woodend, near Melbourne in Australia. It was the day of the annual school outing at Applegate College on the outskirts of the village, and early in the morning a party of schoolgirls and teachers drove out with a picnic to a local beauty spot. By the end of the day four of them had disappeared: three of them were never to be seen again.

This strange story has become a *cause célèbre*, as mysterious as the case of the deserted ship, the *Mary Celeste* or the Bermuda triangle. It has become the subject of countless theories, numerous magazine articles, at least two books and a feature film, *Picnic at Hanging Rock* (1975). But like many historical mysteries the Hanging Rock affair is not all it seems.

The story has it that the party of girls and teachers set out in a hired coach to travel to Hanging Rock for their annual picnic treat. A popular place for picnickers at the turn of the century, Hanging Rock is an unusual geological formation. Of volcanic origin and several million years old, it rises majestically to 500

Above: immense and menacing, the prehistoric volcanic outcrop known as Hanging Rock dominates the surrounding plain like a massive ancient fortress and may be a focal point for paranormal forces. On the sacramental day of St Valentine, were the missing girls caught up by hidden powers and deflected into another dimension?

feet (150 metres) from an otherwise flat plain and terminates in a jumble of miraculously balancing boulders and monoliths that gave it its name. For sightseers a small picnic area had been laid out a short distance from the base of the rock, consisting of some make-shift stone tables and suitably discreet toilet facilities.

The party from the college comprised 19 girls, most of them in their teens, and two teachers. Mlle Diane de Poitiers, the younger of the two teachers, taught French and dancing, and Greta McCraw, a middle-aged Scottish spinster, was the maths mistress. The only other adult in the party was Ben Hussey, the coachmaster from the local livery stables. Mrs Appleyard, the headmistress, remained at the college.

The party set out early that Saturday morning to cover the 4½ miles (7 kilometres) to the picnic site, and arrived just before midday. It was a warm, sunny day, and after their picnic lunch most of the girls seem to have been content to doze under the shade of the trees and boulders. The only other party at the picnic area was encamped some distance away, on the far side of a small stream that ran down from the face of the Rock. This group consisted of Colonel Fitzhubert (formerly of the Indian Army, now retired to more mellow climes), Mrs Fitzhubert, their nephew the Hon. Michael Fitzhubert (on a visit from England) and their groom Albert Crundall.

About 3 p.m. three of the senior girls asked permission from the French teacher to explore the Rock. The three girls – Irma Leopold, Marion Quade and a girl remembered simply as Miranda – were all aged 17 and known to be sensible and responsible. After some discussion with the other adults (during which it was noted that the only two watches with the party – belonging to Ben Hussey and Miss McCraw – had both stopped at noon) it was agreed to allow them to go ahead. As an afterthought Edith Horton, a younger girl aged 14, was given permission to accompany them. All four were warned not to go too far up the Rock, to be careful to avoid its crags, caves and precipices, and to look out for snakes, spiders and other potentially dangerous creepy-crawlies.

The girls walked away from the picnic ground, crossed the stream, and disappeared from sight at about 3.30 p.m. Michael Fitzhubert and Albert Crundall were sitting beside the stream and watched them cross; Irma was first, followed by Marion, Miranda and Edith. Albert let out a wolf-whistle, and Mike got to his feet with the intention of following the girls, but he gave up after only a few yards when they disappeared into a line of trees.

At the picnic site the rest of the school party dozed off. At about 4.30 Mr Hussey became anxious about gathering his charges together. He and Mlle de Poitiers discovered that Miss McCraw was now missing; no one had seen her go, but it was assumed that she

had followed the exploring girls. The Fitzhubert party had by this time packed up and gone home.

Initially with irritation, and eventually with consternation, Hussey and Mlle de Poitiers searched for the absent members of the party. Mr Hussey first checked the toilets, and then organised the girls to search in pairs, calling as they went. A trail of broken bracken and disturbed scrub led to the southern face of the Rock from the east, but beyond that, where the stony ground of the Rock itself began, the traces petered out.

For nearly an hour the distraught picnickers searched; then at about 5.30 Edith Horton suddenly blundered out from the bush on the south-west side of the Rock. She was screaming hysterically and could tell her interrogators nothing of what had happened. Of Miranda, Irma, Marion and Miss McCraw there was no sign.

By now it was getting late and would soon be dark. Mr Hussey lit fires along the creek, and also continued to call out, and to beat upon two billy-cans with a crowbar. But with night-time coming on, the two adults eventually decided to gather up the remainder of their party and return to the college. On the way back they stopped at Woodend police station, where Mr Hussey made a statement to Constable Bumpher.

On the following day, Sunday, the search for the missing women began in earnest. It was assumed that the girls and their teacher had simply got lost in the bush, and the police enlisted the help of local volunteers, including Mike Fitzhubert and Albert

Below: Clyde School for girls, which moved from a Melbourne suburb to this building in Woodend in 1919, was the historical model for Appleyard College, described in Joan Lindsay's novel *Picnic at Hanging Rock* (1967) as a two-storey Italianate mansion built of solid Castlemaine stone

Crundall, to search the Rock. This was no easy task, since the Rock is a treacherous place, with many caves and pits (popularly believed at that time to be bottomless) hidden by rough bush. At the end of the first day's search, nothing had been found.

Meanwhile Woodend's Dr MacKenzie had examined Edith Horton. She appeared to be suffering from mild concussion, and had numerous scrapes, scratches and bruises acquired during her flight through the bush, but no other injuries. She could remember nothing of her time on the Rock. But later in the week, on Wednesday, she was interviewed by Constable Bumpher, when she made the almost casual revelation that on her way back she had passed Miss McCraw heading towards the Rock. Miss McCraw had been some way off, and had paid no attention to Edith's screams. Even worse, Edith bashfully confessed, the normally proper spinster had been improperly dressed; she had no skirt on, only her drawers.

The search continued for several days, while the police systematically interviewed all the witnesses. Young Michael Fitzhubert seemed a prime suspect, if foul play was involved: he had been the last person to see the girls, and admitted to starting out to follow them. But there was no other indication that he might be responsible for the girls' disappearance and, possibly due to pressure from the influential Fitzhuberts, the police abandoned this line of enquiry.

On the Thursday following the picnic the police brought in an Aboriginal tracker and a bloodhound. Given Miss McCraw's scent

Above: the fateful picnic supposedly took place on St Valentine's Day 1900, and the college cook had, according to Joan Lindsay's account, made a 'handsome iced cake in the shape of a heart'. Unfortunately for the authenticity of the story, St Valentine's Day 1900 fell on a Wednesday not, as in the book, on a Saturday

from clothes left in her room, the bloodhound followed a trail up onto the Rock and stood bristling and growling for nearly 10 minutes on a circular platform halfway up. But it failed to find any tangible traces and, convinced that no one could have survived that long in the bush, the police called off the search.

The next day, Friday, Mike Fitzhubert and Albert Crundall decided to make a search of their own. At the end of the day, having found nothing, Mike decided to spend the night on the Rock. Albert returned to Colonel Fitzhubert's residence at Lake View to make Mike's excuses; the next

Right: in a scene from the film *Picnic at Hanging Rock* (1975) the schoolgirls from Appleyard College drink a toast to St Valentine against the threatening background of the primeval Rock. Within a few hours, three members of the party were to vanish for ever

morning, when he returned to the Rock, he followed Mike's trail and discovered him unconscious, suffering from exposure, and with a badly twisted ankle. Mike was carried home and treated by Dr MacKenzie; that night Albert found a hastily scribbled note in Mike's pocket which, though largely incoherent, suggested that Mike had found something on the Rock. On Sunday morning another search was made: to their astonishment, the searchers found Irma Leopold.

She was unconscious. She had several bruises and minor cuts to the head, and her fingernails were broken and torn, but otherwise she seemed to have suffered little as a result of spending over a week in the bush. Her shoeless feet were clean and unmarked. Most extraordinary of all, her corset was missing – but she had not been sexually assaulted. When she revived, she could remember nothing of her ordeal.

And there the story ends. Irma could tell nothing of what happened; Miranda, Marion and Miss McCraw were never seen again. As a result of the episode, pupils were removed from Appleyard College, which was forced to close. Some months later Mrs Appleyard drove out to Hanging Rock and climbed it alone. Her body was subsequently found at the foot of a precipice.

The mystery of Hanging Rock has given rise to endless speculation. For those disinclined to accept a paranormal explanation, there are two possibilities. The girls may simply have got lost and died on the Rock from exposure. Their bodies may have lain hidden in undergrowth at the foot of a cliff or in a cave where they had fallen until disposed of by animals, insects and bacteria (which happens in the Australian bush quite quickly). Edith's amnesia might have been due to hysteria or to a fall; Irma's might have been due to the traumatic experience of

Mike Fitzhubert (above left) and Albert Crundall (right), played by Dominic Guard and John Jarratt in the film *Picnic at Hanging Rock* (1975). One theory to account for the girls' disappearance suggests that the young men may have kidnapped them for sexual purposes. Another theory is that the girls were captured by a UFO, for which the Rock may have acted as an intergalactic beacon like the Devil's Tower (below) in Wyoming in the film *Close encounters of the third kind* (1977)

becoming separated from the others and surviving alone for a week. She may have removed her corset in order to move more freely (this could also be the reason Miss McCraw removed her skirt).

The second possibility is that the girls were the victims of some crime. A theory has been put forward that Mike Fitzhubert and Albert Crundall might have kidnapped the girls (after murdering Miss McCraw) and held them hidden on the Colonel's estate to gratify their sexual desires. Marion and Miranda either died eventually of their injuries, or were murdered; Irma was saved through some chance. If the motive was sexual, then it has been suggested that Mike may have been a 'remittance man' sent to the colonies to keep him out of the way. It may be tempting to think of Mike as a pervert, but

the whole theory falls apart when confronted with Irma's surviving virginity.

Other theories are less earth-bound. It has been suggested that the girls were spirited away by some alien spacecraft. Certainly the Rock itself is distinctive enough – for those inclined to the idea – to serve as some intergalactic beacon, like the Devil's Tower in the film *Close encounters of the third kind* (1977). The presence of a UFO might explain why the watches stopped. When recounting how she had seen Miss McCraw, Edith Horton said she had seen a strange pink cloud around that time: is this evidence of mysterious goings-on in the sky?

Another theory is that the girls slipped into some kind of time travel, emerging in some other time past or future. This theory makes much of the strange pink cloud: both Christian Doppler and Albert Einstein suggested that bodies departing from sight at unnaturally high speed would be seen through a 'red shift' – a distortion of the light spectrum. The pink cloud might have been

Below: the forbidding, jagged crags of Hanging Rock were to claim yet another victim when, according to the novel and the film, Mrs Appleyard, the headmistress of the girls' college, drove out alone to the Rock and threw herself from its heights

Miss McCraw disappearing at high speed as a time traveller.

Other ideas are that the girls crossed into a parallel universe; or that the primeval qualities in the Rock itself spirited the victims away, a theory apparently favoured by the film *Picnic at Hanging Rock*, with its oppressive vision of the Australian landscape, and its positing of the Rock as a giant phallic symbol.

So what exactly did happen on that long-ago St Valentine's Day? Sad to relate, there is no concrete evidence that the disappearances ever took place at all.

Fact or fiction?

Much of the Hanging Rock story is based on Joan Lindsay's novel *Picnic at Hanging Rock* (1967). Although this is a work of fiction, the author obviously hopes her readers will take it to be based on fact. In the preface she says, 'Whether . . . fact or fiction, my readers must decide for themselves.' At the end of the book there is a long quotation, apparently taken from a Melbourne newspaper, describing the outline of the story. Circumstantial evidence has also contrived to mislead recent investigators. All the places mentioned in the story exist, including a Ladies' College at Woodend. The Hussey brothers did run a store near Woodend, and a Dr MacKenzie did practise in the vicinity at the turn of the century. But no contemporary references to the disappearances can be traced.

In fact St Valentine's Day 1900 fell on a Wednesday, not a Saturday. The girls' school (named Clyde College) was opened in 1910 in a Melbourne suburb, and did not move to Woodend until 1919. Neither the local newspaper, the *Woodend Star*, nor the two Melbourne papers, the *Age* and the *Argus*, refer to any disappearances on the Rock during February 1900, nor for several years before or after. The newspaper quoted at the end of the novel suggests that Irma gave several interviews to the Society for Psychical Research; these cannot be traced, nor can the newspaper from which the extract was supposedly taken.

Confronted with this lack of extraneous evidence, Joan Lindsay remains mischievously enigmatic. In an interview with a Melbourne newspaper in 1977 she was asked outright, 'Is *Picnic* fact or fiction?' 'It is an impossible question for me to answer,' she replied. 'Fact and fiction are so closely intertwined.'

Yet it hardly seems to matter whether the story is true or not. It already appears to have passed into modern mythology. People who have read the book or seen the film will assure you that the events described really happened. It seems that the tale has connected powerfully with the Australian collective unconscious; and its characters are already certain of the immortality conferred on the figures in a fairytale.

Index